The dream to travel is a dream about
expanding the landscape around me to also
include that which is beyond the horizon.
- origin unknown.

Drømmen om å reise er en drøm om å utvide
landskapet rundt meg til også å omfatte
det som er bak synsranden.
- av ukjent opprinnelse.

Der Traum zu reisen ist ein Traum,
die Landschaft um mich zu erweitern,
um auch das zu erfassen,
was hinter dem Horizont liegt.
- Herkunft unbekannt.

The Norway
Bed & Breakfast Book

2002  2003

Editor & illustrator:
Anne Marit Bjørgen

PELICAN PUBLISHING COMPANY
Gretna 2002

*The word "Pelican" and the depiction of a pelican are
trademarks of Pelican Publishing Company, Inc., and are
registered in the U.S. Patent and Trademark Office.*

Maps: Source STATENS KARTVERK MAD14010-R108187

If you want to be listed in future editions of this guide, please write to:
Hvis du ønsker å bli presentert i neste utgave av denne boken, vennligst skriv til:
B&B Norway AS, Østerdalsgaten 1J, N - 0658 Oslo, Norway.
Phone: (+47) 22 67 30 80 Fax: (+47) 22 19 83 17
E-mail: bbnorway@online.no
Web: www.bbnorway.com

Cover design: Gustav Dietrichson AS, Bærum, Norway

Printed in Canada
Published by Pelican Publishing Company, Inc.
1000 Burmaster Street, Gretna, Louisiana 70053

Preface

Welcome to the 5th edition of "The Norway Bed & Breakfast Book". Our aim is to make it easy for you to locate friendly and hospitable hosts in cities and in the countryside. Our host families look forward to having you, your family and friends visit them in Norway. Here you will find a diverse selection to choose from. Breakfast is included with most overnight accommodations. However, we also feature rental units with "self-catering" since Norway does not have as long a B&B tradition as some other countries. Breakfast is not served at such places, but guests may prepare meals in well-equipped kitchens.

You choose the type of atmosphere you prefer: houses, cabins, manor homes or old-fashioned storage huts (stabbur), etc.

Prices tend to vary. If you and your family are economizing, you will find some excellent offerings in the Self-catering category and among some of the B&B's. If you are less concerned about price and perhaps more interested in experiences to be enjoyed, you will also find accommodations that are more traditional, cozier, exotic and unique.

Forord

Velkommen til den 5te utgaven av "The Norway Bed & Breakfast Book", (tidligere: "Rom i Norge"). Her finner du vennlige og gjestfrie menneskene i by og på land. Våre vertsfamilier ser fram til å ta imot deg og ditt følge på din neste Norgesferie. Tilbudet er variert. Ved de fleste overnattingsstedene er frokost inkludert i prisen. Men siden vi ikke har den samme lange B&B-tradisjon som i enkelte andre land, har vi også inkludert utleie-enheter med 'selvhushold'. Her serveres ikke frokost, men gjestene kan stelle sine egne måltider på et dertil egnet og utstyrt kjøkken. Du vil kunne velge atmosfære mellom ulike typer hus, hytter, stabbur, villaer etc. Prisene varierer også endel. Hvis du er ute etter de rimeligste alternativene kan du i Selvhusholds-kategorien og enkelte B&B finne gode løsninger. Bryr du deg mindre om pris, men mer om opplevelse, kan du finne de mest tradisjonsrike, koselige, eksotiske og orginale overnattingstilbudene her i samme bok.

Tilbudene er sortert geografisk, fylkesvis. På side 13 ser du en oversikt over fylkene og i hvilken rekkefølge de kommer.

Redaksjonen har stolt på utlei-

Vorwort

Willkommen zur 5. Ausgabe von "The Norway Bed & Breakfast Book". Hier finden Sie nette und gastfreundliche Menschen in Stadt und Land. Unsere Gastgeberfamilien freuen sich, Sie und Ihre Lieben bei Ihrem nächsten Norwegenurlaub zu empfangen. Dieses Buch hält ein vielseitiges Angebot für Sie bereit. Bei den meisten Gastgebern ist Frühstück im Preis enthalten. Da wir jedoch in Norwegen keine so lange "Bed & Breakfast"-Tradition wie in einigen anderen Ländern haben, sind auch Angebote für Selbstversorger aufgeführt. Diese bieten kein Frühstück, dafür aber eine gut ausgestattete Küche für Zubereitung von Mahlzeiten. Sie können unter verschiedenen Häusertypen, "Stabbur" (trad. Speicher), Villen usw. wählen.

Auch die Preise sind unterschiedlich. Preisgünstige Alternativen findet man bei Häusern für "Selbsthaushalt". Ist der Preis nicht so wichtig, sondern das Erlebnis, so finden Sie in diesem Buch viele traditionsreiche, gemütliche, exotische und originelle Übernachtungsmöglichkeiten. Die Angebote sind geografisch und nach Provinzen geordnet.

Accommodations are sorted geographically by county (fylke). On page 13 there is a handy overview of the counties in the same order of presentation as in the book.

The editors have relied upon the honesty and integrity of the hosts, who have provided the information presented. Among those hosts who are members of the NBT (Norwegian organization for rural tourism), a number have been through an official inspection process. You will find more details about the NBT on page 40.

Great effort has been made to ensure accuracy, but the editors and publisher take no responsibility for errors. Likewise, if quality or standard does not fulfill your expectations the editors have no responsibility regarding any agreements or reservations between guests and hosts based on information from this book.

This book undergoes continual change, and we rely on you to help us improve it. We hope you will turn to page 222 and write down and share with us your impressions and experiences as a B&B-guest and as a user of this book.

We wish you happy travels and bid you welcome on behalf of our B&B hosts – all across Norway – the land of majestic mountains and fjords.

ernes ærlighet og redelighet. Opplysningene i boken er basert på informasjon som de har sendt inn til oss. Blandt dem som er medlem i organisasjonen NBT (Norsk Bygdeturisme) har en del vært gjennom et inspeksjonsprogram. Du finner mer informasjon om dette på side 40.

Hvis standardnivå eller øvrig kvalitet ikke står i forhold til forventningene kan ikke vår redaksjon ta noe ansvar, heller ikke ved eventuelle feil. Ethvert leieforhold som baseres på denne boken er en avtale mellom vert og gjest. Vi har kun en informasjonsoppgave.

Denne boken ønsker vi å videreutvikle, og bare du kan fortelle oss hvordan den kan bli bedre. Vi ønsker derfor å høre fra deg. På side 222 kan du skrive noen ord om dine inntrykk og erfaringer. Send det så til vår redaksjon.

Vi håper at du vil få en rik ferieopplevelse ved å treffe nordmenn i sine hjemlige omgivelser. God ferietur og velkommen til våre B&B-verter i det vakre fjell- og fjordlandet Norge.

Übersicht der Provinzen und deren Reihenfolge auf Seite 13. Die Redaktion hat sich auf Ehrlichkeit und Redlichkeit der Vermieter verlassen. Alle Angaben in diesem Buch basieren auf Information, die uns zugesendet wurde. Einige Vermieter sind Mitglieder im Verband NBT (Norsk Bygdeturisme) und dadurch einer Kontrolle unterzogen. Weitere Information finden Sie auf Seite 40.

Sollten Standard oder übrige Qualität nicht den Erwartungen entsprechen, kann unsere Redaktion dafür keine Verantwortung übernehmen. Jedes Mietverhältnis aufgrund dieses Buches ist eine Vereinbarung zwischen Gastgebern und Gästen. Wir erbringen nur die Information.

Wir möchten dieses Buch gerne weiterentwickeln und nur Sie können uns berichten, wie wir es verbessern können. Auf Seite 222 können Sie Ihre Erfahrungen als B&B-Gast und Benützer dieses Buches aufschreiben und an uns schicken. Wir wünschen Ihnen wertvolle Urlaubserlebnisse bei der Begegnung mit Norwegern in deren heimatlicher Umgebung. Willkommen zu unseren "Bed & Breakfast"-Gastgebern in Norwegen, dem herrlichen Land der Fjorde und Berge!

Contents   Innhold   Inhalts-verzeichnis

Sogn & Fjordane:

Møre & Romsdal:

Solvår's B&B, Elverum, page 68

Norumgården B&B, Narvik, page 194

	Symbol reference	**Symbolforklaring**	**Symbolerklärung**

 Bed & Breakfast
open year round — Bed & Breakfast
åpent hele året — Bed & Breakfast
ganzjahrig geöffnet

 Bed & Breakfast
open in summer — Bed & Breakfast
åpent om sommeren — Bed & Breakfast
im Sommer geöffnet

 Selfcatering
open year round — Selvhushold
åpent hele året — Selbsthaushalt
ganzjahrig geöffnet

Selfcatering
open in summer — Selvhushold
åpent om sommeren — Selbsthaushalt
im Sommer geöffnet

The number refers
to page number. — Tallet refererer til
sidetallet i boken. — Die Zahl bezieht sich auf
die Seitenzahl des Buches.

The departments / Fylkene / Die Provinzen

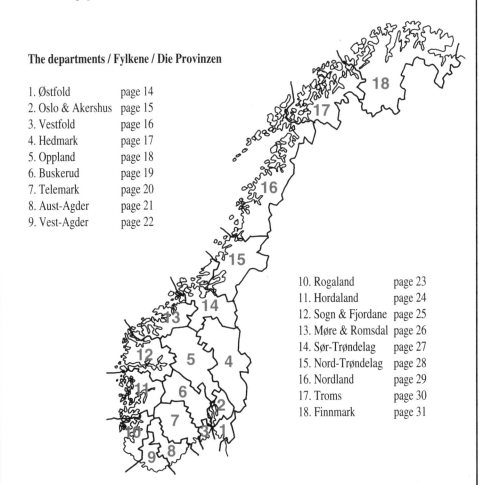

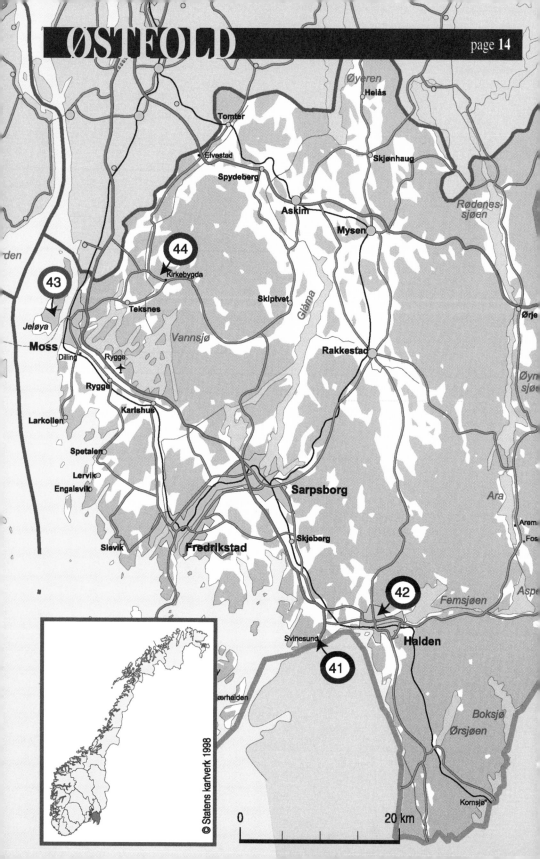

Øyeren

Heiås

Tomter

Elvestad

Spydeberg

Skjønhaug

Rødenes-
sjøen

Askim

Mysen

44

Kirkebygda

Teksnes

Skiptvet

Giåma

Ørje

den

43

Jeløya

Vannsjø

Moss

Dilling

Rygge

Rakkestad

Øyn
sjø

Rygge

Karishus

Larkollen

Spetalen

Lervik

Engalsvllo

Sarpsborg

Ara

Slevik

Fredrikstad

Skjeberg

Aremo

Fos

42

Femsjøen

Aspe

Svinesund

Halden

ærhalden

41

Boksjø

Ørsjøen

© Statens kartverk 1998

Kornsjø

0

20 km

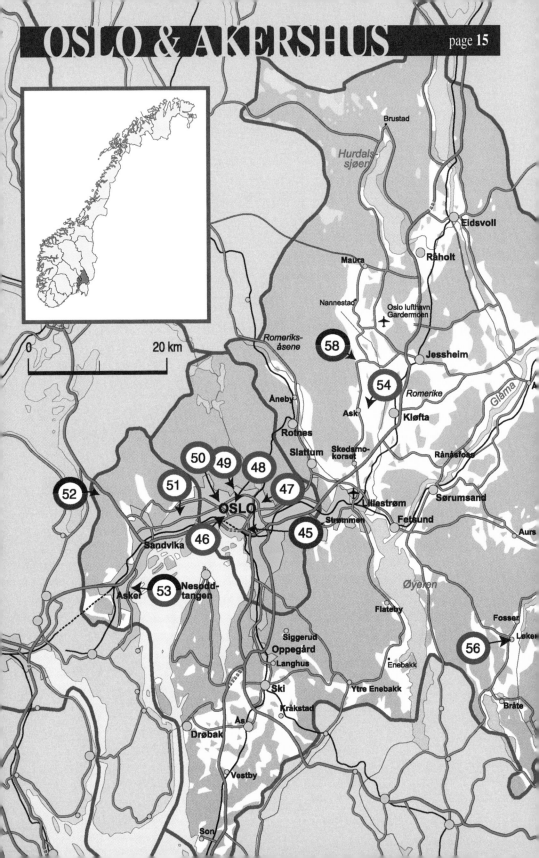

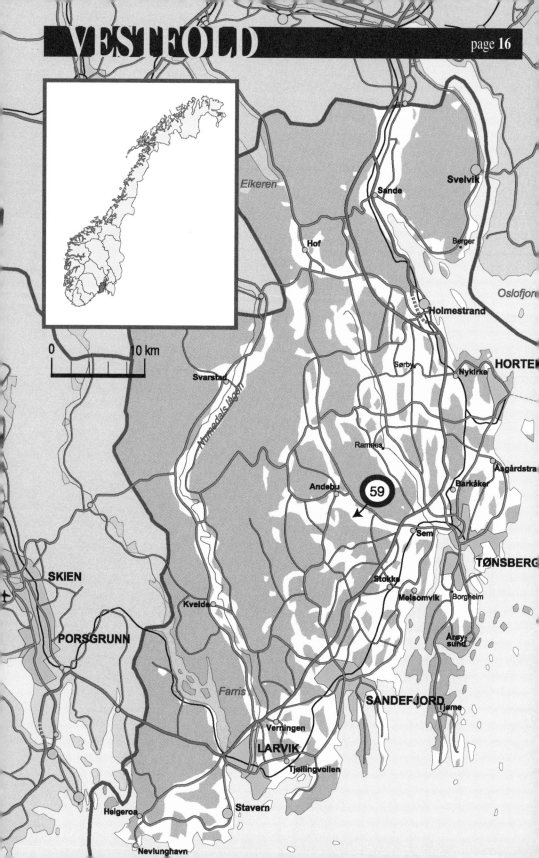

VESTFOLD

Eikeren

Svelvik

Sande

Berger

Hof

Oslofjor

Holmestrand

Sørby

Nykirke

HORTE

Svarstad

Numedalslågen

Ramnes

Åsgårdstra

Andebu

59

Barkåker

Sem

TØNSBERG

SKIEN

Stokke

Melsomvik

Borgheim

Kvelde

PORSGRUNN

Arøy
sund

Farris

SANDEFJORD

Tjøme

Verningen

LARVIK

Tjøllingvollen

Helgeroa

Stavern

Nevlunghavn

0   10 km

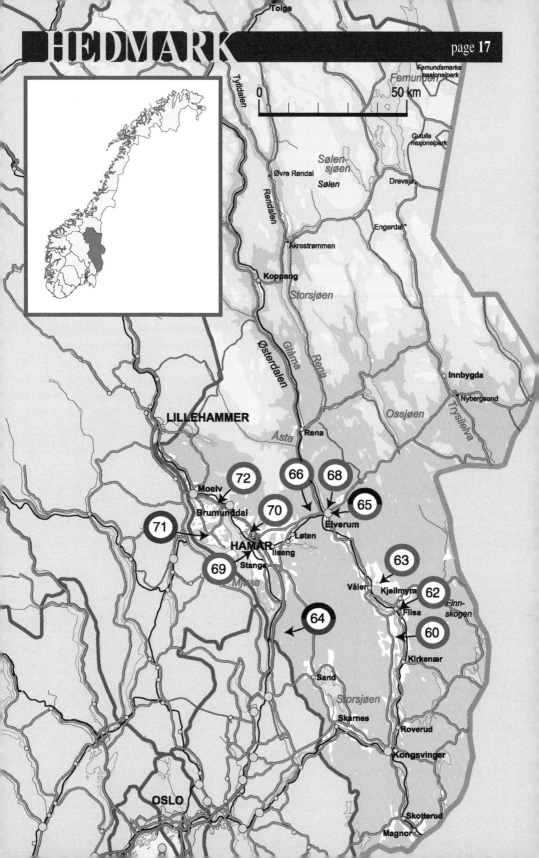

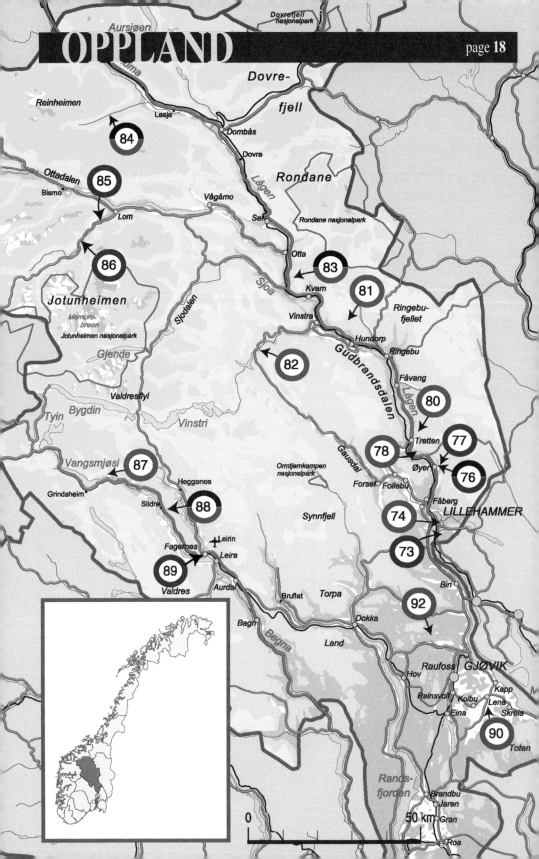

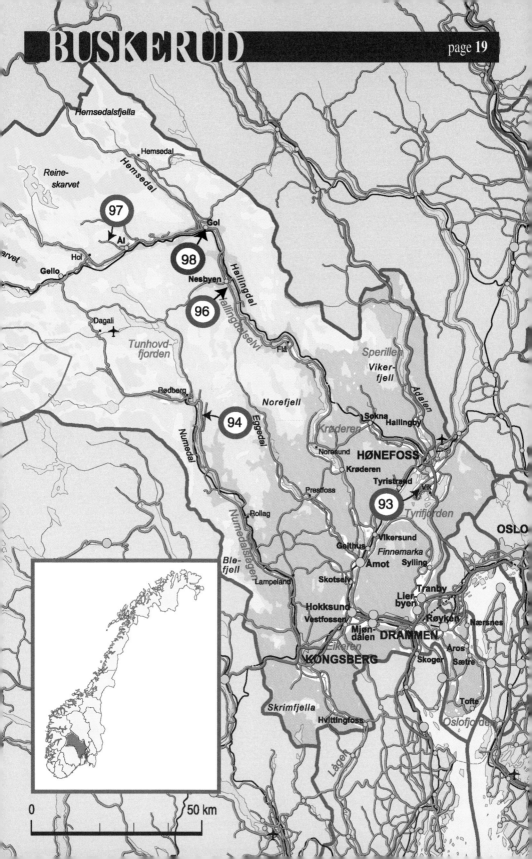

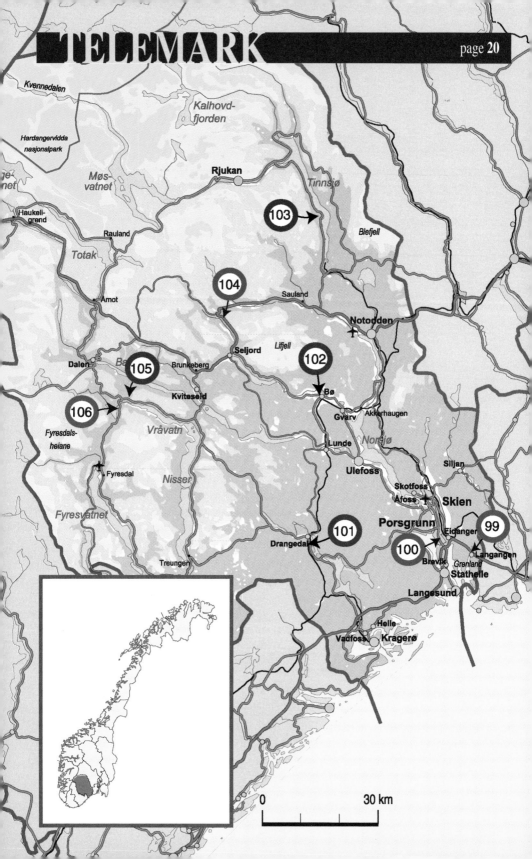

Kvennedalen

Kalhovd-
fjorden

Hardangervidda
nasjonalpark

Møs-
vatnet

Rjukan

Tinnsjø

103

Blefjell

Haukeli-
grend

Rauland

Totak

Amot

104

Sauland

Notodden

Seljord

Lifjell

102

Bø

Dalen

Brunkeberg

105

Kviteseld

Gvarv

Akkerhaugen

106

Fyresdals-
heiane

Vråvatn

Lunde

Norsjø

Siljan

Fyresdal

Nisser

Ulefoss

Skotfoss

Skien

Afoss

Fyresvatnet

101

Porsgrunn

Eidanger

99

100

Langangen

Drangedal

Brevik

Grenland

Stathelle

Treungen

Langesund

Langesund

Helle

Vadfoss

Kragerø

0   30 km

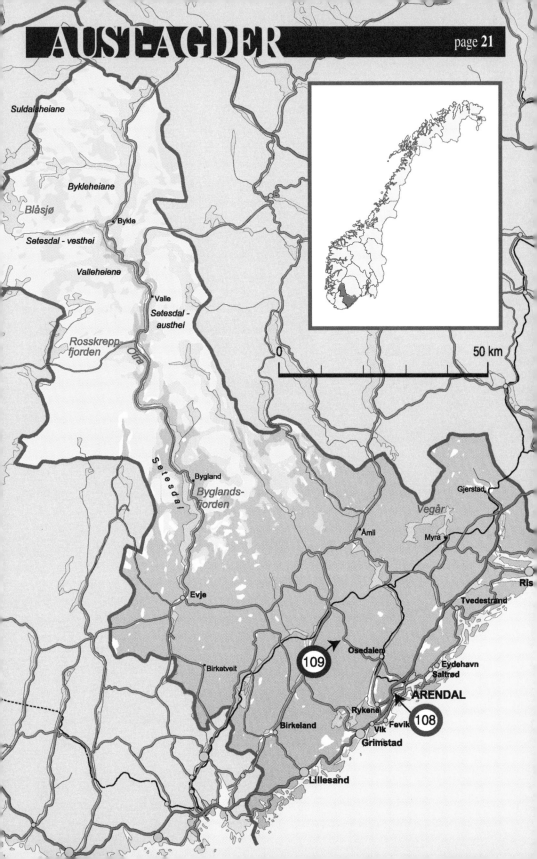

Suldalsheiane

Bykleheiane

Blåsjø

Bykle

Setesdal - vesthei

Valleheiene

Valle

Setesdal - austhei

Rosskrepp-fjorden

Otra

Setesdal

Bygland

Byglands-fjorden

Gjerstad

Vegår

Åmli

Myra

0   50 km

Ris

Tvedestrand

Evje

Osedalen

109

Eydehavn

Saltrød

Birketveit

ARENDAL

Rykene

Vik   Fevik

108

Birkeland

Grimstad

Lillesand

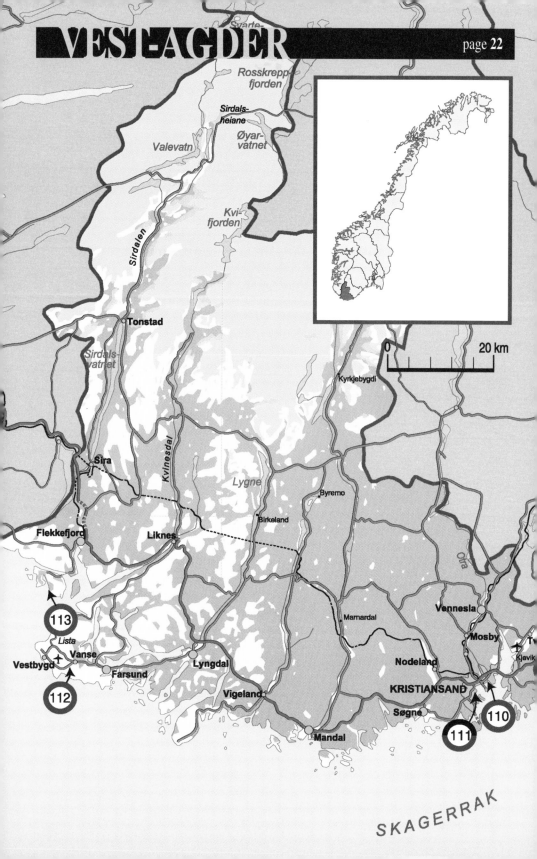

VEST-AGDER

Svarte-

Rosskrepp-
fjorden

Sirdals-
heiane

Øyar-
vatnet

Valevatn

Kvi-
fjorden

Sirdalen

Tonstad

Sirdals-
vatnet

Kyrkjebygdi

0   20 km

Sira

Kvinesdal

Lygne

Byremo

Birkeland

Flekkefjord

Liknes

Otra

Marnardal

Vennesla

113

Mosby

Lista

Vanse

Nodeland

Vestbygd

Farsund

Lyngdal

KRISTIANSAND

Kjevik

112

Vigeland

Søgne

110

111

Mandal

SKAGERRAK

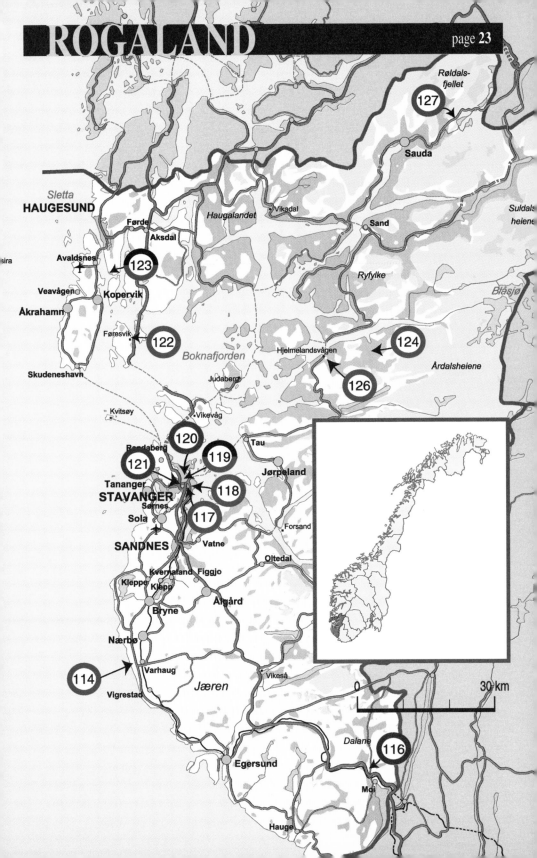

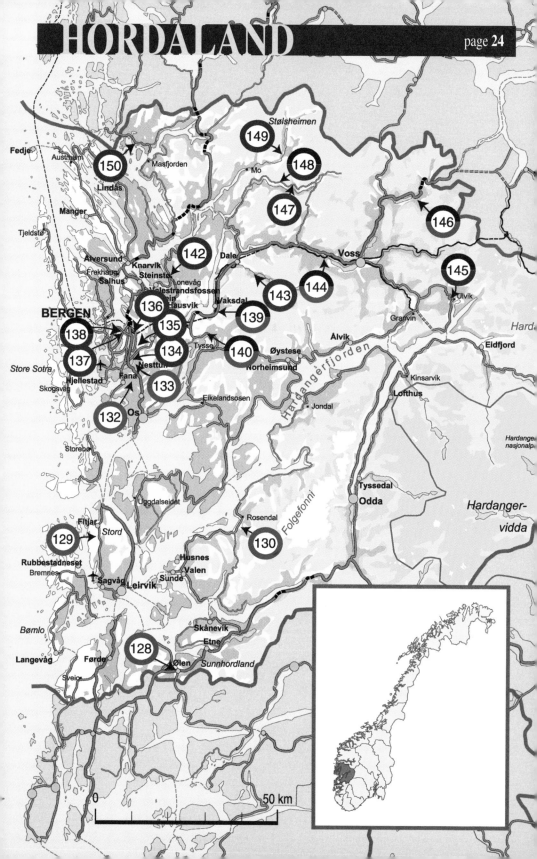

Fedje
Austrheim
Masfjorden
Stølsheimen
Mo
Lindås
Manger
Tjeldstø
Alversund
Frekhaug
Salhus
Knarvik
Steinstø
onevåg
Dale
Voss
Ulvik
Hard
Granvin
Eldfjord
BERGEN
olestrandsfossen
ein
Hausvik
Vaksdal
Ålvik
Kinsarvik
Lofthus
Store Sotra
Tysse
Øystese
Norheimsund
Hardangerfjorden
Hellestad
Nesttun
Fana
Skogsvåg
Eikelandsosen
Jondal
Hardange
nasjonalp
Storebø
Tyssedal
Odda
Hardanger-
vidda
Uggdalseidet
Rosendal
Folgefonni
Fitjar
Stord
Husnes
Valen
Rubbestadneset
Bremnes
Sagvåg
Leirvik
Sunde
Bømlo
Skånevik
Etne
Langevåg
Førde
Ølen
Sunnhordland
Sveio

150
149
148
147
146
142
145
143
144
136
135
139
138
134
140
137
133
132 Os
129
130
128

0   50 km

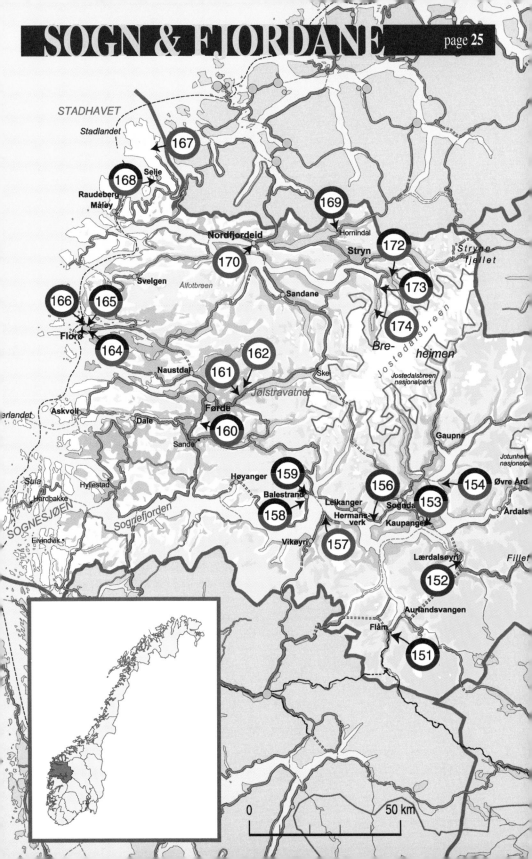

STADHAVET

Stadlandet

167

168 Selje

Raudeberg
Måløy

169

Hornindal

Nordfjordeid

Stryn

Stryne-
fjellet

172

170

173

Svelgen

Ålfotbreen

Sandane

174

Bre-
heimen

166 165

Flora

164

Naustdal

161 162

Jølstravatnet

Skei

Jostedalsbreen

Jostedalsbreen
nasjonalpark

Erlandet

Askvoll

Dale

Førde

Gaupne

160

Sandar

Jotunheim
nasjonalpa

Sula

Hyllestad

Høyanger

159

156

154 Øvre Ård

Hardbakke

Balestrand

Leikanger

Sogndal

153

Årdals

SOGNESJØEN

158

Hermans-
verk

Kaupange

Eivindvik

Sognefjorden

Vikøyri

157

Lærdalsøyri

Fillet

152

Aurlandsvangen

Flåm

151

0   50 km

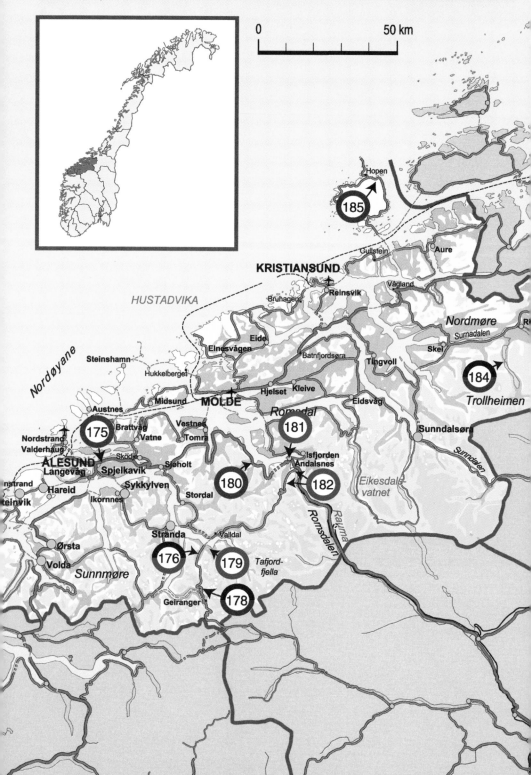

0   50 km

185

Hopen

Gullstein   Aure

KRISTIANSUND

Vågland

Bruhagen   Reinsvik

HUSTADVIKA

Nordmøre

Eide   Batnfjordsøra   Surnadalen

Elnesvågen   Skei

Steinshamn   Tingvoll   184

Nordøyane   Hukkelberget   Hjelset   Kleive   *Trollheimen*

Midsund   **MOLDE**   Eidsvåg

Austnes   *Romsdal*   **Sunndalsøra**

Nordstrand   Brattvåg   Vestnes   181   *Sunndalen*

Valderhaug   175   Vatne   Tomra

Skodje   Isfjorden

ÅLESUND   Sjøholt   Åndalsnes   *Eikesdals-*

Langevåg   Spjelkavik   180   182   *vatnet*

nstrand   Hareid   Sykkylven   Stordal

einvik   Ikornnes

Ørsta   Stranda   Valldal   *Romsdalen*   *Rauma*

Volda   176   179   *Tafjord-*

Sunnmøre   *fjella*

Geiranger   178

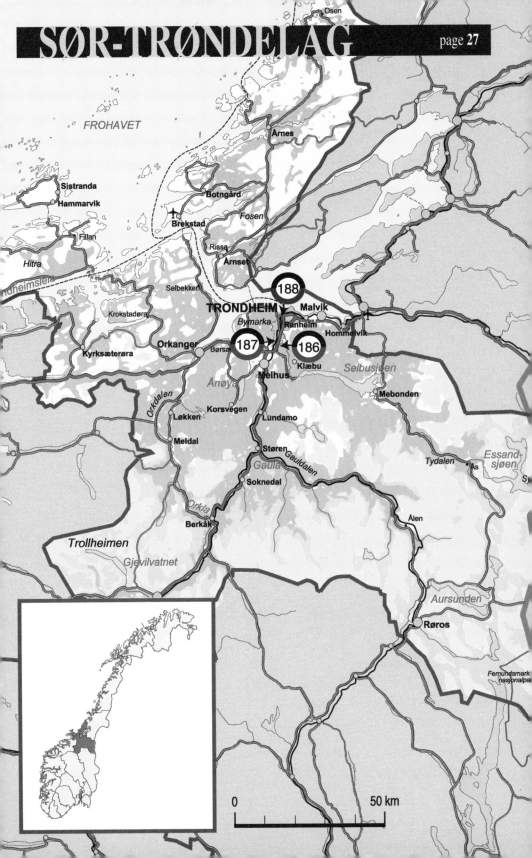

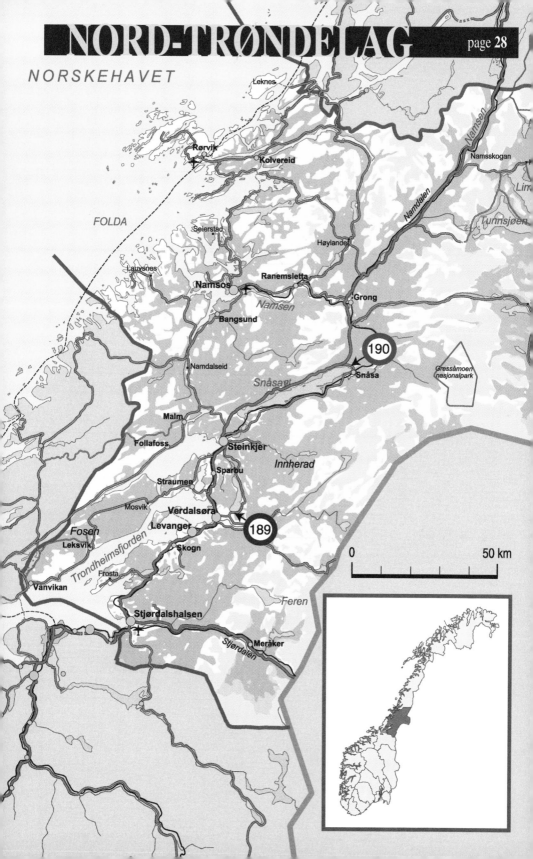

NORSKEHAVET

Vesterålen

Lofoten

Moskenstraumen

VESTFJORDEN

FOLDA

Ofoten

Røsthavet

Svart-
isen

Helgeland

Okstindan

Andenes
Bleik
Andøya
195

Myre
Sortland
Straumsjøen
Bø
Stokmarknes
Melbu
Lødingen

Hol
Bogen
NARVIK
Bjerkvik
Ballangen
194

Svolvær
Leknes
Stamsund
Kabelvåg
Henningsvær
Ramberg
Gravdal
Ballstad
193

Reine
Sørvågen

Kjøpsvik

Oppeid

192

Leinesfjorden

Sørland

Røstlandet

Rago
nasjonalpark

Salten
Løding
Fauske
Straumen

BODØ

Inndyr

Misvær
Moldjorda

Ørnes

Glomfjord

Vågaholmen

Saltfjellet - Svartisen
nasjonalpark

Træna

Lurøy
Storforshei

MO I RANA

Hemnes-
berget

Nesna

Solfjellsjøen
andnessjøen
holmen

Korgen

Leland

0   50 km

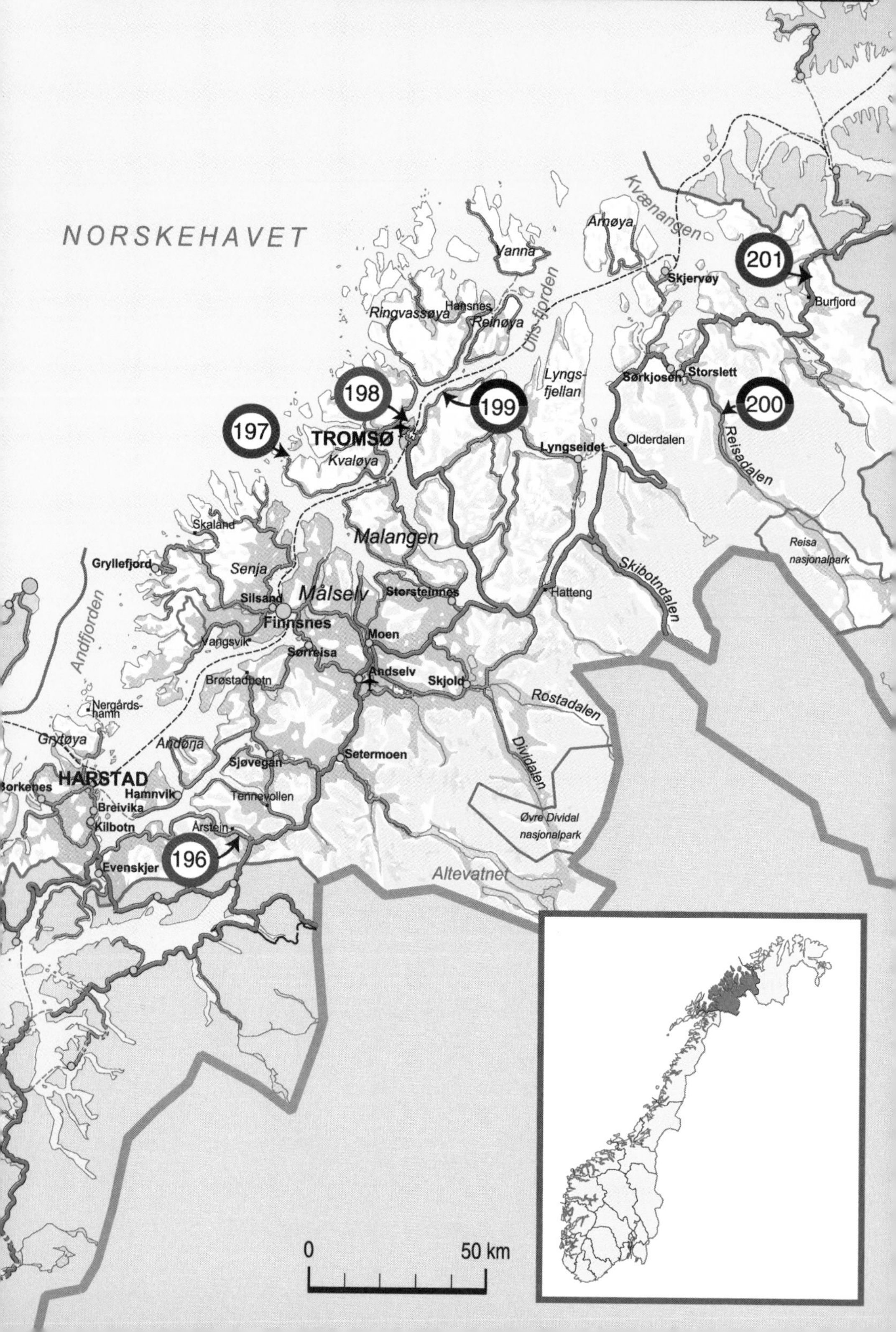

NORSKEHAVET

Yanna

Arnøya

Kvænangen

Skjervøy

201

Burfjord

Ringvassøya
Hansnes
Reinøya

Ullsfjorden

Lyngs-
fjellan

Sørkjosen
Storslett

200

198

199

TROMSØ

Kvaløya

Lyngseidet

Olderdalen

Reisadalen

197

Skaland

Malangen

Reisa
nasjonalpark

Gryllefjord

Senja

Målselv

Storsteinnes

Hatteng

Skibotndalen

Silsand

Finnsnes

Moen

Vangsvik

Sørreisa

Andselv

Skjold

Rostadalen

Brøstadbotn

Andfjorden

Nergårds-
hamn

Andørja

Setermoen

Dividalen

Grytøya

Sjøvegan

Øvre Dividal
nasjonalpark

HARSTAD

Hamnvik

Tennevollen

Borkenes

Breivika

Kilbotn

Årstein

196

Evenskjer

Altevatnet

0   50 km

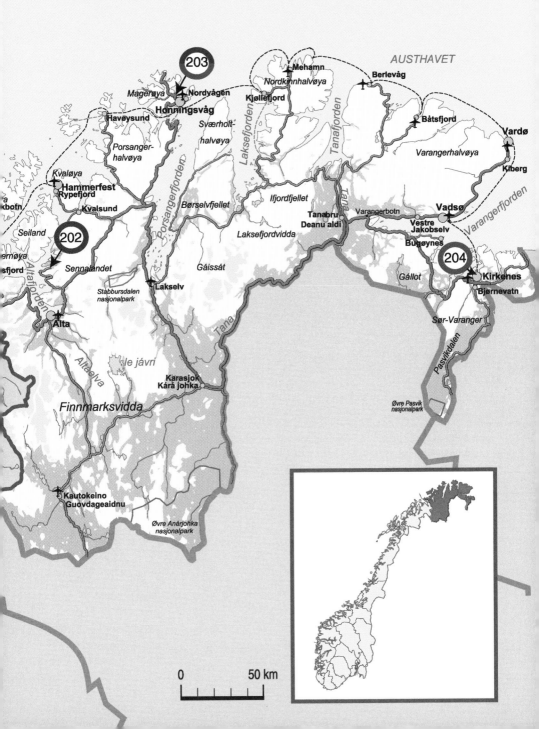

BARENTSHAVET

AUSTHAVET

203

Magerøya **Nordvågen**
Honningsvåg
Havøysund Sværholt-
halvøya

Nordkinnhalvøya **Mehamn**
Kjøllefjord **Berlevåg**

Båtsfjord

Porsanger-
halvøya *Laksefjorden* *Tanafjorden* **Vardø**

Varangerhalvøya

Kiberg

Kvaløya
Hammerfest
Rypefjord *Børselvfjellet* *Ifjordfjellet*

Varangerfjorden

Kvalsund *Laksefjordvidda* **Tanabru**
Deanu aldi Varangerbotn **Vadsø**

Vestre
Jakobselv

202

Seiland *Sennalandet* *Gáissát* **Bugøynes**

Gállot **204**

errnøya
sfjord

Laksek *Tana* **Kirkenes**
Bjørnevatn

Stabbursdalen
nasjonalpark **Lakselv**

Alta

Sør-Varanger

Altaelva *le jávri*

Finnmarksvidda **Karasjok**
Kárá johka

Øvre Pasvik
nasjonalpark

Kautokeino
Guovdageaidnu

Øvre Anárjohka
nasjonalpark

0   50 km

B&B or Self-catering

There are two main categories of lodgings:

1) Bed & Breakfast

2) Self-contained rental units consisting of either rooms, apartments, cabins or houses, all with kitchen access where guests can prepare their own meals. Breakfast is generally not served, but may be available upon request.

For both categories, the hosts live on the premises.

Uppermost on each page is a symbol indicating what is offered:

 Bed & Breakfast

 Self-catering

B&B eller Selvhushold

Det er to hovedkategorier blandt overnattingstilbudene:

1) Rom & Frokost (Bed & Breakfast)

2) Boenheter med selvhushold; det kan være rom, leiligheter, hytter eller hus, alle med kjøkken tilgjengelig hvor gjestene kan stelle sine egne måltider. Her serveres det normalt ikke frokost, men likevel vil du finne at noen kan tilby morgenmat.

Felles for alle tilbudene er at vertsfolket bor på stedet.

Symboler øverst på hver side indikerer hva som tilbys:

 Rom og Frokost

 Selvhushold

B&B oder Selbsthaushalt

Das Angebot ist in zwei Hauptkategorien aufgeteilt:

1) Zimmer und Frühstück (Bed & Breakfast)

2) Wohneinheiten für Selbsthaushalt, d.h. Zimmer, Ferienwohnungen, Hütten oder Ferienhäuser, alle mit Kochmöglichkeit, damit sich die Gäste eigene Mahlzeiten zubereiten können. Von wenigen Ausnahmen abgesehen, wird hier von den Gastgebern kein Frühstück zubereitet.

Bei beiden Kategorien wohnen die Gastgeber an der selben Stelle.

Symbole zuoberst auf jeder Seite geben die Art des Angebotes an:

 Zimmer und Frühstück

 Selbsthaushalt

Standard and quality

In order to provide the readers of our book with a more accurate idea of what each rental location has to offer, we have implemented a grading system for the B&B category. The criteria we use pertain only to the physical facilities being offered such as which items are in the room, how many share a bathroom, etc. The grading system gives no indication as to *quality*, such as the amount of service, cleanliness, decorations, quality of the furniture and equipment, etc. The most important indicator in the grading system for standards is that for *bathroom facilities*. The levels are as follows:

♣ Shared bathroom, where more than 4 people share.

♣ ♣ Shared bathroom with a max. of 4 people, or there is a sink in each of the rooms.

♣ ♣ ♣ Private bath comes with each room.

On the next pages you will find the full designation of requirements for each level of standard.

Standard og kvalitet

For at du som bruker av boken lettere skal få et riktig bilde av hva hvert enkelt utleiested har å tilby har vi innført et graderingssystem for B&B-kategorien. Inndelingen gjelder kun de fysiske faciliteter som tilbys; hva som finnes på rommet, hvor mange som deler bad etc. Graderingssystemet sier ingenting om *kvaliteten* av tilbudet, slik som servicegrad, renhold, dekorering, kvaliteten på møbler og utstyr etc.

Den viktigste indikatoren i graderingssystemet for standard er *baderomsfacilitetene*. Her er en tommelfingerregel for inndelingen:

♣ Delt bad hvor mer enn 4 personer deler bad når det er fullt belegg.

♣ ♣ Delt bad hvor max. 4 personer deler bad, eller det er vaskeservant på hvert av rommene.

♣ ♣ ♣ Hvert rom har eget bad.

På de neste sidene finner du den fulle fortegnelsen av hva som inngår i hvert av standardnivåene.

Standard und Qualität

Um allen Benutzern des Buches einen besseren Überblick über die Qualität des jeweiligen Übernachtungsbetriebs zu verschaffen, haben wir eine Klassifizierung der Angebote vorgenommen. Diese Einstufung bezieht sich allerdings nur auf die Ausstattung der Zimmer; wie z.B. was es im Zimmer gibt, wieviele das Bad teilen usw. Das System berücksichtigt nicht *Qualitäten* wie Dienstbereitschaft, Sauberkeit, Ausschmückung oder Qualität von Möbeln, Ausstattung usw. Das wichtigste Kennzeichen im Einstufungssystem für Standard sind die *Badverhältnisse*. Hier gilt als Grundregel:

♣ Gemeinsames Bad, das bei voller Belegung von mehr als 4 Personen geteilt wird.

♣ ♣ Gemeins. Bad, von höchstens 4 Pers. geteilt, oder Handwaschbecken in jedem der Räume.

♣ ♣ ♣ Jedes Zimmer hat eigenes Bad.

Auf der nächsten Seite finden Sie ein vollständiges Verzeichnis darüber, was jede der Standardstufen erfordert.

Standards for all Bed and Breakfasts

General:
*All guest rooms are clean and tidy. *Local tourist information and transport schedules available. *Regulation fire extinguishing equipment. *Key to the front door and/or room.

In the room:
*Good beds with proper mattresses. *Beds made with clean bed linen. *Extra pillow available. *Good lighting in the room - a night lamp by each bed. *Waste paper basket. *All electrical outlets must be secure and functioning. *Water glass available. *Curtains with functioning / drawing mechanism. *Chest of drawers / cupboards. *Chair(s). *Books and/or periodicals available. *Writing pad and pencil available.

In the bathroom:
*Toilet, hand basin and bath/shower, hot and cold water. *Mirror. *Soap and two hand towels per guest. *Waste paper basket. *Toilet paper. *Bathroom doors that can be locked. *Electrical outlets for shaver and hairdryer.

The Breakfast:
*Tea/coffee, milk and juice. *Bread with 4-6 different sandwich fillings. *Breakfast cereal. *Boiled egg upon request.

In addition to the above:
*Hand basin in the bedroom or max. 4 persons share a bathroom. *Mirror in the room. *Alarm clock in the room. *Iron and ironing board available. *Access to telephone.

In addition to the above:
*Ensuite bathroom. *Shampoo and hair conditioner available. *Coffee and tea making facilities. *Radio in the room. *Minimum one room with a writing desk.

In addition to the above:
*TV in the room. *Own guests' lounge. *Access to laundry. *Accept major credit cards.

Standardinndeling for Rom og Frokost

Generelt:
*Rent og ryddig i alle rom som gjestene benytter. *Lokal turistinformasjon og /eller rutetabeller.
*Forskriftsmessig brannvern. *Nøkkel til ytterdør og/eller rom.

Rommet:
*Gode senger med gode madrasser. *Oppredde senger med rent sengetøy. *Ekstra pute med putetrekk
tilgjengelig. *Godt lys på rommet - nattbordslampe til hver seng. *Avfallskurv. *Alle stikkontakter er
i orden og fungerer. *Vannglass tilgjengelig (på rommet eller på badet). *Gardiner med fortrekks-
mekanisme som fungerer. *Skuffer og/eller skap som er tomme og rene. *Stol(er). *Bøker og/eller
tidsskrift tilgjengelig. *Skriveblokk og blyant tilgjengelig.

Bad og toalett:
*Toalett, håndvask og badekar eller dusj, varmt og kaldt vann. *Speil. *Såpe og håndklær - to til hver
gjest. *Avfallskurv. *Toalettpapir og ekstrarull, boks el. rull m/tørkepapir. *Låsbar dør til baderom og
toalett. *Stikkontakt til barbermaskin el. hårtørrer.

Frokosten:
*Te/kaffe, melk og juice. *Brødmat med 4-6 påleggstyper. *Cornflakes eller kornblandinger el.l.
*Kokt egg ved ønske.

I tillegg til ovenstående oppfylles følgende:
*Håndvask på soverom el. maks 4 pers. deler bad. *Speil på rommet. *Vekkerklokke på rommet.
*Strykemuligheter. *Mulighet for bruk av telefon.

I tillegg til ovenstående oppfylles følgende:
*Eget bad til hvert rom. *Tilgang på shampo og hårbalsam. *Kaffe og te-selvbetjening. *Radio på
rommet. *Minst ett rom med skrivebord.

I tillegg til ovenstående oppfylles følgende:
*TV på rommet. *Egen stue/oppholdsrom til gjestene. *Mulighet for klesvask. *Kan ta kreditt-kort.

Standardeinteilung für Zimmer und Frühstück

Allgemein:
*Sauber und aufgeräumt in allen Räumen, die der Gast benutzt. *Örtliche Touristinformation und Fahrpläne. *Vorschriftsmässiger Brandschutz. *Schlüssel zu Haus- oder Zimmertür.

Das Zimmer:
*Gute Betten mit guten Matratzen. *Bezogene Better mit sauberer Bettwäsche. *Zusätzliches Kopfkissen mit Bezug zugänglich. *Ausreichendes Licht im Zimmer, Bettlampe über jedem Bett. *Abfalleimer. *Alle Steckdosen müssen in Ordnung sein. *Wasserglas zugänglich. *Gardinen, die sich vorziehen lassen. *Schublade und/oder Schrank müssen leer und sauber sein. *Stuhl(e). *Bücher und/oder anderes Lesematerial zugänglich. *Schreibmaterial zugänglich.

Toilette und Bad:
*Toilette, Handwaschbecken und Badewanne oder Dusche, W & K Wasser. *Spiegel. *Seife und Handtuch - 2 Handtücher für jeden Gast. *Abfalleimer. *Toilettenpapier und Extrarolle, Behälter oder Rolle mit Papierhandtüchern. *Abschliessbare Tür zu Bad und Toilette. *Stecker für Rasierapparat und Haarfön.

Das Frühstück:
*Tee/Kaffee, Milch und Saft. *Brot mit 4-6 verschiedenen Belägen. *Cornflakes, Müsli usw. *Gekochtes Ei oder Spiegelei nach Wunsch.

Zusätzlich wird folgendes geboten:
*Handwaschbecken aut dem Zimmer, oder max. 4 Personen teilen ein Bad. *Spiegel im Zimmer. *Wecker im Zimmer. *Möglichkeit zum Bügeln. *Telefonbenutzung.

Zusätzlich wird folgendes geboten:
*Eigenes Bad auf dem Zimmer. *Shampoo und Haarbalsam zugänglich. *Kaffee und Tee - Selbstbedienung. *Radio auf dem Zimmer. *Mindestens ein Zimmer mit Schreibtisch.

Zusätzlich wird folgendes geboten:
*Fernsehapparat auf dem Zimmer. *Aufenthaltsraum für die Gäste. *Möglichkeit zur Kleiderwäsche. *Kreditkarten werden angenommen.

How to use this book

All hosts are presented in this book by name, address and telephone/fax number and e-mail address for those having such. You are welcome to contact them directly. Most hosts prefer reservations in advance; they are then prepared to welcome you, and you are assured of lodging.

Not all hosts are available by telephone at all times. The "time to call" is given for each host. When you reserve a room, remember to give your expected time of arrival. B&B hosts do not have a 24-hr reception service: they are private individuals who are occasionally very busy.

Give your host as precise an arrival time as possible and you will be doing yourself a huge service. This allows your host to plan his daily routine and ensures that someone will be home when you arrive.

Reserving a room

When you send your reservation via mail, fax, or e-mail, please provide the following information:

*Name of guest along with the address, fax-/phone number and e-mail address *Arrival date and time of day *Date of

Hvordan bruke boken

Alle vertsfolk som er presentert i boken står oppført med navn, adresse, telefon-/faxnummer og e-post adresse for dem som har. Du er velkommen til å ta direkte kontakt med den enkelte tilbyder. De fleste foretrekker å motta forhåndsbestillinger. Vertsfolket liker å være forberedt på din ankomst og rom står klar til deg.

Ikke alle tilbydere er tilgjengelig på telefon til enhver tid. "Best tid å ringe" er indikert for hver tilbyder. Når du bestiller rom, husk alltid å nevne hvilken tid på dagen du forventer å ankomme. B&B-verter har ingen 24-timers resepsjonsbetjening, de er privatpersoner som til tider kan ha mye å gjøre.

Gi verten et mest mulig nøyaktig tidspunkt for din ankomst da gjør du deg selv en tjeneste. Verten kan planlegge sin dag og du kan være sikker på at det er folk tilstede når du ankommer.

Bestilling av rom

Når du sender din bestilling pr. brev, fax eller e-post, oppgi følgende opplysninger:

*Navn og adresse samt telfon-/faxnummer og evt. e-post

Gebrauch des Buches

Alle Gastgeber in diesem Buch sind mit Name, Straße, PLZ o. Ort, Telefon-/Faxnummer und E-Mail-Adresse (soweit vorhanden) aufgeführt. Sie können somit direkt mit dem einzelnen Vermieter Kontakt aufnehmen. Die meisten bevorzugen Voranmeldungen, damit sie sich auf den Empfang der Gäste vorbereiten können. Und für Sie ist dann die Unterkunft gesichert. Nicht alle Vermieter sind zu jeder Zeit telefonisch erreichbar.

"Zeit für Anrufe" ist für jeden Vermieter angeführt. Geben Sie, bitte, bei einer Bestellung immer Ihre voraussichtliche Ankunftszeit an. Die B&B-Gastgeber haben keinen 24-Stunden-Empfangsdienst, sondern sind Privatpersonen, die oft viel zu tun haben.

Bitte teilen Sie dem Vermieter den möglichst genauen Zeitpunkt Ihrer Ankunft mit. Sie tun sich damit auch selbst einen Gefallen. Ihr Vermieter kann dann seinen Tagesablauf genau planen und Sie bei Ihrer Ankunft empfangen.

Zimmerbuchung

Bitte, geben Sie bei Bestellung per Brief, Fax oder E-Post folgendes an:

departure *Number in party *Number of rooms/beds needed *Smoker or non smoker *Age of children *Special requirements.

Prices

All prices are given in Norwegian currency, on a per day basis.

Bed & Breakfast

For the B&B category, the price includes beds made with linen and breakfast for the number of people the room is designed for.

It is often possible to have an extra bed put in the room for an additional fee. Some B&B's also offer family rooms or rooms with several beds. Ask the host about prices.

Self catering

For the self-catering category, prices are given either for the whole unit or per person. Wherever a charge for bed linen is specified as an additional cost item, the charge pertains to each complete set per person for the first night's stay. You may subsequently use your own bed linen. When breakfast prices are listed, they represent a per person charge.

The book's organization

The included establishments are organized by county. Individual homes are marked on

---

adresse *Ankomstdato og tidspunkt for ankomst *Avreisedato *Antall personer i reisefølget *Antall rom/senger *Røker eller ikke-røker *Barns alder *Spesielle behov.

Priser

Alle priser er oppgitt pr. døgn, i norske kroner.

Bed & Breakfast

For B&B-kategorien inkluderer prisen oppredde senger og frokost for det antall personer som rommet er beregnet for. Det er i mange tilfeller mulig å få inn en ekstraseng på rommet for et tillegg i prisen. Noen B&B tilbyr også familierom eller flersengsrom. Spør vertskapet om pris.

Selvhushold

For utleie-enheter med selvhushold er prisene gitt enten for hele enheten eller pr. person. Der hvor sengetøy er spesifisert som tilleggspris, gjelder prisen pr. oppredning, altså pr. person, den første natten. Man kan eventuelt benytte medbrakt sengetøy.
Der hvor frokost er spesifisert gjelder prisen pr. person.

Bokens organisering

Tilbudene er sortert fylkesvis. På kartsidene finner du tall som refererer til de sidetallene hvor tilbyderne er presentert. Helt bakerst i boken finnes en

---

*Name, Adresse, Telefon-/Faxnummer und evt. E-Postadresse *Datum und Uhrzeit Ihrer Ankunft *Abreisedatum *Anzahl Zimmer/Betten *Raucher/Nichtraucher *Alter der Kinder *Besondere Anforderungen

Preise

Alle Preise sind pro Tag in norwegischen Kronen angegeben.

Bed & Breakfast

Für die B&B-Kategorie schliesst der Preis bezogene Betten und Frühstück für die Zahl der Personen, für die das Zimmer berechnet ist, ein. Gegen Preiszuschlag kann oft ein Extrabett erstellt werden. Bei einigen B&B gibt es auch Familienzimmer oder Mehrbettzimmer. Fragen Sie die Vermieter nach dem Preis.

Selbsthaushalt

Für Objekte mit Selbsthaushalt gelten die Preise für die ganze Einheit oder pro Person. Wenn für Bettwäsche ein zusätzlicher Preis angegeben ist, gilt der Preis pro Person und Bettwäsche-Set. Eventuell kann mitgebrachte Bettwäsche benutzt werden.
Wenn Frühstück aufgeführt ist, gilt der Preis pro Person.

Aufbau des Buches

Die Angebote sind nach Pro-

the maps by a number that refers to the page number where you will find their presentation. More detailed directions is given in the back of the book.

liste med veibeskrivelser for de av tilbyderne hvor det ikke ble plass nok på presentasjonssiden.

vinzen geordnet. Auf den Karten sind sie mit einer Zahl angegeben, die sich auf die Seitenzahl der jeweiligen Beschreibung bezieht. Ganz hinten im Buch gibt es eine Liste mit Zufahrtbeschreibungen zu den meisten Angeboten, in dieser Ausgabe leider nur Norwegisch und Englisch.

From Reisa National Park, Troms
Accommodation in the area: 'Laksefiskerens krypinn', page 200

Norsk Bygdeturisme (NBT)

This newly established special interest organization functions independently and works towards the development of Bed & Breakfasts along with various other small-scale vacation concepts in Norway. NBT has initiated a program for inspecting B&B's. The stamp "NBT Inspected", which you find at the top of each B&B presentation page is your guaranty that the description of each rental offer corresponds with actual facilities.

Please bear in mind that those B&B's you find in this book that do not have the NBT label are not necessarily of lower standard, but rather have not yet chosen to participate in the organization. Wherever you see "NBT Inspected", you already have your guaranty.

Norsk Bygdeturisme (NBT)

Den nystartede interesseorganisasjonen NBT er en uavhengig organisasjon som jobber for å utvikle Bed & Breakfast så vel som en rekke andre småskala reiselivskonsepter i Norge. NBT har introdusert et inspeksjonsprogram for B&B. Markeringen "NBT Inspected" som du finner øverst på B&B-presentasjonssidene er din garanti for at beskrivelsen av tilbudet er i samsvar med det som faktisk tilbys.

Når du i denne boken finner B&B som ikke er inspisert betyr ikke det nødvendigvis at de er dårligere, men at de foreløpig ikke har valgt å delta i organisasjonen NBT. Men der du finner "NBT Inspected" har du allerede din garanti.

Norsk Bygdeturisme (NBT)

Die neugegründete Interessenvereinigung NBT ist eine unabhängige Organisation, die es sich zum Ziel gesetzt hat, Bed & Breakfast sowie einige andere, kleinere Fremdenverkehrsbetriebe in Norwegen zu unterstützen.

Besonders wichtig erschien es, eine Qualitätskontrolle bei den Betrieben einzuführen. Der Begriff "NBT Inspected", den Sie ganz oben auf den Präsentationsseiten finden, dient als Garantie dafür, daß die aufgeführte Ausstattung auch tatsächlich vorhanden ist.

Wenn Sie in dieser Ausgabe noch Betriebe finden, die nicht mit dem Begriff "NBT Inspected" versehen sind, heißt das nicht, daß diese schlechter sind, sondern nur, daß sie vorläufig noch nicht an der Organisation NBT teilnehmen wollen. Bei allen anderen gilt die Garantie schon jetzt.

"Change is the law of life. Those who look only to the past or present are certain to miss the future."

-John F. Kennedy

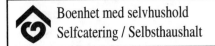
Villa Antique

Your host:
Victor & Renate Dahle

Address:
Svinesund
N - 1789 Berg i Østfold
Phone: 69 19 51 90
Fax: 69 19 51 90
Mobil: 92 62 55 56 / 90 79 71 57

Best time to call:
07.00 - 10.00 / 17.00 - 23.00

Apartment for 2-7 persons	Leilighet for 2-7 personer	Wohnung für 2-7 Personen
No. of bedrooms: 1 1/2	Antall soverom: 1 1/2	Anzahl Schlafräume: 1 1/2
Own bath, kitchen nook and LR	Eget bad, kjøkkenkrok og stue	Eig. Bad, Küchenecke und Stube
Price for whole unit: **500,-**	Pris for hele enheten: **500,-**	Ganze Einheit: **500,-**
Price per pers.: **150,-**	Pris pr. pers.: **150,-**	Preis pro Pers.: **150,-**
Bed linen fee: **40,-**	Tillegg for sengetøy: **40,-**	Mieten von Bettwäsche: **40,-**
Open 1 May - 30 Oct.	Åpent 1. mai - 30. okt.	Geöffnet 1. Mai - 30. Okt.
Pets accepted	Husdyr tillatt	Haustiere erlaubt
VISA and MC accepted	Vi tar VISA og MC	Wir nehmen VISA und MC
Handicap access	Handikappvennlig	Behindertengerecht
English spoken		Sprechen Englisch

The Dahle Family consists of two adults, two children, one dog and a rabbit. They operate Dahle's Antique Shop in the same locality and here you will find all sorts of items both inside and outside the house. The rental apartment is situated in the bottom level.

Directions:
The house is located near the Swedish border, 900 m from the Svinesund bridge. The house is easily visible from highway E-6, near the Shell gas station.

Familien Dahle består av to voksne, to barn, hund og kanin. De driver Dahles Antikvitetshandel i samme hus, hvor man finner mye rart både inne og ute. Utleieleiligheten ligger i underetasjen.

Veibeskrivelse:
Huset ligger 900 meter inn på norsk side fra Svinesundbroen. Huset er lett synlig fra E-6, ved Shell bensinstasjon.

Die Gastgeberfamilie Dahle besteht aus zwei Erwachsenen, zwei Kindern, einem Hund und einem Kaninchen! Im gleichen Haus befindet sich das Antiquitätengeschäft der Familie. Besucher finden hier innen wie außen bemerkenswerte Kaufgegenstände. Die Ferienwohnung befindet sich im Untergeschoss.

Wegbeschreibung:
Das Haus liegt von der Svinesundbrücke aus 900 m auf norwegischem Gebiet. Es ist von der E-6 aus leicht zu erkennen (in der Nähe der Shell-Tankstelle).

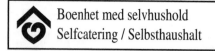
Pia's Gjestehus

Your host:
**Inger Liv Hansteen
& Svein Osborg**

Address:
**Brattveien 15
N - 1772 Halden**
Phone/Fax: **69 17 64 12**
Mobil: **90 03 30 42 / 90 66 51 66**
E-mail: **ing-liv@frisurf.no**

Best time to call:
09.00 - 17.00

Guesthouse for 2-8 persons	Gjestehus for 2-8 personer	Gästehaus für 2-8 Personen
No. of bedrooms: 4	Antall soverom: 4	Anzahl Schlafräume: 4
Own bath, kitchen, LR	Eget bad, kjøkken, stue	Eig. Bad, Küche, Stube
Price per pers.: **200,-/300,-**	Pris pr. pers.: **200,-/300,-**	Preis pro Pers.: **200,-/300,-**
Bed linen included	Sengetøy er inkludert	Inkl. Bettwäsche
Open 1 June - 31 Aug.	Åpent 1. juni - 31. aug.	Geöffnet 1. Juni - 31. Aug.
Off season upon request	Forøvrig på forespørsel	Nebelsaisson auf Anfrage
TV in all rooms	TV på alle rom	TV auf allen Zimmern
Yard/terrace/dekk access	Hage/terrasse/uteplass	Garten/Terrasse/Aussenplatz
Breakfast service available **100,-**	Frokost kan serveres **100,-**	Frühstück auf Bestellung **100,-**
English spoken		Sprechen etwas Deutsch

In the past, Halden has been held under siege by Sweden. Because of this, a fortress looms over the city, and history permeates the entire area.

A trip by private boat, canoe or "route boat" through Halden's chain of lakes will unveil many natural wonders. The dam and lock system here are North Europe's highest.

The hosts are a retired sea captain, and an ex-telegraphist and four stray cats who found a new home.

Halden har flere ganger gjennom historien vært beleiret av svenskene. Festningsverket ruver over byen. Det er historie i hver stein og tue i området.

Reiser du med båt gjennom Haldenvassdraget, kan du oppleve naturperler på nært hold. Sluseanlegget er Nord-Europas høyeste.

Vertskapet i Pias Gjestehus er en pensjonert sjøkaptein og en hjemmeværende telegrafist, samt fire bakgårdskatter som fant seg et nytt hjem.

Halden ist früher mehrmals von den Schweden belagert worden. Die Festung überragt die Stadt und jeder Stein zeugt von ihrer Geschichte. Mit dem eigenen Boot oder mit dem Ausflugsschiff kann man auf dem "Haldenvassdraget" Naturperlen erleben. Es gibt eine Schleusenanlage, die 28 m hoch und somit Nord-Europas höchste ist.

Die Gastgeber sind ein pensionierter Seekapitän und eine ehemalige Telegrafistin. Ausserdem gibt es 4 Katzen im Haus.

If you can dream it, you can do it. -Walt Disney

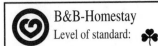
Bed & Breakfast in Moss

Your host:
Siri & Gjermund Wæhre

Address:
Stjerneveien 10
N - 1513 Moss
Phone: 69 27 23 17
E-mail: sirwah@frisurf.no

Best time to call:
08.00 - 23.00

Double-/Twin room:	**450,-**	Dobbelt-/tosengsrom:	**450,-**	Doppel-/Zweibettzi.:	**450,-**
1 pers. in double room:	**350,-**	1 pers. i dobbeltrom:	**350,-**	1 Pers. im Doppelzi.:	**350,-**
No. of rooms: 3		Antall rom: 3		Anzahl Zimmer: 3	
Full breakfast		Full frokost		Volles Frühstück	
Laid breakfast table or -tray		Dekket frokostbord el. frokostbrett		Serv.: Frühstückstisch o. -tablett	
Open year round		Åpent hele året		Ganzjährig geöffnet	
TV available		TV tilgjengelig		Zugang zu TV	
No smoking inside		Ingen røking innendørs		Kein Rauchen im Haus	
Discount for children		Rabatt for barn		Ermässigung für Kinder	
Selfcatering possible		Selvhushold er mulig		Selbsthaushalt möglich	
English & French spoken				Sprechen Deutsch	

You are a welcome guest in the home of a family of four situated in a peaceful neighborhood adjacent to a woodsy area. This single-family dwelling is located on the island of Jeløy, which features excellent swimming and recreational opportunities. Rental accommodation includes two good-sized bedrooms and a large family room. A large room with an open fireplace and TV is available for guest use. Jeløya is located just outside of the Moss city center, and from here the distance out to the Wæhre Family is 3 km.

I et fredelig villastrøk nært inntil skogen inviteres du som gjest hos familie på fire. Eneboligen ligger på øya Jeløy som byr på gode bade- og rekreasjonsmuligheter. For utleie er to middels store soverom og et stort familierom. En stor peisestue med TV står til gjestenes disposisjon. Jeløya ligger like utenfor Moss sentrum, og fra sentrum er det 3 km ut til fam. Wæhre.

In einer ruhigen Wohngegend, nahe am Wald, begrüßt die vierköpfige Familie ihre Gäste. Das Einfamilienhaus liegt auf der Insel Jeløya, die für ihre guten Bade- und Erholungsmöglichkeiten bekannt ist.
Vermietet werden zwei mittelgroße Schlafräume und ein großes Familienzimmer. Eine große Kaminstube mit TV steht ebenfalls für die Gäste bereit. Jeløya ist eine der Stadt Moss vorgelagerte Insel. Vom Zentrum aus sind es ca. 3 km bis zur Familie Wæhre.

Østre Tveter Gård

Your host:
Thor & Liv Scott Anstensrud

Address:
N - 1592 Våler
Phone: 69 28 98 23
Fax: 69 28 98 66
Mobil: 91 39 67 33
E-mail: eanstens@online.no

Best time to call:
11.00 - 13.00 / 20.00 - 23.00

A: Guesthouse for 2-6 persons	**A:** Gjestehus for 2-6 personer	**A:** Gästehaus für 2-6 Personen
No. of bedrooms: 3	Antall soverom: 3	Anzahl Schlafräume: 3
2 baths, kitchen, LR	2 bad, kjøkken og stue	2 Bäder, Küche, Stube
Price for whole unit: **1.320,-**	Pris for hele enheten: **1.320,-**	Ganze Einheit: **1.320,-**
Price per pers.: **220,-**	Pris pr. pers.: **220,-**	Preis pro Pers.: **220,-**
B: 'Store-house' for 2-5 persons	**B:** Stabbur for 2-5 personer	**B:** 'Vorratshaus' für 2-5 Personen
No. of bedrooms: 1	Antall soverom: 1	Anzahl Schlafräume: 1
Bath in annex, kitch. in store-house	Bad i sidebygn., kjøkken i stabbur	Bad im Annex, Küche im V.haus
Price for whole unit: **880,-**	Pris for hele enheten: **880,-**	Ganze Einheit: **880,-**
Price per pers.: **220,-**	Pris pr. pers.: **220,-**	Preis pro Pers.: **220,-**
Bed linen fee: **50,-**	Tillegg for sengetøy: **50,-**	Mieten von Bettwäsche: **50,-**
Open year round	Åpent hele året	Ganzjährig geöffnet
TV in guesthouse (A)	TV i gjestehuset (A)	TV im Gästehaus (A)
Yard/terrace/dekk access	Hage/terrasse/uteplass	Garten/Terrasse/Aussenplatz
No smoking inside	Ingen røking innendørs	Kein Rauchen im Haus
English spoken		Sprechen etwas Deutsch

Beautiful rural countryside and forest are the setting for this cosy farm in full operation with sheep, horses, Shetland ponies, pigs, hens, geese, ducks, rabbits, cats and dogs. Additionally, there is a sawmill, sign shop and gallery. You may help take care of the animals or enjoy the nice hiking trails in the forest.
Horseback-riding. A golf course is the nearest neighbour. A protected waterway is 7 km away, at Vansjø.

Omkranset av vakkert kulturlandskap og skog finner du denne trivelige bondegården som er i full drift med sau, hest, shetlandsponier, gris, høner, gjess, ender, kaniner, katter og hund. I tillegg er her et sagbruk, skiltverksted og galleri.
Her kan du få ta del i dyrestellet eller benytte deg av det flotte turterrenget i skogen. Muligheter for ridning. En golfbane er nærmeste nabo. 7 km til Vansjø som er et vernet vassdrag.

Einladender Bauernhof, umgeben von reizvoller Kulturlandschaft und Wäldern. Landwirtschaftlicher Betrieb mit Schafen, Pferden, Shetlandponys, Schweinen, Hühnern, Gänsen, Enten, Kaninchen, Katzen und Hunden. Sägewerk, Schilderwerkstatt, Galerie. Wer möchte, kann bei der Pflege der Tiere mithelfen oder das Wandergebiet ringsum erkunden. Reiten, Golfplatz in der Nähe, 7 km zum See Vansjø, einem unter Schutz stehenden Gewässer.

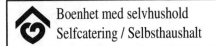
Den Blå Dør

Your host:
Anne Gutu

Address:
**Skedsmogata 7
N - 0655 Oslo**
Phone: **22 19 99 44**

Best time to call:
09.00 - 21.00

Room for 2 pers.:	**450,-**	Rom for 2 pers.:	**450,-**	Zimmer für 2 Pers.:	**450,-**
Room for 1 pers.:	**300,-**	Rom for 1 pers.:	**300,-**	Zimmer für 1 Pers.:	**300,-**
Shared bath and kitchen		Delt bad og kjøkken		Gemeins. Bad und Küche	
No. of rooms: 3		Antall rom: 3		Anzahl Zimmer: 3	
Bed linen included		Sengetøy er inkludert		Inkl. Bettwäsche	
Breakfast available:	**50,-**	Frokost kan serveres:	**50,-**	Frühstück:	**50,-**
Open year round		Åpent hele året		Ganzjährig geöffnet	
TV in rooms		TV på rommene		TV in den Zimmern	
Yard		Hage		Garten	
No smoking in rooms		Ingen røking på rom		Kein Rauchen im Zimmer	
Discount for children		Rabatt for barn		Ermässigung für Kinder	
English spoken				Sprechen etwas Deutsch	

Den Blå Dør (The Blue Door) is a pleasant place to stay at Kampen, one of the most attractive parts of Oslo. You will find closely built, old timber houses in a popular neighborhood where the owners have taken pride in restoring their homes over the decades. The Blue Door is 10 minutes by bus from Oslo centre, close to Tøyen and the Munch Museum. Take bus No. 60, get off at Kampen Church. Skedsmogata is two blocks from the bus stop, along Bøgata.

Den Blå Dør er et sjarmerende overnattingssted på Kampen, en av de triveligste bydelene i Oslo. Her står gamle trehus tett i tett, et populært område hvor omsorgsfulle huseiere har pusset opp og restaurert i årtier.
Stedet ligger 10 min. med buss fra Oslo sentrum, nær Tøyen og Munchmuseet. Ta buss nr. 60 til Kampen kirke. Skedsmogata ligger to kvartaler fra kirken, langs Bøgata.

Den Blå Dør ist eine gemütliche Übernachtungsmöglichkeit in Kampen, einem der nettesten Stadtteile Oslos. Dort findet man alte Holzhäuser dicht aneinander in einem beliebten Gebiet, wo umsichtige Besitzer seit Jahrzehnten ihre Häuser liebevoll restaurieren. Das Haus liegt in der Nähe vom Munch-Museum und den Tøyen-Museen und ist nach 10 Min. Busfahrt vom Zentrum Oslo aus zu erreichen. Bus Nr. 60 bis Kampen Kirche. Die Skedsmo-Strasse erreicht man nach zwei Häuserblocks der Bøgata.

Frognerparken Bed & Breakfast

Your host:
Claudia Debrunner
& Jørn A. Jensen

Address:
Kirkevn. 15, N - 0260 Oslo
Phone: 22 44 31 41
Mobil: 97 56 23 87
E-mail: bb-oslo@online.no
Web: http://bb-oslo.home.online.no

Best time to call:
08.00 - 23.00

Double room:	**500.-**	Dobbeltrom:	**500,-**	Doppelzimmer:	**500,-**
1 pers. in double room:	**400,-**	1 pers. i dobbeltrom:	**400,-**	1 Pers. in Doppelzimmer:	**400,-**
Single room:	**250,-**	Enkeltrom:	**250,-**	Einzelzimmer:	**250,-**
Surcharge for one night stay:	**25,-**	Tillegg for kun én natt:	**25,-**	Zuschlag, nur eine Noche:	**25,-**
No. of rooms: 2		Antall rom: 2		Anzahl Zimmer: 2	
Full breakfast		Full frokost		Volles Frühstück	
Laid breakfast table		Dekket frokostbord		Serv.: Frühstückstisch	
Open year round		Åpent hele året		Ganzjährig geöffnet	
Garden		Hage		Garten	
Discount for children		Rabatt for barn		Ermässigung für Kinder	
No smoking indoors		Ingen røking innendørs		Kein Rauchen im Haus	
Access to telephone/fax/Internet		Tilgang på telefon/faks/Internett		Zugang Telefon/Fax/Internet	
Pets welcome		Kjæledyr tillatt		Haustiere willkommen	
English and some French spoken				Sprechen Deutsch	

Young, easy-going Norwegian/ Swiss family with 3 children and a people-friendly cat welcome guests to a 100 year-old wooden manor home situated in quiet and peaceful surroundings adjacent to a large park near Oslo city center and the Vigeland Park. Short walk to the trolley, subway and many Oslo attractions. Your hosts have long experience in travel services.

Vi er en ung, ukomplisert norsk/ sveitsisk familie med tre barn og en menneskekjær katt. Vi inviterer til opphold i en 100 år gammel trevilla, med stille og fredelig beliggenhet i en stor hage sentralt i Oslo, like ved Vigelandsparken. Kort vei til trikk, T-bane og alle byens tilbud. Vertskapet har lang erfaring fra reiselivsbransjen

Wir sind eine junge, unkompli- zierte, norwegisch-schweizerische Familie mit 3 Kindern und einer freundlicher Katze. Wir laden Sie in unserer 100 Jahre alten Holzvilla ein. Ruhige Lage (großer Garten), zentral in Oslo und in unmittel- barer Nähe des Vigelandparks. Kurze Entfernung zu Straßenbahn, U-Bahn sowie allen Angeboten der Großstadt. Als Gastgeber blicken wir auf eine lange Erfahrung im Reisefach zurück.

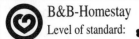
Solveig's Bed & Breakfast

Your host:
Roy Everson

Address:
Tåsen Terrasse 11
N - 0873 Oslo
Phone: 22 23 60 41
E-mail: raeverso@online.no
Web: http://solveigs.com

Best time to call:
08.00 - 22.00

Double-/Twin room:	**500,-**	Dobbelt-/tosengsrom:	**500,-**	Doppel-/Zweibettzimmer:	**500,-**
1 pers. in double room:	**375,-**	En pers. i dobbeltrom:	**375,-**	1 Pers. im Doppelzimmer:	**375,-**
Single room:	**300,-**	Enkeltrom:	**300,-**	Einzelzimmer:	**300,-**
Extra bed:	**100,-/50,-**	Ekstraseng:	**100,-/50,-**	Extra Bett:	**100,-/50,-**
No. of rooms: 3		Antall rom: 3		Anzahl Zimmer: 3	
Continental breakfast		Kontinental frokost		Kontinentales Frühstück	
Laid breakfast table		Dekket frokostbord		Serv.: Frühstückstisch	
Open year round		Åpent hele året		Ganzjährig geöffnet	
Terrace/deck access/yard		Terrasse/uteplass/hage		Terrasse/Aussenplatz/Garten	
No smoking		Ingen røking		Kein Rauchen	
English spoken		Snakker litt norsk		Sprechen Englisch	

Solveig's B&B has its name from mother Solveig who emigrated to America in 1948 after growing up in the house during WWII. Her son, your host, Roy, has now moved from America to Norway and opened the doors to Solveig's house for guests from far and near. The house lies on a hillside 5 km north of downtown and enjoys a nice view of the city and fjord. The quiet neighborhood is near Sognsvann lake and Nordmarka forest with easy access to public transport and the local shopping center nearby.

Solveigs B&B har navn etter mor Solveig som utvandret til Amerika i 1948 etter å ha vokst opp i huset under 2.verdenskrig. Verten Roy, hennes sønn, har nå utvandret fra Amerika til Norge og har åpnet dørene i Solveig's hus for gjester fra fjern og nær.
Huset ligger i en åsside i nordre del av Oslo og har fin utsikt over byen og fjorden. Det er et stille boligstrøk nær Sognsvann og Nordmarka. Det er gode offentlige transportmuligheter og kort vei til lokalt kjøpesenter.

Solveigs Bed and Breakfast wurde nach der Mutter Solveig benannt, die während des 2. Weltkriegs in diesem Haus aufwuchs und im Jahre 1948 nach Amerika auswanderte. Der Gastgeber Roy, ihr Sohn, ist nun von Amerika nach Norwegen gezogen und hat die Pforten in Solveig's Haus wieder für Gäste aus nah und fern geöffnet. Das Haus liegt an einem Hügel im nördlichen Teil Oslos und bietet eine reizvolle Aussicht auf Stadt und Fjord. Es liegt in einer ruhigen Wohngegend nahe des Waldgebiets Nordmarka und des Sees Sognsvann. Kurze Entfernung zu öffentlichen Verkehrsmitteln sowie zum Einkaufszentrum.

Evjen
Bed & Breakfast

Your host:
Esther & Knut Evjen

Address:
Holmenveien 16 B
N - 0374 Oslo
Phone: 22 92 10 59
Fax: 22 92 10 59
Mobil: 41 01 81 79
E-mail: eevjen@start.no

Best time to call:
09.00 - 18.00

Double room/Suite:	**650,-/750,-**	Dobbeltrom/suite:	**650,-/750,-**	Doppelzi./Suite:	**650,-/750,-**
Suite for 3 persons:	**900,-**	Suite for 3 personer:	**900,-**	Suite für 3 Personen:	**900,-**
1 pers. in double room:	**600,-**	En pers. i dobbeltrom:	**600,-**	1 Pers. im Doppelzi.:	**600,-**
Single room:	**425,-**	Enkeltrom:	**425,-**	Einzelzimmer:	**425,-**
No. of rooms: 2		Antall rom: 2		Anzahl Zimmer: 2	
Continental breakfast		Kontinental frokost		Kontinentales Frühstück	
Meals: Self-service		Servering: Selvbetjening		Serv.: Selbstbedienung	
Open year round		Åpent hele året		Ganzjährig geöffnet	
TV available		TV tilgjengelig		Zugang zu TV	
Yard/terrace/deck access		Hage/terrasse/uteplass		Garten/Terrasse/Aussenplatz	
Bike for rent		Sykkelutleie		Fahrrad zu mieten	
No smoking inside		Ingen røking innendørs		Kein Rauchen im Haus	
Selfcatering possible		Selvhushold er mulig		Selbsthaushalt möglich	
English spoken				Sprechen Englisch	

In a townhouse with a lush garden a short distance from Oslo town center you'll find comfortable rooms with a personal atmosphere and with an elegant shower-bathroom.
Its location along the Holmenkollen metroline makes it convenient to visit Holmenkollen, Vigeland Park and Oslo city center. Good variety of nearby stores, bank, post office, cafés and restaurants. Ample parking, washing of laundry is available. Your hosts are a retired attorney and a part-time teacher.

I en villa med flott hage, i kort avstand fra Oslo sentrum, finner du koselige rom med personlig atmosfære og eget elegant dusj-bad.
Villaen ligger på Vindern langs Holmenkollbanen, noe som gjør det enkelt å besøke både Holmenkollen, Vigelandsparken og sentrum av byen. Vindern byr også på et godt utvalg av butikker, bank, post, kaféer og restauranter. Det er gode parkeringsmuligheter, muligheter for klesvask.
Vertskapet er en pensjonert advokat og en deltids lærer.

Eine Villa in Vindern an der Holmenkollenbahn mit schönem Garten, nicht weit vom Zentrum Oslos entfernt. Gemütliche Zimmer mit persönlicher Atmosphäre und elegantem Bad.
Man kann also sehr gut sowohl den Holmenkollen, den Vigelandpark und das Zentrum Oslos besuchen. Man erreicht sehr schnell den Holmenkollen, den Vigelandpark sowie Oslo Zentrum. Vindern bietet mehrere Geschäfte, Bank, Post, Cafès und Restaurants. Gute Parkmöglichkeiten. Waschmaschine vorhanden. Gastgeber sind ein pensionierter Rechtsanwalt und eine Lehrerin.

Mary's
Bed & Breakfast

Your host:
Mary & Kjell Pedersen

Address:
Jerpefaret 15 B
N - 0788 Oslo
Phone: 22 92 17 71
E-mail: kjell.pedersen@chello.no

Best time to call:
09.00 - 11.00 / 18.00 - 23.00

Double room w/waterbed:	**600,-**	Dobbeltrom m/vannseng:	**600,-**	Doppelzi. m/Wasserbett	**600,-**
Single room:	**350,-**	Enkeltrom:	**350,-**	Einzelzimmer:	**350,-**
1 pers. in double room:	**350,-**	En pers. i dobbeltrom:	**350,-**	1 Pers. im Doppelzi.:	**350,-**
No. of rooms: 2		Antall rom: 2		Anzahl Zimmer: 2	
Full breakfast		Full frokost		Volles Frühstück	
Laid breakfast table		Dekket frokostbord		Serv.: Frühstückstisch	
Open year round		Åpent hele året		Ganzjährig geöffnet	
Terrace/deck access		Terrasse/uteplass		Terrasse/Aussenplatz	
No smoking inside		Ingen røking innendørs		Kein Rauchen im Haus	
English spoken				Sprechen Englisch	

350 meters above sea level and west of Holmenkollen, Mary and Kjell welcome both Norwegian and foreign guests to their home. A 25-minute metro ride from downtown Oslo (line no. 1) and you are close to city offerings while enjoying peaceful surroundings and beautiful views of Oslo Fjord and nearby countryside.
A short distance away is Holmen-kollen National Ski Centre (ski-jump, Nordic skiing, summer concerts, Norwegian Ski Museum). Go on foot or via metro.

350 meter over havet, på Holmen-kollens vestside, ønsker Mary og Kjell gjester fra inn- og utland velkommen til sin enebolig. 25 minutter med T-bane nr. 1 fra Oslo sentrum bor du nært byen med alle dens tilbud, samtidig som du har rolige omgivelser og nydelig utsikt til Oslofjorden og nærliggende landskap.
Det er kort avstand til Holmen-kollen riksanlegg (langrenn, skihopp m/konserter om sommeren og Norsk Skimuseum) enten til fots eller med T-bane.

Auf der Westseite des Holmen-kollen, 350 Meter hoch gelegen, heißen Mary und Kjell ihre Gäste aus dem In- und Ausland in ihrem Einfamilienhaus willkommen. Nur 25 Minuten mit der U-Bahn nr. 1 von Oslo Zentrum entfernt, kann man die Angebote einer Großstadt jederzeit nutzen. Gleichzeitig wohnen Sie in einer ruhigen Umgebung mit einer sehr schönen Aussicht auf den Oslo-fjord und die angrenzende Landschaft. Auch zur Holmen-kollen-Anlage (Skispringen, Langlauf, Norwegisches Ski-museum, im Sommer Konzerte) ist es zu Fuß oder mit der U-Bahn nicht weit.

Oslo
Bed & Breakfast

Your host:
Ida Løchen

Address:
Gråkamveien 20
N - 0779 Oslo
Mobil: **91 60 01 13**

Best time to call:
09 00 - 22.00

Double room:	**500,-**	Dobbeltrom:	**500,-**	Doppelzimmer:	**500,-**
1 pers. in double room:	**400,-**	1 pers. i dobbeltrom:	**400,-**	1 Pers. in Doppelzimmer:	**400,-**

No. of rooms: 2	Antall rom: 2	Anzahl Zimmer: 2
Full breakfast	Full frokost	Volles Frühstück
Laid breakfast table	Dekket frokostbord	Serv.: Frühstückstisch
Open year round	Åpent hele året	Ganzjährig geöffnet
TV available	TV tilgjengelig	Zugang zu TV
Yard/garden/terrace/deck access	Hage/terrasse/uteplass	Garten/Terrasse/Aussenplatz
No smoking in rooms	Ingen røking på rom	Kein Rauchen im Zimmer
English spoken		Sprechen Englisch

Wooden house built in 1905 with a fantastic location and surroundings. Situated 200 m above sea level with a view of the Oslo Fjord. Large garden. Five min. to Metro (T-bane) and 15 min. via Metro to downtown. Short distance to Holmenkollen and nearby forest and lakes. Good cross-country ski trails, alpine ski slopes and swimming areas. Parking on private courtyard.

Trehus fra 1905 med fantatisk beliggenhet og atmosfære, 200 m over havet med utsikt over Oslofjorden. Stor, viltvoksende hage. Fem min. til T-bane og femten minutter med banen til sentrum. Kort vei til Holmenkollen og omkringliggende skogsområder og vann. Gode langrennsløyper, alpintbakker og bademuligheter. Parkering på privat gårdsplass.

Ein reizvoll auf 200 m Meereshöhe gelegenes Holzhaus von 1905. Besondere Atmosphäre. Schöne Aussicht über den fjord. Großer Garten. 5 Min. zur U-Bahn, 15 Min. mit der Bahn ins Stadtzentrum. Kurze Entfernung zum Holmenkollen und den umliegenden Seen und Waldgeb. Loipen und Alpinhänge, im Sommer Bademöglichkeiten. Parkmöglichkeit auf einem privaten Hof.

The person who goes farthest is generally the one
who is willing to do and dare.
The sure-thing boat never gets far from shore.
- Dale Carnegie

Anna's Place

Your host:
Anna Borg

Address:
Myrveien 2 B
N - 1358 Jar
Phone: 67 58 92 68
Mobil: 93 69 56 14
E-mail: annasplacenorway@
hotmail.com

Best time to call:
08.00 - 10.00 / 19.00 - 22.00

Double-/Twin room:	**800,-**	Dobbelt-/tosengsrom:	**800,-**	Doppel-/Zweibettzi.:	**800,-**
Price for family of 4:	**1.000,-**	Pris for fam. på 4:	**1.000,-**	Preis für Fam. 4 Pers.	**1.000,-**
Price for 4 adults	**1.100,-**	Pris for 4 voksne:	**1.100,-**	Preis für 4 Erw.	**1.100,-**

Apartment w/own bath, kitchen, LR with double bed and bedroom w/bunk-beds	Leilighet m/eget bad, kjøkken, stue med dobbeltseng og soverom m/køyesenger	Wohnung mit eig. Bad, Küche, Stube mit Doppelbett und Schlafzimmer mit Kojenbetten
Full breakfast	Full frokost	Volles Frühstück
Laid breakfast table	Dekket frokostbord	Serv.: Frühstückstisch
Open year round	Åpent hele året	Ganzjährig geöffnet
TV in appartment	TV i leiligheten	TV in der Wohnung
Yard/terrace/deck access	Hage/terrasse/uteplass	Garten/Terrasse/Aussenplatz
No smoking inside	Ingen røking innendørs	Kein Rauchen im Haus
Selfcatering possible	Selvhushold er mulig	Selbsthaushalt möglich
English and Czeck spoken		Sprechen Deutsch

This modern and spacious detached home is situated in a quiet neighborhood in Bærum, just outside Oslo's city limits, 15 min. drive by car or trolley from downtown. You will enjoy a full-featured and very comfortable basement apartment. You have your own entrance and a private garden and sitting area. A ping-pong table on the patio may be used. Your hostess is Swiss and her husband Norwegian. They have settled down in Norway after many years in Switzerland.

I et rolig villastrøk i Bærum, like utenfor Oslo's bygrense, 15 min. med bil eller trikk fra sentrum, ligger denne moderne og romslige eneboligen. Her tilbys en fullt utstyrt og meget komfortabel utleieleilighet i underetasjen . Den har egen inngang og egen hageflekk med sitteplass. Et ping-pong bord på terrassen kan også benyttes.
Vertinnen er sveitsisk og mannen norsk. De har nå slått seg ned i Norge etter mange år i Sveits.

Das moderne, geräumige Einfamilienhaus liegt in einer ruhigen Wohngegend in Bærum, direkt hinter der Stadtgrenze Oslos, mit dem Auto bzw. der Straßenbahn ca. 15 min vom Zentrum entfernt. Den Gast erwartet eine sehr gut ausgestattete, komfortable Einlieger-Ferienwohnung mit eigenem Eingang und einem Fleckchen Garten mit Sitzmöbeln. Tischtennisplatte auf der Terrasse zur Verfügung. Die Gastgeberin stammt aus der Schweiz, ihr Mann ist Norweger. Nach vielen Jahren in der Schweiz haben sie sich nun in Norwegen niedergelassen.

Sölvhölen Cottages

Your host:
fam. Smithurst

Address:
**Ringeriksveien 278
N - 1340 Skui**
Phone: **67 13 33 56 / 67 13 68 56**
Fax: **67 13 13 07**
E-mail: **stephen.smithurst@
nif.idrett.no**

Best time to call:
16.30 - 23.00

Guesthouse for 2-4 persons	Gjestehus for 2-4 personer	Gästehaus für 2-4 Personen
No. of bedrooms: 1	Antall soverom: 1	Anzahl Schlafräume: 1
Own bath, kitchenette, LR	Eget bad, tekjøkken, stue	Eig.Bad, kleine Küche, Stube
No. of guesthouses: 2	Antall gjestehus: 2	Anzahl Gästehauser: 2
Price per pers.: **150,-**	Pris pr. pers.: **150,-**	Preis pro Pers.: **150,-**
Bed linen fee: **50,-**	Tillegg for sengetøy: **50,-**	Mieten von Bettwäsche: **50,-**
Open 1 June - 15 Sept.	Åpent 1. juni - 15. sept.	Geöffnet 1. Juni - 15. Sept.
Yard/terrace/deck access	Hage/terrasse/uteplass	Garten/Terrasse/Aussenplatz
Bike for rent	Sykkelutleie	Fahrrad zu mieten
Discount for children	Rabatt for barn	Ermässigung für Kinder
Breakfast service available **30,-**	Frokost kan serveres **30,-**	Frühstück auf Bestellung **30,-**
English and some French spoken		Sprechen etwas Deutsch

Sølvhølen's atmosphere: a country setting with free ranging hens, located just off E-16, between Oslo and Hønefoss.
Home-made rolls beckon guests in the morning. Lovely surroundings summon one to hikes or bicycle trips (borrow from the Smithursts). Swim at nearby Oslofjord beach. Food stores close by.
Directions:
Take the exit in the direction of Hønefoss (E-16) from E-18 at Sandvika. After driving 7 km, you come to the village of Skui. Continue past the Skui sign and drive 2 km until you see a white house on the left and a sign that reads "Rooms & Cottage".

Sölvhölen ligger i landlige omgivelser og har frittgående høner i hagen. Du finner stedet like ved E-16, mellom Oslo og Hønefoss.
Det vanker ferske rundstykker til gjestene om morgenen.
Fint turterreng i området, muligheter for leie av sykkel. Badestrand i Oslofjorden. Kort avstand til butikker.

Veibeskrivelse:
Fra E-18, Sandvika; ta av mot Hønefosss, E-16. Kjør 7 km til tettstedet Skui. Etter skiltet Skui kjører du videre 2 km og ser huset på venstre hånd, hvitmalt med skiltet "Rooms & Cottage".

Sølvhølen, mit freilaufenden Hühnern im Garten, liegt in ländlicher Umgebung. Sie finden es an der E16 zw. Oslo und Hønefoss.
Jeden Morgen warten duftende Brötchen auf die Gäste. Die Umgebung lädt zu Touren ein, Fahrräder können Sie leihen. Der Badestrand ist am Oslofjord. Unweit zu Geschäften.

Wegbeschreibung:
Von der E-18 (Sandvika): Abzweigung nach Hønefoss (E-16). Nach 7 km erreichen Sie den Ort Skui. 2 km hinter dem Ortsschild liegt ein weißes Haus auf der linken Seite. Auf dem Schild steht "Rooms & Cottage".

The Blue Room

Your host:
**Tone K. Mamen
& Asgeir Mamen**

Address:
**Nesåsen 11C
N - 1394 Nesbru**
Phone: **66 84 90 10 / 57 67 63 25**
Mobil: **90 86 12 03**
E-mail: **tmamen@attglobal.net**
Web: **http://pws.preserv.net/the
blueroom**

Best time to call:
09.00 - 23.00

Double-/Twin room:	**600,-**	Dobbelt-/tosengsrom:	**600,-**	Doppel-/Zweibettzimmer:	**600,-**
1 pers. in double room:	**400,-**	En person i dobbeltrom:	**400,-**	1 Pers. im Doppelzimmer:	**400,-**
No. of rooms: 2		Antall rom: 2		Anzahl Zimmer: 2	
Full breakfast		Full frokost		Volles Frühstück	
Laid breakfast table		Servering: Dekket frokostbord		Serv.: Frühstückstisch	
Open 1 May - 1 September		Åpent 1. mai - 1. sept.		Geöffnet 1. Mai - 1. Sept.	
Yard/terrace/deck access		Hage/terrasse/uteplass		Garten/Terrasse/Aussenplatz	
Indoor swimmingpool		Innendørs svømmebaseng		Schwimmbad im Haus	
Boat for rent		Båtutleie		Boot zu mieten	
Bike for rent		Sykkelutleie		Fahrrad zu mieten	
No smoking inside		Ingen røking innendørs		Kein Rauchen im Haus	
Discount for children		Rabatt for barn		Ermässigung für Kinder	
Selfcatering possible		Selvhushold er mulig		Selbsthaushalt möglich	
Some English spoken				Sprechen etwas Deutsch	

On the outskirts of Oslo, Tone and Asgeir offer you airy, pleasant rooms with view in their large, modern manor home. The house has an indoor swimming pool and sauna, and ample parking nearby. Nesåsen is a residential area featuring detached homes with gardens and greenery, and your hosts also offer boat and bicycle rental. This allows you to combine a city holiday with outdoor activities.
It is a short way to public transport and the marina.

I utkanten av Oslo tilbyr Tone og Asgeir lyse og trivelige rom med utsikt i deres store moderne villa. Boligen har innendørs svømmebasseng og sauna, og det er gode parkeringsmuligheter ved huset. Nesåsen er et boligområde bestående av eneboliger med hager og grøntareal, og vertskapet kan også tilby båt- og sykkel-utleie. På denne måten kan man kombinere storbyferien med friluftsopplevelser.
Det er kort vei til offentlig kommunikasjon og båthavn.

Am Rande Oslos vermieten Tone und Asgeir in ihrer großen und modernen Villa helle und einladende Zimmer mit Aussicht. Schwimmbad und Sauna im Haus vorhanden, gute Parkmöglichkeiten direkt am Haus. Nesåsen ist ein Wohngebiet, in dem Einfamilienhäuser mit Vorgarten und viel Grün dominieren. Boots- und Fahrradverleih durch die Gastgeber. Idealer Ort, um einen Großstadturlaub mit Erholung im Grünen zu kombinieren.
Kurze Entfernung zu öffentlichen Verkehrsmitteln sowie zum Bootshafen.

B&B-Homestay
Level of standard: ♣ ♣

NBT-member
NBT-inspected

page **54**
Akershus

Smedstad Gård

Your host:
Randi E. Skallerud &
Laila H. Skallerud

Address:
Smedstad Gård
N - 2022 Gjerdrum
Phone: 63 99 10 90
Fax: 63 99 01 44
E-mail:
smedstad.gaard@online.no

Best time to call:
08.00 - 22.00

Twin room:	**620,-**	Tosengsrom:	**620,-**	Zweibettzimmer:	**620,-**
Single room:	**450,-**	Enkeltrom:	**450,-**	Einzelzimmer:	**450,-**
No. of rooms: 8		Antall rom: 8		Anzahl Zimmer: 8	
Full breakfast		Full frokost		Volles Frühstück	
Breakfast buffet		Servering: Frokost buffét		Serv.: Frühstücksbüfett	
Open 1 Jan. - 20 Dec.		Åpent 1. jan. - 20. des.		Geöffnet 1. Jan. - 20. Des.	
TV available		TV tilgjengelig		Zugang zu TV	
Terrace/yard		Terrasse/hage		Terrasse/Garten	
No smoking in rooms		Ingen røking på rom		Kein Rauchen im Zimmer	
Smoking room available		Røykerom		Raucherzimmer	
Phone/fax/Internet available		Tilgang på tlf./fax/Internett		Tel., Fax und Internet vorhanden	
Hot meals: min. 8 persons		Varme måltider: min. 8 personer		Warme Mahlzeiten; min. 8 Pers.	
English spoken				Sprechen Englisch	

Three generations welcome you to Smedstad Farm which is in the country side, 30 km north of Oslo, and approx. 15 km south of Oslo Airport Gardermoen.

The rooms are in the Main House, where the guests also have a common sitting-room. Eight rooms share two bathrooms. Washbasin with hot/cold water in each room. The farm has livestock which can be experienced at close hand.

Tre generasjoner ønsker velkommen til Smedstad gård som ligger i landlige omgivelser, 3 mil nord for Oslo og ca. 15 km. sør for Oslo Lufthavn Gardermoen. Rommene er i hovedhuset hvor gjestene også har en felles gjestestue. Åtte rom deler to bad, det er vaskeservant med varmt og kaldt vann på alle rom.

Det er dyr på gården som kan oppleves på nært hold.

Der Hof Smedstad liegt in lieblichem Bauernland, 30 km nördlich von Oslo und etwa 15 km südlich vom neuen Osloer Flughafen Gardermoen. Die drei Generationen des Hofes heissen Gäste willkommen.

Die Räume, sowie ein gemeinsamer Aufenthaltsraum, befinden sich im Haupthaus. 2 Bäder für insgesamt 8 Zimmer, Waschbecken (fl. w. u. k. Wasser) auf allen Zimmern. Möglichkeit für Kontakt mit Haustieren.

Room for 2 pers.:	Rom for 2 pers.: **460,-**	Zimmer für 2 Pers.:
Room for 1 pers.:	Rom for 1 pers.: **380,-**	Zimmer für 1 Pers.:
Shared bath, kitchen, DR and LR	Delt bad, kjøkken, spisestue, stue	Gem. Bad, Küche, Esszi.u. Stube
Bed linen included	Sengetøy er inkludert	Inkl. Bettwäsche
Open 1 Jan. - 20 Dec.	Åpent 1. jan. - 20. des.	Geöffnet 1. Jan. - 20. Des.
TV available	TV tilgjengelig	Zugang zu TV
Yard/terrace/dekk access	Hage/terrasse/uteplass	Garten/Terrasse/Aussenplatz
No smoking in rooms	Ingen røking på rom	Kein Rauchen im Zimmer
Smoking room availab	Røykerom	Raucherzimmer
English spoken		Sprechen Englisch

Close by the farm you have Romeriksåsen which has some lovely walks, cycle paths, fishing and swimming. In the winter there is a lit Nordic skiing circuit and downhill skiing. 18-hole golf course recently completed - 5 km from farm.

Directions:
From Oslo: Take E-6 north towards Hamar/Trondheim. Exit in Skedsmokorset and then take RV 120 towards Nannestad and Gjerdrum until you reach Ask. Turn right towards Kløfta and the Gjerdrum church. Look for a sign marked "Smedstad Gård" about 3 km from Ask on the left-hand side.

From Hamar or Oslo Airport:
Follow E6 towards Oslo and exit towards Kløfta. Turn right in the roundabout and continue towards Kløfta town center. Drive straight ahead through two roundabouts and stay on this road until it ends. Then turn left towards Ask and drive for about 1 km. Look for the sign for Smedstad Gård on the right side of the road.

I nærheten av gården ligger Romeriksåsen med fine turstier for fotturer og sykkelturer, fiskemuligheter og badevann. På vinteren er det lysløype og alpinbakke. 5 km unna ligger en nylig anlagt 18-hulls golfbane.

Veibeskrivelse:
Fra Oslo: Følg E-6 nordover i retning Hamar/Trondheim. Ta av i Skedsmokorset og følg RV 120 mot Nannestad og Gjerdrum helt til du kommer til Ask. Ta til høyre mot Kløfta og Gjerdrum kirke. Ca. 3 km fra Ask finner du skiltet "Smedstad Gård" inn til venstre.

Fra Hamar eller Oslo lufthavn:
Følg E-6 i retning Oslo og ta av E-6 mot Kløfta, ta til høyre i rundkjøringen og fortsett mot Kløfta sentrum. Kjør rett fram i to rundkjøringer og følg denne veien helt til enden. Ta så til venstre mot Ask og etter ca. 1 km vil du se skiltet med Smedstad Gård på høyre side av veien.

Nahe zum Gebiet Romeriksåsen für Wanderungen, Radtouren, Angeln und Baden. Im Winter Flutlichtloipe und Alpinanlage. 5 km entfernt befindet sich ein neu angelegter 18-Loch-Golfplatz.

Wegbeschreibung:
Ab Oslo: Folgen Sie der E-6 in Richtung Norden (Hamar/Trondheim). Bei Skedsmokorset biegen Sie ab auf die Str.120 in Richtung Nannestad und Gjerdrum. Im Ort Ask geht es rechts ab gegen Kløfta und Gjerdrum kirke. 3 km nach Ask links dem Schild "Smedstad Gård" folgen.

Aus Richtung Hamar oder Flughafen Oslo:
Folgen Sie der E 6 in Richtung Oslo und biegen Sie dann bei Kløfta ab. Im Kreisverkehr zweigen Sie nach rechts in Richtung Kløfta Zentrum ab. Sie durchqueren 2 weitere Kreisel (geradeaus halten) und folgen der Straße bis zum Ende. Dort geht es nach links in Richtung Ask, nach ca. 1 km sehen Sie das Schild „Smedstad Gård" (rechte Straßenseite).

Høland Bed & Breakfast

Your host:
Torunn & Tom Rolfson

Address:
Elverhøy
N - 1960 Løken
Phone: 63 85 05 55
Fax: 63 85 04 17
Mobil: 90 06 31 71
E-mail: tom.rolfson@ablecon.no

Best time to call:
08.00 - 22.00

Double room:	**600,-**	Dobbeltrom:	**600,-**	Doppelzimmer:	**600,-**
Loft with bed:	**500,-**	Sovehems:	**500,-**	Schlafboden:	**500,-**
1 pers. in double room:	**300,-**	1 pers. i dobbeltrom:	**300,-**	1 Pers. in Doppelzimmer:	**300,-**
1 pers in loft with bed:	**250,-**	1 pers på sovehems:	**250,-**	1 Person auf Schlafboden:	**250,-**
No. of rooms: 4		Antall rom: 4		Anzahl Zimmer: 4	
Other meals served on request		Ándre måltider etter avtale		Serv.: Andere Mahlzeiten	
Open year round		Åpent hele året		Ganzjährig geöffnet	
TV available		TV tilgjengelig		Zugang zu TV	
Terrace/deck access/yard/garden		Terrasse/uteplass/hage		Terrasse/Aussenplatz/Garten	
Bike for rent		Sykkelutleie		Fahrrad zu mieten	
Discount for children 50%		Rabatt for barn 50%		Ermäßigung für Kinder 50%	
Selfcatering possible		Selvhushold mulig		Selbsthaushalt möglich	
No smoking inside		Ingen røking innendørs		Kein Rauchen im Haus	
Pets welcome		Kjæledyr tillatt		Haustiere willkommen	
VISA accepted		Vi tar VISA		Wir nehmen VISA	
English spoken				Sprechen etwas Deutsch	

Directions:

From Oslo: Follow E-6 towards Trondheim and then RV159 towards Strømmen/Lillestrøm. Continue until Fetsund (signs are marked Bjørkelangen). Exit RV22 towards Mysen. Exit onto RV169 towards Løken and look for the sign to Bransrud after about 20 km. Turn left at the sign and drive 50 m. The farm is on the right-hand side.

Veibeskrivelse:

Fra Oslo. Følg E-6 i retning Trondheim til deretter RV 159 til Strømmen/Lillestrøm. Kjør videre til Fetsund (skiltet mot Bjørke-langen). Ta RV 22 i retning Mysen. Ta av til RV169 mot Løken, etter 20 km se etter skilt til Bransrud. Sving til venstre ved skilt, kjør 50 m. Gården ligger på høyre side.

Wegbeschreibung:

Fahren Sie ab Oslo auf der E-6 in Richtung Trondheim und biegen Sie dann auf die Str. 159 nach Strømmen/ Lillestrøm ab. Fahren Sie weiter bis Fetsund (Ausschil-derung nach Bjørkelangen), um dort auf die Str. 22 nach Mysen abzuzw. Anschließend geht es weiter auf Str. 169 in Richtung Løken. Nach ca. 20 km erreichen Sie die Ausschilderung nach Bransrud. Am Schild links ab-biegen, dann ca. 50 m zum Hof, rechts.

Guesthouse for 4-9 persons	Gjestehus for 4-9 personer	Gästehaus für 4-9 Personen
No. of bedrooms: 3 + loft	Antall soverom: 3 + hems	Anzahl Schlafzi.: 3 + Schlafboden
4 baths, kitchen, dining room, LR	4 bad, kjøkken, spisestue, stue	4 Bäder, Küche, Sp.Zi., Stube
Price for whole unit: **1.000,-**	Pris for hele enheten: **1.000,-**	Ganze Einheit: **1.000,-**
Price per pers.: **250,-**	Pris pr. pers.: **250,-**	Preis pro Pers.: **250,-**
Bed linen fee: **50,-**	Tillegg for sengetøy: **50,-**	Mieten von Bettwäsche: **50,-**
Open year round	Åpent hele året	Ganzjährig geöffnet
TV available	TV tilgjengelig	Zugang zu TV
Yard/Terrace/Deck access	Terrasse/uteplass/hage	Garten/Terrasse/Aussenplatz
Bike for rent.	Sykkelutleie	Fahrrad zu mieten
Pets welcome	Kjæledyr tillatt	Haustiere willkommen
No smoking indoors.	Ingen røking innendørs	Kein Rauchen im Haus
VISA accepted	Vi tar VISA	Wir nehmen VISA
Discount for children 50%	Rabatt for barn 50%	50% Ermäßigung für Kinder
Suitable for handicapped	Handikapvennlig	Behindertengerecht
English spoken		Sprechen etwas Deutsch

The vacation farm consists of four dwelling structures. The younger members in our family live in or the main dwelling while Grandma lives in the old house. The old storage house offers a fun overnight experience for kids. In the Stable, you will find a 170 m² guest house – alongside ten horses who still have their home here. The rooms have tiled floors with inlaid heating elements and AC. Høland features horseback-riding for children and touring for experienced riders. Here you will come across rabbits, chickens, cats and dogs, along with a large garden area that includes a fish pond, outdoor grill area with gas grills, trampoline, trees to climb and sandbox. Activities include Moose Safaris, transportation to a wetlands area where you can go bird watching. Take walks in the woods, and pick berries and mushrooms. Close by you will find lighted ski trails and small lakes. Close to soccer field, museum, grocery store and bus stop. All basic services within 1 km.

Feriegården på Høland består av fire bygninger. I "Hovedhuset" bor den yngre delen av familien, mens mormor bor i "Gamlebygningen". "Stabburet" er et spennende overnattingssted for barn som vil sove i høyet og i "Stallen" er det innrettet et 170 kvm stort komplett utstyrt gjestehus - ved siden av at ti hester fortsatt har sitt hjem her.
Rommene har flislagte gulv med varmekabler og air-condition. Høland tilbyr barneridning på ridebane og turridning for erfarne ryttere. Her er kaniner, høner, katter og hund, samt en stor hage med fiskedam, grillplass med gassgriller, trampoline, klatretre og sandkasse.
Tilbud om elgsafari, transport til fredet våtmarksområde med fugletitting og skogsturer med plukking av bær og sopp. I nærheten finnes det skogsveier og stier, lysløype og badevann med toaletter og fiskebrygge. Det er kjørevei til vannet. Fotballplass 500 m, gårdsmuseum 1,5 km. Butikk, landhandel 150 m, bussholdeplass 150 m.

Der Ferienbauernhof auf Høland besteht aus vier Gebäuden. Im "Haupthaus" wohnt der jüngere Teil der Familie, während Oma im "Altenhaus" lebt. Im Speicherhaus fühlen sich besonders die jüngsten Gäste, die gern im Heu schlafen möchten, sehr wohl.
Im "Stall" wurde ein 170 m² großes, komplettes Gästehaus eingerichtet – außerdem sind dort noch 10 Pferde untergebracht! Alle Zimmer verfügen über Fußbodenheizung und Klimaanlage. Kinder können auf dem Hof Reitstunden nehmen, für erfahrene Reiter sind sogar Ausritte möglich. Weitere Angebote: Kaninchen, Hühner, Katzen, Hunde, außerdem ein großer Garten mit Angelteich, Grillplatz, Trampolin, Kletterbaum und Sandkasten. Elchsafaris, Vogelexkursionen, Waldausflüge (Beeren und Pilze sammeln). Beleuchtete Loipe, Badesee mit Toiletten und Angelstelle. Geschäft 150 m, Bushaltestelle 150 m. 1 km zu allen wichtigen Serviceangeboten.

Trugstadloftet

Your host:
Grethe & Lars Chr. Kjærstad

Address:
Trugstad gård
N - 2034 Holter
Phone: 63 99 50 45
Mobil: 93 42 01 54 / 97 56 89 69

Best time to call:
16.00 - 22.00

'Store-house' for 2-8 persons	Stabbur for 2-8 personer	'Vorratshaus' für 2-8 Personen
No. of rooms: 4	Antall rom: 4	Anzahl Zimmer: 4
Two baths and one kitchen	To bad og ett kjøkken	2 Bäder, 1 Küche
Price per pers.: **275,-**	Pris pr. pers.: **275,-**	Preis pro Pers.: **275,-**
Bed linen included	Sengetøy er inkludert	Inkl. Bettwäsche
Open April - October	Åpent april - oktober	Geöffnet April - Oktober
TV available	TV tilgjengelig	Zugang zu TV
Yard/deck access	Hage/uteplass	Garten/Aussenplatz
No smoking inside	Ingen røking innendørs	Kein Rauchen im Haus
Breakfast service available	Frokost kan serveres	Frühstück auf Bestellung
Some English spoken		Sprechen etwas Deutsch

Trugstadloftet, an old storehouse which has been remodelled with antique farm furniture and canopy beds from the 1800's. Here you can make your own meals in the kitchen. Trugstadloftet is located in Holter, west of Jessheim, 15 min. from Oslo Airport.
Directions:
From Oslo: Take E-6 north towards Skedsmokorset where you will take RV 120 towards Nannestad. Drive through Gjerdrum until you come to the roundabout near the Rimi grocery store/gas station. Continue straight ahead about 2 km towards Nannestad. Turn left at the sign marked "Trugstad gård". Drive 800 m and you have arrived!

Trugstadloftet er et gammelt stabbur som er ombygd og innredet med gamle bondemøbler og himmelsenger fra 1800-tallet.
Her kan gjester stelle sine egne måltider i et enkelt kjøkken. Trugstadloftet ligger i Holter, vest for Jessheim, 15 min. fra Oslo flyplass.

Veibeskrivelse:
Fra Oslo: Følg E-6 nordover til Skedsmokorset hvor du tar RV 120 mot Nannestad. Kjør gjennom Gjerdrum til rundkjøring ved Rimi-butikk og bensinstasjon. Fortsett rett fram mot Nannestad, ca. 2 km. Ta så av til venstre hvor skilt sier Trugstad gård. Kjør 800 m og du er framme.

Trugstadloftet ist ein altes Vorratshaus (Stabbur), mit alten Bauernmöbeln (Himmelbetten anno 1880) eingerichtet. Hier können Gäste selbst ihre Mahlzeiten (kleine Küche) zubereiten. Holter liegt westlich vom Ort Jessheim, 15 Min. vom Flughafen Oslo entfernt. Wegbeschreibung: Ab Oslo: Folgen Sie der E-6 in Richtung Norden bis Skedsmokorset. Dort biegen Sie ab auf die Str.120 in Richtung Nannestad und Gjerdrum. Fahren Sie durch Gjerdrum bis zum Kreisel am Rimi-Supermarkt u. Tankstelle. Anschließend geradeaus in Richtung Nannestad (ca. 2 km), beim Schild "Trugstad Gård" links abbiegen. Nach 800 m ist das Ziel erreicht.

Aarholt-tunet

Your host:
Ingfrid Weydahl &
Svein Aarholt

Address:
N - 3160 Stokke
Phone: 33 33 90 96
Fax: 33 33 90 97
E-mail: aarholt@online.no
Web: www.aarholt-tunet.com

Best time to call:
09.00 - 22.00

4-bedded rooms:	**700,-**	4-sengsrom:	**700,-**	4-Bettzimmer:	**700,-**
Price per pers.:	**200,-**	Pris pr. pers.:	**200,-**	Preis pro Pers.:	**200,-**
No. of rooms: 2		Antall rom: 2		Anzahl Zimmer: 2	
Own bath, kitchen nook in rooms		Eget bad og kjk.krok på rommet		Eig. Bad, Küchenecke im Zimmer	
Bed linen fee:	**50,-**	Tillegg for sengetøy:	**50,-**	Mieten von Bettwäsche:	**50,-**
Open year round		Åpent hele året		Ganzjährig geöffnet	
Terrace/deck access		Terrasse/uteplass		Terrasse/Aussenplatz	
No smoking inside		Ingen røking innendørs		Kein Rauchen im Haus	
English spoken				Sprechen etwas Deutsch	

The Aarholt-tunet is a newly restored, old family farm with cozy little timber houses. In summertime you can experience a genuine ecological farming vacation program with activities such as animal care, making garments of wool, glazing bread, grilling pancakes, beaver safaris, etc., for those who are interested. Evening entertainment is included. The farm has donkeys, goats, sheep, rabbits, ducks, hens and cats. Other events during the year include various seminars, leadership training and overnight parties for groups.

Aarholt-tunet er en nyrestaurert gammel slektsgård med koselige små tømmerhus. Her drives økologisk landbruk. Om sommeren tilbys også et eget bondegårdsferieprogram med aktiviteter som dyrestell, karding og toving av ull, grisling av brød, lappesteking på takke, beversafari etc. for dem som vil være med på det. Kveldsunderholdning følger også med. På gården er det esel, geit, sauer, kaniner, ender, høner og katter. Ellers i året drives det her ulike kurs, leirskole, selskaper med overnatting og lignende for grupper.

Aarholt-tunet ist ein kürzlich restaurierter, historischer Generationenhof mit gemütlichen kleinen Blockhäusern. Hier wird ökologischer Landbau betrieben. Den Sommer über wird ein Bauernhof-Ferienprogramm angeboten, z.B. Tierpflege, Krempeln, Kämmen von Rohwolle, Brotbacktechniken (z.B. Vorbacken von Brotlaiben, damit sie eine gleichmäßige Kruste bekommen), Bibersafaris usw. Auch am Abend ist für ein Programm gesorgt. Auf dem Hof leben Esel, Ziegen, Schafe, Kaninchen, Enten, Hühner und Katzen. Das ganze Jahr über werden verschiedene Kurse angeboten, außerdem Ferienlager, Gesellschaften (mit Übernachtung) oder ähnliche Gruppenarrangements.

Strandsjø kurs-gård og potetkafé

Your host:
Åse Lund Støen/Ole Egil Støen
Address:
N - 2266 Arneberg
Phone: 62 95 34 47
Fax: 62 95 34 31
E-mail: strandsjo@strandsjo.no
Web: www.strandsjo.no
Best time to call:
08.00 - 22.00

Double-/Twin room:	**560,-**	Dobbelt-/tosengsrom:	**560,-**	Doppel-/Zweibettzi.:	**560,-**
1 pers. in double room:	**350,-**	1 pers. i dobbeltrom:	**350,-**	1 Pers. im Doppelzi.:	**350,-**
No. of rooms: 7		Antall rom: 7		Anzahl Zimmer: 7	
Full breakfast		Full frokost		Volles Frühstück	
Served in the kitchen		Serveres på kjøkkenet		Serv.: im "Kartoffelcafé"	
or in the "Potato Café"		eller i potetkaféen		oder in der Küche	
Open year round		Åpent hele året		Ganzjährig geöffnet	
Boat for rent		Båtutleie		Boot zu mieten	
No smoking in rooms		Ingen røking på rom		Kein Rauchen im Zimmer	
VISA accepted		Vi tar VISA		Wir nehmen VISA	
Phone/fax/Internet available		Tilgang til tlf./fax/Internett		Tel., Fax und Internet vorhanden	
Member of Norsk Gardsmat		Medlem av Norsk Gardsmat		Mitglied v. Norsk Gardsmat	
English spoken				Sprechen etwas Deutsch	

By Strandsjøen Lake, next to RV 210 between Eleverum and Kongsvinger, your hosts eager to welcome you to a small farm of character. The farm has been in the family for 6 generations. The guests live in a straw house, a timber frame house and in the main house. Breakfast is served in a renovated kitchen from the 1700s or in the "Potato Café". This Café is Norway's first. Open to the public on Saturdays and Sundays during the summer season.
There is livestock on the farm.
Unique fishing and bird watching possibilities.

Ved Strandsjøen, like ved RV 210 mellom Elverum og Kongsvinger, tar vertskapet imot gjester på et småbruk med særpreg. De er 6te generasjon på gården. Gjestene bor i halmhus, tømmerhus og i våningshuset.
Frokosten serveres i et restaurert 1700-tallskjøkken, eller i "Potetkaféen" som er Norges første og åpen for publikum hver lørdag og søndag i sommerhalvåret.
Det er husdyr på gården.
Unikt fugleliv og fiskemuligheter.

Bei Strandsjø, nahe der Strasse 210 zwischen Elverum und Kongsvinger, empfängt man Gäste auf einem kleinen Hof besonderer Art, den die 6. Generation bewirtschaftet. Die Gäste wohnen in Häusern aus Stroh und Blockholz, sowie im Haupthaus. Das Frühstück wird in einer restaurierten Küche aus dem 18. Jahrhundert serviert, oder im „Potetkaféen" (Kartoffelcafé), dem ersten in Norwegen (den Sommer über samstags und sonntags geöffnet). Es gibt Haustiere am Hof und in der Umgebung eine Vielfalt an Vögeln, sowie Angelmöglichkeiten.

A: "Halmkroken"
Straw-cabin for 2-9 persons
No. of bedrooms: 4
Two bathrooms and kitchen
Price for whole unit: **1.100,-**

B: "Halmstrået"
Straw-cabin for 2-3 persons
No. of bedrooms: 1
Own kitchenette, bath in other bld.
Price for whole unit: **400,-**

C: "Haljestugua"
Guesthouse for 2-6 persons
No. of bedrooms: 2
Own bath, kitchen and LR
Price for whole unit: **600,-**

Applies to all rental units:
Bed linen fee: **60,-**
Open year round
Yard
Boat for rent
No smoking in rooms
VISA accepted
English spoken

A: "Halmkroken"
Halmhus for 2-9 personer
Antall soverom: 4
To bad og kjøkken
Pris for hele enheten: **1.100,-**

B: "Halmstrået"
Halmhus for 2-3 personer
Antall soverom: 1
Eget tekjøkken, bad i annet hus
Pris for hele enheten: **400,-**

C: "Haljestugua"
Gjestehus for 2-6 personer
Antall soverom: 2
Eget bad, kjøkken og stue
Pris for hele enheten: **600,-**

For alle enhetene gjelder:
Tillegg for sengetøy: **60,-**
Åpent hele året
Hage
Båtutleie
Ingen røking på rom
Vi tar VISA

A: "Halmkroken"
Strohhaus für 2-9 Personen
Anzahl Schlafräume: 4
Zwei Bäder und Küche
Ganze Einheit: **1.100,-**

B: "Halmstrået"
Strohhaus für 2-9 Personen
Anzahl Schlafräume: 1
Kleine Küche, Bad in anderem Haus
Ganze Einheit: **400,-**

C: "Haljestugua"
Gästehaus für 2-6 Personen
Anzahl Schlafräume: 2
Eig. Bad, Küche und Stube
Ganze Einheit: **600,-**

Für alle Einheiten gilt:
Mieten von Bettwäsche: **60,-**
Ganzjährig geöffnet
Garten
Boot zu mieten
Kein Rauchen im Zimmer
Wir nehmen VISA
Sprechen etwas Deutsch

Directions:
Drive south from Elverum or
north from Kongsvinger on RV
210 about 45 km. Turn in the
direction of "Strandsjøen" at the
only Esso station along this route.
Proceed to follow the signs to
Strandsjø kursgård og potetkafé.

Veibeskrivelse:
Fra Elverum sørover eller fra
Kongsvinger nordover følges RV
210 ca. 45 km. Ved eneste Esso-
stasjon på denne strekningen, tar
du av mot "Strandsjøen". Følg
deretter skilting til Strandsjø
kursgård og potetkafé.

Wegbeschreibung:
Aus Richtung Elverum folgen Sie
der Straße 210 in südlicher, aus
Richtung Kongsvinger in
nördlicher Richtung, jeweils ca.
45 km. An der einzigen Esso-
Tankstelle auf dieser Strecke
abbiegen in Richtung "Strandsjøen". Folgen Sie dann der
Beschilderung bis zum Haus.

You can surmount the obstacles in your path if you are
determined, courageous and hardworking. Do not fear to
pioneer, to venture down new paths of endeavor.
-Ralph J. Bunche

Heggelund's rom og frokost

Your host:
Berit & Lars Petter Heggelund

Address:
Negardssvingen 3
N - 2270 Flisa
Phone: 62 95 16 27
Mobil: 91 19 15 59
E-mail: berit.heggelund@c2i.net
Web: www.heggelund.no

Best time to call:
09.00 - 22.00

Double room:	**450,-/550,-**	Dobbeltrom:	**450,-/550,-**	Doppelzimmer:	**450,-/550,-**
Twin room:	**450,-**	Tosengsrom:	**450,-**	Zweibettzimmer:	**450,-**
1 pers. in double room:	**325,-/425,-**	En pers. i dobbeltrom:	**325,-/425,-**	1 Pers. im Doppelzi.:	**325,-/425,-**
No. of rooms: 3		Antall rom: 3		Anzahl Zimmer: 3	
Full breakfast		Full frokost		Volles Frühstück	
Laid breakfast table		Dekket frokostbord		Serv.: Frühstückstisch	
Open year round		Åpent hele året		Ganzjährig geöffnet.	
TV available		TV tilgjengelig		Zugang zu TV	
Yard/terrace/deck access		Hage/terrasse/uteplass		Garten/Terrasse/Aussenplatz	
No smoking inside		Ingen røking innendørs		Kein Rauchen im Haus	
English and some French spoken				Sprechen etwas Deutsch	

Berit and Lars Petter bid you welcome to their newly restored Swiss villa from the early 1900s in a large garden at Flisa, between Kongsvinger and Elverum. They are determined to preserve the house's uniqueness and style, and the dining room is all original. Excellent opportunities for hiking tours, including nearby Finnskogen woods. If desired and weather permitting, breakfast may be served on the terrace or in the garden.

I en stor hage på Flisa, mellom Kongsvinger og Elverum, ønsker vertskapet Berit og Lars Petter deg velkommen til sin nyrestaurerte sveitservilla fra århundreskiftet. De har satset på å bevare husets stil og særpreg, og spisestua er helt uendret.
Det er fine muligheter for turgåing med blant annet Finnskogen i nærheten.
Om ønskelig og om været tillater det, kan frokosten serveres på terrassen eller i hagen.

In Flisa, zwischen Kongsvinger und Elverum, heißen Sie die Gastgeber Berit und Lars Petter in ihrer frisch renovierten Villa im Schweizerstil aus der Jahrhundertwende willkommen. Das Ehepaar hat es verstanden, den besonderen Stil des Hauses zu bewahren, so ist z.B. das Eßzimmer nahezu unverändert geblieben.
Die Region bietet mit dem in der Nähe liegenden Waldgebiet Finnskogen sehr gute Wandermöglichkeiten. Nach Absprache - und wenn das Wetter es zuläßt - kann das Frühstück auch im Garten oder auf der Terrasse serviert werden.

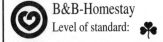
Ulfsbøl Søndre

Your host:
Wiebke Hartmann

Address:
Ulfsbøl Søndre
N - 2435 Braskereidfoss
Phone: 62 43 79 20
Fax: 62 43 79 21
Mobil: 90 55 47 21
E-mail: wiebke@c2i.net

Best time to call:
18.00 - 21.00

Double-/Twin room: **420,-**	Dobbelt-/tosengsrom: **420,-**	Doppel-/Zweibettzimmer: **420,-**
No. of rooms: 2	Antall rom: 2	Anzahl Zimmer: 2
Full breakfast	Full frokost	Volles Frühstück
Laid breakfast table	Dekket frokostbord	Serv.: Frühstückstisch
Other meals available	Andre måltider kan bestilles	Andere Mahlzeiten auf Anfrage
Open year round	Åpent hele året	Ganzjährig geöffnet
TV available	TV tilgjengelig	Zugang zu TV
Terrace/deck access/yard/garden	Terrasse/uteplass/hage	Terrasse/Aussenplatz/Garten
Bike for rent	Sykkelutleie	Fahrrad zu mieten
Swimming pool	Svømmebasseng	Schwimmbecken
Access to telephone/fax/Internet	Tilgang på telefon/faks/Internett	Zugang Telefon/Fax/Internet
Pets welcome	Kjæledyr tillatt	Haustiere willkommen
English spoken		Sprechen Deutsch

Old farm in idyllic surroundings with view of Glomdalen valley. Overhanging balcony, cozy sitting room with fireplace, large garden area with swimming pool. Forest with berries, mushrooms and wildlife just behind the house. Excellent area for hikes and bicycling. Fishing. Homemade cakes and preserves.

Gammel gård i idylliske omgivelser med utsikt over Glomdalen. Overbygget terrasse, hygglig peisestue, stor hage med svømmebasseng. Skog med bær, sopp og dyreliv like bak huset. Fint fottur- og sykkelområde. Finnskogen like ved. Fiske. Norsk Trafikksenter 3 km. Hjemmelagde kaker og syltetøy.

Idyllisch gelegener alter Bauernhof. Schöne Aussicht von überdachter Terrasse. Kamin im Aufenthaltsraum. Grosser Garten. Hinterm Haus der Wald mit Beeren, Pilzen und regem Tierleben. Zahlreiche Bäche und Seen mit Angelmöglichkeiten. Hausgemachte Kuchen und Marmelade.

They succeeded, because they did not know it was impossible.
–Origin unknown

Experience is the best teacher.
–Proverb

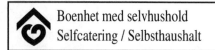

Spitalengen

Your host:
Lasse Knudsen, Elisabeth
Sandnes, Anne Mari Sletli

Address:
Spitalengen
N - 2338 Espa
Phone: 62 58 08 64
Phone/Fax: 62 58 08 58
Mobil: 41 10 24 65 / 94 36 06 77
E-mail: lajok@online.no

Best time to call:
08.00 - 23.00

Cabin for 2-7 persons	Hytte for 2-7 personer	Hütte für 2-7 Personen
No. of bedrooms: 2	Antall soverom: 2	Anzahl Schlafräume: 2
Own kitchen, LR	Eget kjøkken, stue	Eig. Küche, Stube
No running water, outhouse	Ikke innlagt vann, utedo	Kein fl. Wasser, Aussentoilette
Price for whole unit: **300,-**	Pris for hele enheten: **300,-**	Ganze Einheit: **300,-**
Bed linen fee: **50,-**	Tillegg for sengetøy: **50,-**	Mieten von Bettwäsche: **50,-**
Open 1 June - 31 Aug.	Åpent 1. juni - 31. aug.	Geöffnet 1. Juni - 31. Aug.
Winter: reservations required	Vinter: forhåndsbestilling nødv.	Winter: Vorbestellung nötig
TV available	TV tilgjengelig	Zugang zu TV
Indoor patio, garden	Innebygd terrasse, hage	Überdachte Terrasse, Garten
Boat and bike for rent	Båt- og sykkelutleie	Boot und Fahrrad zu mieten
Horseback Riding; advanced level	Ridning for øvet rytter	Reiten f. geübte Reiter
No smoking inside	Ingen røking innendørs	Kein Rauchen im Haus
Discount for children	Rabatt for barn	Ermässigung für Kinder
English spoken		Sprechen Deutsch

Spitalengen is a small, ecologically run farm in the quaint village of Spitalen. A family of 6 lives here and keeps busy with forestry and caring for their sheep and horses. Beautiful walking trails with a variety of summer and winter activities. To the south lie several small lakes. Families with children will enjoy swimming in Granerudsjøen.
45 km from Hamar and 10 km from Mjøsa. Note: water is fetched from an outside pump and the outhouse is situated about 10 meters from the guest cottage.

Spitalengen er et lite, økologisk småbruk i ei lita bygd - Spitalen. Her bor en familie på 6 som driver med litt skogbruk, sau og hest. I bygda er det et flott turterreng med muligheter for skogsturer, jakt, fiske og bading. På Granerudsjøen er det anlagt badeplass som er ypperlig for barnefamilier. Beliggenhet 45 km fra Hamar og 6 km fra Mjøsa.
Merk: vann hentes fra pumpe ute, og det er utedo i skjul ca 10 m fra hytta.

Kleiner, ökologisch wirtschaftender Bauernhof in der Gemeinde Spitalen. Die sechsköpfige Familie betreibt Forstwirtschaft sowie Schaf- und Pferdezucht. Spitalen bietet im Sommer wie im Winter sehr gute Wandermöglichkeiten. Im Süden der Gemeinde gibt es viele kleine Seen, z.B. Granerudsjøen mit Bademöglichkeiten insbesondere für Familien.
45 km bis Hamar, 10 km zum See Mjøsa. Bitte beachten: Wasser aus Pumpe (außen), Außentoilette im Schuppen (10 m).

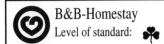
Skogholtet utleie

Your host:
Marit Nesset

Address:
Dagfinn Grønosetsveg 12B
N - 2400 Elverum
Phone: 62 41 54 42

Best time to call:
08.00 - 11.00 / 16.00 - 22.00

Twin room:	**390,-**	Tosengsrom:	**390,-**	Zweibettzimmer:	**390,-**
Single room:	**210,-**	Enkeltrom:	**210,-**	Einzelzimmer:	**210,-**
No. of rooms: 2		Antall rom: 2		Anzahl Zimmer: 2	
Continental breakfast		Kontinental frokost		Kontinentales Frühstück	
Open 1 June - 31 Aug.		Åpent 1. juni - 31. aug.		Geöffnet 1. Juni - 31. Aug.	
Deck access/yard		Uteplass/hage		Aussenplatz/Garten	
Selfcatering possible		Selvhushold er mulig		Selbsthaushalt möglich	
English spoken				Sprechen Englisch	

Skogholtet is situated 1.7 km. south-east of Elverum Church, a short distance from Elverum center, the Forestry Museum and a swimming beach. Fine hiking in the woods directly behind the house.

Directions:
From Norsk skogbruksmuseum take a left onto RV 20, then make two rights. Follow Grindals-bakken for 1 km passing block apartments on the left. Take the first right which is Dagfinn Grønn-osets vei. Take an immediate left and look for a light brown town-house in the road's curve.

Skogholtet utleie ligger 1,7 km sør-øst for Elverum kirke. Kort vei til Elverum sentrum, til Skog-bruksmuseet og til badeplass. Fine turmuligheter i skogen rett bak huset.

Veibeskrivelse:
Fra Norsk skogbruksmuseum; ta til venstre ut på RV 20, så til høyre to ganger. Følg Grindals-bakken 1 km forbi boligblokker på venstre side. Ta første til høyre som er Dagfinn Grønnosets vei. Ta så straks til venstre og finn en brunbeiset tomannsbolig i svingen.

Skogholtet utleie liegt 1,7 km südöstlich von der Kirche in Elve-rum. Unweit zum Zentrum von Elverum, zum Forstwirtschafts-museum und zum Badeplatz. Gute Wandermöglichkeiten in Waldge-lände direkt vom Haus aus.

Wegbeschreibung:
Vom Norwegischen Forstwirt-schaftsmuseum: biegen Sie nach links auf die Straße 20 ab, dann zweimal nach rechts. Folgen Sie der Straße Grindalsbakken bis ca. 1 km hinter einige Wohnblocks (linke Seite). Anschließend in die erste Straße rechts abzweigen (Dagfinn Grønnosets vei). Dann sofort wieder nach links, und Sie erreichen in der Kurve ein braunes Haus.

Midtskogen gård

Your host:
Eva Avkjern & Karl Espenes

Address:
Midtskogen gård
N - 2411 Elverum
Phone: **62 41 75 94**
E-mail: eva-av@online.no
Web: www.midtskogen.no

Best time to call:
08.30 - 09.30 / 17.00 - 18.00 /
22.00 - 23.00

Four bed room:	**700,-/800,-**	Firesengsengsrom:	**700,-/800,-**	Vierbettzimmer:	**700,-/800,-**
2 p. in four bed room:	**600,-/500,-**	2 pers. i firesengsrom:	**600,-/500,-**	2 Pers. in Vierbettzi.:	**600,-/500,-**
Two bed room:	**500-,**	Tosengsrom:	**500-,**	Zweibettzimmer:	**500-,**
Single room:	**300,-**	Enkeltrom:	**300,-**	Einzelzimmer:	**300,-**

No. of rooms: 4	Antall rom: 4	Anzahl Zimmer: 4
Full breakfast	Full frokost	Volles Frühstück
Laid breakfast table	Dekket frokostbord	Serv.: Frühstückstisch
Open year round	Åpent hele året	Ganzjährig geöffnet
TV available	TV tilgjengelig	Zugang zu TV
Deck access	Uteplass	Aussenplatz
No smoking inside	Ingen røking innendørs	Kein Rauchen im Haus
Access to telephone/fax/Internet	Tilgang på telefon/faks/Internett	Zugang Telefon/Fax/Internet
Pets welcome	Kjæledyr tillatt	Haustiere willkommen
English, Finnish and some French		Sprechen Deutsch

Simple, practical rooms in the main dwelling with private entrances to each room. Accommodations consist of cabins, apartments, campingrooms and loft. Personal service, peaceful atmosphere and good food made with top grade homegrown fruits and vegetables. Operational farm with free-roaming livestock, horse-based forestry activity, felt goods workshop. Ideal for families with children between the ages of 3-14 years. Activities: family-based games, forest hikes, creative learning for children, tours with horse and wagon or sleigh.

Enkle, praktiske rom i hovedbygningen med egen inngang til rommene. Hytter, leilighet, campingrom og soveloft utfyller tilbudet. Personlig service, fredelig atmosfære og god mat av førsteklasses råvarer fra gården. Levende gårdsmiljø med frittgående husdyr, skogbruk med hest, filtverksted.
Ideelt for familier med barn 3-14 år. Aktiviteter, familieleker, skogturer, kreativ forming for barn, kjøring med hest og vogn eller slede.

Einfache und praktische Zimmer im Hauptgebäude (eigener Eingang). Übernachtungen in Hütten, Ferienwohnungen, Campingzimmern sowie auf einem Schlafboden. Persönlicher Service, ruhige Atmosphäre, sehr gutes Essen (erstklassige Lebensmittel vom Hof). Echtes Bauernhofmilieu mit frei umherlaufenden Tieren, Forstwirtschaft (m. Pferd) und Filzwerkstatt. Ideal für Familien mit Kindern von 3 - 14 Jahren. Aktivitäten: Familienspiele, Waldtouren, kreatives Werken für Kinder, Touren mit Pferdewagen bzw. –schlitten.

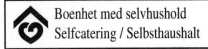
A: Apartment for 8 persons
No. of bedrooms: 3
Own bath, kitchen, LR
Price for whole unit: **800,-**
Price for 4 pers.: **600,-**

B: Cabin for 4 persons
No. of bedrooms: 1
Own bath, kitchen, LR
Price for whole unit: **500,-**

C: Campingrooms for 4 pers. (2x)
No. of bedrooms: 1.
Common access to guest kitchen
and sanitary facilities
Price per pers.: (min. 2 p.) **100,-**

D: Loft dormitory
60 m² dormitory offers basic
budget accommodation for
groups. We supply mattresses, the
guests must bring their own sleeping bags or a duvet and a pillow.
Common access to guest kitchen
and sanitary facilities.
Price per pers.: **70,-**
Group rebate

Applies to all rental units:
Bed linen fee: **40,-**
Open all year
Dormitory open 1 May - 1 Oct.

A: Leilighet for 8 personer
Antall soverom: 3
Eget bad, kjøkken, stue
Pris for hele enheten: **800,-**
Pris for 4 pers.: **600.-**

B: Hytte for 4 personer
Antall soverom: 1
Eget bad, kjøkken, stue
Pris for hele enheten: **500,-**

C: Campingrom for 4 pers. (2x)
Antall soverom: 1
Adgang felles gjestekjøkken og
sanitærrom m/dusj, vask og WC
Pris pr. person: (min. 2 p.) **100,-**

D: Soveloft
60 m² soveloft gir enkel og billig
innkvartering for grupper.
Madrasser finnes, gjester må ta
med soveposer, eventuelt dyne og
pute. Det er adgang til felles
gjestekjøkken og sanitæranlegg
med dusj, WC og vaskeservanter.
Pris pr. person: **70,-**
Grupperabatt

For alle enhetene gjelder:
Tillegg for sengetøy: **40,-**
Åpent hele året
Soveloft åpent 1. mai -1. okt.

A: Wohnung für 8 Personen
Anzahl Schlafräume: 3
Eig. Bad, Küche, Stube
Ganze Einheit: **800,-**
Preis für 4 Pers.: **600,-**

B: Hütte für 4 Personen
Anzahl Schlafräume: 1
Eig. Bad, Küche, Stube
Ganze Einheit: **500,-**

C: Campingzi. für 4 Pers. (2x)
Anzahl Schlafräume: 1
Gemeins. Gästeküche
und Sanitäranlage
Preis pro Pers.: (min. 2 P.) **100,-**

D: Schlafboden
Der 60 m² große Schlafboden
bietet Gruppen eine einfache und
preiswerte Übernachtungsmög-
lichkeit. Matrazen sind vorhanden,
Schlafsack bzw. Bettzeug muss
mitgeführt werden. Gemeins.
Gästeküche und Sanitäranlage.
Preis pro Person: **70,-**
Gruppenrabatt möglich

Für alle Einheiten gilt:
Mieten von Bettwäsche: **40,-**
Ganzjährig geöffnet
Schlafboden: 1. Mai – 1. Okt.

Directions:
Located on RV 3, five km west of
Elverum, toward Hamar. Signposts well in advance. Look for
sign "Midtskogen Gård" at
entrance.

Veibeskrivelse:
Ved RV 3, fem km vest for Elverum retning Hamar. Forvarslings-
skilting. Skilt "Midtskogen Gård"
ved innkjørselen.

Wegbeschreibung:
An der Str. 3 gelegen, 5 km
westlich von Elverum (Richtung
Hamar). Schild "Midtskogen
Gård" an der Einfahrt.

Don't be afraid to take a big step if one is indicated.
You can't cross a chasm in two small jumps.
-David Lloyd George

Solvår's Bed & Breakfast

Your host:
Solvår & Jan Viggo Oppegård

Address:
Barbra Ringsvei 14
N - 2407 Elverum
Phone: 62 41 49 48
Mobil: 97 72 75 27 / 99 61 20 26

Best time to call:
08.00 - 23.00

Double room:	**480,-**	Dobbeltrom:	**480,-**	Doppelzimmer:	**480,-**
Single room:	**290,-**	Enkeltrom:	**290,-**	Einzelzimmer:	**290,-**
No. of rooms: 2		Antall rom: 2		Anzahl Zimmer: 2	
Full breakfast		Full frokost		Volles Frühstück	
Laid breakfast table		Dekket frokostbord		Serv.: Frühstückstisch	
Open year round		Åpent hele året		Ganzjährig geöffnet	
TV available		TV tilgjengelig		Zugang zu TV	
Terrace/deck access/yard		Terrasse/uteplass/hage		Terrasse/Aussenplatz/Garten	
No smoking inside		Ingen røking innendørs		Kein Rauchen im Haus	
Discount for children		Rabatt for barn		Ermässigung für Kinder	
Selfcatering possible		Selvhushold mulig		Selbsthaushalt möglich	
English, some French				Sprechen etwas Deutsch	
& some Greek spoken					

In Elverum, Solvår's Bed & Breakfast is within walking distance of the Forestry Museum and Glåmdal Museum. Behind the property lies a forest area with good hiking terrain. The rooms are in the host's own home and in a guest cottage next door.
If you are celebrating something, the host will gladly offer something special.

Directions:
Follow RV 20 towards Kongsvinger. Look for a sign marked B&B 1 km after passing Norsk Skogbruksmuseum (Norwegian Forestry Museum) and proceed to follow the sign.

Solvårs Bed & Breakfast ligger i Elverum med gangavstand til Skogbruksmuseet og Glåmdalsmuseet. Bak eiendommen ligger skogen med turterreng.
Ett av utleierommene er i vertskapets egen bolig og ett i gjestehytten like ved.
Har du noe å feire, steller de gjerne i stand noe ekstra.

Veibeskrivelse:
Følg RV 20 mot Kongsvinger. 1 km etter at du har passert Norsk Skogbruksmuseum; se etter B&B-skilt, følg skilt videre.

Solvårs Bed & Breakfast liegt in Elverum, in Reichweite des Forstwirtschaftsmuseums und des Glåmdalsmuseums. Wandermöglichkeiten im nahen Wald. Ein Mietzimmer befindet sich im Haus des Besitzers, und das andere in einer Gasthütte daneben. Wenn Sie etwas feiern wollen, helfen die Gastgeber gerne.

Wegbeschreibung:
Folgen Sie der Straße 20 in Richtung Kongsvinger. 1 km hinter dem Norwegischen Forstwirtschaftsmuseum auf das B&B-Schild achten. Folgen Sie weiter diesem Schild.

Overskott's Bed & Breakfast

Your host:
Ingrid & Svein Overskott

Address:
Buevegen 2
N - 2312 Ottestad
Phone/Fax: 62 57 61 86
Mobil: 97 72 15 73
E-mail: sv-ove@online.no

Best time to call:
16.00 - 24.00

Double-/Twin room:	**450,-**	Dobbelt-/tosengsrom:	**450,-**	Doppel-/Zweibettzi.:	**450,-**
Single room:	**250,-**	Enkeltrom:	**250,-**	Einzelzimmer:	**250,-**
No. of rooms: 5		Antall rom: 5		Anzahl Zimmer: 5	
Full breakfast		Full frokost		Volles Frühstück	
Laid breakfast table		Dekket frokostbord		Serv.: Frühstückstisch	
Open year round		Åpent hele året		Ganzjährig geöffnet.	
TV available		TV tilgjengelig		Zugang zu TV	
Terrace/yard		Terrasse/hage		Terrasse/Garten	
Bike for rent		Sykkelutleie		Fahrrad zu mieten	
No smoking in rooms		Ingen røking på rom		Kein Rauchen im Zimmer	
Discount for children		Rabatt for barn		Ermässigung für Kinder	
Selfcatering possible		Selvhushold er mulig		Selbsthaushalt möglich	
English spoken				Sprechen etwas Deutsch	

Overskott´s B&B is located just south of Hamar. Follow the signs from E-6 to Ottestad.
The house is a large villa built in 1971. Short distances to beaches, "Vikingskipet" (Olympic site, 1994) and the Norwegian Emigrant Museum. Downtown Hamar, 4 km away, offers historical sites, museums, shopping and restaurants.
Enjoy a living room with open fireplace and TV for guests, smoking allowed.
The Overskotts can arrange for a summer BBQ.

Overskotts B&B finner du like sør for Hamar. Langs E-6 tar man av hvor skilt viser Ottestad.
Huset er en stor og komfortabel villa fra 1971. Det er kort vei til badeplasser, Vikingskipet og Utvandrermuseet. Hamar sentrum ligger 4 km unna og tilbyr historie, museer, shopping og spisesteder.
Det er en egen peisestue med TV for gjestene, og her er det tillatt å røyke.
Fam. Overskott kan etter avtale servere grillmat i egen hage sommerstid.

Südlich von Hamar gelegen. Von E-6 bei Schild Ottestad abzweigen.
Grosse, komfortable Villa, gebaut 1971. Unweit zu Badeplätzen, dem bekannten Wikingerschiff und dem Auswanderermuseum. 4 km nach Hamar mit Museum, historischen Stätten, Geschäften und Restaurants.
Für die Gäste steht eine eigene Kaminstube mit TV zur Verfügung. Dort ist auch das Rauchen gestattet.
Grillgerichte können im Garten serviert werden.

Bellevue
Bed & Breakfast

Your host:
S. Bjørge

Address:
Aluveien 65
N - 2319 Hamar
Phone: 62 52 34 77
Fax: 62 52 66 30

Best time to call:
10.00 - 17.00

Double room:	**595,-/750,-**	Dobbeltrom:	**595,-/750,-**	Doppelzimmer:	**595,-/750,-**
Single room:	**545,-**	Enkeltrom:	**545,-**	Einzelzimmer:	**545,-**
Double room:	**450,-/600,-**	Dobbeltrom:	**450,-/600,-**	Doppelzimmer:	**450,-/600,-**
Single room:	**395,-**	Enkeltrom:	**395,-**	Einzelzimmer:	**395,-**
No. of rooms: 20		Antall rom: 20		Anzahl Zimmer: 20	
Full breakfast		Full frokost		Volles Frühstück	
Laid breakfast table or -tray		Dekket frokostbord eller -brett		Serv.: Frühstückstisch oder -tablett	
Open year round		Åpent hele året		Ganzjährig geöffnet	
TV available		TV tilgjengelig		Zugang zu TV	
Terrace/deck access/yard		Terrasse/uteplass/hage		Terrasse/Aussenplatz/Garten	
VISA, DC, AmEx accepted		Vi tar VISA, DC, AmEx		Wir nehmen VISA, DC	
Discount for children		Rabatt for barn		Ermässigung für Kinder	
Selfcatering possible		Selvhushold er mulig		Selbsthaushalt möglich	
English spoken		Sprechen Deutsch		Sprechen Deutsch	

Bellevue Bed & Breakfast is located 5 min. from Hamar city center by car; northwest Hamar near Ankerskogen, swimming hall, Hedmarkstoppen, Hamar Olympic Amphitheatre and Domkirkeodden with the Hedmark County Museum.

Bellevue Bed & Breakfast ligger 5 min. fra Hamar sentrum med bil; nord-vest i Hamar. Kort vei til Ankerskogen, svømmehall, Hedmarkstoppen, Hamar OL-amfi og Domkirkeodden med Hedmarksmuseet.

Bellevue Bed & Breakfast liegt 5 Autominuten von Hamar Zentrum entfernt, und zwar in nordwestlicher Richtung bei Ankerskogen. Aktivitäten: Schwimmhalle, Olympiahalle (Amphi), Landzunge Domkirkeodden und Hedmarkmuseum (Auswanderermuseum).

Be bold with your dreams. Nurture the dreams that inspire you to go beyond your limits.
-Author Unknown

Strandhagen

Your host:
Berte & Trygve Tørud

Address:
Skavangvegen 218
N - 2350 Nes, Hedmark
Phone: 62 35 31 14
Fax: 62 35 52 97
Mobil: 95 14 30 47
E-mail: berted@frisurf.no
Web:
http://home.no.net/skavang/
Best time to call:
07.00 - 22.00

Guesthouse for 2-8 persons	Gjestehus for 2-8 personer	Gästehaus für 2-8 Personen
No. of bedrooms: 2	Antall soverom: 2	Anzahl Schlafräume: 2
No. of sleeping alcoves: 2	Antall sovealkover: 2	Anzahl Schlafalkoven: 2
Own bath, kitchen, LR	Eget bad, kjøkken, stue	Eig. Bad, Küche, Stube
High season (week 26-31):	Høysesong (uke 26-31):	Hochsaison (Woche 26-31):
Price for whole unit: **900,-**	Pris for hele enheten: **900,-**	Ganze Einheit: **900,-**
Part of unit for 2 persons: **600,-**	Del av enhet for 2 pers.: **600,-**	Teil einer Einheit 2 Pers.: **600,-**
Low season:	Lavsesong:	Nebensaison:
Price for whole unit: **800,-**	Pris for hele enheten: **800,-**	Ganze Einheit: **800,-**
Part of unit for 2 persons: **500,-**	Del av enhet for 2 pers.: **500,-**	Teil einer Einheit 2 Pers.: **500,-**
Bed linen fee: **50,-**	Tillegg for sengetøy: **50,-**	Mieten von Bettwäsche: **50,-**
Open year round	Åpent hele året	Ganzjährig geöffnet
TV	TV	TV
Yard/terrace/deck access	Hage/terrasse/uteplass	Garten/Terrasse/Aussenplatz
Boat and bike available	Båt og sykkel kan lånes	Boot u. Fahrrad zu leihen
No smoking inside	Ingen røking innendørs	Kein Rauchen im Haus
Breakfast service available	Frokost kan serveres	Frühstück auf Bestellung
English spoken		Sprechen Englisch

Experience the idyllic island on Mjøsa Lake, "Helgøya", where hiking and bicycling trails are scenic beyond imagination and the lake invites you in on warm summer days. 23 km from Brumunddal and 3 km from Nes, the farm is one of the island's oldest, producing grain, potatoes and sod. Animals: cats and a dog. Private beach, boat and bikes available. The steamboat "Skibladner" stops close to the bridge.	Strandhagen ligger på den idylliske Helgøya, den eneste øya i Mjøsa. Det er 23 km fra Brumunddal og 3 km fra Nes. Garden er en av øyas eldste. Det er badestrand, båt og sykler til disposisjon. Tur- og sykkelterreng. Ved brua legger Skibladner til. En tur med den gamle dampbåten kan anbefales. På garden dyrkes det korn, poteter og grasfrø. Der er katter og en hund på gården.	Skavang liegt auf der idyllischen Insel Helgøya, 23 km von Brumunddal u. 3 km von Nes. Helgøya lädt zu schönen Ausflügen mit dem Dampfboot Skibladner u. mit dem Rad ein. Der Hof ist einer der ältesten auf der Insel. Badestrand und Bootbrücke. Fahrrad zu leihen. Auf dem Hof werden Getreide, Kartoffeln u. Grassamen angebaut, es gibt Katzen und einen Hund.

Solbakken Gjestegård

Your host:
Karen & Rolf Rønnekleiv

Address:
Solbakken, Veldre
N - 2380 Brumunddal
Phone: 62 35 55 43
Fax: 62 35 45 97
E-mail: roennek@online.no
Web: http://hjem.sol.no/roennek

Best time to call:
15.00 - 23.00

Double-/Twin room:	425,-	Dobbelt-/tosengsrom:	425,-	Doppel-/Zweibettzi.:	425,-
Single room:	240,-	Enkeltrom:	240,-	Einzelzimmer:	240,-
No. of rooms: 5		Antall rom: 5		Anzahl Zimmer: 5	
Full breakfast		Full frokost		Volles Frühstück	
Laid breakfast table		Dekket frokostbord		Serv.: Frühstückstisch	
Open year round		Åpent hele året		Ganzjährig geöffnet	
TV available		TV tilgjengelig		Zugang zu TV	
Terrace/yard		Terrasse/hage		Terrasse/Garten	
No smoking inside		Ingen røking innendørs		Kein Rauchen im Haus	
Discount for children		Rabatt for barn		Ermässigung für Kinder	
Selfcatering possible		Selvhushold er mulig		Selbsthaushalt möglich	
English spoken				Sprechen Deutsch	

Solbakken Guest House was once a pension. The Guest House is beautifully situated at Veldre in Ringsaker Municipality, 3 km from highway E6 and 5 km from Brumunddal railway station. The poet Alf Prøysen's childhood home is only 6 km. away. Close by is a beach for swimming. Ringsaker Mountain and Sjusøen ski slopes and hiking terrain are 30-40 minutes away by car.

Solbakken gjestegård har tidligere vært drevet som pensjonat. Gjestegården ligger idyllisk til i Veldre i Ringsaker kommune, 3 km fra E6 og 5 km fra Brumunddal jernbanestasjon. Alf Prøysens barndomshjem, Prøysenstua, er bare 6 km unna. Det er kort vei til badestrand. Ringsakerfjellet og Sjusjøen, flott ski- og turterreng kan man nå på 30-40 min. med bil.

Solbakken gjestegård wurde früher als Pension betrieben. Das Haus liegt idyllisch in Veldre bei Ringsaker, 3 km von E6, 5 km von Brumunddal. Das Elternhaus des norw. Poeten Alf Prøysen liegt 6 km entfernt. Unweit zum Badestrand. 30-40 Min. Autofahrt zu den Bergen von Ringsaker und Sjusjøen mit herrlichem Wander- und Skigelände.

Trust that still, small voice that says,
'This might work and I'll try it.'
-Diane Mariechild

Hindklev Gård

Your host:
**Eivind Mæhlum &
Anne Mari Råbøl**

Address:
**Kongsveien 23
N - 2614 Lillehammer**
Phone: 61 25 06 24
Fax: 61 26 99 03
E-mail: hindklev@c2i.net

Best time to call:
08.00 - 21.00

A: Apartment for 2-3 persons
Own bath and kitchenette
Price for whole unit: **400,-**

B: Apartment for 4-5 persons
Own bath and LR w/kitchenette
Price for whole unit: **600,-**

Bed linen fee: **60,-**
No. of apartments: 7
Open year round
TV available
Yard
No smoking in rooms
English spoken

A: Leilighet for 2-3 personer
Eget bad og minikjøkken
Pris for hele enheten: **400,-**

B: Leilighet for 4-5 personer
Eget bad og stue m/minikjøkken
Pris for hele enheten: **600,-**

Tillegg for sengetøy: **60,-**
Antall leiligheter: 7
Åpent hele året
TV tilgjengelig
Uteplass
Ingen røking på rom

A: Wohnung für 2-3 Personen
Eig. Bad und Küchenecke
Ganze Einheit: **400,-**

B: Wohnung für 4-5 Personen
Eig. Bad u. Stube mit Küchenecke
Ganze Einheit: **600,-**

Mieten von Bettwäsche: **60,-**
Anzahl Wohnungen: 7
Ganzjährig geöffnet
Zugang zu TV
Aussenplatz
Kein Rauchen im Zimmer
Sprechen etwas Deutsch

Just outside of Lillehammer you will find Hindklev Gård enjoying a lovely view of Lake Mjøsa. There is an excellent trail down to the water. All 7 of the rental cottages have their own bathroom and kitchenette. On the large courtyard you will find toys for children and outdoor furniture. The farm has rabbits and hens. Your hosts are a family of five.

Directions:
From Lillehammer: Follow RV 213 southward. After driving 5-6 km, look for the sign for Hindklev. Exit to the right and you are there.

Like utenfor Lillehammer ligger Hindklev Gård med flott utsikt over Mjøsa. Det går en fin sti ned til vannet.
De sju utleieleilighetene har alle eget bad og minikjøkken. På den store gårdsplassen er det leker for barna og utemøbler. På gården er det kaniner og høner.
Vertskapet er en familie på fem.

Veibeskrivelse:
Fra Lillehammer, følg RV 213 sørover. Etter 5-6 km finner du skilt til Hindklev, Ta av til høyre og du er framme.

Der Hof liegt etwas ausserhalb von Lillehammer und bietet schöne Aussicht auf den Mjøsa-See. Ein kleiner Pfad führt hinunter zum See. 7 Ferienwohnungen, alle mit eigenem Bad und Miniküche. Auf dem großen Vorplatz stehen Gartenmöbel und Spielgeräte für Kinder. Kaninchen und Hühner am Hof. Fünfköpfige Gastgeberfamilie.

Wegbeschreibung:
Von Lillehammer: Straße 213 südwärts. Nach 5-6 km Schild nach Hindklev folgen. Rechts abbiegen, und Sie sind am Ziel.

Øvergaard

Your host:
Egil Sorgendal & Åse Skarbø

Address:
Jernbanegaten 24
N - 2609 Lillehammer
Phone: 61 25 99 99
Fax: 61 26 02 26
Mobil: 92 61 47 00
E-mail: overgaard-overnatting@
Web: c2i.net
http://home.c2i.net/overgaard

Best time to call:
17.00 - 21.00

Double room:	**550,-/750,-**	Dobbeltrom:	**550,-/750,-**	Doppelzimmer:	**550,-/750,-**
Twin room:	**550,-/750,-**	Tosengsrom:	**550,-/750,-**	Zweibettzimmer:	**550,-/750,-**
1 pers. in double room:	**390,-**	1 pers. i dobbeltrom:	**390,-**	1 Pers. im Doppelzi.:	**390,-**
Single room:	**330,-**	Enkeltrom:	**330,-**	Einzelzimmer:	**330,-**
No. of rooms: 4		Antall rom: 4		Anzahl Zimmer: 4	
Full breakfast		Full frokost		Volles Frühstück	
Laid breakfast table or br.fast tray		Dekket frokostbord el. frokostbrett		Serv.: Frühstückstisch o. -tablett	
Open year round		Åpent hele året		Ganzjährig geöffnet	
TV/Radio available		TV/radio tilgjengelig		Zugang zu TV/Radio	
Terrace/dekk access		Terrasse/uteplass		Terrasse/Aussenplatz	
Canoe for rent		Kanoutleie		Kanu zu mieten	
No smoking inside		Ingen røking innendørs		Kein Rauchen im Haus	
Discount for children		Rabatt for barn		Ermässigung für Kinder	
English spoken				Sprechen Deutsch	

Øvergaard features a tastefully renovated, luxurious farmhouse dating from around 1850 and is located in quiet and peaceful surroundings in the middle of the town center. It is a 2 min. walk to the pedestrian-only shopping street. Good parking facilities. Lillehammer is popular and tourist attractions includes: "Maihaugen", an open-air museum and craftshop museum, the old steamboat, "Skibladner", touring on Mjøsa Lake. For skiing enthusiasts Olympic City '94 has an enviable assortment of lit tracks for both Nordic and alpine skiing.

Øvergaard med deres restaurerte herskapelige gårdsbygning fra 1850-tallet ligger i stille og rolige omgivelser midt i sentrum av byen. Det er 2 min. gangavstand til gågaten. Gode parkeringsmuligheter.
Lillehammer er en typisk turistby med mange og varierte turistattraksjoner; Maihaugen med friluftsmuseum og De Sandvigske Samlinger. Skibladner, den gamle dampbåten, går i turisttrafikk på Mjøsa. OL-byen er godt utstyrt med lysløyper og slalåmbakker.

Das frisch renovierte Hofgebäude von Øvergaard von ca. 1850 liegt im Zentrum der Stadt in ruhiger und friedlicher Umgebung. In nur 2 Minuten gelangt man in die Fußgängerzone. Gute Parkmöglichkeiten.
Lillehammer ist ein typischer Touristenort mit vielerlei Angeboten: Maihaugen mit Freilichtmuseum und den Sandvigschen Sammlungen. Das alte Dampfschiff Skibladner verkehrt im Sommer auf dem Mjøsa-See. Für Wintersportler bietet die Olympia-Stadt Flutlichtloipen und Alpinpisten.

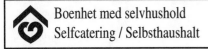
Apartment for 2-4 persons	Leilighet for 2-4 personer	Wohnung für 2-4 Personen
No. of bedrooms: 2	Antall soverom: 2	Anzahl Schlafräume: 2
Own bath and kitchen	Eget bad og kjøkken	Eig. Bad und Küche
Common LR access	Fellesstue tilgjengelig	Gemeinschaftsraum vorhanden
Price for whole unit: **900,-**	Pris for hele enheten: **900,-**	Ganze Einheit: **900,-**
Bed linen included	Sengetøy er inkludert	Inkl. Bettwäsche
Open year round	Åpent hele året	Ganzjährig geöffnet
TV	TV	TV
Terrace/dekk access	Terrasse/uteplass	Terrasse/Aussenplatz
No smoking inside	Ingen røking innendørs	Kein Rauchen im Haus
Discount for children	Rabatt for barn	Ermässigung für Kinder
English spoken		Sprechen Deutsch

Directions:

From Oslo (Driving north): Via E-6, take the first exit marked Lillehammer, drive through the tunnel and under the railroad tracks, then straight ahead through the first stoplight, turn right at the second stoplight then left at the third stoplight and here you will see Kulturhuset Banken with a dome on the right side. Drive straight ahead up the hill and turn left at the fourth intersection past Kulturhuset, which puts you on Mejdellsgaten. Øvergaard is the fourth house on the right side at the point where Mejdellsgate turns into Jernbanegaten.
From Trondheim (Driving south): Via E-6, take the second exit marked Lillehammer, and then follow the above directions.

Veibeskrivelse:

Fra Oslo: E-6, ta av ved første avkjøring til Lillehammer, kjør gjennom tunnel og under jernbanelinjen, rett fram i første lyskryss, til høyre i andre lyskryss, til venstre i tredje lyskryss, her ser du på høyre side Kulturhuset Banken med kuppel. Kjør rett fram opp bakken og sving til venstre i fjerde kryss fra Kulturhuset. Du er nå i Mejdellsgaten. Øvergaard ligger som hus nr. 4 på høyre side idet Mejdellsgate slutter og Jernbanegaten begynner.
Fra Trondheim: E-6, ta av ved andre avkjøring til Lillehammer, følg så beskrivelsen over.

Wegbeschreibung:

Ab Oslo: Befahren Sie die E-6 bis zur ersten Abfahrt Lillehammer. Anschließend geht es durch einen Tunnel (unter der Bahnlinie), an der ersten Ampelkreuzung geradeaus, an der nächsten Ampelkreuzung rechts, wieder an der nächsten Ampelkreuzung links (auf der rechten Seite sieht man die Kuppel des Kulturhauses Banken). Weiter geradeaus fahren, den Hang hinauf und an der vierten Kreuzung hinter dem Kulturhaus links abbiegen. Sie befahren nun die Straße "Mejdellsgaten". Øvergaard befindet sich als Haus Nr. 4 auf der rechten Seite, dort wo die Mejdallsgate endet und die Jernbanegate beginnt.
Von Trondheim: Befahren Sie die E-6 bis zur zweiten Abfahrt Lillehammer und folgen Sie dann der oben angegebenen Beschreibung.

Dare to begin! He who postpones living rightly is like the rustic who waits for the river to run out before he crosses.
–Horace

Høvren Gård

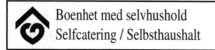

Your host:
Gudrun & Laurits Høvren

Address:
N - 2636 Øyer
Phone: **61 27 81 57**
Fax: **61 27 42 32**
Mobil: **95 77 81 57**
E-mail: **l-hoevre@online.no**

Best time to call:
08.00 - 23.00

A: Guesthouse for 2-9 persons
3 bedrooms, 1 sleeping alcove
Own bath, kitchen, LR
Price for whole unit: **750,-**

B: Apartment for 2-7 persons
No. of bedrooms: 2
Own bath, kitchen, LR
Price for whole unit: **700,-**

Bed linen fee: **50,-**
Open 1 May - 1 October
TV in both units
Yard/terrace/deck access
No smoking inside
English spoken

A: Gjestehus for 2-9 personer
3 soverom, 1 sovealkove
Eget bad, kjøkken, stue
Pris for hele enheten: **750,-**

B: Leilighet for 2-7 personer
Antall soverom: 2
Eget bad, kjøkken, stue
Pris for hele enheten: **700,-**

Tillegg for sengetøy: **50,-**
Åpent 1. mai - 1. oktober
TV i begge enheter
Hage/terrasse/uteplass
Ingen røking innendørs

A: Gästehaus für 2-9 Personen
3 Schlafräume, 1 Schlafalkoven
Eig. Bad, Küche, Stube
Ganze Einheit: **750,-**

B: Wohnung für 2-7 Personen
Anzahl Schlafräume: 2
Eig. Bad, Küche, Stube
Ganze Einheit: **750,-**

Mieten von Bettwäsche: **50,-**
Geöffnet 1. Mai - 1. Oktober
TV in beiden Einheiten
Garten/Terrasse/Aussenplatz
Kein Rauchen im Haus
Sprechen etwas Deutsch

Høvren Gård has an open overview of Øyerbygda. The farm, originally established way back in the 1300s, has been in this family for five generations. "Kårhuset", unit A, is from around 1750 and is carefully renovated. Unit B, a cellar apartment built in 1985 is part of the farmhouse. A stay at Høvren Gård allows you to experience traditional farming including both milk and meat production. You will also see other animals on the farm such as goats, hens, miniature pigs and rabbits. Your hosts are a family of five. The pilgrimage route passes by.

Høvren Gård ligger høyt med fritt utsyn over Øyerbygda. Gården har vært i slekten i fem generasjoner, men har sin opprinnelse helt tilbake til 1300-tallet.
Kårhuset, enhet A, er fra ca. 1750 og er restaurert etter dagens behov. Enhet B er en kjellerleilighet bygget i 1985 i hovedhuset på gården.
På Høvren Gård kan du oppleve gårdsdrift på tradisjonelt vis med melke- og kjøttproduksjon. Ellers er det en del dyr på gården som geiter, høner, minigris og kanin. Vertskapet er en familie på fem. Pilgrimsleden går gjennom her.

Hochgelegener Hof mit freier Aussicht auf die Gemeinde Øyer. Familienbetrieb seit 5 Generationen, die Spuren reichen zurück bis ins 14. Jahrhundert. Das ehemalige Altenteil (Wohneinheit A) stammt von 1750 und wurde für heutige Anforderungen umgebaut. Wohneinheit B ist eine Kellerwohnung aus 1985 im Hauptgebäude des Hofes. Traditionelle Vieh- und Milchwirtschaft. Ziegen, Hühner, Ferkel und Kaninchen. Fünfköpfige Gastgeberfamilie. Der Pilgerpfad Pilgrimsleden führt am Hof vorbei.

Skåden Gård

Your host:
Anne Marie & Trond Skåden

Address:
Skåden Gård
N - 2636 Øyer
Phone: 61 27 81 60
Fax: 61 27 83 12
Mobil: 97 65 93 01

Best time to call:
08.00 - 16.00 / 18.00 - 23.00

Apt./cabins for 2-6 persons	Leil./hytter for 2-6 personer	Wohn./Hütten für 2-6 Pers.
No. of units: 8	Antall boenheter: 8	Anzahl Einheiten: 8
Own bath, kitchen, LR	Eget bad, kjøkken, stue	Eig. Bad, Küche, Stube
Shared bath for smallest utnits	De minste enhetene deler bad	Gemeins. Bad f. die kleinsten Einh.
Price for up to 3 pers.: **190,-**	Pris opp til 3 pers.: **190,-**	Preis für 3 Pers.: **190,-**
Price for up to 4 pers.: **500,-**	Pris opp til 4 pers.: **500,-**	Preis für 4 Pers.: **500,-**
Price for up to 6 pers.: **700,-**	Pris opp til 6 pers.: **700,-**	Preis für 5 Pers.: **700,-**
Price for up to 6 pers.: **750,-**	Pris opp til 6 pers.: **750,-**	Preis für 6 Pers.: **750,-**
Bed linen fee: **50,-**	Tillegg for sengetøy: **50,-**	Mieten von Bettw.: **50,-**
Open year round	Åpent hele året	Ganzjährig geöffnet
TV in most rental units	TV i de fleste enheter	TV in den meisten Einheiten
Terrace/deck access/yard	Terrasse/uteplass/hage	Terrasse/Aussenplatz/Garten
Discount off-season	Rabatt utenom sesong	Ermässigung Nebensaison
Some English spoken		Sprechen etwas Englisch

Skåden Gård is located 20 km north of Lillehammer, a farm which is steeped in tradition tracing its family roots back to 1734. The farm lies high up in the valley with an incredible view of the valley. The Trondheim pilgrim route passes through the farm courtyard.

Through many generations artifacts have been collected and today are exhibited in a small farm museum.

The farm is a dairy and breeds pigs.

20 km nord for Lillehammer ligger Skåden Gard, en gammel og tradisjonesrik gård med slektsrøtter tilbake til 1734. Den ligger høyt oppe i dalsiden med storslått utsikt over Øyerbygda. Gjennom flere generasjoner er det samlet gamle bruksgjenstander som idag utgjør et lite gårdsmuseum.

Gården er i full drift med ku og smågrisproduksjon.

Pilegrimsleden mot Trondheim går gjennom gårdstunet.

Der alte, traditionsreiche Hof Skåden liegt 20 km nördlich von Lillehammer, hoch oben am Hang mit grossartiger Aussicht über das Tal. Die seit 1734 ansässige Familie hat viele alte Gegenstände zu einem kleinen Hofmuseum gesammelt.

Der Hof wird mit Rinder- und Schweinezucht betrieben.

Der alte Pilgerpfad nach Trondheim geht mitten durch den Hof.

B&B-Inn
Level of standard: ✿ ✿ & ✿ ✿ ✿

NBT-member
NBT-inspected

page **78**
Oppland

Skarsmoen Gård

Your host:
Marit & Anders Bleka

Address:
N - 2635 Tretten
Phone: 61 27 63 13
Fax: 61 27 64 66
E-mail: info@skarsmoen.no
Web: www.skarsmoen.no

Best time to call:
08.00 - 24.00

Double-/Twin room:	**690,-**	Dobbelt-/tosengsrom:	**690,-**	Doppel-/Zweibettzi.:	**690,-**
Single room:	**475,-**	Enkeltrom:	**475,-**	Einzelzimmer:	**475,-**
No. of rooms: 8		Antall rom: 8		Anzahl Zimmer: 8	
Full breakfast		Full frokost		Volles Frühstück	
Breakfast tray		Servering: Frokostbrett		Serv.: Frühstückstablett	
or breakfast buffet		eller Frokostbufffét		oder Frühstücksbüfett	
Open year round		Åpent hele året		Ganzjährig geöffnet	
TV available		TV tilgjengelig		Zugang zu TV	
Yard/garden		Hage		Garten	
No smoking inside		Ingen røking innendørs		Kein Rauchen im Haus	
VISA, MC accepted		Vi tar VISA, MC		Wir nehmen VISA, MC	
Discount for children		Rabatt for barn		Ermässigung für Kinder	
Some English spoken				Sprechen etwas Deutsch	

The Skarsmoen Farm is located in an idyllic wilderness area between Øyer and Tretten. The main house, from 1760, is now fully restored and renovated.
The farm has a dairy herd.
On marked walking trails you chance sightings of elk and deer. The flora is exceptional. 500 m from farm is Lågen in which you can fish trout and pike.
In the winter there are prepared Nordic skiing trails.
This is the place for quiet contemplation, in inviting and well equipped rooms and huts.

I et idyllisk skogområde mellom Øyer og Tretten ligger gården Skarsmoen, med hovedhus fra 1760, nå restaurert og ombygd. På gården er det melkeproduksjon.
På merkede turstier kan du møte elg og småvilt. Floraen kan by på mange overraskelser. Det er 500 m til Lågen, hvor du kan fiske ørret, sik og harr.
Oppkjørte skiløyper på vinteren.
Vil du ha det stille og fredelig, ønsker vi deg velkommen til hyggelige og velutstyte rom og hytter.

Der Hof Skarsmoen liegt idyllisch in einer Waldgegend zwischen Øyer und Tretten und wird mit Milchwirtschaft betrieben. Das restaurierte, angebaute Haupthaus stammt aus 1760. Auf markierten Wanderpfaden mit reicher Flora kann man Elchen und Kleinwild begegnen. 500 m zum Angelfluss Lågen mit Forellen, Felchen und Äschen. Präparierte Loipen im Winter. Ruhiger, friedlicher Ferienplatz mit gemütlichen, wohlausgestatteten Zimmern und Hütten.

A: Guesthouse for 2-6 persons	**A:** Gjestehus for 2-6 personer	**A:** Gästehaus für 2-6 Personen
No. of bedrooms: 2	Antall soverom: 2	Anzahl Schlafräume: 2
LR with kitchen- and diningnook, own bath	Stue med kjøkkenkrok og spisekrok, og eget bad	Stube mit Küchen- und Essecke, eigenes Bad.
Price for whole unit: **850,-**	Pris for hele enheten: **850,-**	Ganze Einheit: **850,-**
Bed linen fee: **70,-**	Tillegg for sengetøy: **70,-**	Mieten von Bettwäsche: **70,-**
B: Apartment for 2-3 persons	**B:** Leilighet for 2-3 personer	**B:** Wohnung für 2-3 Personen
No. of bedrooms: 1	Antall soverom: 1	Anzahl Schlafräume: 1
Kitchen nook and bath	Kjøkkenkrok og bad	Bad und kleine Küche
Price for whole unit: **550,-**	Pris for hele enheten: **550,-**	Ganze Einheit: **550,-**
Bed linen fee: **70,-**	Tillegg for sengetøy: **70,-**	Mieten von Bettwäsche: **70,-**
Applies to both rental units:	Gjelder begge enheter:	Gilt für beide Einheiten:
Open year round	Åpent hele året	Ganzjährig geöffnet
TV	TV	TV
Yard/terrace/dekk access	Hage/terrasse/uteplass	Garten/Terrasse/Aussenplatz
No smoking inside	Ingen røking innendørs	Kein Rauchen im Haus
VISA, MC accepted	Vi tar VISA, MC	Wir nehmen VISA, MC
Breakfast service available: **60,-**	Frokost kan serveres: **60,-**	Frühstück auf Bestellung: **60,-**
Some English spoken		Sprechen etwas Deutsch

Directions:
Follow E-6 north to a point about 25 km north of Lillehammer. Look for the sign marked "Skarsmoen 0,7" situated in a large woodsy area. Follow the sign. From the north: Follow E-6 southwards past Otta and Kvitfjell look for the "Skarsmoen 0,7" sign about 6 km past.

Veibeskrivelse:
Følg E-6 ca. 25 km nord for Lillehammer. Se etter skiltet "Skarsmoen 0,7" inne i en stor skog. Følg skilt videre. Fra nord følges E-6 forbi Otta, Kvitfjell og 6 km forbi Tretten og finn skiltet "Skarsmoen 0,7".

Wegbeschreibung:
Folgen Sie der E-6 bis ca. 25 km nördlich von Lillehammer. Achten Sie in einem großen Waldgebiet auf die Beschilderung "Skarsmoen 0,7". Folgen Sie der Beschilderung.
Anreise aus Norden: Folgen Sie der E-6 über Otta und Kvitfjell bis 6 km nach Tretten, anschließend der Beschilderung "Skarsmoen 0,7" folgen.

What is the difference between an obstacle and
an opportunity? Our attitude toward it.
Every opportunity has a difficulty,
and every difficulty has an opportunity.
-J. Sidlow Baxter

B&B-Inn
Level of standard: ♣ ♣

NBT-member
NBT-inspected

page **80**
Oppland

Glomstad Gård

Your host:
Odd Pedersen &
Janna Glomstad

Address:
N - 2635 Tretten
Phone: 61 27 62 57
Fax: 61 27 69 77
Mobil: 91 79 98 50
E-mail: glogap@online.no
Web: www.glomstad.com

Best time to call:
09.00 - 23.00

Double room:	**550,-/785,-**	Dobbeltrom:	**550,-/785,-**	Doppelzimmer:	**550,-/785,-**
Twin room:	**550,-**	Tosengsrom:	**550,-**	Zweibettzimmer:	**550,-**
1 pers. in double room:	**345,-**	En pers. i dobbeltrom:	**345,-**	1 Pers. im Doppelzi.:	**345,-**
Single room:	**345,-/525,-**	Enkeltrom:	**345,-/525,-**	Einzelzimmer:	**345,-/525,-**
No. of rooms: 27		Antall rom: 27		Anzahl Zimmer: 27	
Full breakfast		Full frokost		Volles Frühstück	
Breakfast buffet		Servering: Frokost buffét		Serv.: Frühstücksbüfett	
Lunch and dinner possible		Mulighet for lunsj og middag		Mittag-/Abendessen auf Wunsch	
Open year round		Åpent hele året		Ganzjährig geöffnet	
Yard/garden		Hage		Garten	
TV available		TV tilgjengelig		Zugang zu TV	
VISA accepted		Vi tar VISA		Wir nehmen VISA	
Discount for children		Rabatt for barn		Ermässigung für Kinder	
English & Dutch spoken				Sprechen Deutsch	

Glomstad Gård, 5 km from Tretten, has traditions dating back to the 16th century. Janna is the 12th generation on the farm. Janna's mother started hosting guests in 1942. Today you find a modern vacation spot characterized by Gudbrandsdalen's rich village heritage, and Norwegian tradition is present in both interior design and local cuisine. The delicious food has been featured in newspaper articles. Friendly, homey and relaxed atmosphere. Short distance to Lillehammer, Hunderfossen Family Park, ski center, Rondane and Jotunheimen.

Glomstad Gård, 5 km fra Tretten, har tradisjoner tilbake til det 16. århundre, og Janna er 12. generasjon på gården. Jannas mor startet å ta imot gjester i 1942.
I dag er det et moderne feriested preget av Gudbrandsdalens rike bygdekultur, og norsk tradisjon preger såvel interiøret som kokkekunsten. Den gode maten har også ført til reportasjer i ukepressen. Her er det en vennlig, hjemmekoselig og avslappet atmosfære. Kort avstand til Lillehammer, Hunderfossen familiepark, skianlegg, Rondane og Jotunheimen.

Glomstad Gård, 5 km von Tretten entfernt, ist ein Traditionsbetrieb mit Wurzeln bis ins 16. Jahrhundert. Übernachtungsgäste kamen erstmals 1942. Heute ist Glomstad ein moderner Urlaubsort, geprägt von der bäuerlichen Kultur des Gudbrandsdals. Norwegische Tradition ebenfalls bei Interieur und Kochkunst. Das schmackhafte Essen wurde in der Wochenpresse vorgestellt. Freundliche und gemütliche Atmosphäre. Unweit nach Lillehammer, zum Hunderfossen-Fam.park, zu Skigebieten sowie, zu den Nationalparks Rondane und Jotunheimen.

Valberg Fjellgard

Your host:
Reidun & Bård Valberg

Address:
Kvarvet
N - 2647 Sør-Fron
Phone: 61 29 64 42
Mobil: 48 15 27 86
E-mail: baar-val@online.no

Best time to call:
08.00 - 23.00

Double room:	**400,-**	Dobbeltrom:	**400,-**	Doppelzimmer:	**400,-**
Single room:	**300,-**	Enkeltrom:	**300,-**	Einzelzimmer:	**300,-**
Fam.apt. for 2-5 pers.:	**450,-/600,-**	Fam.leil. for 2-5 pers.:	**450,-/600,-**	Wohn. für 2-5 Pers.:	**450,-/600,-**
No. of rooms: 3		Antall rom: 3		Anzahl Zimmer: 3	
Full breakfast		Full frokost		Volles Frühstück	
Laid breakfast table/buffet		Dekket frokostbord/-buffé		Serv.: Frühstückstisch/-büfett	
Open year round		Åpent hele året		Ganzjährig geöffnet	
TV in appartment		TV i leilighet		TV in Wohnung	
Terrace/deck access/yard		Terrasse/uteplass/hage		Terrasse/Aussenplatz/Garten	
No smoking inside		Ingen røking innendørs		Kein Rauchen im Haus	
VISA, MC accepted		Vi tar VISA, MC		Wir nehmen VISA, MC	
Discount for children		Rabatt for barn		Ermässigung für Kinder	
Selfcatering possible		Selvhushold er mulig		Selbsthaushalt möglich	
English spoken				Sprechen etwas Deutsch	

Valberg Mountain Farm is located 850 meters above sea level, with a great view, 12 km from the E-6 signpost "Kvarvet".
Good possibilities for experiencing nature. Nature trails suited for both short and long hikes in the Rondane area, elk safaries.
You'll also find a rural community and historical sites nearby.
The farm is mainly for sheep and fodder production. Meet a happy little dog running round the farmstead.

Valberg Fjellgard ligger 850 m.o.h. med storslått utsikt, 12 km fra E-6 ved skiltet "Kvarvet". Her er gode muligheter for å oppleve naturen. Naturstier for korte og lange fotturer i Rondane, elgsafari. Her er også bygdetun og severdigheter i bygda.
På garden er det sau-, kjøtt- og grasproduksjon. Her er også en glad liten hund.

Der Gebirgshof Valberg liegt auf 850 m Höhe, 12 km von E-6 Schild «Kvarvet», und bietet grossartige Aussicht. Er wird mit Schaf- und Mastviehzucht, sowie Heuwirtschaft betrieben und es gibt einen netten, kleinen Hund.
Kürzere oder längere Naturlehrpfade durch den Nationalpark Rondane, Elchsafari, sowie das Heimatmuseum.

Skåbu Hytter og Camping

Your host:
Arnhild & Arne Evjen

Address:
N - 2643 Skåbu
Phone: 61 29 56 24
Web:
www.gudbrandsdalsnett.net/
skabuhytterogcamping
Best time to call:
08.00 - 22.00

A: Cabins for 4-6 persons
No. of bedrooms: 1-2
Kitchen or kitchen nook in LR
Price for whole unit: **300,-**

B: Cabins for 2-4 persons
Kitchenette
Price for whole unit: **200,-**

Bed linen fee: **50,-**
Cabins do not have running water
Common kitchen for all cabins
Shared sanitary facilities

Open year round
Yard
No smoking inside
Breakfast service available
English spoken

A: Hytter for 4-6 personer
Antall soverom: 1-2
Separat kjk. el. kjk.krok i stuen
Pris for hele enheten: **300,-**

B: Hytter for 2-4 personer
Kjøkkenkrok
Pris for hele enheten: **200,-**

Tillegg for sengetøy: **50,-**
Hyttene har ikke innlagt vann
Felles sanitæranlegg og oppvask-
kjøkken for alle hyttene

Åpent hele året
Uteplass
Ingen røking innendørs
Frokost kan serveres

A: Hütten für 4-6 Personen
Anzahl Schlafräume: 1-2
Küche oder Küchenecke in Stube
Ganze Einheit: **300,-**

B: Hütten für 2-4 Personen
Küchenecke
Ganze Einheit: **200,-**

Mieten von Bettwäsche: **50,-**
Kein fließendes Wasser in den
Hütten. Sanitäranlage und Spül-
küche stehen allen Gästen zur
Verfügung.

Ganzjährig geöffnet
Aussenplatz
Kein Rauchen im Haus
Frühstück auf Bestellung
Sprechen Englisch

Idyllic country farm with courtyard in Gudbrandsdalen. At 800 metres above sea level, Skåbu is one of Norway's loftiest village communities and is rich in cultural and outdoor activities, summer and winter. Mountain trails for walks and bicycling. Convenient for car vacations. Large, groomed Nordic ski complex. The 3 large cabins include fireplaces/free wood for cozy evenings after a hike. Nice view of countryside. Peaceful with fresh mountain air.

Idyllisk sted på gårdstun i Gudbrandsdalen. Skåbu er et av Norges høyestliggende bygdesamfunn på 800 m.o.h. og er rikt på kultur- og naturopplevelser både sommer og vinter. Fjellterreng for fotturer og med sykkel. Sentralt for bilturer også. Skientusiaster kan benytte et stort preparert løypenett. De tre store hyttene har vedfyring med gratis ved for kveldskosen etter fjellturen. Fin utsikt over landskapet. Stillhet og frisk fjell-luft.

Skåbu liegt idyllisch auf einem Gudbrandsdal-Gehöft und ist mit 800 m Meereshöhe einer der höchstgelegenen Orte Norwegens. Kulturelle und landschaftliche Schönheiten im Sommer wie im Winter. Ruhe, frische Gebirgsluft, Fahrrad- und Wandermöglich-keiten, Autoausflüge, für Lang-lauffans zahlreiche präparierte Loipen. Die drei großen Hütten bieten durch Holzofen gemütliche Wärme (Brennholz kostenlos). Schöne Aussicht auf die Umgebung.

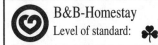
Storrusten Gjestegård & Camping

Your host:
Ingrid Kjørum

Address:
Varphaugen
N - 2670 Otta
Phone/Fax: 61 23 52 20

Best time to call:
09.00 - 23.00 (summer)
17.00 - 23.00 (off season)

Double-/Twin room:	**460,-**	Dobbelt-/tosengsrom:	**460,-**	Doppel-/Zweibettzi.:	**460,-**
1 pers. in double room:	**230,-**	1 pers. i dobbeltrom:	**230,-**	1 Pers. im Doppelzi.:	**230,-**
No. of rooms: 7		Antall rom: 7		Anzahl Zimmer: 7	
Coin-operated hot water shower		Myntapparat for varmtvann i dusj		Münzautomat für Dusche	
Full breakfast		Full frokost		Volles Frühstück	
Laid breakfast table		Dekket frokostbord		Serv.: Frühstückstisch	
Open 15 June - 15 Aug.		Åpent 15. juni - 15. aug.		Geöffnet 15. Juni - 15. Aug.	
Terrace/deck access/yard		Terrasse/uteplass/hage		Terrasse/Aussenplatz/Garten	
VISA accepted		Vi tar VISA		Wir nehmen VISA	
Discount for children		Rabatt for barn		Ermässigung für Kinder	
Selfcatering possible		Selvhushold mulig		Selbsthaushalt möglich	
English spoken				Sprechen etwas Deutsch	

Storrusten Gjestehus (Guesthouse) & Camping are found along highway E-6, about 7 km south of Otta and 3 km north of Sjoa. It is a quiet, little place offering beautiful natural attractions and numerous local activities. There is a rafting base nearby and the pilgrimage route to Trondheim passes by here. It is not far to the river, convenient for those who are interested in fishing. The guesthouse has a sauna in the woods and its own camping ground and open fire pit. The area offers activities for children with a trampoline and swings.

Storrusten Gjestehus & Camping finner du langs E-6 ca. 7 km sør for Otta og 3 km nord for Sjoa. Det er et rolig, lite sted med flott natur og flere aktivitetstilbud i nærheten. Det er en raftingplass i nærheten og pilgrimsleden går forbi her. Det er ikke langt fra elva, og den som har ønske om å fiske har muligheten til det. Gjestehuset har et badstuhus i skogen og en egen leirplass/bålplass.
Stedet er også barnevennlig med trampoline og huske.

Storrusten Gjestehus & Camping befindet sich an der E-6, ca. 7 km südlich von Otta und 3 km nördlich von Sjoa. Ein ruhiger kleiner Ort inmitten reizvoller Landschaft und mit vielen Freizeitangeboten in der Umgebung. Eine Rafting-Anlegestelle und ein historischer Pilgerpfad (Pilegrimsleden) liegen ganz in der Nähe. Auch bis zum Fluß ist es nicht weit, so daß auch Angelfreunde auf ihre Kosten kommen. Zum Gästehaus gehört ein eigenes Saunagebäude im Wald sowie ein Lagerplatz mit Feuerstelle. Für Kinder stehen Trampolin und Schaukel zur Verfügung.

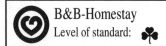
Brenden Seter

Your host:
Bergljot Brenden

Address:
Postboks 2
N - 2665 Lesja
Phone: 61 24 37 32
Mobil: 94 14 93 28

Best time to call:
08.00 - 12.00 / 16.00 - 23.00

Price per pers.:	**230,-**	Pris pr. pers.:	**230,-**	Preis pro Pers.:	**230,-**
Children under 12 years:	**175,-**	Barn under 12 år:	**175,-**	Kinder unter 12:	**175,-**
No. of beds: 4		Antall sengeplasser: 4		Anzahl Betten: 4	
Full breakfast		Full frokost		Volles Frühstück	
Laid breakfast table		Dekket frokostbord		Serv.: Frühstückstisch	
Full board:	**500,-**	Fullpensjon:	**500,-**	Vollpension:	**500,-**
Full board; children u.12:	**350,-**	Fullpensjon barn under 12:	**350,-**	Vollpension; Kinder u.12:	**350,-**
Open 24 June - 18 Aug.		Åpent 24. juni - 18. aug.		Geöffnet 24. Juni - 18. Aug.	
Yard		Uteplass		Aussenplatz	
English spoken				Sprechen Deutsch	

This beautiful pasture is farmed the traditional way every summer. The cows are milked and the dairy products are processed in the traditional pasture way. Guests are welcome to enjoy the taste of fresh dairy staples. Nowhere will you taste better sour cream porridge.
The guest cottage on the pasture has one bedroom and one living room with fireplace. There is no running water, but guests have access to hot & cold water, a washing basin and there is a nice outhouse for the guests.
The pasture is situated in the middle of wide-open countryside with excellent hiking trails, good fishing spots, mountain walks and moose safaris.

Denne nydelige gamle seteren drives på tradisjonelt vis hver sommer. Dyrene melkes og melkeprodukter tilberedes på tradisjonelt setervis. Gjestene er velkomne til å nyte smaken av seterkost. Ingen steder får du bedre rømmegrøt.
Seterhuset for gjestene har ett soverom og en peisestue. Det er ikke innlagt vann, men det er tilgang på kaldt/varmt vann, vaskevannsfat og det er en fin utedo til bruk for gjestene.
Seteren ligger midt i et åpent landskap med flott turterreng, gode fiskemuligheter, fjellturer og elgsafari.

Die gemütliche Alm wird jeden Sommer auf traditionelle Art und Weise bewirtschaftet. Die Tiere werden von Hand gemolken, die Milchprodukte auf traditionelle Art zubereitet. Alle Gäste sind willkommen, die Spezialitäten der Alm zu probieren. Nirgendwo anders bekommt man ein besseres Rømmegrøt (Sauerrahmbrei). Für die Gäste steht ein Schlafraum und eine Kaminstube zur Verfügung. Es gibt kein fließendes Wasser im Haus, Kalt-/Warmwasser, Waschschüssel und gute Außentoilette können aber genutzt werden. Die Alm liegt in einer offenen Landschaft mit Wander- und Angelmöglichkeiten. Bergtouren und Elchsafaris können organisiert werden.

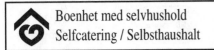

Strind Gard

Your host:
Anne Jorunn & Trond Dalsegg

Address:
Strind Gard
N - 2686 Lom
Phone: 61 21 12 37
Fax: 61 21 18 94
Mobil: 91 87 52 48
E-mail: trondals@frisurf.no
Web: www.strind-gard.no

Best time to call:
16.00 - 23.00

A: Barn (apartment) for 5 persons	**A:** "Låvebrua", leil. for 5 personer	**A:** Scheune (Wohnung), 5 Pers.
Price for whole unit: **380,-**	Pris for hele enheten: **380,-**	Ganze Einheit: **380,-**
Extra per pers. over 3 pers.: **40,-**	Tillegg pr. pers. over 3 pers.: **40,-**	Extra pro Person ü. 3 Pers.: **40,-**
B: "Eldhus" for 2 persons	**B:** Eldhus for 2 personer	**B:** hist. Backhaus für 2 Pers.
Price for whole unit: **180,-**	Pris for hele enheten: **180,-**	Ganze Einheit: **180,-**
C: Store-house for 2-3 persons	**C:** Stabbur for 2-3 personer	**C:** Vorratshaus für 2-3 Personen
Price for whole unit: **250,-**	Pris for hele enheten: **250,-**	Ganze Einheit: **250,-**
D: Apartment for 5 persons	**D:** Gammelstugu, 1 etg., 5 pers.	**D:** Wohnung für 5 Personen
Price for whole unit: **380,-**	Pris for hele enheten: **380,-**	Ganze Einheit: **380,-**
Extra per pers. over 3 pers.: **40,-**	Tillegg pr. pers. over 3 pers.: **40,-**	Extra pro Person ü. 3 Pers.: **40,-**
E: Apartment for 3 persons	**E:** Gammelstugu, 2 etg., 3 pers.	**E:** Wohnung für 3 Personen
Price for whole unit: **250,-**	Pris for hele enheten: **250,-**	Ganze Einheit: **250,-**
F: Apartment for 6 persons	**F:** Leilighet for 6 personer	**F:** Wohnung für 6 Personen
Price for whole unit: **600,-**	Pris for hele enheten: **600,-**	Ganze Einheit: **600,-**
Extra per pers. over 4 pers.: **50,-**	Tillegg pr. pers. over 4 pers.: **50,-**	Extra pro Person ü. 4 Pers.: **50,-**
G: Cabin for 4 persons	**G:** Hytte for 4 personer	**G:** Hütte für 4 Personen
Price for whole unit: **600,-**	Pris for hele enheten: **600,-**	Ganze Einheit: **600,-**
Bed linen fee: **40,-**	Tillegg for leie sengetøy: **40,-**	Mieten von Bettwäsche: **40,-**
Open year round	Åpent hele året	Ganzjährig geöffnet.
Terrace/garden and grill	Terasse/uteplass/hage og grill	Terr./Aussenplatz und Grill
Sauna	Sauna	Sauna
No smoking inside	Ingen røyking innendørs	Kein Rauchen im Haus
English spoken		Sprechen etwas Deutsch

Cozy farmyard with a pleasant mix of old and new structures. Great base for day-trips, by foot or car, to Jotunheimen. Livestock includes sheep and horses.

Koselig gardstun med blanding av eldre og nyere bebyggelse. Fint utgangspunkt for dagsturer i Jotunheimen til fots eller bilturer. Det er sau og hest på garden.

Gemütlicher Bauernhof mit einer Mischung aus älteren und neueren Gebäuden. Schöner Ausgangspunkt für Tagestouren ins Jotunheimen-Gebirge zu Fuß oder mit Auto.

Storhaugen

Your host:
Marit & Magnar Slettede

Address:
Storhaugen
N - 2687 Bøverdalen
Phone: 61 21 20 69
Fax: 61 21 20 69
Mobil: 95 70 31 27

Best time to call:
08.00 - 20.00

A: Log cabin for 2-6 personer
No. of bedrooms: 2
Bathroom, kitchen, LR
Price for whole unit: **550,-**

B: Apartments for 4-9 pers. (4x)
No. of bedrooms: 1-2
Bathroom, kitchen/living room
Price for whole unit: **525,-/700,-**

C: One-room cabin for 3 pers.
Bathroom, kitchenette
Price for whole unit: **300,-**

D: Log cabin for 14 persons
No. of bedrooms: 5
For whole unit: **1.000,-/1.200,-**

Applies to all rental units:
Bed linen fee: **50,-**
Breakfast service available: **70,-**
Cleaning fee: **150,-/300,-**
Open Easter - 1 Nov.
TV available
Terrace/deck access
Pets welcome
Some English spoken

A: Tømmerhytte for 2-6 personer
Antall soverom: 2
Bad, kjøkken, stue
Pris for hele enheten: **550,-**

B: Leiligheter for 4-9 pers. (4x)
Antall soverom: 1-2
Bad, kjøkken/stue
Pris for hele enheten: **525,-/700,-**

C: Ettromshytte for 3 personer
Eget bad og tekjøkken
Pris for hele enheten: **300,-**

D: Tømmerhytte for 14 personer
Antall soverom: 5
For hele enheten: **1.000,-/1.200,-**

For alle enhetene gjelder:
Tillegg for sengetøy: **50,-**
Frokost kan serveres: **70,-**
Rengjøring: **150,-/300,-**
Åpent: Påske - 1. nov.
TV tilgjengelig
Terrasse/uteplass
Kjæledyr tillatt

A: Blockhütte für 2-6 Personen
Anzahl Schlafräume: 2
Eig. Bad, Küche, Stube
Ganze Einheit: **550,-**

B: Wohnung für 4-9 Personen
Anzahl Schlafräume: 1-2
Eig. Bad, Küche/Stube
Ganze Einheit: **525,-/700,-**

C: Hütte (1 Raum) für 3 Pers.
Eig. Bad, Teeküche
Ganze Einheit: **300,-**

D: Blockhütte für 14 Personen
Anzahl Schlafräume: 5
Ganze Einheit: **1.000,-/1.200,-**

Für alle Einheiten gilt:
Mieten von Bettwäsche: **50,-**
Frühstück auf Bestellung: **70,-**
Endreinigung: **150,-/300,-**
Geöffnet Ostern - 1. Nov.
Zugang zu TV
Terrasse/Aussenplatz
Haustiere willkommen
Sprechen etwas Deutsch.

Mountain farm with active farm life including goats and other livestock. On the outskirts of Jotunheimen with excellent hiking areas. Rich in cultural activities. Summer ski center 13 km. Cave and glacier tours.

Fjellgård med levende gårdsmiljø, geiter og andre dyr. I utkanten av Jotunheimen med turmuligheter og kulturopplevelser. Sommerskisenter 13 km, grottebesøk og brevandring. Maiferie med skitur på Sognefjellet.

Berghof mit typischer Bauernhofatmosphäre. Am Rande des Jotunheimen gelegen, gute Wandermöglichkeiten und kult. Sehenswürdigkeiten. 13 km zum Sommerskizentrum, außerdem Grotten- und Gletscherwanderungen.

B&B-Inn
Level of standard:

NBT-member
NBT-inspected

page **87**

Oppland

Sørre Hemsing

Your host:
Berit & Arne Nefstad

Address:
Heensgarda
N - 2975 Vang i Valdres
Phone: 61 36 72 70 / 61 36 70 73
Fax: 61 36 77 71
Mobil: 97 16 84 58
E-mail: shemsing@frisurf.no

Best time to call:
09.00 - 22.00

Double room:	**700,-**	Dobbeltrom:	**700,-**	Doppelzimmer:	**700,-**
1 pers. in double room:	**400,-**	1 pers. i dobbeltrom:	**400,-**	1 Pers. im Doppelzi.:	**400,-**
No. of rooms: 5		Antall rom: 5		Anzahl Zimmer: 5	
Full breakfast		Full frokost		Volles Frühstück	
Laid breakfast table		Dekket frokostbord		Serv.: Frühstückstisch	
Open year round		Åpent hele året		Ganzjährig geöffnet	
TV available		TV tilgjengelig		Zugang zu TV	
Terrace/deck access		Terrasse/uteplass		Terrasse/Aussenplatz	
Boat for rent		Båtutleie		Boot zu mieten	
No smoking inside		Ingen røking innendørs		Kein Rauchen im Haus	
Discount for children		Rabatt for barn		Ermässigung für Kinder	
VISA accepted		Vi tar VISA		Wir nehmen VISA	
Phone/Fax/Internet available		Tilgang på telefon/fax/Internett		Tel., Fax und Internet vorhanden	
Some English spoken				Sprechen etwas Englisch	

Sørre Hemsing is a beautiful example of a Norwegian historical landmark. The farm consists of two farmhouses, barn, stall, millhouse, smithy and drying hut. Some of the structures are newly renovated while others are not quite finished. The farm's unique character is well preserved in its interiors and furnishings. The kitchen and bathrooms are both modern and comfortable. Vang is a mountain village whose main activities are sheep, goat and cattle raising. Mountain dairy farming is a summertime activity that often brings livestock to Sørre Hemsing.

Sørre Hemsing er et vakkert eksempel på norsk kulturhistorie. Gården består av to våningshus, fjøs, bu, låve, kvernhus, smie og tørkehus. Noen av husene er nyrestaurerte, mens noen ikke er helt ferdige ennå. Det unike særpreget ved gården er godt bevart i interiør og møblement, dog er kjøkken og bad både moderne og lekre.
Vang er ei fjellbygd der næringsveien er sau, geit og ku. På sommerstid er det en del stølsdrift, og da er det gjerne dyr på Sørre Hemsing.

Das Gehöft ist ein schönes Beispiel für die bäuerliche Kultur Norwegens. zwei Wohnhäuser, Stall, Speicher, Scheune, Mühlenhaus, Schmiede und Darre (hist. Trockenanlage für Getreide). Die meisten Gebäude wurden in den letzten Jahren restauriert. Die besondere Atmosphäre wurde auch bei der Möblierung beibehalten. Modern und einladend sind Küche und Bad.
Vang ist eine Siedlung mit Schaf-, Ziegen- und Viehwirtschaft. Während der bewirtschafteten Zeit im Sommer sind auf Sørre Hemsing viele Tiere zu sehen.

Opslidre Bed & Breakfast

Your host:
Nils-Olav Nordby

Address:
Opslidre
N - 2966 Slidre
Phone: 61 34 32 87
Fax: 61 34 32 87
Mobil: 93 04 32 87

Best time to call:
08.00 - 22.00

Double room:	**600,-**	Dobbeltrom:	**600,-**	Doppelzimmer:	**600,-**
No. of rooms: 2		Antall rom: 2		Anzahl Zimmer: 2	
Continental breakfast		Kontinental frokost		Kontinentales Frühstück	
Laid breakfast table		Dekket frokostbord		Serv.: Frühstückstisch	
Open 1 June - 31 Aug.		Åpent 1. juni - 31. aug.		Geöffnet 1. Juni - 31. Aug.	
TV available		TV tilgjengelig		Zugang zu TV	
Terrace/deck access/garden		Terrasse/uteplass/hage		Terrasse/Aussenplatz/Garten	
Boat for rent		Båtutleie		Boot zu mieten	
No smoking		Ingen røking innendørs		Kein Rauchen im Haus	
Access to telephone/fax/Internet		Tilgang på telefon/faks/Internett		Zugang Telefon/Fax/Internet	
Selfcatering possible		Selvhushold er mulig		Selbsthaushalt möglich	
English spoken				Sprechen Englisch	

Self-catering: Apt. for 2-4 pers.		Selvhushold: Leil. for 2-4 pers.		Selbsthaushalt: Wohnung, 2-4 P.	
No. of bedrooms: 1		Antall soverom: 1		Anzahl Schlafräume: 1	
Bath, kitchenette, LR		Bad, tekjøkken, stue		Eig. Bad, Teeküche, Stube	
Price for whole unit:	**750,-**	Pris for hele enheten:	**750,-**	Ganze Einheit:	**750,-**
Bed linen fee:	**75,-**	Tillegg for sengetøy:	**75,-**	Mieten von Bettwäsche:	**75,-**
Breakfast service available:	**50,-**	Frokost kan serveres:	**50,-**	Frühstück auf Bestellung:	**50,-**

Well-maintained farm with view of valley and Jotunheimen. Historical interesting area featuring stave churches, rock carvings, runic stone carvings and burial mounds. Excellent conditions for walking tours year round. Fishing possibilities. 30-40 min. drive to ski complex.

Velstelt gard med utsikt over dalføret og Jotunheimen. Historisk interessant område med stavkirker, helleristninger, runestein og gravrøyser. Fine turmuligheter hele året. Fiskemuligheter. 30-40 min. til skianlegg.

Gepflegter Hof mit Aussicht über das Tal und die Gebirgszüge von Jotunheimen. Historisch interessante Region: Stabkirchen, Felszeichnungen, Runenstein, Steingräber. Das ganz Jahr über gute Wandermöglichkeiten. Angelmöglichkeiten. 30 bis 40 Minuten zum Skizentrum.

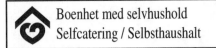

Fagernes
Bed & Breakfast

Your host:
Bente Brenna

Address:
Gamleveien 4
N - 2900 Fagernes
Phone: 61 36 15 12
Fax: 61 36 13 47
Mobil: 90 65 08 06
E-mail: b-brem@frisurf.no
Best time to call:
08.00 - 22.00

A: Apartment for 2 persons	**A:** Leilighet for 2 personer	**A:** Wohnung für 2 Personen
No. of bedrooms: 1	Antall soverom: 1	Anzahl Schlafräume: 1
Own bath, kitchen	Eget bad, kjøkken,	Eig. Bad, Küche
Price for whole unit: **600,-**	Pris for hele enheten: **600,-**	Ganze Einheit: **600,-**
B: Room for 2 persons **450,-**	**B:** Rom for 2 personer **450,-**	**B:** Zimmer für 2 Personen **450,-**
1 pers. in double room: **250,-**	1 pers. i dobbeltrom: **250,-**	1 Pers. in Doppelzimmer: **250,-**
Shared bath and kitchen	Delt bad og kjøkken	Gemeins. Bad und Küche
Applies to all rental units:	For alle enhetene gjelder:	Für alle Einheiten gilt:
Open year round	Åpent hele året	Ganzjährig geöffnet
Bed linen fee: **60,-**	Tillegg for sengetøy: **60,-**	Mieten von Bettwäsche: **60,-**
Terrace/deck access/yard/garden	Terrasse/uteplass/hage	Terrasse/Aussenplatz/Garten
Boat and bike rental nearby	Båt- og sykkelutleie i nærheten	Boot u. Fahrrad zu mieten
Discount for children	Rabatt for barn	Ermäßigung für Kinder
No smoking inside	Ingen røking innendørs	Kein Rauchen im Haus
Access to telephone/fax/Internet	Tilgang på tlf./faks/Internett	Zugang Telefon/Fax/Internet
English and some French spoken		Sprechen etwas Deutsch

Fagernes is the community center in the Valdres region. Idyllically situated along the Strande Fjord with thriving commerce, folk museum and a wide variety of outdoor activities. Distance to alpine ski facilites: 10 and 20 km plus many cross-country trails nearby. Rental and instruction for ski sailing at Vaset. Equestrian center 20 km. Also enjoy Fagernesmarken fair in January; Valdresmarken fair in July; folk music festival in July and the Cured Fish (rakfisk) Festival in November.

Bygdebyen Fagernes er sentrum i Valdresregionen. Stedet ligger idyllisk til ved Strandefjorden med livlig handelsvirksomhet, folkemuseum og mange muligheter for friluftsaktiviteter av alle typer. Alpintanlegg 10 og 20 km unna og mange langrennsløyper i nærområdet. Utleie og undervisninging i skiseiling på Vaset. Hestesenter 20 km. Opplev også Fagernesmarken i januar, Valdresmarken i juli, Jørn Hilme-stemnet (folkemusikk) i juli og rakfiskfestival i november.

Fagernes ist der Zentralort der Valdres-Region. Hier kann man nicht nur sehr gut einkaufen, auch das örtliche Museum ist einen Besuch wert. Alpinzentrum 10 bzw. 20 km, viele Loipen in der näheren Umgebung. Kurse im "Skisegeln" in Vaset. Reitzentrum 20 km. Besondere Erlebnisse sind die Jahrmärkte "Fagernesmarken" im Januar,"Valdresmarken" im Juli sowie das Volksmusikfestival im Juli und das "Rakfiskfestival" (Gärforelle) im November.

Holthe Gård

Your host:
Inger Johanne & Ole Holthe

Address:
N - 2847 Kolbu
Phone/Fax: **61 16 72 10**
Mobil: **91 30 00 32**

Best time to call:
08.00 - 09.00 / 17.00 - 23.00

Double room:	**480,-/600,-**	Dobbeltrom:	**480,-/600,-**	Doppelzimmer:	**480,-/600,-**
Single room:	**380,-**	Enkeltrom:	**380,-**	Einzelzimmer:	**380,-**
No. of rooms: 6		Antall rom: 6		Anzahl Zimmer: 6	
Full breakfast		Full frokost		Volles Frühstück	
Laid breakfast table		Dekket frokostbord		Serv.: Frühstückstisch	
or breakfast buffet		eller frokost buffét		oder Frühstücksbüfett	
Open year round		Åpent hele året		Ganzjährig geöffnet	
TV available		TV tilgjengelig		Zugang zu TV	
Terrace/deck access/yard		Terrasse/uteplass/hage		Terrasse/Aussenplatz/Garten	
Bike for rent		Sykkelutleie		Fahrrad zu mieten	
No smoking in rooms		Ingen røking på rom		Kein Rauchen im Zimmer	
Discount for children		Rabatt for barn		Ermässigung für Kinder	
Some English spoken				Sprechen etwas Englisch	

Directions:
From Gjøvik: Drive towards
Minnesund (Lena) for 15 km and
exit from roundabout towards
Lena on RV 246 and drive about 1
km. Take RV 244 in to Lena city
center and continue on RV 244
about 12-13 km. Look for sign to
Holthe Gård near S-markedet.
From Oslo: RV 4 towards Gjøvik.
Exit in direction Lena after 90 km.

Veibeskrivelse:
Fra Gjøvik; Kjør mot Minnesund
(Lena), etter 15 km, i en
rundkjøring; ta av mot Lena RV
246 og kjør ca 1 km. Ta RV 244
inn til Lena sentrum og følg RV
244 videre ca. 12-13 km. Ved S-
markedet står skilt til Holthe Gård.
Fra Oslo: RV-4 mot Gjøvik, etter
90 km tar du av mot Lena.

Wegbeschreibung:
Von Gjøvik: Richtung Minnesund
(Lena), nach 15 km biegen Sie in
einem Kreisverkehr ab Richtung
Lena (Straße 246) und fahren Sie
ca. 1 km. Dann auf der Straße 244
Richtung Zentrum. Weiter auf der
Straße 244 durch Lena hindurch.
Nach ca. 12-13 km steht an einem
Supermarkt ein Schild nach
Holthe Gård.
Von Oslo: Auf der Straße 4 Rich-
tung Gjøvik, nach ca. 90 km ab-
biegen Richtung Lena.

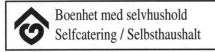
A: 'Store-house' for 2-10 pers.	**A:** Stabbur for 2-10 personer	**A:** 'Vorratshaus' für 2-10 Pers.
No. of bedrooms: 4	Antall soverom: 4	Anzahl Schlafräume: 4
4 baths, kitchen, LR	4 bad, kjøkken, stue	4 Bäder, Küche, Stube
Price for whole unit: **1.800,-**	Pris for hele enheten: **1.800,-**	Ganze Einheit: **1.800,-**
Price per pers.: **300,-**	Pris pr. pers.: **300,-**	Preis pro Pers.: **300,-**
B: Guesthouse for 2-6/7 persons	**B:** Gjestehus for 2-6/7 personer	**B:** Gästehaus für 2-6/7 Personen
No. of bedrooms: 3	Antall soverom: 3	Anzahl Schlafräume: 3
3 baths, 1 kitchen	3 bad, 1 kjøkken	3 Bäder, 1 Küche
Price for whole unit: **1.500,-**	Pris for hele enheten: **1.500,-**	Ganze Einheit: **1.500,-**
Price per pers.: **300,-**	Pris pr. pers.: **300,-**	Preis pro Pers.: **300,-**

Bed linen included	Sengetøy er inkludert	Inkl. Bettwäsche
Open year round	Åpent hele året	Ganzjährig geöffnet
Yard/terrace/deck access	Hage/terrasse/uteplass	Garten/Terrasse/Aussenplatz
Boat for rent	Sykkelutleie	Boot zu mieten
No smoking in rooms	Ingen røking på rom	Kein Rauchen im Zimmer
Discount for children	Rabatt for barn	Ermässigung für Kinder
Some English spoken		Sprechen etwas Englisch

Holthe Gård is beautifully situated in Toten and is the ideal place for both children and adults who like to be active. There is a large yard with children's play facilities including a large trampoline, swings, basketball, table tennis and horseback riding. The farm is quite proud of its peacock. In the cellar is the farm's own country café where you can buy dinner and there is also a pleasant common area where guests may meet.
Swimming facilities and nearby Raufoss Badeland Swim Center.

Holthe Gård ligger vakkert til på Toten, og er et ideelt sted for såvel barn som voksne som trenger å bevege seg. Her er det stor hage med leketilbud til barna; blant annet en stor trampoline, husker, kurvball, bordtennis og muligheter for å ri på hester. En av gårdens stoltheter er en påfugl i hagen. I kjelleren finnes det en egen gårdskro hvor middag kan kjøpes, og ellers er det hyggelige oppholdsrom hvor gjestene kan møtes.
Bademuligheter og kort vei til Raufoss Badeland.

Der Hof Holthe Gård liegt reizvoll in der Landschaft Toten und ist ideal für alle, die im Urlaub ihr Bedürfnis nach Bewegung ausleben möchten. Den Gast erwartet ein großes Gartengrundstück mit Spielmöglichkeiten für Kinder, u.a. ein großes Trampolin, Schaukel, Basketball, Tischtennis u. sogar Reitmöglichkeiten. Der Stolz des Hofes ist ein prächtiger Pfau. Im Kellergeschoß gibt es eine kleine Wirtschaft, die warme Mahlzeiten anbietet. Darüber hinaus stehen den Gästen gemütliche Aufenthaltsräume zur Verfügung. In der Nähe Bademöglichkeiten; kurze Entfernung zum Raufoss Badeland.

> The biggest mistake people make in life is not trying to make a living at doing what they most enjoy.
> - Malcomb S. Forbes

Kronviksætra
Bed & Breakfast

Your host:
Jorunn Bjørnslien
& Geir Raaum

Address:
Landåsveien 949
N - 2861 Landåsbygda
Phone/Fax: 61 12 68 85
Mobil: 90 17 47 90 / 90 51 42 37
E-mail: post@kronviksetra.com
Web: www.kronviksetra.com
Best time to call: 17.00 - 23.00

Double-/Twin room:	**400,-**	Dobbelt-/tosengsrom:	**400,-**	Doppel-/Zweibettzi.:	**400,-**
Single room:	**250,-**	Enkeltrom:	**250,-**	Einzelzimmer:	**250,-**
No. of rooms: 5		Antall rom: 5		Anzahl Zimmer: 5	
Full breakfast		Full frokost		Volles Frühstück	
Laid breakfast table		Dekket frokostbord		Serv.: Frühstückstisch	
Open year round		Åpent hele året		Ganzjährig geöffnet	
TV available		TV tilgjengelig		Zugang zu TV	
Terrace/deck access		Terrasse/uteplass		Terrasse/Aussenplatz	
Boat for rent		Båtutleie		Boot zu mieten	
Bike for rent		Sykkelutleie		Fahrrad zu mieten	
Some English spoken				Sprechen etwas Deutsch	

Kronviksætra lies quietly situated 20 km west of Gjøvik. There is a view over Landås Lake, hiking, swimming or fishing. For winter sports enthusiasts: crosscountry ski trails.

Kronviksætra was originally built as a boarding house in 1936. It is now fully renovated in its original style with the atmosphere still intact. Charming wood stoves in the rooms. Cozy living room, fireplace and TV. This farm features dogs, donkeys, sheep and hens.

Directions:
From Gjøvik: follow RV-33 towards Fagernes/Dokka 14 km. Exit in direction Kronviksætra/Landåsbygda and drive 6 km on road 132. Follow posted signs.

Kronviksætra ligger landlig og fredelig til 20 km vest for Gjøvik. Det er fin utsikt ned til Landåsvannet med bade- og fiskemuligheter. For vintersportsinteresserte har Landåsbygda lysløype og flott turterreng.

Kronviksætra ble bygd i 1936 som pensjonat, nå restaurert, hvor stil og atmosfære er bevart. Gamle vedovner i alle rom. Peisestue og TV-stue disponible for gjester. Det er hunder, esler, sauer og høner på gården.

Veibeskrivelse:
Fra Gjøvik; følg RV 33 mot Fagernes/Dokka 14 km. Ta av mot Kronviksætra/Landåsbygda på fylkesvei 132, følg denne 6 km. Det er skiltet helt frem.

Kronviksætra liegt ländlich und ruhig, 20 km westl. von Gjøvik. Herrliche Aussicht auf den See Landåsvann mit Bade- und Angelmögl. Schönes Gelände für Skiwandern mit Flutlichtloipe.

Kronviksætra wurde 1936 als Pension gebaut, nun modernisiert, aber Stil und Atmosphäre bewahrt. Kamin- und TV-Stube für Gäste. Auf dem Hof gibt es Hunde, Esel, Schafe und Hühner.

Wegbeschreibung:
Von Gjøvik: 14 km auf der Str. 33 in Richtung Fagernes/Dokka, dann abbiegen auf Str. 132 in Richtung Kronviksætra/Landåsbygda. Etwa 6 km weiter auf dieser Straße. Die Strecke ist bis zum Ziel ausgeschildert.

B&B-Homestay
Level of standard: ✿✿ & ✿✿✿

NBT-member
NBT-inspected

page **93**
Buskerud

Frøhaug Gård

Your host:
Ellen & Arne Fjeldstad

Address:
N - 3530 Røyse
Phone/Fax: 32 15 71 09
E-mail: arnfje@online.no

Best time to call:
15.00 - 22.00

Double room:	**600,-**	Dobbeltrom:	**600,-**	Doppelzimmer:	**600,-**
3-bedded room:	**800,-**	3-sengs rom:	**800,-**	3-Bettzimmer:	**800,-**
Twin room:	**400,-**	Tosengsrom:	**400,-**	Zweibettzimmer:	**400,-**
No. of rooms: 5		Antall rom: 5		Anzahl Zimmer: 5	
Full breakfast		Full frokost		Volles Frühstück	
Breakfast buffet		Servering: Frokost buffét		Serv.: Frühstücksbüfett	
or laid breakfast table		eller dekket frokostbord		oder Frühstückstisch	
Open year round		Åpent hele året		Ganzjährig geöffnet	
TV available		TV tilgjengelig		Zugang zu TV	
Terrace/deck access/yard		Terrasse/uteplass/hage		Terrasse/Aussenplatz/Garten	
No smoking inside		Ingen røking innendørs		Kein Rauchen im Haus	
VISA accepted		Vi tar VISA		Wir nehmen VISA	
Some English spoken				Sprechen etwas Deutsch	

Frøhaug Farm, located in a quiet area 5 km from Vik in Hole, with view of Tyrifjorden and Krokskogen forest. The "Main House," from 1766, the second floor room is in Biedermeier style. A large farm kitchen offers large farm style breakfasts. The hosts' son runs the farm. There are farm animals and a large quiet yard, safe for children.

Directions:
Follow E-16 to Vik about 10 km south of Hønefoss. Take the exit towards Røyse and proceed straight ahead 5 km. Look for the sign alongside the highway.

Frøhaug gård, 5 km fra Vik i Hole, ligger høyt og fritt med utsikt over Tyrifjorden og med Krokskogen i bakgrunnen. Hovedbygningen er fra 1766, TV-stuen i 2. etg. er i biedermeierstil. Stor frokost serveres i stort gårdskjøkken.
Vertskapets sønn har overtatt driften av gården. Det er noen dyr. Stor hage og uteplass ved husene, stille og barnevennlig.

Veibeskrivelse:
Kjør E-16 til Vik ca. 10 km sør for Hønefoss. Ta av mot Røyse og kjør rett frem 5 km. Det står skilt ved veien.

Der Hof Frøhaug, 5 km von Vik in Hole, liegt hoch und frei, mit Aussicht über den See Tyrifjord, umgeben vom Waldgebiet Krokskogen. Das Haupthaus ist aus 1766, die TV-Stube im Biedermeierstil. In der grossen Bauernküche gibt es ein reichhaltiges Frühstück. Der Sohn hat den Hof mit einigen Tieren übernommen. Grosser Garten, ruhig u. kinderfreundlich. Wegbeschreibung: Fahren Sie die E-16 bis Vik, ca. 10 km südlich von Hønefoss. Dort biegen Sie ab in Richtung Røyse und fahren 5 km geradeaus. Anschließend der Beschilderung an der Straße folgen.

B&B-Homestay
Level of standard: ♣ ♣ ♣

NBT-member
Inspected by NBT

page **94**
Buskerud

Sevletunet

Your host:
Gro Sevle

Address:
N - 3630 Rødberg
Phone: 32 74 15 86
Fax: 32 74 36 36
Mobil: 97 66 56 38
E-mail: sevletunet@fentun.net
Web:
www.numedal.net/sevletunet

Best time to call:
08.00 - 23.00

Double room/Apt.:	**790,-**	Dobbeltrom/leilighet:	**790,-**	Doppelzi./Wohn.:	**790,-**
Twin room/Apt.:	**790,-**	Tosengsrom/leilighet:	**790,-**	Zweibettzi./Wohn.:	**790,-**
1 pers. in double room:	**530,-**	1 pers. i dobbeltrom:	**530,-**	1 Pers. im Doppelzi.:	**530,-**
No. of rooms: 3		Antall rom: 3		Anzahl Zimmer: 3	
Full breakfast		Full frokost		Volles Frühstück	
Breakfast buffet		Frokostbufffét		Serv.: Frühstücksbüfett	
Birch firewood is included		Bjørkeved til peisen er inkludert		Brennholz im Preis enthalten	
Open year round		Åpent hele året		Ganzjährig geöffnet	
TV available		TV tilgjengelig		Zugang zu TV	
Terrace/deck access/yard		Terrasse/uteplass/hage		Terrasse/Aussenplatz/Garten	
Boat and bike for rent		Båt- og sykkelutleie		Boot u. Fahrrad zu mieten	
No smoking insideble		Ingen røking innendørs		Kein Rauchen im Haus	
English spoken				Sprechen etwas Deutsch	

Rustic and cozy guestrooms in a barn from the 1700s, situated in a farmhouse grouping of historical landmark status. You will find a place rich in Norwegian cultural heritage. It was renovated and restored to original condition in 1998. The various structures are of very high standard and this farm received the Norwegian Heritage Society's "Olav's Rose" in 1999. There are numerous activities offered nearby: swimming, fishing, wilderness park, mountain areas. In addition, your hosts will gladly tell stories about the old days on the farm.

Rustikt, koselig gjestehus i låve fra 1700-tallet på tun blant fredede bygninger. Vertskapet legger høy vekt på service og trivsel, og her vil du finne noe av det som særpreger norsk kulturarv. Restaurert og ombygget i 1998. Gjestehuset har høy standard og den historiske gården fikk Norsk Kulturarvs "Olavsrosa" i 1999. Det finnes flere aktivitetstilbud i nærheten; badestrand, fiske, villmarkspark, fjellområder. I tillegg forteller vertskapet gjerne historier fra gamledager på gården.

Rustikales, gemütliches Ferienhaus. Es handelt sich um eine historische Scheune als eines von mehreren denkmalgeschützten Gebäuden auf einem Gehöft aus dem 17. Jahrhundert. Die Gastgeber legen besonderen Wert auf Service und Wohlbefinden der Gäste und berichten gerne aus der Hofgeschichte. Der Hof vermittelt einen guten Eindruck von der bäuerlichen Kultur Norwegens. Das Gehöft wurde 1998 restauriert und erhielt 1999 den Preis "Olavsrosa". Freizeitangebote: Badestrand, Angelmöglichkeiten, Wildnispark, Gebirgsregionen.

A: Room for 2 persons
Own bath, shared kitchen, LR
Price per unit: **580,-**
No. of units: 3

Families/groups:
Price for 4-5 pers./2 rooms: **875,-**
Price for 6-8 pers./3 rooms: **1.150,-**
Birch firewood is included
TV available

B: "Rallarstua"
Cabin for 2-4 persons
No. of bedrooms: 2
Own bath and kitchen
Simple standard
Price for whole unit: **500,-**

Applies to both rental units:
Bed linen fee: **55,-**
Open year round
Deck access
No smoking inside

A: Rom for 2 personer
Eget bad, delt kjøkken, stue
Pris pr. enhet: **580,-**
Antall enheter: 3

Familier/grupper:
Pris for 4-5 pers./2 rom: **875,-**
Pris for 6-8 pers./3 rom: **1.150,-**
Bjørkeved til peisen er inkludert
TV tilgjengelig

B: "Rallarstua"
Hytte for 2-4 personer
Antall soverom: 2
Eget bad og kjøkken
Enkel standard
Pris for hele enheten: **500,-**

Gjelder for begge enheter:
Tillegg for sengetøy: **55,-**
Åpent hele året
Uteplass
Ingen røking innendørs

A: Zimmer für 2 Personen
Eig. Bad, gemeins.Küche u. Stube
Preis pro Einheit: **580,-**
Anzahl Einheiten: 3

Familien/Gruppen:
Preis für 4-5 Pers./2 Zi.: **875,-**
Preis f. 6-8 Pers./3 Zi.: **1.150,-**
Brennholz im Preis enthalten
Zugang zu TV

B: "Rallarstua"
Hütte für 2-4 Personen
Anzahl Schlafräume: 2
Eig. Bad und Küche
Einfacher Standard
Ganze Einheit: **500,-**

Für alle Einheiten gilt:
Mieten von Bettwäsche: **55,-**
Ganzjährig geöffnet
Aussenplatz
Kein Rauchen im Haus

Sevletunet you will find unique old buildings and be sure not to miss a chance to hear the exciting history of the farm. Situated in the medieval valley Numedal where there are 4 stave churches and numerous medieval structures. Langedrag is a nature reserve with wolves and lynx, which is only a one-hour drive from the farm.

Directions:
Sevletunet is located 89 km from Kongsberg, 69 km from Geilo and 4.5 km from Rødberg. From Kongsberg drive towards Rødberg on RV 40, and slow down near the upper end of Norefjorden, to the right you will see the farm with its old wooden buildings. From Rødberg: After crossing the bridge to Vrenne/Gvammen/Fjordgløtt, turn left at the first exit in the clearing.

Sevletunet ligger i Middelalderdalen Numedal med 4 stavkirker og utallige middelalderbygninger. Naturparken Langedrag, med ulv og gaupe, ligger en times kjøring fra gården.

Veibeskrivelse:
Sevletunet ligger 89 km fra Kongsberg, 69 km fra Geilo og 4,5 km fra Rødberg.
Fra Kongsberg kjør RV 40 mot Rødberg, ved øvre enden av Norefjorden, sakne farten, titt inn til høyre og dere ser gården med de gamle tømmerhusene.
Fra Rødberg: På sletta etter broen over til Vrenne/Gvammen/Fjordgløtt skal du ta første avkjørsel til venstre.

Sevletunet liegt im Numedal, dem „Mittelaltertal", bekannt für seine 4 Stabkirchen sowie zahlreiche mittelalterliche Gebäude. Nur ca. 1 Stunde Autofahrt entfernt öffnet der Erlebnishof und Naturpark Langedrag seine Tore (Wölfe und Luchse).

Wegbeschreibung:
Sevletunet liegt 89 km von Kongsberg, 69 km von Geilo und 4,5 km von Rødberg entfernt.
Sie ab Kongsberg die Straße 40 in Richtung Rødberg. Verlangsamen Sie am oberen Ende des Norefjords die Fahrt und biegen Sie nach rechts ab, bis Sie den Hof mit den alten Blockhütten erreichen.
Ab Rødberg: Nach der Brücke (Richtung Vrenne/Gvammen/ Fjordgløtt) die erste Abzweigung nach links.

Hagale Gjestegård

Your host:
Sigrunn Bæra Svenkerud

Address:
**Alfarvegen
N - 3540 Nesbyen**
Phone: 32 07 10 07
Mobil: 41 41 92 16
E-mail: tol-sven@online.no

Best time to call:
12.00 - 22.00

Double room:	**470,-/670,-**	Dobbeltrom:	**470,-/670,-**	Doppelzimmer:	**470,-/670,-**
Twin room:	**520,-**	Tosengsrom:	**520,-**	Zweibettzimmer:	**520,-**
1 pers. in double room:	**÷100,-**	1 pers. i dobbeltrom:	**÷100,-**	1 Pers. in Doppelzimmer:	**÷100,-**
No. of rooms: 5		Antall rom: 5		Anzahl Zimmer: 5	
Full breakfast		Full frokost		Volles Frühstück.	
Laid breakfast table		Dekket frokostbord		Serv.: Frühstückstisch	
Open year round		Åpent hele året		Ganzjährig geöffnet	
TV available		TV tilgjengelig		Zugang zu TV	
Terrace/deck access/yard/garden		Terrasse/uteplass/hage		Terrasse/Aussenplatz/Garten	
Selfcatering possible		Selvhushold er mulig		Selbsthaushalt möglich	
No smoking in rooms		Ingen røking på rom		Kein Rauchen im Zimmer	
Access to telephone		Tilgang på telefon		Zugang Telefon	
English spoken				Sprechen etwas Deutsch	

Ancestral farm featuring old Halling-style houses and restored storage houses from the 1600's for overnight accommodations in an traditional environment. Rental units of good standard – restored in the style of olden days. Local activities/attractions: Folk museum, meteorite craters, bicyling, fishing, walking trails, alpine ski center, outdoor swimming facility, mountain farm complex, bear park.

Gammel slektsgård med hallingstugu og stabbur fra 1600-tallet tilbyr overnatting i tradsjonsrikt miljø. Boenheter med god standard, restaurert i gammel stil. Aktiviteter i området: Folkemuseum, meterorittkrater, sykling, fiske, merkede turstier, alpintanlegg, friluftsbad, Langedrag fjellgård, bjørnepark.

Alter Erbhof mit "Hallingstugu" (Hütte) und Speicherhaus aus dem 17. Jahrhundert bietet Übernachtungen in traditionsreicher Atmosphäre an. Wohneinheiten mit hohem Standard. Zahlreiche Aktivitäten in der Umgebung: Volksmuseum, Meteoritenkrater, Angeln, Wanderwege, Alpinzentrum, Freibad, Langedrag Bergbauernhof, Bärenpark.

It's never too late - in fiction or in life - to revise.
-Nancy Thayer

B&B-Homestay
Level of standard: ♣ ♣

NBT-member
NBT-inspected

page **97**
Buskerud

Laa Gjestestugu

Your host:
Lise Laa

Address:
Øvre Ål
N - 3570 Ål
Phone: **32 08 12 12**

Best time to call:
08.00 - 23.00

Double room:	**600,-**	Dobbeltrom:	**600,-**	Doppelzimmer:	**600,-**
Single room:	**300,-**	Enkeltrom:	**300,-**	Einzelzimmer:	**300,-**
No. of rooms: 2		Antall rom: 3		Anzahl Zimmer: 2	
Full breakfast		Full frokost		Volles Frühstück	
Breakfast tray		Servering: Frokostbrett		Serv.: Frühstückstablett	
Open year round		Åpent hele året		Ganzjährig geöffnet	
TV available		TV tilgjengelig		Zugang zu TV	
Terrace/deck access		Terrasse/uteplass		Terrasse/Aussenplatz	
No smoking inside		Ingen røking innendørs		Kein Rauchen im Haus	
Discount for children		Rabatt for barn		Ermässigung für Kinder	
Selfcatering possible		Selvhushold er mulig		Selbsthaushalt möglich	
No indoor pets		Ikke husdyr innendørs		Keine Haustiere drinnen	
Member of Norsk Gardsmat		Medlem av Norsk Gardsmat		Mitglied v. Norsk Gardsmat	
English spoken				Sprechen etwas Deutsch	

In the country farm courtyard are 9 houses: the oldest being from 1706. For rent is a recent wooden guesthouse which offers high standard with a fireplace and Jacuzzi, washing machine and dish washer. The farm is situated 720 m. above sea level on the sunny side of the valley with a view. Neighboring farm offers horseback riding throughout the year except during school vacation. Hiking facilities with marked trails. Directions: Follow the signs to Kvinnegardslia. 3.5 km from Ål town center. Brown wooden house with brown barn at the crossroad.

Nybygget gjestehus i tømmer. Gårdstun med ni hus; det eldste er fra 1706. Hytten/gjestehuset har høy standard med peis og boblebad, vaskemaskin og oppvaskmaskin.
Gården ligger på solsiden av dalen, på 720 m.o.h, med fin utsikt. Det er muligheter for å ri på hester hos en nabo hele året untatt i skoleferien. Muligheter for foturer på merkede stier.

Veibeskrivelse:
Følg skilting til Kvinnegardslia. 3,5 km fra Ål sentrum. Brun låve, brun tømmerhytte ved veikryss.

Neuerbautes Gästeblockhaus auf einem Gehöft mit 9 Gebäuden; das älteste von 1706.
Hütte/Gästehaus ist komfortabel und hat Kamin und Whirlpool, Waschmaschine u. Spülmaschine. Der Hof liegt auf der Sonnenseite des Tals auf 720 m ü. d. M. mit schöner Aussicht. Ganzjährige (exkl. Schulferien) Reitmöglichkeiten beim Nachbarn. Markierte Wanderpfade.
Wegbeschreibung:
Folgen Sie Schild Kvinnegardslia. 3,5 km vom Ort entfernt an einer Kreuzung braune Scheune und ein braunes Blockhaus.

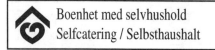

Norbooking

Address:
Gamlevegen 6
N - 3550 Gol
Phone: 32 07 30 70
Fax: 32 07 30 71
E-mail:
booking@norbooking.com
Web: www.norbooking.com

Best time to call:
09.00 - 17.00

Through Norbooking you can make reservations for accommodation in cabins, apartments or guest houses, you can also reserve daytrips for farm visits and other activities, all throughout Norway. Norbooking is mainly using Internet as information- and distribution-channel with an online-booking system. Response time at online requests: Within two workdays. It is also possible to inquire by phone.

Gjennom Norbooking kan du bestille overnatting i hytter, leiligheter og i gjestegårder, du kan også bestille ferieaktiviteter og gårdsbesøk, i hele Norge. Norbooking bruker i hovedsak Internett som informasjons- og distribusjonskanal med et 'online' bookingsystem. Respons ved bestilling: inntil to arbeidsdager. Det er også mulig å bestille på telefon.

Über Norbooking können Sie Übernachtungen in Hütten, Ferienwohnungen und Gästehäusern, sowie Ferienaktivitäten in ganz Norwegen bestellen. Norbooking verwendet hauptsächlich Internett als Informations- und Distributionskanal mit einem "online" -Buchungssystem. Antwort auf Bestellung kommt innerhalb von zwei Arbeitstagen. Bestellung üter Telefon ist auch möglich.

Many people have the wrong idea about what constitutes true happiness. It is not attained through self-gratification but through fidelity to a worthy purpose.

-Helen Keller

Nothing can stop the man with the right mental attitude from achieving his goal; nothing on earth can help the man with the wrong mental attitude.

-Thomas Jefferson

Fjellheim
Bed & Breakfast

Your host:
Solveig Wiersdalen

Address:
Bedehusbakken 8
N - 3947 Langangen
Phone: 35 56 83 64

Best time to call:
09.00 - 21.00

Double room:	**550,-**	Dobbeltrom:	**550,-**	Doppelzimmer:	**550,-**
Double room w/extra bed:	**750,-**	Dobbeltrom m/ekstra seng:	**750,-**	Doppelzi. m/Extrabett:	**750,-**
1 pers. in double room:	**300,-**	En pers. i dobbeltrom:	**300,-**	1 Pers. im Doppelzimmer:	**300,-**

No. of rooms: 3	Antall rom: 3	Anzahl Zimmer: 3
Full breakfast	Full frokost	Volles Frühstück
Breakfast buffet	Servering: Frokost buffét	Serv.: Frühstücksbüfett
Open year round	Åpent hele året	Ganzjährig geöffnet
TV available	TV tilgjengelig	Zugang zu TV
Common LR for guests	Eget oppholdsrom	Eigener Aufenthaltsraum
Yard/terrace/deck access	Hage/terrasse/uteplass	Garten/Terrasse/Aussenplatz
English spoken		Sprechen Englisch

The beginning of Southern Norway marks the spot where you can enjoy food and lodging with your hostess Solveig and her 5 cats. She wishes you welcome to her large and comfortable detached home in the small village of Langangen, right between Porsgrunn and Larvik. It's 5 min. from the house down to the sea and there are good swimming and fishing facilities, along with excellent hiking areas nearby. Among other local attractions, you might visit Porsgrunn's porcelain factory and museum, founded in 1887. Ferry connections from Larvik to Denmark.

Der Sørlandet starter kan du søke kost og losji hos Solveig og hennes 5 katter. Hun ønsker dere velkommen til sin store og koselige enebolig i den lille bygda Langangen, midt i mellom Porsgrunn og Larvik.
Fra huset er det 5 minutter til sjøen med gode bade- og fiskemuligheter, og det er også fine turområer i nærheten.
Av attraksjoner i nærheten har man bl.a. muligheten til å besøke Porsgrunns porselensfabrikk og museum, grunnlagt i 1887.
Fra Larvik er det ferjeforbindelse til Danmark.

Vor den Toren Südnorwegens freuen sich Solveig und ihre 5 Katzen auf die Gäste. Die Gastgeberin heißt Sie in ihrem gemütlichen Einfamilienhaus im kleinen Ort Langangen, auf halber Strecke zwischen Porsgrunn und Larvik willkommen. Vom Haus sind es nur 5 Minuten bis zum Meer mit guten Bade- und Angelmöglichkeiten, und in der Umgebung kann man schöne Wanderungen unternehmen. Eine interessante Sehenswürdigkeit ist die Porzellanfabrik in Porsgrunn (seit 1887) mit angrenzendem Museum.
Von Larvik aus gibt es eine Fährverbindung nach Dänemark (Frederikshavn).

Åkerveien Bed & Breakfast

Your host:
Ruth & David Tenden

Address:
Åkerveien 11
N - 3929 Porsgrunn
Phone: 35 51 08 70
Mobil: 99 77 27 43
E-mail: tende@online.no

Best time to call:
09.00 - 23.00

Twin room:	400,-	Tosengsrom:	400,-	Zweibettzimmer:	400,-
1 pers. in twin room:	300,-	1 pers. i tosengsrom:	300,-	1 Pers. im Zweibettzimmer:	300,-
Extra bed:	100,-/200,-	Ekstraseng:	100,-/200,-	Extra Bett:	100,-/200,-
No. of rooms: 1		Antall rom: 1		Anzahl Zimmer: 1	
Full breakfast		Full frokost		Volles Frühstück	
Laid breakfast table		Dekket frokostbord		Serv.: Frühstückstisch	
Open year round		Åpent hele året		Ganzjährig geöffnet	
TV available		TV tilgjengelig		Zugang zu TV	
Yard/terrace/deck access		Hage/terrasse/uteplass		Garten/Terrasse/Aussenplatz	
English spoken				Sprechen Englisch	

Åkerveien Bed & Breakfast can offer you a pleasantly furnished basement apartment with a small sleeping alcove in a detached home, 3 km south of Porsgrunn city center. The cellar apartment has windows facing southwest, overlooking the garden. Guests have their own bathroom, both cable-TV and radio in the living room. Your hosts are both retired after long, active careers. Sites of interest include the Porsgrunn porcelain factory and museum, definitely worth a visit!
Located 10 km from Skien, where it is possible to begin a tour by boat on the Telemarkskanalen.

Åkerveien Bed & Breakfast kan tilby en hyggelig møblert kjellerstue med en liten sovealkove i enebolig 3 km syd for Porsgrunn sentrum.
Kjellerstuen har vinduer mot sydvest, og utenfor er det hage. Her er det også et bad som bare brukes av gjestene, og i stuen er det kabel-TV og radio.
Vertskapet er begge pensjonister etter et langt yrkesaktivt liv.
Av severdigheter er et besøk på Porsgrunn Porselensfabrikk og museum å anbefale. Det er 10 km til Skien hvor man kan starte turen med båt på Telemarkskanalen.

Åkerveien Bed & Breakfast liegt 3 km südlich von Porsgrunn und bietet seinen Gästen in einem Einfamilienhaus eine gemütlich möblierte Kellerwohnung mit einem kleinen Schlafalkoven und Bad. Die Fenster liegen in südwestlicher Richtung, vor dem Haus steht ein Garten zur Verfügung. Der Wohnraum verfügt über Kabel- und Radioanschluß.
Die Gastgeber sind nach einem langen Berufsleben nun beide Rentner. Eine interessante Sehenswürdigkeit ist die Porzellanfabrik in Porsgrunn mit angrenzendem Museum. Bis Skien, wo die Bootsfahrt auf dem Telemarkskanal beginnt, sind es 10 km.

Hulfjell Gård & Hytteutleie

Your host:
Tellef Moland & Britt Eide

Address:
Hulfjell Gård,
N - 3750 Drangedal
Phone: 35 99 92 54
Mobil: 41 30 90 52
E-mail: tollak@c2i.net

Best time to call:
08.00 - 22.00

Cabin for 2-8 persons	Hytte for 2-8 personer	Hütte für 2-8 Personen
No. of bedrooms: 2	Antall soverom: 2	Anzahl Schlafräume: 2
Own bath, kitchen	Eget bad, kjøkken	Eig. Bad, Küche
Yard/terrace/deck access	Terrasse/uteplass	Terrasse/Aussenplatz
Price for whole unit: **650,-**	Pris for hele enheten: **650,-**	Ganze Einheit: **650,-**
Bed linen fee: **75,-**	Tillegg for sengetøy: **75,-**	Mieten von Bettwäsche: **75,-**
Open year round	Åpent hele året	Ganzjährig geöffnet
Pets welcome	Kjæledyr tillatt	Boot zu mieten.
Boat for rent	Båtutleie	Haustiere willkommen
Some English spoken		Sprechen etwas Englisch

Hulfjell is a pleasant farm with lots of animals: cows, horses, ponies, miniature pigs, goats, sheep, rabbits and geese. The cabin is situated 5 meters from the edge of the lake with a large deck area extending down towards the shoreline. Here you will enjoy excellent swimming in a lake that gets nice and warm during the summertime. Guests can also fish and the farm rents out canoes. Guests may take care of the hens, which entitles them to help themselves to fresh eggs in the hen house.
Directions:
Exit E-18 towards Drangedal. About 5 km before Drangedal town center, exit highway at the sign "Hulfjell Gård, hytte, gårdssalg og kanoutleie". Farm 1.5 km.

Hulfjell er en trivelig gård med mange dyr; ku, hest, ponni, minigris, geit, sau, kanin, and og gjess. Hytten ligger fem meter fra vannet, med en stor terrasse ned mot strandkanten.
Her er det fine bademuligheter i vann som blir godt og varmt om sommeren. Gjestene kan også fiske, og gården leier ut kanoer. Om gjestene ønsker det kan de ta seg av hønsene, og får da selv fritt hente friske egg i hønsehuset.
Veibeskrivelse:
Ta av fra E-18 retning Drangedal. Ca. 5 km før Drangedal sentrum, ta av ved skilt merket "Hulfjell Gård, hytte, gårdssalg og kanoutleie". Det er da 1,5 km til gården.

Gemütlicher Bauernhof mit vielen Tieren. Es gibt Kühe, Pferde, Ponys, kleine Ferkel, Ziegen, Schafe, Kanin- chen, Enten und Gänse. Die Hütte liegt nur 5 m vom See entfernt und bietet eine große Terrasse bis hinunter zur Wasserkante. Die Wassertemperatur ist im Sommer angenehm mild. Angelmöglichkeiten, darüber hinaus werden auf dem Hof Kanus vermietet. Wenn die Gäste mögen, dürfen sie sich selbst um die Hühner kümmern und morgens kostenlos ihre Frühstückseier im Hühnerstall holen.
Wegbeschreibung:
Zweigen Sie von der E-18 in Richtung Drangedal ab. Folgen Sie ca. 5 km vor Drangedal dem Schild "Hulfjell Gård, hytte, gårdssalg og kanoutleie". Hof ca. 1,5 km.

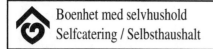
Bø gardsturisme

Your contact:
Bergit Askildt Myrjord

Address:
Askildtvgen 60
N - 3800 Bø
Phone: **35 95 21 55**
Fax: **35 95 21 17**
Mobil: **99 23 62 15**
E-mail: **post@gardsturisme.no**
Web: **www.gardsturisme.no**

Best time to call:
10.00 - 13.00

Rental units for 2-12 persons:
Price per unit: **550,- up to 1.250,-**
Bed linen fee: **50,-**
Open year round

Boenheter for 2-12 personer:
Pris pr. enhet: **550,- opp til 1.275,-**
Tillegg for leie sengetøy: **50,-**
Åpent hele året

Einheiten für 2-12 Personen:
Pro Einheit: **550,- zu 1.250,-**
Mieten von Bettwäsche: **50,-**
Ganzjährig geöffnet

Management of 24 rental units among 18 farms in and around Bø. The farms are in normal operation and many have livestock. All units include outdoor grills and garden furniture along with play areas. Short distance to walking trails, swimming and fishing areas. Central Telemark is an interesting area with many sources of vacation fun and cultural experiences. Among these are: Heddal Stave Church, Bø Country Museum, The Telemark Canal and Telemark Summerland. Good variety of outdoor activities and fishing nearby.

Farm visit:
Røysland, the uppermost farm among the Stoklandheia uplands is ready to receive day visits by groups or individual guests. Horseback tours and riding lessons all year round. Advance reservations required.

Bø Gardsturisme formidler 24 boenheter fordelt på 18 garder i Bø og omegn. Gardene er i vanlig drift, og mange har husdyr. Alle enhetene har grill og hagemøbler, samt lekeområder. Kort vei til tur, bade- og fiskemuligheter. Midt-Telemark er et interessant område med masse feriemoro og kulturopplevelser. Vi kan nevne, Heddal Stavkyrkje, Bø bygdemuseum, Telemarkkanalen og Telemark Sommarland. Gode muligheter for alle typer friluftsliv og fiske i området.

Gardsbesøk:
Røysland, den øverste garden på Stoklandheia i Bø, med utsikt over "sju prestegjeld", tar imot dagsbesøk av grupper og enkeltgjester. Rideturer og ridetimer hele året. Forhåndsbestilling.

Bø Gardsturisme bietet 24 Wohneinheiten, die sich auf 18 Bauernhöfe in Bø und Umgebung verteilen. Alle Höfe sind bewirtschaftet, auf vielen leben Tiere. Alle Wohnungen sind mit Grill und Gartenmöbeln ausgestattet. Kurze Entf. zu Wander-, Bade- und Angelmöglichkeiten. Midt-Telemark ist eine interessante Region, mit viel Ferienspaß, und kulturellen Erlebnissen. Als Beispiele sollen die Stabkirche von Heddal und der Freizeitpark genannt werden. Gute Möglichkeiten zu allen Arten der Betätigung an der frischen Luft sowie zum Angeln.

Bauernhofbesuche:
Røysland ist der oberste Hof auf Stoklandheia bei Bø. Tagesausflügler (Gruppen und Einzelgäste) sind willkommen. Reitstunden und Reittouren ganzjährig möglich. Voranmeldung.

Sanden

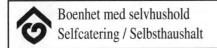

Your host:
Knut Erik Grønskei
& Annik Bothner

Address:
Sanden
N - 3691 Gransherad
Phone: 35 01 89 12
Mobil: 41 67 33 99
E-mail: k-e-g@online.no
Web: home.online.no/~k-e-g/

Best time to call:
17.00 - 22.00

A: Guesthouse for 6-8 persons
No. of bedrooms: 2
Own bath, kitchen, LR
Price per pers.:   **100,-/150,-**

B: Guesthouse for 2 pers.
No. of bedrooms: 1
Shared bath
Price per pers.:   **75,-**

Bed linen included
Open year round
TV available
Boat for rent
No smoking inside
Suitable for handicapped
Breakfast service available: **50,-**
English and some French spoken

A: Gjestehus for 6-8 personer
Antall soverom: 2
Eget bad, kjøkken, stue
Pris pr. pers.:   **100,-/150,-**

B: Gjestehus (Stabbur) for 2 pers.
Antall soverom: 1
Delt bad
Pris pr. pers.:   **75,-**

Sengetøy er inkludert
Åpent hele året
TV tilgjengelig
Båtutleie
Ingen røking innendørs
Handikapvennlig
Frokost kan serveres: **50,-**

A: Gästehaus für 6-8 Personen
Anzahl Schlafräume: 2
Eig. Bad, Küche, Stube
Preis pro Pers.:   **100,-/150,-**

B: Gästehaus für 2 Pers.
Anzahl Schlafräume: 1
Gemeins. Bad
Preis pro Pers.:   **75,-**

Inkl. Bettwäsche
Ganzjährig geöffnet
Zugang zu TV
Boot zu mieten
Kein Rauchen im Haus
Behindertengerecht
Frühstück auf Bestellung: **50,-**
Sprechen etwas Deutsch

Overnight accommodations at a farm near Tinnsjøen. Winter activities: Ski/mountain tours, ice fishing. Summer activities: Fishing and hunting, mountain hikes, food preparation with homegrown products: Fish, berries and vegetables.

Directions:
From Rjukan: Drive towards Tinnsjøen and turn right at the crossing near the lake. Drive to Sanden. Distance to Rjukan: 35 km.

Overnatting på gård ved Tinnsjøen i Telemark. Vinteraktiviteter: Ski- og fjellturer, isfiske. Sommeraktiviteter: Fiske og fangst, fjellturer, matlaging av egne produkter: Fisk, bær og grønnsaker.

Veibeskrivelse:
Fra Rjukan, kjør mot Tinnsjøen og ta til høyre i kryss ved sjøen. Kjør til Sanden. Avstand Rjukan, 35 km.

Übernachtung auf einem Hof am See Tinnsjøen in Telemark. Winteraktivitäten: Ski- u. Bergtouren, Eisangeln. Sommeraktivitäten: Angeln, Bergwanderungen, Zubereitung eigener Lebensmittel: Fisch, Beeren und Gemüse.

Wegbeschreibung:
Fahren Sie von Rjukan in Richtung Tinnsjøen und zweigen Sie am See an der Kreuzung rechts ab nach Sanden. 35 km bis Rjukan.

Huldrehaug

Your host:
Elinor Igelkjøn

Address:
N - 3841 Flatdal
Phone: 35 05 22 87
Fax: 35 05 21 16
Mobil: 97 04 29 80

Best time to call:
09.00 - 23.00

Double room:	**350,-/500,-**	Dobbeltrom:	**350,-/500,-**	Doppelzimmer:	**350,-/500,-**
1 pers. in dbl room:	**200,-/375,-**	1 pers. i dobbeltrom:	**200,-/375,-**	1 Pers. im Doppelzi.:	**200,-/375,-**
Family room 3-4 pers.:	**650,-/700,-**	Familierom 3-4 pers:	**650,-/700,-**	Familienzi. 3-4 Pers.:	**650,-/700,-**
No. of rooms: 4		Antall rom: 4		Anzahl Zimmer: 4	
Full breakfast		Full frokost		Volles Frühstück	
Laid breakfast table		Dekket frokostbord		Serv.: Frühstückstisch	
Open year round		Åpent hele året		Ganzjährig geöffnet	
TV available		TV tilgjengelig		Zugang zu TV	
Terrace/yard		Terrasse/hage		Terrasse/Aussenplatz	
No smoking inside		Ingen røking innendørs		Kein Rauchen im Haus	
VISA accepted		Vi tar VISA		Wir nehmen VISA	
Discount for children under 12		Rabatt for barn under 12 år		Ermässigung für Kinder unter 12	
English spoken				Sprechen Deutsch	

Flatdal is a distinctive valley, completely flat between steep mountain walls. Huldrehaug is in the midst of Telemark's many cultural and historical attractions; only 200 m. from Nutheim, with a café, a gallery and an outdoor pool.
With Elinor as your hosts, there likely will be both hiking and dinner invitations.

Flatdal er en særegen dal og er, som navnet forteller, helt flat i bunnen. På begge sider stiger fjellene bratt opp.
Med Elinor som vertskap vanker det både tur- og middagsinvitasjoner.
Du befinner deg midt blandt Telemarks mange kulturelle og historiske opplevelsestilbud. Like ved ligger Nutheim, med kafé, galleri og et flott utendørs svømmebasseng.

Flatdal ist ein eigenartiges Tal und wie der Name andeutet ganz flach im Grund mit zu beiden Seiten steil aufragenden Bergen.
Bei Elinor wird man auch zu Touren und Mittagessen eingeladen. Günstiger Ausgangspunkt zu vielen kulturellen und historischen Erlebnissen in Telemark. 200 m nach Nutheim mit Galerie, Cafè und schönem Schwimmbecken.

Be couragous, it is the only place yet not crowded.
-Anita Roddick

Naper Gård

Your host:
Solveig & Ådne Naper

Address:
Naper Gård
N - 3849 Vråliosen
Phone: 35 05 51 89
Fax: 35 05 51 89
Mobil: 98 46 95 42
E-mail: anaper@online.no

Best time to call:
09.00 - 21.00

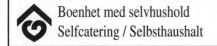

Guesthouse for 2-6 persons		Gjestehus for 2-6 personer		Gästehaus für 2-6 Personen	
Own bath, kitchen, LR, DR		Eget bad, kjøkken, stue, spisestue		Eig. Bad, Küche, Sp.Zi., Stube	
Bedrooms: 2		Soverom: 2		Anzahl Schlafräume: 2	
Price for whole unit:	**500,-**	Pris for hele enheten:	**500,-**	Ganze Einheit:	**500,-**
Or price per pers.:	**300,-**	Eller pris pr. pers.:	**300,-**	Oder pro Person:	**300,-**
Bed linen fee:	**70,-**	Tillegg for sengetøy:	**70,-**	Mieten von Bettwäsche:	**70,-**
Breakfast service available:	**70,-**	Frokost kan serveres:	**70,-**	Frühstück nur nach Vorbest.:	**70,-**
Open year round		Åpent hele året		Ganzjährig geöffnet	
Yard/terrace/deck access		Terrasse/uteplass/hage		Garten/Terrasse/Aussenplatz	
Boat: free use		Båt inkludert i leie		Boot zu mieten	
Pets welcome		Kjæledyr tillatt		Haustiere willkommen	
English spoken				Sprechen Deutsch	

Old ancestral farm (forestry-based) situated in a beautiful area for walking tours in nearby forests and meadows. Fishing/boat trips and swimming. The only residents are the couple who run the farm, plus their dog and three cats, and they all enjoy meeting the nice people who come to visit the farm.

Gammel slektsgård (skogsgård) beliggende i flott område for turer i skog og mark. Fiske/båtturer og bading. Kun ekteparet som driver gården bor der nå, sammen med hund og tre katter, og de syntes det er hyggelig å treffe nye mennesker som kommer på besøk på gården.

Alter Familienbetrieb in reizvoller Lage. Gute Möglichkeiten zu Ausflügen durch Wald und Feld. Angeln, Bootstouren und Baden möglich. Auf dem Hof wohnt heute nur noch das Gastgeber-Ehepaar mit ihrem Hund und Katzen. Beide sind Begegnungen ihren Gästen gegenüber aufgeschlossen.

Directions:
E-134 from Drammen towards Brunkeberg. Exit onto RV 41 towards Kvitseid/Vrådal. From Vrådal: RV 38 towards Vråliosen. Turn left just after passing Vråliosen (towards Nordbø). From here it is only 500 m to Naper Gård.

Veibeskrivelse:
E-134 fra Drammen til Brunkeberg. Ta av mot Kvitseid/Vrådal, RV 41. Fra Vrådal RV 38 til Vråliosen. Ta til venstre rett etter Vråliosen (mot Nordbø). Da er det ca 500 m til Naper Gård.

Wegbeschreibung:
Fahren Sie die E-134 von Drammen in Richtung Brunkeberg. Biegen Sie anschließend auf die Str. 41 nach Kviteseid/Vrådal ab. Ab Vrådal geht es weiter auf der Str. 38, bis Sie Vråliosen erreichen. Direkt hinter der Siedlung zweigen Sie in Richtung Nordbø ab. Hof 500 m.

Fossum Kurs- & feriesenter

Your host:
Dierk & Birgitte Rengstorf

Address:
Hauggrend
N - 3870 Fyresdal
Phone: 35 04 25 14
Fax: 35 04 25 64
E-mail: fossum@fyresdal.online.no
Web: www.fossumferie.com

Best time to call:
0800 - 22.00

Double room/Twin room:	**450,-**	Dobbeltrom/tosengsrom:	**450,-**	Doppel-/Zweibettzimmer:	**450,-**
1 pers. in double room:	**290,-**	1 pers. i dobbeltrom:	**290,-**	1 Pers. in Doppelzimmer:	**290,-**
No. of rooms: 9		Antall rom: 9		Anzahl Zimmer: 9	
Full breakfast		Full frokost		Volles Frühstück	
Laid breakfast table		Servering: Frokostbord		Serv.: Frühstückbuffet	
Other meals served by agreement		Andre måltider etter avtale		Andere Mahlzeiten auf Best.	
Open year round		Åpent hele året		Ganzjährig geöffnet	
Terrace/Deck access/Yard/Garden		Terrasse/uteplass/Hage		Terrasse/Aussenplatz/Garten	
Boat for rent		Båtutleie		Boot zu mieten	
Discount for children u. 13 yrs.		Rabatt for barn u. 13 år		Ermäßigung für Kinder u. 13 J.	
Selfcatering possible		Selvhushold er mulig		Selbsthaushalt möglich	
No smoking inside		Ingen røking innendørs		Kein Rauchen im Haus	
VISA accepted		Vi tar VISA		Wir nehmen VISA	
Access to telephone/fax		Tilgang på telefon/telefaks		Zugang Telefon/Fax	
Pets welcome		Kjæledyr tillatt		Haustiere willkommen	
Sauna. Horseback riding.		Sauna. Ridemuligheter		Sauna. Reitmöglichkeiten	
Suitable for handicapped		Handikapvennlig		Behindertengerecht	
English and French spoken				Sprechen Deutsch	

Holiday center with plenty of indoor and outdoor activities. Workshop for arts and handicraft, weaving/weaving looms, courses in Yoga, Reiki, and meditation. Skiing, climbing, survival, horseback riding. Sightseeing nearby: stave church, museums and mines. Geologically interesting area.

Ferieanlegg med et bredt spekter aktivitetstilbud. Atelierer for kunst/ håndverk, veving, meditasjon/ yogakurs. Svært gode friluftslivmuligheter sommer og vinter. Betydelige severdigheter i nærområdet, blant annet stavkirke, kanalanlegg, gruver, museer og interessante geologiske formasjoner.

Ferienhof mit breit gefächertem Aktivitätenangebot. Atelier für Kunst und Kunsthandwerk, Webstube. Kursangebot für Yoga, Reiki, Meditation. Gute Möglichkeiten für naturnahe Freizeitgestaltung. Sehenswürdigkeiten in der Nähe, u.a. Stabkirche, Bergwerke, Museen, Telemarkkanal. Geologisch interessantes Gebiet.

Directions:
Via RV 355, 15 km north of Fyresdal.

Veibeskrivelse:
Ved RV 355, 15 nord for Fyresdal.

Wegbeschreibung:
An der Str. 355 gelegen, 15 km nördlich von Fyresdal.

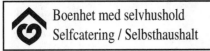

A: 4 Cabins for 4 persons	**A:** 4 Hytter for 4 personer	**A:** 4 Hütten für 4 Personen
Own kitchen/LR	Egen stue/kjøkken	Eig. Küche/Stube
Price for whole unit: **220,-**	Pris for hele enheten: **220,-**	Ganze Einheit: **220,-**

B: 1 Cabin for 2 persons	**B:** 1 Hytte for 2 personer	**B:** 1 Hütte für 2 Personen
Own kitchen/LR	Egen stue/kjøkken	Eig. Küche/Stube
Price for whole unit: **250,-**	Pris for hele enheten: **250,-**	Ganze Einheit: **250,-**

C: 3 Cabins for 3 persons	**C:** 3 Hytter for 3 personer	**C:** 3 Hütten für 3 Personen
Own kitchen/LR	Egen stue/kjøkken	Eig. Küche/Stube
Price for whole unit: **280,-**	Pris for hele enheten: **280,-**	Ganze Einheit: **280,-**

D: 2 Cabins for 4 persons	**D:** 2 Hytter for 4 personer	**D:** 2 Hütten für 4 Personen
No. of bedrooms: 1	Antall soverom: 1	Anzahl Schlafräume: 1
Own kitchen/LR	Egen stue/kjøkken	Eig. Küche/Stube
Price for whole unit: **380,-**	Pris for hele enheten: **380,-**	Ganze Einheit: **380,-**

E: 1 Cabin for 5-6 persons	**E:** 1 Hytter for 5-6 personer	**E:** 1 Hütte für 5-6 Personen
No. of bedrooms: 2	Antall soverom: 2	Anzahl Schlafräume: 2
Own kitchen/LR	Egen stue/kjøkken	Eig. Küche/Stube
Price for whole unit: **480,-**	Pris for hele enheten: **480,-**	Ganze Einheit: **480,-**

F: 2 Cabins for 6 persons	**F:** 2 Hytter for 6 personer	**F:** 2 Hütten für 6 Personen
No. of bedrooms: 3	Antall soverom: 3	Anzahl Schlafräume: 3
Own kitchen/LR	Egen stue/kjøkken	Eig. Küche/Stube
Price for whole unit: **550,-**	Pris for hele enheten: **550,-**	Ganze Einheit: **550,-**

G: 1 Cabin for 10 persons	**G:** 1 Hytte for 10 personer	**G:** 1 Hütte für 10 Personen
No. of bedrooms: 5	Antall soverom: 5	Anzahl Schlafräume: 5
Own kitchen/LR	Egen stue/kjøkken	Eig. Küche/Stube
Price for whole unit: **800,-**	Pris for hele enheten: **800,-**	Ganze Einheit: **800,-**

H: 1 Apartment for 2 persons	**H:** Leilighet for 2 personer	**H:** 1 Wohnung für 2 Personen
Own kitchen/LR, DR and bath	Egen stue/kjk., spiserom og bad	Eig. Bad, Küche, Stube, Sp.Zi.
No pets please	Merk: ikke husdyr	Keine Haustiere
Price for whole unit: **550,-**	Pris for hele enheten: **550,-**	Ganze Einheit: **550,-**

Applies to all rental units:	For alle enhetene gjelder:	Für alle Einheiten gilt:
Bed linen fee: **60,-**	Tillegg for sengetøy: **60,-**	Mieten von Bettwäsche: **60,-**
Breakfast service available: **70,-**	Frokost kan serveres: **70,-**	Frühstück auf Bestellung: **70,-**
Other meals served on request	Andre måltider kan bestilles	Andere Mahlzeiten auf Best.
Yard/terrace/deck access/garden	Terrasse/uteplass/hage	Garten/Terrasse/Aussenplatz

> You must have courage, whatever the test, however many
> times you fall, stand up just once more.
> -Author Unknown

Templen Bed & Breakfast

Your host:
Britt Egeland

Address:
Vestre Bievei 6
N - 4825 Arendal
Phone: 37 09 59 81
Mobil: 90 75 02 88

Best time to call:
08.00 - 12.00 / 17.00 - 23.00

Double-/Twin room:	**700,-**	Dobbelt-/tosengsrom:	**700,-**	Doppel-/Zweibettzi.:	**700,-**
1 pers. in double room:	**450,-**	En pers. i dobbeltrom:	**450,-**	1 Pers. im Doppelzi.:	**450,-**
No. of rooms: 3		Antall rom: 3		Anzahl Zimmer: 3	
Full breakfast		Full frokost		Volles Frühstück	
Laid breakfast table		Dekket frokostbord		Serv.: Frühstückstisch	
Open year round		Åpent hele året		Ganzjährig geöffnet	
TV available in the loft		TV tilgjengelig i loftsstue		Zugang zu TV	
Terrace/deck access/garden		Terrasse/uteplass/hage		Terrasse/Aussenplatz/Garten	
No smoking inside		Ingen røking innendørs		Kein Rauchen im Haus	
Discount for children		Rabatt for barn		Ermässigung für Kinder	
Parking		Parkeringsplass		Parkplatz	
Some English spoken				Sprechen etwas Deutsch	

Templen, a small farming complex on 95 hectares, is situated among peaceful surroundings about 5 km west of Arendal. There is excellent hiking in the nearby woods, and a short distance to nice beaches, golf course and museums. Kristiansand Dyrepark (animal park) is about a 45 min drive. Easy ferry connections to the continent, including Denmark. Rhododendron and perennial garden nearby. Tours upon request.

Templen, et lite gardsbruk på 95 mål, ligger i rolige omgivelser ca. 5 km vest for Arendal. Her er fine turmuligheter i skogen like ved, og det er kort avstand til fine badestrender, golfbane og museer. Til Kristiansand Dyrepark tar det ca 45 min. med bil. Gode ferjeforbindelser til kontinentet og Danmark.
Rododendron- og staudehage like ved. Visning etter avtale.

Templen ist ein kleiner Bauernhof von 95 Dekar, der in ruhiger Umgebung ca. 5 km westlich von Arendal liegt. Schöne Wandermöglichkeiten im nahegelegenen Wald, kurze Entfernung zu reizvollen Badestränden, Golfplatz und Museen. 45 Minuten mit dem Auto bis zum Tierpark in Kristiansand. Gute Fährverbindungen nach Dänemark und Mitteleuropa. Rhododendron- und Staudengarten nebenan. Führungen nach Absprache.

Honesty is the best image.
-Ziggy (Tom Wilson)

Bjorvatn Resort

Your host:
Harald Lunderød

Address:
Bjorvatn
N - 4828 Mjåvatn
Phone: 37 03 98 09
Fax: 37 03 98 09
Mobil: 41 20 17 77

Best time to call:
08.00 - 23.00

Guesthouse for 2-6 persons	Gjestehus for 2-6 personer	Gästehaus für 2-6 Personen
No. of bedrooms: 2	Antall soverom: 2	Anzahl Schlafräume: 2
Own bath, kitchen/dining room	Eget bad, kjøkken/spisestue	Eig. Bad, Küche/Sp.Zi.
Price for whole unit: **500,-**	Pris for hele enheten: **500,-**	Ganze Einheit: **500,-**
Price per pers.: **200,-**	Pris pr. pers.: **200,-**	Preis pro Pers.: **200,-**
Bed linen fee: **50,-**	Tillegg for sengetøy: **50,-**	Mieten von Bettwäsche: **50,-**
Terrace/deck access	Terrasse/uteplass	Garten/Terrasse/Aussenplatz
Open year round	Åpent hele året	Ganzjährig geöffnet
TV available.	TV tilgjengelig	Zugang zu TV
Boat: Free use	Båt kan lånes	Boot inkl.
Breakfast service available: **50,-**	Frokost kan serveres: **50,-**	Frühstück auf Bestellung: **50,-**
English and some Spanish spoken		Sprechen etwas Deutsch

Apartment in an old barn. Sunny location with view of a large lake. Dock with nearby swimming area and free use of boat. Hunting and fishing. Excellent sledding hill and skiing from deck area and down towards the lake. Bjorvatn is a little cluster of farms including four dwellings. Winter sports complex w/groomed ski trails: 3-4 km.

Directions:
From Kristiansand: Follow the signs towards the airport then continue on RV 41 to Birkeland. Exit towards Mjåvatn/Øynaheia. 8 km to the exit "Bjorvatn 1". Drive via Arendal route in case of difficult weather conditions.

Leilighet i gammel låve på gårdstun. Solrik beliggenhet, med utsikt over et stort vann. Brygge med badeplass og gratis båt. Mulighet-er for jakt og fiske. Fin ake- og skibakke fra terrassen og ned mot vannet. Bjorvatn er en liten grend med fire boliger. Nærmeste vintersportssted med løyper: 3-4 km.

Vegbeskrivelse
Fra Kristiansand: Følg skilt til flyplassen, fortsett på RV 41 til Birkeland.Ved Herefoss, ta av mot Mjåvatn/Øynaheia. Kjør 8 km til avkjørsel Bjorvatn 1. Kjør evt. via Arendal ved vanskelige kjøreforhold.

Ferienwohnung in einer alten Scheune. Sonnige Lage, Aussicht auf einen großen See. Kai mit Badestelle und Boot. Jagd- und Angelmöglichkeiten. Reizvoller Schlitten- und Skihang von der Terrasse bis hinunter zum See. Bjorvatn ist eine kleine Siedlung mit 4 Häusern. 3-4 km zu Skiloipen.

Wegbeschreibung
Ab Kristiansand: Dem Schild zum Flughafen folgen, dann Str. 41 nach Birkeland. Bei Herefoss nach Mjåvatn/Øynaheia abbiegen. Nach 8 km Abzweigung Bjorvatn (1 km). Bei schwierigen Straßenverhältnissen: Anreise über Arendal.

Sjøgløtt
Det lille hotell

Your host:
Helene Ranestad

Address:
Østre Strandgate 25
N - 4610 Kristiansand
Phone/Fax: 38 02 21 20
Mobil: 90 57 23 32
E-mail: booking@sjoglott.no
Web: http://sjoglott.no

Best time to call:
07.00 - 22.30

Double room:	**590,-/780,-**	Dobbeltrom:	**590,-/780,-**	Doppelzimmer:	**590,-/780,-**
Single room:	**350,-/590,-**	Enkeltrom:	**350,-/590,-**	Einzelzimmer:	**350,-/590,-**
No. of rooms: 12		Antall rom: 12		Anzahl Zimmer: 12	
Full breakfast		Full frokost		Volles Frühstück	
Breakfast buffet		Servering: Frokost buffét		Serv.: Frühstücksbüfett	
Open year round		Åpent hele året		Ganzjährig geöffnet	
TV available		TV tilgjengelig		Zugang zu TV	
Yard/terrace/deck access		Hage/terrasse/uteplass		Garten/Terrasse/Aussenplatz	
No smoking inside		Ingen røking innendørs		Kein Rauchen im Haus	
VISA, MC, DC accepted		Vi tar VISA, MC, DC		Wir nehmen VISA, MC, DC	
English spoken				Sprechen Deutsch	

Sjøgløtt Hotell is a small, family-run hotel with 12 rooms and is a place where your hosts do their best to create an atmosphere in which you can feel welcome and at home. You find the hotel in a quiet part of downtown Kristiansand, near the guest marina and the old fortress. Walking distance (3 min.) to Markensgate, which is the city's main shopping thoroughfare with restaurants and nightspots. Also close to the ocean and the beachside "promenade". Some of the rooms feature ocean views and the hotel also has its own garden area where children can safely play. Welcome to an enjoyable stay at "The Little Hotel"!

Sjøgløtt er et lite familiedrevet hotell med 12 rom, der vertskapet forsøker å skape et sted der du kan føle deg hjemme og velkommen. Hotellet finner du i et rolig område i sentrum av Kristiansand, i nærheten av gjestehavnen og den gamle festningen. Kort avstand (3 min. gange) til Markensgate som er byens handlegate med restauranter og utesteder. Det er også kort vei til sjøen og "strandpromenaden".
Noen av rommene har utsikt mot sjøen, og hotellet har også egen hage hvor barna kan leke trygt. Velkommen til et hyggelig opphold på "Det lille hotell"!

Ein kleines, familienbetriebenes Hotel mit 12 Zimmern. Die Gastgeber möchten ihren Gästen einen Aufenthaltsort bieten, an dem man sich richtig heimisch fühlen kann. Das Hotel liegt in einem ruhigen Viertel im Zentrum von Kristiansand; in der Nähe Gästehafen und historische Festung. Nur 3 Minuten Fußweg zur Fußgängerzone (Markensgate) mit Restaurants und Lokalen. Ebenfalls in unmittelbarer Nähe liegt das Meer und die "Strandpromenade".
Einige Zimmer bieten Aussicht aufs Meer. Ein hoteleigener Garten, in dem Kinder sicher spielen können, ist vorhanden. Willkommen zu einem gemütlichen Aufenthalt im "Kleinen Hotel"!

Hos tante Gerd

Your host:
Gerd Reibrå

Address:
**Sørlibakken 16
N - 4621 Kristiansand S**
Phone: **38 01 13 73**

Best time to call:
07.00 - 10.00

Twin room:	**360,-**	Tosengsrom:	**360,-**	Zweibettzimmer:	**360,-**
Single room:	**180,-**	Enkeltrom:	**180,-**	Einzelzimmer:	**180,-**
Room for 3 persons:	**540,-**	Rom til tre personer:	**540,-**	Zimmer für 3 Pers.:	**540,-**
No. of rooms: :	3	Antall rom: 3		Anzahl Zimmer: 3	
Laid breakfast table		Dekket frokostbord		Serv.: Frühstückstisch	
Open 1 May - 31 Sept.		Åpent 20. mai - 15. sept.		Geöffnet 1. Mai - 31. Sept.	
Terrace/deck access/yard/garden		Terrasse/uteplass/hage		Terrasse/Aussenplatz/Garten	
Discount for children (7 yrs.)		Rabatt for barn (7 år)		Ermäßigung für Kinder (b. 7	
No smoking indoors		Ingen røking innendørs		Jahre). Kein Rauchen im Haus	
Access to telephone		Tilgang på telefon		Zugang Telefon	
English spoken				Sprechen Deutsch	

Hos tante Gerd (Aunt Gerd's Place) offers B&B in a house with ocean view and nearby marina and bathing areas. Single rooms with private entrances from the terrace or deck. Common bathroom. Cozy garden patio area. Regular bus service to the animal park. Many popular attractions near the city. Hos Tante Gerd is about three km from Kristiansand city center.

Directions:
Follow E-18 towards Mandal and exit onto FV 456 towards Vågsbygd after the tunnel. Continue until you reach the shop "Arthur Jernvare" and make your first left onto Skyllingsheia. The first right turn will be onto Sørlibakken.

Bolig med sjøutsikt, nær små-båthavn og badeplass. Enkle rom med egen inngang fra terrasse el. veranda. Felles bad. Deilig hage og terrasse. Direktebuss til dyre-parken (Kaptein Sabeltann!). Mange aktuelle steder i byens omegn. Hos Tante Gerd ligger vel tre km fra Kristiansand sentrum.

Veibeskrivelse:
Følg E-18 retning Stavanger/Mandal, ta av til FV 456 retning Vågsbygd etter tunellen. Fortsett gjennom rundkjøring ved Texaco, til Arthur Jernvare og ta første vei til venstre (Skyllingsheia). Første vei til høyre er Sørlibakken.

Wohnhaus mit Meerblick, in der Nähe eines Kleinboothafens und einer Badestelle. Einfache Zimmer mit eigenem Eingang von der Terrasse bzw. Veranda. Gemeinsames Bad. Sehr schöner Garten bzw. Terrasse. Direkte Busverbindung zum Tierpark. "Hos Tante Gerd" liegt ca. 3 km vom Stadtzentrum in Kristiansand entfernt.

Wegbeschreibung:
Folgen Sie der E 18 in Richtung Mandal. Biegen Sie hinter dem Tunnel auf die Straße 456 in Richtung Vågsbygd ab. Fahren zum Laden "Arthur Jernvare" und die erste Straße links hinauf. Dann Erste Straße rechts.

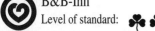

B&B-Inn
Level of standard: ♣ ♣ ♣

NBT-member
NBT-inspected

page **112**
Vest-Agder

Vatne Gård

Your host:
Lars & Lise Sandnes

Address:
Østre Vatne
N - 4560 Vanse
Phone/Fax: **38 39 32 90**
Mobil: **90 54 40 95**
E-mail: **vatneg@online.no**

Best time to call:
08.00 - 22.00

Double-/Twin room:	**650,-**	Dobbelt-/tosengsrom:	**650,-**	Doppel-/Zweibettzi.:	**650,-**
Single room:	**440,-**	Enkeltrom:	**440,-**	Einzelzimmer:	**440,-**
No. of rooms: 2		Antall rom: 2		Anzahl Zimmer: 2	
Full breakfast		Full frokost		Volles Frühstück	
Laid breakfast table or -tray		Dekket frokostbord el. -brett		Serv.: Frühstückstisch o. -tablett	
Open year round		Åpent hele året		Ganzjährig geöffnet	
TV in all rooms		TV på alle rom		TV in allen Zimmern	
Terrace/deck access/yard		Terrasse/uteplass/hage		Terrasse/Aussenplatz/Garten	
Boat for rent		Båtutleie		Boot zu mieten	
Outdoor jacuzzi for rent		Utendørs massasjebad til leie		Massagebad im Freien zu mieten	
VISA, MC accepted		Vi tar VISA, MC		Wir nehmen VISA, MC	
Discount for children		Rabatt for barn		Ermässigung für Kinder	
Selfcatering possible		Selvhushold er mulig		Selbsthaush. möglich	
Garage for motorbikes		Garasje for motorsykler		Garage für Motorräder	
English spoken				Sprechen Deutsch	

Vatne Gård is located at unique Lista, a popular and exciting stop along Nordsjøveien (North Sea Highway). Here you will enjoy 10 km of sandy beaches, fishing and marked walking trails: idyllic Southern Norway at its best. Guests stay in comfortable, well-equipped and attractive rooms or apartments. Outdoor Jacuzzi with 36C (102F) degree water year round. Many of the past guests come back year after year and your hosts hope that you will be among them! Pets are unfortunately not allowed.

Vatne Gård ligger på særpregede Lista, et populært og spennende stoppested langs Nordsjøveien. Her er 10 km med sandstrender, fiskemuligheter og oppmerkede turstier, sørlandsidyll på sitt beste. Gjestene bor i komfortable, vel-utstyrte og lekre rom eller leilig-heter. Utendørs massasjebad med 36 grader hele året.
Mange av gjestene kommer til-bake år etter år, og vertskapet håper at også du blir en av dem! Egne dyr kan dessverre ikke tas med.

Schöne Lage auf der Insel Lista, einem beliebten Reiseziel entlang der Nordseestraße. 10 km lange Sandstrände, Angelmöglichkeiten und markierte Wanderwege - eine Sørlandidylle wie aus dem Bilder-buch! Komfortable, gut aus-gestattete und geschmackvoll ein-gerichtete Zimmer oder Ferien-wohnungen. Das ganze Jahr über verwöhnt ein 36 Grad warmer Whirlpool die Urlauber. Viele der Gäste kommen Jahr für Jahr wieder. Sie vielleicht auch bald? Haustiere dürfen leider nicht mit-gebracht werden.

Skipperhuset
Seng & Mat

Your host:
Leif & Grethe Waage Larsen

Address:
N - 4432 Hidrasund
Phone/Fax: 38 37 22 72

Best time to call:
07.00 - 22.00

Double-/Twin room:	**1.400,-**	Dobbelt-/tosengsrom:	**1.400,-**	Doppel-/Zweibettzi.:	**1.400,-**
Single room:	**800,-**	Enkeltrom:	**800,-**	Einzelzimmer:	**800,-**
Full board		Full pensjon		Vollpension	
No. of rooms: 7		Antall rom: 7		Anzahl Zimmer: 7	
Fully-licensed		Alle rettigheter		Alle Schankrechte	
Open year round		Åpent hele året		Ganzjährig geöffnet	
Terrace/yard/quay		Terrasse/hage/brygge		Terrasse/Garten/Bootsteg	
Boat for rent		Båtutleie		Boot zu mieten	
Sauna		Badstu		Sauna	
No smoking in rooms		Ingen røking på rom		Kein Rauchen im Zimmer	
English, some French				Sprechen etwas Deutsch	
& Spanish spoken					

Skipperhuset ("The Skipper's House"), has housed four generations of sea captains. Grethe and Leif, your hosts, have left the shipping for the welfare of their guests. They combine top service with culinary pleasures, often including seafood.

The dwelling is a typical white-painted south coast house with adjacent boathouse on dock. Boat available. Dock fishing. Seafarers are welcome to spend the night, have a hot bath and a gourmet meal.

Skipperhuset is an ideal and somewhat different "hiding place".

I Skipperhuset har det bodd skipsførere i fire generasjoner.

Vertskapet, Grethe og Leif, har forlatt skipsfarten til fordel for sine gjester som får topp service med høydepunktene i måltidenes kulinariske opplevelser, ofte med havets ingredienser.

Huset er et typisk hvitmalt sørlandshus med brygge og sjøbu. Båt stilles til disposisjon. Fiske er mulig fra bryggekanten. Seilere og lystbåtfolk er velkommen innom for en natt i land, et bad og et godt måltid.

Skipperhuset er et ideelt og litt annerledes "gjemmested".

Skipperhuset wird seit Generationen von Kapitänen bewohnt. Die jetzigen Besitzer, Grethe und Leif, bieten Spitzenservice mit kulinarischen Erlebnissen, oft mit Zutaten aus dem Meer.

Das Gebäude ist ein typisches Sörlandshaus mit eigenem Kai und Bootshaus. Boot zur Verfügung. Angeln von der Kaikante. Bootsleute und Segler sind auch für 1 Nacht, eine gute Mahlzeit und ein Bad, willkommen.

Skipperhuset ist der ideale, etwas andere "Schlupfwinkel"!

B&B-Homestay
Level of standard: ♣ ♣

NBT-member
Inspected by NBT

page **114**
Rogaland

Huset ved havet

Your host:
Jytte & Oddvar Varhaug

Address:
Ægrå
N - 4360 Varhaug
Phone: 51 43 03 83
Fax: 51 43 11 86

Best time to call:
15.00 - 22.00

Double-/Twin room:	**400,-**	Dobbelt-/tosengsrom:	**400,-**	Doppel-/Zweibettzimmer:	**400,-**
1 pers. in double room:	**350,-**	1 pers. i dobbeltrom:	**350,-**	1 Pers. in Doppelzimmer:	**350,-**
Single room:	**250,-**	Enkeltrom:	**250,-**	Einzelzimmer:	**250,-**

No. of rooms: 7	Antall rom: 7	Anzahl Zimmer: 7
Open year round	Åpent hele året	Ganzjährig geöffnet
TV available	TV tilgjengelig	Zugang zu TV
Terrace/deck access/yard/garden	Terrasse/uteplass/hage	Terrasse/Aussenplatz/Garten
Bike for rent	Sykkelutleie	Fahrrad zu mieten
No smoking indoors	Ingen røking innendørs	Kein Rauchen im Haus
Pets welcome by agreement	Kjæledyr tillatt etter avtale	Haustiere nach Absprache
English spoken		Sprechen etwas Deutsch

Your hosts at 'Huset ved havet' (House by the Sea) have been receiving guests for 5-6 years and no longer keep animals on the Ægrå farm. Situated about 500 m from the sea and 3 km from Varhaug. 'Huset ved havet' is near Nordsjøvegen scenery route, and is conveniently located for trips to Kongeparken, Lysefjord, Ryfylke and Dalane. Havana Badeland (Swimming Complex) in Sandnes, the monument at Hafrsfjord and the Petroleum Museum in Stavanger are other nearby attractions.

Vertskapet har drevet med turisme i 5-6 år, og har ikke lengre dyr på gården Ægrå. Beliggenhet ca 500 m fra havet og 3 km fra Varhaug. Huset ved havet ligger ved Nordsjøvegen, og har praktisk nærhet til Kongeparken, Lysefjord, Ryfylke og Dalane. Havana Badeland i Sandnes, monumentet ved Hafrsfjord og Oljemuseet i Stavanger er andre severdigheter i nærheten.

Seit die Gastgeber Übernachtungsgäste aufnehmen (5-6 Jahre), gibt es auf dem Hof Aegrå keine Tiere mehr. Reizvolle Lage, ca. 500 m vom Meer und 3 km von der Siedlung Varhaug entfernt. "Huset ved havet" (das Haus am Meer) liegt direkt an der Nordseestraße. Außerdem in der Nähe: Königspark, Lysefjord, Ryfylke und Dalane. Weitere Sehenswürdigkeiten: "Havana Badeland" (Sandnes), Monument am Hafrsfjord, Ölmuseum Stavanger.

English

A: "Loftet"
Apartment for 2-6 persons
In new building, high standard
No. of bedrooms: 2
Own bath, kitchen, LR, DR
Price for whole unit: **800,-**

B: "Gurihuset"
Guesthouse for 2-8 persons
Preservation-worthy Jæren-style h.
No. of bedrooms: 3
Bath, kitchen, LR, DR
Price for whole unit: **700,-**

C: "Eldhuset"
Guesthouse for 2 persons
Antall soverom: 1
Bath, kitchen/LR
Price for whole unit: **450,-**

Applies to all rental units:
Bed linen fee: **50,-**
Breakfast service available: **50,-**
Open year round
TV available
Yard/terrace/deck access
Bike for rent
No smoking indoors
Pets welcome by agreement
English spoken

Norsk

A: "Loftet"
Leilighet for 2-6 personar
Ny bygning med høg standard
Antall soverom: 2
Bad, kjøkken, stue, spisestue
Pris for hele enheten: **800,-**

B: "Gurihuset"
Gjestehus for 2-8 personar
Verneverdig jærhus
Antall soverom: 3
Bad, kjøkken, stue, spisestue
Pris for hele enheten: **700,-**

C: "Eldhuset"
Gjestehus for 2 personar
Antall soverom: 1
Eget bad, kjøkken/stue
Pris for hele enheten: **450,-**

For alle enhetene gjelder:
Tillegg for sengetøy: **50,-**
Frokost kan serveres: **50,-**
Åpent hele året
TV tilgjengelig
Hage/terrasse/uteplass
Sykkelutleie
Ingen røking innendørs
Kjæledyr tillatt etter avtale

Deutsch

A: "Loftet"
Wohnung für 2-6 Personen
Neues Gebäude, hohem Standard
Anzahl Schlafräume: 2
Eig. Bad, Küche, Stube, Sp.Zi.
Ganze Einheit: **800,-**

B: "Gurihuset"
Gästehaus für 2-8 Personen
Denkmalgeschütztes Jærenhaus
Anzahl Schlafräume: 3
Eig. Bad, Küche, Stube, Sp.Zi.
Ganze Einheit: **700,-**

C: "Eldhuset" (Backhaus)
Gästehaus für 2 Personen
Anzahl Schlafräume: 1
Bad, Küche/Stube
Ganze Einheit: **450,-**

Für alle Einheiten gilt:
Mieten von Bettwäsche: **50,-**
Frühstück auf Bestellung: **50,-**
Ganzjährig geöffnet
Zugang zu TV
Garten/Terrasse/Aussenplatz
Fahrrad zu mieten
Kein Rauchen im Haus
Haustiere nach Absprache
Sprechen etwas Deutsch

Directions:
From E-39: Exit FV 504 at Bøe
and follow the road to RV 44.
Follow RV 44 about 400 meters
towards Stavanger then turn left.
Drive 400 meters to "Huset ved
havet". Alternative route: Take the
train to Varhaug.

Veibeskrivelse:
Fra E-39: Ta av FV 504 ved Bøe,
følg vegen til RV 44. Følg RV 44
400 m retning Stavanger, ta til
venstre. Kjør 400 m til Huset ved
havet. Alternativ: Ta tog til
Varhaug.

Wegbeschreibung:
Str. 39: Biegen Sie bei Bøe auf
Str. 504 ab und folgen Sie ihr bis
Str. 44. Diese führt nach Stavan-
ger. Nach ca. 400 m biegen Sie
links ab, nach weiteren 400 m
erreichen Sie das Haus am Meer.
Alternative: Mit der Bahn bis
Varhaug.

Make it a rule of life never to regret and never to look back.
Regret is an appalling waste of energy; you can't build on it;
it's only good for wallowing in.
-Katherine Mansfield

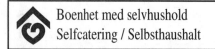
Magne Handeland

Your host:
Magne Handeland

Address:
Handeland
N - 4462 Hovsherad
Phone: 51 40 21 24
E-mail: magnh@online.no

Best time to call:
08.00 - 22.00

Guesthouse for 2-6 persons	Gjestehus for 2-6 personer	Gästehaus für 2-6 Personen
No. of bedrooms: 2	Antall soverom: 2	Anzahl Schlafräume: 2
Own bath, kitchen, LR	Eget bad, kjøkken, stue	Eig. Bad, Küche, Stube
Price per pers.: **200,-**	Pris pr. pers.: **200,-**	Preis pro Pers.: **200,-**
Bed linen included	Sengetøy er inkludert	Inkl. Bettwäsche
Open year round	Åpent hele året	Ganzjährig geöffnet
TV available	TV tilgjengelig	Zugang zu TV
Terrace/garden	Terrasse/uteplass/Hage	Terrasse/Aussenplatz/Garten
Rowboat and canoe available	Robåt- og kanoutlån	Ruderboot und Kanu zu leihen
English spoken		Sprechen Englisch

Magne Handeland's guest house was built in 1978 and is well equipped with freezer, washing machine, telephone, and a full kitchen. It has a private outdoor terrace, grill and garden furniture. Handeland is a short ways from E-39, just north of the village of Moi.
Fresh-water swimming and fishing opportunities nearby. The farm has cows, hens and cats and guests may arrange to assist in tending. Magne also has a wood workshop where beautiful bowls and candlesticks are designed and handcrafted.

Gjestehuset hos Magne Handeland ble bygget i 1978 og er godt utstyrt med både fryseboks, vaskemaskin, telefon, fullt utstyrt kjøkken og en terrasse med grill og utemøbler som er til gjestenes disposisjon.
Handeland ligger på en liten avstikker fra E-39, like nord for Moi.
Badeplasser i ferskvann og muligheter for fiske.
På gården er det både kyr og høns og gårdskatter. Etter nærmere avtale kan gjestene få være med på å stelle husdyrene.
Magne har også et tredreiingsverksted og lager vakre staker og boller.

Das Gästehaus wurde 1978 gebaut und ist gut ausgerüstet mit Kühlschrank, Tiefkühler, Waschmaschine, Telefon und komplett eingerichteter Küche. Ungestörte Terrasse mit Grill und Sitzmöbeln. Handeland liegt einen kleinen Abstecher von E-39, nördlich von Moi. Badeplätze am See und Möglichkeit zum Angeln. Der Hof hat Grossvieh, Hühner und Katzen. Die Gäste können nach Absprache bei der Tierpflege teilnehmen.
Magne hat eine Drechsler-Werkstatt, wo die schönsten Schüsseln und Kerzenhalter entstehen.

The Thompsons' Bed & Breakfast

Your host:
Sissel & Roger Thompson

Address:
Muségtaten 79
N - 4010 Stavanger
Phone: 51 52 13 29
Mobil: 91 55 65 24

Best time to call:
08.00 - 23.00

Double room:	**450.-**	Dobbeltrom:	**450,-**	Doppelzimmer:	**450,-**
Single room:	**250,-**	Enkeltrom:	**250,-**	Einzelzimmer:	**250,-**
No. of rooms: 4		Antall rom: 4		Anzahl Zimmer: 4	
Full breakfast		Full frokost		Volles Frühstück	
Laid breakfast table		Dekket frokostbord		Serv.: Frühstückstisch	
Open year round		Åpent hele året		Ganzjährig geöffnet	
TV in all rooms		TV i alle rom		TV in allen Zimmern	
Terrace/yard/garden		Terrasse/hage		Terrasse/Garten	
No smoking in rooms.		Ingen røking på rom		Kein Rauchen im Zimmer	
English spoken				Sprechen Deutsch	

English/Norwegian couple invites you to a lovely old villa from 1910 about 10 min. walk from city center. Large rooms, high ceiling. 5 min. walk to lovely walking areas. Close to museums, shops, harbor etc. Sissel & Roger maintain a very hospitable family home. Both are classic car enthusiasts. TV, hairdryer, tea/ coffee in rooms. Breakfast in family dining room. Cyclists welcome.

Directions:
From Stavanger city center to Muségate: Straight up the hill, with Rogaland theater and the Stavanger Museum on your left-hand side. Look for the beige house with green trim, about 800 m from city center.

Engelsk/norsk ektepar ønsker deg velkommen til en nydelig gammel villa fra 1910, ca ti min. spasertur fra sentrum. Store rom med stor takhøyde. Fem minutter fra vakkert turterreng. Nær museer, butikker, havnen etc. Sissel og Roger er begge veteranbilentusiaster, og driver et meget gjestefritt hjem. TV, hårtørker og kaffe/te på rommene. Frokost i familiens spisestue. Syklister ønskes velkommen.

Veibeskrivelser:
Fra Stavanger sentrum til Muségaten: Opp bakken, med Rogaland Teater og Stavanger Museum på venstre side. Se etter beige hus med grønne lister, ca 800 m fra sentrum.

Die englisch-norweg. Gastgeber heissen ihre Gäste in einer gemütlichen alten Villa willkommen, die nur ca. 10 Minuten vom Stadtzentrum liegt. Große Zimmer mit hohen Decken. 5 Minuten bis zu einem schönen Wandergebiet. In der Nähe Museen, Geschäfte, Hafen usw. Sissel und Roger sind "Oldtimerfans" und sehr gastfreundlich. TV, Fön und Kaffee/Tee auf allen Zimmern. Frühstück im Esszimmer der Familie. Radfahrer sind ebenfalls willkommen.

Stavanger Zentrum bis Muségate: den Hang hinauf (Rogaland Theater und Stavanger Museum linkerhand). Achten Sie auf ein beigefarbenes Haus mit grünen Fensterrahmen, ca. 800 m vom Zentrum entfernt.

B&B-Homestay
Level of standard: ♣ ♣

NBT-member
Inspected by NBT

page **118**
Rogaland

Stavanger B&B

Your host:
Michael A. Peck

Address:
Vikedalsgaten 1
N - 4093 Stavanger
Phone: 51 56 25 00
Fax: 51 56 25 01
Mobil: 90 63 12 58
E-mail: peck@online.no
Web: www.stavangerbedand
breakfast.no
Best time to call:
08.00 - 23.00

Double room:	**590,-**	Dobbeltrom:	**590,-**	Doppelzimmer:	**590,-**
Single room:	**450,-**	Enkeltrom:	**450,-**	Einzelzimmer:	**450,-**
No. of rooms: 14		Antall rom: 14		Anzahl Zimmer: 14	
Full breakfast		Full frokost		Volles Frühstück	
Open year round		Åpent hele året		Ganzjährig geöffnet	
TV in all rooms		TV i alle rom		TV in allen Zimmern	
VISA, MC accepted		Vi tar VISA, MC		Wir nehmen VISA, MC	
Access to telephone/fax/Internet		Tilgang til tlf./fax/Internett		Tlf., Fax und Internet vorhanden	
Pets welcome		Kjæledyr tillatt		Haustiere willkommen	
English spoken				Sprechen Deutsch	

Stavanger B&B is located about 5 min. walk from the train station, bus, ferry and express boat. 14 newly renovated rooms including: refrigerator, shower, wash basin, TV, laundry service and ample parking. Guests gather each evening at 21.00 (9 pm) to enjoy Norwegian-style waffles served with sour cream, jam and coffee.

Directions:
Exit E-39 towards the town center and drive straight through three roundabouts. Inside the Bergjeland tunnel, turn left in the roundabout and drive straight ahead to the next roundabout. Turn left in this roundabout and drive 600 meter to Vikedalsgaten 1.

Ca. 5 min. gange fra jernbane, buss, ferge og hurtigbåt ligger Stavanger B&B. 14 nyoppussede rom med kjøleskap, dusj, håndvask, TV, vaskeriservice og god parkering. Hver kveld kl. 21.00 samles alle til vafler med rømme og syltetøy og kokekaffe.

Veibeskrivelser:
Fra E-39 mot sentrum kjør rett frem gjennom tre rundkjøringer. Inn i Bergjelandstunellen, ta til venstre i rundkjøring, kjør rett frem til neste rundkjøring. Ta til venstre i denne og kjør 600 meter til Vikedalsgaten 1.

Stavanger B&B liegt nur ca. 5 Min. von Bahn, Bus, Fähre und Schnellboot. Den Gast erwarten 14 renovierte Zimmer mit Kühlschrank, Dusche, Waschbecken, TV und Wäscheservice. Gute Parkmöglichkeiten. Allabendlich treffen sich die Gäste gegen 21.00 Uhr zu Waffeln mit "rømme" (Sauerrahm) und Marmelade, dazu wird frisch gebrühter Kaffee serviert.

Wegbeschreibung:
Fahren Sie auf der E-39 immer geradeaus in Richtung Zentrum (3x Kreisverkehr). Sie gelangen zum Tunnel "Bergjelandstunnelen", biegen im Kreisverkehr links ab und erreichen den nächsten Kreisverkehr. Dort zweigen Sie wieder links ab und fahren 600 m bis Vikedalsgaten 1.

Tone's Bed & Breakfast

Your host:
Tone Bourrec

Address:
Peder Claussønsgate 22
N - 4008 Stavanger
Phone: 51 52 42 07
Mobil: 92 65 65 96
E-mail: ton-bour@online.no
Web: www.home.master
        sites.com/tone/
Best time to call:
09.00 - 20.00

Double-/Twin room:	**420,-**	Dobbelt-/tosengsrom:	**420,-**	Doppel-/Zweibettzi.:	**420,-**
Single room:	**250,-**	Enkeltrom:	**250,-**	Einzelzimmer:	**250,-**
1 pers. in double room:	**350,-**	1 pers. i dobbeltrom:	**350,-**	1 Pers. im Doppelzi.:	**350,-**

No. of rooms: 3	Antall rom: 3	Anzahl Zimmer: 3
Full breakfast	Full frokost	Volles Frühstück
Open 1 May - 1 October	Åpent 1. mai - 1. oktober	Geöffnet 1. Mai - 1. Oktober
Patio/garden	Uteplass/hage	Aussenplatz/Garten
No smoking inside	Ingen røking innendørs	Kein Rauchen im Haus
VISA accepted	Vi tar VISA	Wir nehmen VISA
English, French & some Italian spoken		Sprechen etwas Deutsch

Swiss house from 1894 with a small garden, in the middle of the city. Quiet surroundings.	Sveitserhus fra 1894 med liten hage. Midt i byen. Rolige omgivelser.	Haus im Schweizer Stil aus 1894 mit kleinem Garten. Mitten in der Stadt, doch ruhige Umgebung.
Directions: Ask for Løkkeveien. Peder Claussønsgate crosses Løkkeveien.	Veibeskrivelse: Spør etter Løkkeveien. Peder Claussønsgate er en tverrgate til Løkkeveien.	Wegbeschreibung: Fragen Sie nach der Straße "Løkkeveien". Die "Peder Claussønsgate" kreuzt den Løkkeveien.

The world is full of hopeful analogies and handsome, dubious eggs, called possibilities. -George Eliot

Something which we think is impossible now will not be impossible in another decade. -Constance Baker Motley

Den Gamle Stallen

Your host:
Else & Arne Sørlie

Address:
Villa Blidensol
Øvre Strandgate 112
N - 4005 Stavanger
Phone: 51 52 53 46
Web: www.ostvoll.net/stallen

Best time to call:
08.00 - 23.00

Guesthouse for 2-6 persons	Gjestehus for 2-6 personer	Gästehaus für 2-6 Personen
No. of bedrooms: 1 + 2 loft rooms	Antall soverom: 1 + 2 loftsrom	Anzahl Schlafräume: 1 + 2 Schlaf-
Own bath, kitchen, LR	Eget bad, kjøkken, stue	böden, Eig. Bad, Küche, Stube
Price for whole unit,	Pris for hele enheten,	Preis für der Ganze Einheit,
up to 4 persons: **1.000,-**	opptil 4 personer: **1.000,-**	bis 4 Personen: **1.000,-**
Per person for extra beds: **200,-**	Ekstraoppredning pr. pers.: **200,-**	Extrabett pro Pers: **200,-**
Bed linen included	Sengetøy er inkludert	Inkl. Bettwäsche
Open year round	Åpent hele året	Ganzjährig geöffnet
TV available	TV tilgjengelig	Zugang zu TV
VISA, MC accepted	Vi tar VISA, MC	Wir nehmen VISA, MC
Breakfast service available: **30,-**	Frokost kan serveres: **30,-**	Frühstück auf Bestellung: **30,-**
English and some Italian spoken		Sprechen etwas Deutsch

You will find Den Gamle Stallen (The Old Stable) in the historical part of Old Stavanger. It is an old stable that has been carefully renovated into a pleasant rental home with traces of modern comforts. In addition to the bedroom, there are 2 guest beds in the living room. The house is 50 m². Small, white-washed wooden cottages are tightly situated here just as they were in all southern Norwegian coastal towns in days of old. The Stable is about 300 years old and may well be the town's oldest structure. Downtown lies just on the other side of Vågen, about 3 min. walk.

I den vernede bydelen Gamle Stavanger finner du Den Gamle Stallen. Dette er en gammel stall som er gjort om til et hyggelig utleiehus etter pietetsfull restaurering med innslag av moderne komfort. I tillegg til soverommet er det 2 gjestesenger i stuen. Huset er på 50 m².
Her ligger små hvitmalte trehus tett i tett som det gjorde i alle våre sørnorske kystbyer i gamle dager. Stallen er ca. 300 år gammel og er muligens det eldste huset i byen. Sentrum ligger like på andre siden av Vågen, ca. 3 min. spasertur.

In der unter Denkmalschutz stehenden Altstadt "Gamle Stavanger" befindet sich "Den Gamle Stallen", ein historischer Stall, der nach einer stilvollen Restaurierung komfortabel zur Vermietung umgebaut wurde. Das Gebäude ist ca. 50 qm groß. Zusätzlich zum Schlafraum stehen im Wohnraum zwei Gästebetten zur Verfügung. In der Umgebung gibt es zahlreiche weißgestrichene Holzhäuser, die - wie damals an der Küste Südnorwegens üblich - dicht aneinandergebaut wurden. Der Stall ist ca. 300 Jahre alt und gilt als ältestes Gebäude der Stadt. Das Stadtzentrum liegt gleich auf der anderen Seite des Hafenbeckens Vågen (ca. 3 Minuten Fußweg).

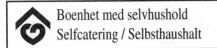
Byhaugen

Your host:
Judith Kristin & Harald Asche

Address:
Bruveien 6
N - 4024 Stavanger
Phone: 51 53 57 85
E-mail: harald.asche@c2i.net
Web: www.byhaugen.no

Best time to call:
08.00 - 22.00

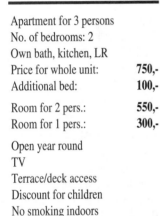

Apartment for 3 persons		Leilighet for 3 personer		Wohnung für 3 Personen	
No. of bedrooms: 2		Antall soverom: 2		Anzahl Schlafräume: 2	
Own bath, kitchen, LR		Eget bad, kjøkken, stue		Eig. Bad, Küche, Stube	
Price for whole unit:	**750,-**	Pris for hele enheten:	**750,-**	Ganze Einheit:	**750,-**
Additional bed:	**100,-**	Ekstraseng:	**100,-**	Zusätzlich Bett:	**100,-**
Room for 2 pers.:	**550,-**	Rom for 2 pers.:	**550,-**	Zimmer für 2 Pers.:	**550,-**
Room for 1 pers.:	**300,-**	Rom for 1 pers.:	**300,-**	Zimmer für 1 Pers.:	**300,-**

Open year round	Åpent hele året	Ganzjährig geöffnet
TV	TV	TV
Terrace/deck access	Terrasse/uteplass	Terrasse/Aussenplatz
Discount for children	Rabatt for barn	Ermäßigung für Kinder
No smoking indoors	Ingen røking innendørs	Kein Rauchen im Haus
Pets welcome	Kjæledyr tillatt	Haustiere willkommen
English, some French and Italian		Sprechen etwas Deutsch

Near both downtown and nature. Your host is glad to assist with reservations for tours, transportation, etc. Member of Cyclists Welcome and B&B Circle Stavanger. The unit was built in 2000 and is of high standard. Car parking in yard and bicycle parking i garage.

Nær både sentrum og naturen. Eieren er behjelpelig med å bestille turer, transport etc. Medlem av Cyclists Welcome og B&B Circle Stavanger. Enheten ble ferdig i 2000 og holder høy standard. Bilparkering i gården og sykkelparkering i garasje.

Gute Lage in Zentrums- und Naturnähe. Der Besitzer hilft gern beim Transport oder beim Buchen von Touren usw. Die Wohnung bietet einen hohen Standard. Parken im Hof. Garage für Fahrräder vorhanden.

Good thoughts are no better than good dreams,
unless they are executed.
-Ralph Waldo Emerson

B&B-Homestay
Level of standard: ♣ ♣

NBT-member
NBT-inspected

page **122**
Rogaland

Kleivå Gardscamping

Your host:
Svanhild & Sigmund Alvestad

Address:
N - 5561 Bokn
Phone: 52 74 84 24
Fax: 52 74 82 82
Mobil: 99 51 39 72
E-mail: kleivaa@online.no
Web: www.kleivaa.no

Best time to call:
08.00 - 23.00

Double room:	**550,-**	Dobbeltrom:	**550,-**	Doppelzimmer:	**550,-**
1 pers. in double room:	**400,-**	1 pers. i dobbeltrom:	**400,-**	1 Pers. im Doppelzi.:	**400,-**
No. of rooms: 2		Antal rom: 2		Anzahl Zimmer: 2	
Full breakfast		Full frukost		Volles Frühstück	
Breakfast tray		Servering: Frukostbrett		Serv.: Frühstückstablett	
Open year round		Ope heile året		Ganzjährig geöffnet	
TV available		TV tilgjengeleg		Zugang zu TV	
Terrace		Terrasse/uteplass		Terrasse/Aussenplatz	
Boat for rent		Båtutleige		Boot zu mieten	
Bike for rent		Sykkelutleige		Fahrrad zu mieten	
No smoking inside		Inga røyking innomhus		Kein Rauchen im Haus	
Phone/fax/Internet available		Tilgang til tlf./fax/Internett		Tel., Fax und Internet vorhanden	
Guests with pets are welcome		Kjæledyr tillatt		Haustiere erlaubt	
Discount for children		Rabatt for born		Ermässigung für Kinder	
Selfcatering possible		Sjølvhushald er mogeleg		Selbsthaushalt möglich	
English spoken				Sprechen etwas Deutsch	

Kleivå farm is approx. 3.5 km from E-39, on the island of Vestre Bokn.
Plentiful opportunity for hiking, fishing, biking, canoeing, looking after animals etc. The nearby Haugaland area offers over 30 activities, and it is not far to Skudeneshavn, one of Norway's most unique old town areas.
The farm has cows, pigs, cats, lambs and rabbits.

Kleivå gard finn du 3,5 km frå E-39, på øya Vestre Bokn.
Gode høve til fotturer, kano-padling, fiske, sykkelturer, stell av dyr og anna. Haugalandet rundt kan by på over 30 aktivitetar, og det er kort veg til Skudeneshavn, eit av Noregs mest særprega gamle byområder.
På garden er det kyr, griser, katter, lam og kaniner.

Der Hof Kleivå liegt 3,5 km von der Strasse E-39 auf der Insel Vestre Bokn. Gute Möglichkeiten für Wandern, Kanupaddeln, Angeln, Radfahren, Tierbetreuung u.a. In Haugalandet kann man mehr als 30 verschiedenen Aktivitäten nachgehen. Unweit entfernt liegt Skudeneshavn mit seiner historischen Altstadt, architektonisch eine der interessantesten Städte des Landes. Auf dem Hof gibt es Kühe, Schweine, Katzen, Lämmer und Kaninchen.

Anne Grete's Husrom

Your host:
Anne Grete Hausvik

Address:
Soldalveien 3
N - 5546 Røyksund
Phone: 52 83 65 93
Mobil: 94 60 52 33
E-mail: viggo@iname.com

Best time to call:
08.00 - 20.00

Apartment for 2-4 persons	Leilighet for 2-4 personer	Wohnung für 2-4 Personen
Own bath, sleeping alcove and LR w/kitchen	Eget bad, sovealkove og stue m/kjøkken	Eig. Bad, Schlafalkoven und Stube mit Küche
Price for whole unit: **300,-**	Pris for hele enheten: **300,-**	Ganze Einheit: **300,-**
Bed linen fee: **25,-**	Tillegg for sengetøy: **25,-**	Mieten von Bettwäsche: **25,-**
Open May - October	Åpent mai - oktober	Geöffnet Mai - Oktober
TV available	TV tilgjengelig	Zugang zu TV
Yard/terrace/deck access	Hage/terrasse/uteplass	Garten/Terrasse/Aussenplatz
No smoking inside	Ingen røking innendørs	Kein Rauchen im Haus
Discount for children	Rabatt for barn	Ermässigung für Kinder
Some English & Spanish spoken		Sprechen etwas Deutsch

Anne Grete is an experienced hostess, and you find her on the mainland, 12 km south of Hauge-sund. The house has a lovely view of the fjord and neighboring wilderness. Good hiking opportunities, abundant seasonal berry and mushroom picking, swimming and fishing. motorized rowboat for rent.

From Anne Grete's you can venture on day trips to visit the quaint villages of Skudenes and Koper-vik with their historical wooden buildings, visit Avaldsnes Church, or take the boat from Haugesund to Utsira, an ocean island, Norway's most western point.

Anne Grete har tatt imot turister i mange år. Du finner stedet på fast-landet 12 km sør for Haugesund. Huset har fin utsikt over fjord og friområde.

I området er det fint turterreng, bra med skogsbær og sopp. Fine steder for bading og fisking i fjorden.

Fra Anne Gretes husrom kan man legge ut på dagsturer for å besøke de idylliske småstedene Skudenes og Kopervik med gammel trehus-bebyggelse, beskue Avaldsnes kirke eller ta båten fra Haugesund til Utsira, et lite samfunn på ei øy ute i havgapet som er Norges vestligste bosetning.

Anne Grete nimmt seit vièlen Jahren Gäste auf.

Gausvik liegt 12 km südlich von Haugesund. Das Haus hat eine schöne Aussicht über Fjord und Umgebung. Reizvolles Wanderge-lände, reich an Waldbeeren und Pilzen. Schöne Stellen zum Baden und Angeln im Fjord.

Ausflüge nach Skudenes oder Koppervik, kleine idyllische Orte mit Holzhäusern. Zu empfehlen sind der Besuch der Avaldsnes-Kirche und Fahrt mit Schiff von Haugesund nach Utsira, der west-lichsten Siedlung von Norwegen auf einer Insel in der Nordsee.

Fossane

Your host:
Kari & Sven Egil Sørensen

Address:
Fossane, Vormedalen
N - 4130 Hjelmeland
Phone: 51 75 15 32
E-mail: fossane@online.no
Web: www.fossane.no

Best time to call:
08.00 - 23.00

Double room:	**600,-**	Dobbeltrom:	**600,-**	Doppelzimmer:	**600,-**
Single room:	**300,-**	Enkeltrom:	**300,-**	Einzelzimmer:	**300,-**
Children:	**200,-**	Born:	**200,-**	Kinder:	**200,-**
No. of rooms: 3		Antal rom: 3		Anzahl Zimmer: 3	
Laid breakfast table		Dekka frukostbord		Serv.: Frühstückstisch	
Open year round		Ope heile året		Ganzjährig geöffnet	
Terrace/deck access/yard/garden		Terrasse/uteplass/hage		Terrasse/Aussenplatz/Garten	
No smoking inside		Inga røyking innomhus		Kein Rauchen im Haus	
English spoken				Sprechen Deutsch	

Rental rooms are available in the main farm dwelling where your hosts live. The farm also features 3 restored houses available for rente on a self-catering basis. The farm is a place that is full of culture and history. There are numerous cascades with old-style and modern hydroelectric stations and a restored grinding mill. The river includes an exciting swimming spot and you can fish in your host's own part of the waterway. Tour the lake in our rowboat or canoe. Fossane is situated in a beautiful wilderness area, near both fjord and mountain. 1.5 hour drive to the starting point for walking tours to Preikestolen.

Rom til leigei gardhuset, der vertskapet bur sjølv. Tre restaurerte hus på garden er også til leige med sjølvhushald.
Garden er fylt med kultur og historie. Her er det fossefall med gamalt og nytt elektrisitetsverk, og eit restaurert kvernhus. I elva er det ein spennande badeplass og tilbod om stangfiske i eigars del av vassdraget. Robåt og kano kan nyttast til turar på vatnet.
Fossane ligg i eit flott naturområde, nært både fjord og fjell. Det er 1,5 time med bil til utgangspunktet for tur til Preikestolen.

Zimmer im Hauptgebäude des Hofes zur Verfügung. Dort wohnen auch die Gastgeber. Darüber hinaus können auf dem Hof 3 renovierte Ferienhäuser gemietet werden. Ein Aufenthalt auf dem Hof ist kulturell und geschichtlich sehr reizvoll. Sehenswürdigkeiten: ein Wasserfall, ein altes und ein neues E-Werk sowie historische, restaurierte Mühlen. Schöne Badestelle. Der dem Besitzer gehörige Flussabschnitt lädt zum Rutenangeln ein, außerdem stehen Ruderboot und Kanu zur Verfügung. Fossane ist in eine sehr reizvolle Landschaft eingebettet, in der Nähe von Fjorden und Gebirge. Der Ausgangspunkt zur Wanderung auf den Preikestolen ist mit dem Auto nur ca. 1,5 Stunden entfernt.

A: "Johnsenhuset"
Guesthouse for 2-8 persons:
No. of bedrooms: 3
Own bath, kitchen, LR
Price for whole unit: **500,-/600,-**
Price per pers. over 6 pers.:   **50,-**

B: "Folgå"
Guesthouse for 2-6 persons:
No. of bedrooms: 3
Own bath, kitchen, LR
Price for whole unit: **500,-/600,-**

C: "Bjødlandsfolgå"
Guesthouse for 2-4 persons:
No. of bedrooms: 2
Own bath, kitchen, LR
Price for whole unit: **500,-/600,-**

Applies to all rental units:
Open year round
Garden/yard/terrace/deck access
Boat for rent
Pets welcome
Cleaning not included,
option for cleaning: **500,-**
Bed linen fee: **50,-**
English spoken

A: "Johnsenhuset"
Gjestehus for 2-8 personar:
Antall soverom: 3
Bad, kjøkken, stova
Pris for heile eininga: **500,-/600,-**
Pris pr. person over 6 pers.:   **50,-**

B: "Folgå"
Gjestehus for 2-6 personar:
Antall soverom: 3
Bad, kjøkken, stova
Pris for heile eininga: **500,-/600,-**

C: "Bjødlandsfolgå"
Gjestehus for 2-4 personar:
Antall soverom: 2
Bad, kjøkken, stova
Pris for heile eininga: **500,-/600,-**

Gjeld alle einingar:
Ope heile året
Hage/terrasse/uteplass
Båtutleige
Kjæledyr tillatt
Reingjering er ikkje inkludert,
kan gjerast av vertskapet: **500,-**
Tillegg for sengetyg: **50,-**

A: "Johnsenhuset"
Gästehaus für 2-8 Personen
Anzahl Schlafräume: 3
Eig. Bad, Küche, Stube
Ganze Einheit: **500,-/600,-**
Preis pro Pers. über 6 Pers.:   **50,-**

B: "Folgå"
Gästehaus für 2-6 Personen
Anzahl Schlafräume: 3
Eig. Bad, Küche, Stube
Ganze Einheit: **500,-/600,-**

C: "Bjødlandsfolgå"
Gästehaus für 2-4 Personen
Anzahl Schlafräume: 2
Eig. Bad, Küche, Stube
Ganze Einheit: **500,-/600,-**

Für alle Einheiten gilt:
Ganzjährig geöffnet
Garten/Terrasse/Aussenplatz
Boot zu mieten
Haustiere willkommen
Reinigung nicht im Preis,
Angebot: Reinigung: **500,-**
Mieten von Bettwäsche: **50,-**
Sprechen Deutsch

Directions:
From Stavanger: Take the ferry to
Tau, then follow RV 13 to Hjelmeland. Turn toward Vormedalen,
you see the sign just before the
ferry quay at Hjemeland. To
Vormedalen the distance is ca. 20
km drive and turn right over the
bridge towards Fundingsland for 1
km or turn right on the 3rd road
after the bridge.

Vegforklaring:
Frå Stavanger. Ta ferge til Tau,
følg RV 13 til Hjelmeland.
Du finn skilt til Vormedalen rett
før fergekaia i Hjelmeland. Kjør
mot Vormedalen, ca. 20 km, veg
over bru til høgre (Fundingsland)
1 km mot Fundingsland eller 3.
veg til høgre etter bru.

Wegbeschreibung:
Ab Stavanger: Nehmen Sie die
Fähre nach Tau, und folgen Sie
der Straße 13 nach Hjelmeland.
Direkt vor dem Fähranleger ist der
Weg nach Vormedalen
ausgeschildert (Hjelmeland –
Vormedalen: ca. 20 km). Dort
geht es über eine Brücke und
anschließend nach rechts
(Fundingsland). Nach ca. 1 km
biegen Sie in die 3. Straße rechts
ab (3. Straße hinter der Brücke).

All knowledge should be translated into action.
–Albert Einstein

Hotel Nøkling
Hjelmeland Camping

Your host:
Per Anker Bergh Nøkling
& Åse Tone Nøkling

Address:
Hjelmeland
Postboks 4
N - 4148 Hjelmeland
Phone: 51 75 02 30
Fax: 51 75 02 30

Best time to call:
08.00 - 23.00

Double room:	**590,-/650,-**	Dobbeltrom:	**590,-/650,-**	Doppelzimmer:
Single room:	**400,-/470,-**	Enkeltrom:	**400,-/470,-**	Einzelzimmer:

Double room: **590,-/650,-**
Single room: **400,-/470,-**
No. of rooms: 24
Full breakfast.
Laid breakfast table or buffet
Other meals served on request
Open year round
TV available
Terrace/deck access/yard/garden
Boat for rent
Bike for rent
Discount for children
Self-catering possible (+ 8 cabins)
Access to telephone/fax
English and French spoken

Dobbeltrom: **590,-/650,-**
Enkeltrom: **400,-/470,-**
Antall rom: 24
Full frokost
Dekket frokostbord el. -buffet
Andre måltider serveres
Åpent hele året
TV tilgjengelig
Terrasse/uteplass/hage
Båtutleie
Sykkelutleie
Rabatt for barn
Selvhushold er mulig (+ 8 hytter)
Tilgang på telefon/faks

Doppelzimmer: **590,-/650,-**
Einzelzimmer: **400,-/470,-**
Anzahl Zimmer 24
Volles Frühstück.
Frühstückstisch oder -büfett
Andere Mahlzeiten nach Vereinb.
Ganzjährig geöffnet
Zugang zu TV
Terrasse/Aussenplatz/Garten
Boot zu mieten
Fahrrad zu mieten
Ermässigung für Kinder
Selbsthaushalt mögl. (+ 8 Hütten)
Zugang Telefon/Fax
Sprechen Deutsch

Centrally, yet beautifully situated near the fjord in Hjelmeland. Excellent fishing spots and hiking trails. Row boats, swimming area. Local attractions: Breathtaking Prekestolen, Skomakenibba. Meals served to overnight guests.

Stedet ligger vakkert til ved fjorden sentralt i Hjelmeland. Gode fiskemuligheter og turterreng. Robåter, badestrand. Attraksjoner i nærområdet: Prekestolen, Skomakenibba, servering for overnattingsgjester.

Landschaftlich reizvolle Lage am Fjord, zentral in Hjelmeland. Gute Angelmöglichkeiten. Wandergebiet, Ruderboote, Badestrand. Sehenswürdigkeiten in der Umgebung: Der Berg Prekestolen und Skomakenibba. Bewirtung für Übernachtungsgäste.

Directions:
About 300 m from ferry quay in Hjelmeland along RV 13. Signposts lead to hotel. Travel time from Stavanger via Tau: about 85 min.

Veibeskrivelse:
Ca. 300 m fra fergekaien i Hjelmeland ved riksveg 13. Skiltanvisning til hotellet. Reisetid fra Stavanger via Tau: ca. 85 min.

Wegbeschreibung:
Ca. 300 m vom Fähranleger in Hjelmeland entfernt (Str. 13). Der Beschilderung bis zum Hotel folgen. Fahrzeit ab Stavanger über Tau (Fähre!): ca. 85 Minuten.

Øysteinbu

Your host:
Margoth P. Aas &
Øystein O. Årthun
Address:
Hellandsbygd
N - 4200 Sauda
Phone: 52 78 06 34
Best time to call:
08.00 - 23.00

Guesthouse for 2-8 persons	Gjestehus for 2-8 personer	Gästehaus für 2-8 Personen
No. of bedrooms: 4	Antall soverom: 4	Anzahl Schlafräume: 4
Own bath, kitchen, LR	Eget bad, kjøkken, stue	Eig. Bad, Küche, Stube
Price for whole unit: **600,-**	Pris for hele enheten: **600,-**	Ganze Einheit: **600,-**
Bed linen fee: **50,-**	Tillegg for sengetøy: **50,-**	Mieten von Bettwäsche: **50,-**
Open year round	Åpent hele året	Ganzjährig geöffnet
TV available	TV tilgjengelig	Zugang zu TV
Terrace/deck access	Terrasse/uteplass	Terrasse/Aussenplatz
Boat for rent	Båtutleie	Boot zu mieten
Bike for rent	Sykkelutleie	Fahrrad zu mieten
No smoking inside	Ingen røking innendørs	Kein Rauchen im Haus
English and some French spoken		Sprechen Deutsch

Øysteinbu was built around 1860. Parts of the house could be older. The house has since been converted and extended several times. Hellandsbygd is located 260 m above the sea, 16 km from Sauda in the direction of Røldal. In the summer there are fishing and hiking opportunities, and superb conditions for winter sports. Sauda is an old industrial community; of interest is Sauda Smelteverk, industrial museum and guided tour of an abandoned zinc mine.

Øysteinbu ble bygget omkring 1860. Deler av huset kan være eldre. Der er også siden blitt ombygget og påbygget flere ganger. Hellandsbygd ligger 260 m.o.h., 16 km fra Sauda i retning Røldal. Fiske- og turmuligheter om sommeren og gode forhold for vintersport på vinterstid. Sauda er et gammelt industrisamfunn hvor man kan besøke Sauda Smelteverk, Industriarbeidermuseumet og få omvisning i nedlagte sinkgruver.

Øysteinbu wurde 1860 gebaut, doch können Teile des Hauses älter sein. Es wurde mehrmals um- und angebaut. Hellandbygd liegt 260 m.ü.d.M., 16 km von Sauda in Richtung Røldal. Im Sommer Angel- und Wandermöglichkeiten, doch auch günstig für Wintersport. Sehenswürdigkeiten im alten Industrieort Sauda: E-Werk und Zink-Gruben, Industriearbeitermuseum und Sauda Schmelzwerk. Führungen.

Eide Gard

Your host:
Johanne Marie Heggebø

Address:
Eide
N - 5580 Ølen

Phone: 53 76 82 23
Fax: 53 76 83 01
Mobil: 90 19 53 10

Best time to call:
15.00 - 21.00

Double-/Twin room:	**600,-**	Dobbelt-/tosengsrom:	**600,-**	Doppel-/Zweibettzimmer:	**600,-**
1 pers. in double room:	**500,-**	1 pers. i dobbeltrom:	**500,-**	1 Pers. in Doppelzimmer:	**500,-**
Single room:	**500,-**	Enkeltrom:	**500,-**	Einzelzimmer:	**500,-**
No. of rooms: 3		Antal rom: 3		Anzahl Zimmer: 3	
Laid breakfast table		Dekka frukostbord		Serv.: Frühstückstisch	
Open year round		Ope heile året		Ganzjährig geöffnet	
TV available		TV tilgjengeleg		Zugang zu TV	
Terrace/deck access/yard/garden		Terrasse/uteplass/hage		Terrasse/Aussenplatz/Garten	
Boat for rent.		Båtutleige		Boot zu mieten	
No smoking inside		Inga røyking innomhus		Kein Rauchen im Haus	
English spoken				Sprechen etwas Deutsch	

Eide Gard is the place for anyone who is seeking the uncomplicated, original atmosphere of Western Norway. Farm facilities dating from around 1800 are restored in the traditional Norwegian style. Here you will find an old cookhouse with a hearth and an old woodshed that has been converted for use as an old-style gathering hall. Fjord view from the rooms, walking distance to Ølen town center, marked walking trails.

Eide Gard er staden for deg som søkjer den enkle og tradisjonelle stemninga frå Vestlandet. Gardstunet, som stammer frå rundt år 1800 er satt i stand i tradisjonell norsk stil. På garden finn du óg eit eldhus med grue, og eit vedskjul som er omgjort til gildeskål (trad. selskapslokale). Fjordutsikt frå romma, gangavstand til Ølen sentrum, merka turløyper.

Der Hof Eide Gard ist genau der richtige Ort für alle Gäste, die die einfache und ursprüngliche Atmosphäre Westnorwegens mögen. Der Hof stammt ca. von 1800, die Gebäude sind im traditionellen norwegischen Stil erbaut und eingerichtet. Unter anderem gibt es ein altes Backhaus mit Feuerstelle sowie einen Holzschuppen, der zu einem sogenannten "Gildeskål" umgebaut wurde, einem trad. Gesellschaftsraum. Fjordblick aus den Zimmern, Fußweg nach Zentrum, markierte Wanderwege.

Fate chooses your relations, you choose your friends.
–Jacques Delille (1738 – 1813)

Koløen's Gårdsferie

Your host:
Amarjit & Helge Koløen

Address:
Helland
N - 5419 Fitjar
Phone: 53 49 91 96
Mobil: 91 38 61 56

Best time to call:
16.00 - 23.00

Guesthouse for 2-6 persons	Gjestehus for 2-6 personar	Gästehaus für 2-6 Personen
No. of bedrooms: 3	Antal soverom: 3	Anzahl Schlafräume: 3
Own bath, kitchen, LR	Eige bad, kjøken, stove	Eig. Bad, Küche, Stube
Price for whole unit: **700,-**	Pris for heile eininga: **700,-**	Ganze Einheit: **700,-**
Bed linen fee: **60,-**	Tillegg for sengetyg: **60,-**	Mieten von Bettw.: **60,-**
Open year round	Ope heile året	Ganzjährig geöffnet
TV	TV	TV
Yard/garden/terrace	Terrasse/uteplass/hage	Garten/Terrasse/Aussenplatz
Boat for rent	Båtutleige	Boot zu mieten
No smoking inside	Inga røyking innomhus	Kein Rauchen im Haus
Breakfast service available: **60,-**	Frukost kan serverast: **60,-**	Frühstück auf Bestellung: **60,-**
English & Punjabi spoken		Sprechen etwas Deutsch

Fitjar is an island community consisting of as many islands as one finds days in a year. The tiny village, Fitjar, is located in the northwest of Stord. The Koløens' Farm has existed since 1626 and is located 6 km south of Fitjar. Sea and fresh water fishing. Sailing in renovated sailing vessel, visit local museum or hike in the mountains.
You'll find cows, hens and other animals on the farm along with a dairy, vegetable farming, berries and homemade jams.
Helge is farmer and carpenter. Amarjit works in a bank.

Fitjar er ein øykommune som har like mange øyar som det er dagar i året. Tettstaden Fitjar ligg på nordvestre del av Stord. Koløens gard har vore i drift sidan 1626 og ligg 6 km sør for Fitjar. Her kan ein fiske i sjø og i vatn, sigla i restaurert seglskute, vitja museum eller ta seg fram langs turløyper i fjellet.
På garden er det kyr, høns, og andre dyr. Det vert produsert mjølk, grønsaker, egg, bær og heimelaga syltetøy. Debio økologisk urtehage. Sal av urter.
Helge er bonde og snikkar, Amarjit er bankfunksjonær.

Fitjar ist eine Inselgemeinde mit so vielen Inseln wie Tage im Jahr. Der Ort Fitjar liegt im Nordw. der Insel Stord. Der Hof Koløen, 6 km südlich von Fitjar, wird seit 1626 betrieben. Hier können Sie fischen, segeln, ein Museum besuchen oder in den Bergen wandern. Auf dem Hof gibt es Kühe, Hühner u. andere Tiere, Milchwirtschaft, Eier, Gemüseanbau, Beeren und selbstgem. Marmelade. Ökologischer Kräutergarten, Verkauf von Kräutern.
Helge ist Bauer und Tischler, Amarjit arbeitet in der Bank.

Guddalstunet

Your host:
Kirsten & Johannes Guddal

Address:
N - 5470 Rosendal
Phone: **53 48 11 27**
Fax: **53 48 47 42**
Mobil: **95 16 91 66**
E-mail: **guddalst@online.no**

Best time to call:
08.00 - 23.00

Double room:	**600,-**	Dobbeltrom:	**600,-**	Doppelzimmer:	**600,-**
1 pers. in double room:	**550,-**	1 pers. i dobbeltrom:	**550,-**	1 Pers. im Doppelzimmer:	**550,-**
No. of rooms: 2		Antall rom: 2		Anzahl Zimmer: 2	
Full breakfast		Full frokost		Volles Frühstück	
Laid breakfast table		Dekket frokostbord		Serv.: Frühstückstisch	
Open year round		Åpent hele året		Ganzjährig geöffnet	
TV available		TV tilgjengelig		Zugang zu TV	
Yard/garden		Hage		Garten	
No smoking inside		Ingen røking innendørs		Kein Rauchen im Haus	
Awarded the qualitymark 'Olavsrosa'		Er tildelt kvalitetsmerket Olavsrosa		Erhielt den Preis 'Olavsrosa'	
English spoken				Sprechen Deutsch	

In old and new houses and huts you will be welcomed to a generation farm with traditions. The farm has been awarded the "Olavsrosa" by the national cultural foundation for the historic environmental quality which the place represents, through careful restoration.
Rosendal is known for its renaissance/baroque chateau from the 17th century barony, which is now a museum.

I gamle og nye hus og hytter ønskes du velkommen til en generasjonsgård med tradisjoner. Guddalstunet er tildelt Olavsrosa fra den nasjonale kulturminnestiftelsen for den historiske miljøkvaliteten som anlegget representerer, gjennom pietetsfullt restaureringsarbeide.
Rosendal er kjent for sitt renessanse/barokkslott Baroniet, fra 1600-tallet, som nå er museum.

Auf dem traditionsreichen Erbhof werden Gäste in alten und neuen Häusern und Hütten willkommen geheissen.
Der Hof wurde vom nationalen Kulturdenkmalsfond für pietätsvolle Restaurierung und geschichtliche. Milieuqualität ausgezeichnet. Das Renaissance/Barock Schloss Rosendal aus 1600 ist jetzt Museum.

The greatest mistake you can make in life is to be
continually fearing you will make a mistake.
-Elbert Hubbard

Cabins for 2-5 persons	Hytter for 2-5 pers.	Hütten für 2-5 Pers.
Own bath, kitchen, LR	Eget bad, kjøkken, stue	Eig. Bad, Küche, Stube
Price per cabin: **700,-**	Pris pr. hytte: **700,-**	Preis pro Hütte: **700,-**
Bed linen fee: **50,-**	Tillegg for sengetøy: **50,-**	Mieten von Bettw.: **50,-**
Open year round	Åpent hele året	Ganzjährig geöffnet
TV	TV	TV
Terrace/dekk access/yard/garden	Terrasse/uteplass/hage	Terrasse/Aussenplatz/Garten
Boat for rent	Båtutleie	Boot zu mieten
No smoking inside	Ingen røking innendørs	Kein Rauchen im Haus
No smoking in rooms	Ingen røking på rom	Kein Rauchen im Zimmer
Breakfast service available: **85,-**	Frokost kan serveres: **85,-**	Frühstück auf Bestellung: **85,-**
English spoken		Sprechen Deutsch

Directions:	Veibeskrivelse:	Wegbeschreibung:
3 km south of Rosendal along RV 13, you come to Seimsfoss. Exit the main highway near the Fokus store and follow the sign towards Guddal. Stay to the left when the road forks after 1 km. Drive to the left over the bridge where there is a sign marked Guddal. One more kilometer and you have arrived at Guddalstunet. Drive into the courtyard with the homemade sign for "Guddalstunet".	Langs RV 13, 3 km sør for Rosendal kommer du til Seimsfoss. Ta av i veikryss ved Fokusforretningen hvor skilt viser til Guddal. Etter 1 km deler veien seg i to. Ta til venstre, over brua, med skilt til Guddal. Så 1 km til, og du er framme i Guddalstunet. Kjør opp i tunet med privat skilt "Guddalstunet".	Auf der Straße 13 gelangen Sie ca. 3 km südlich von Rosendal nach Seimsfoss. Biegen Sie am Geschäft „Fokus" an der Kreuzung ab und folgen Sie der Beschilderung nach Guddal. Nach ca. 1 km teilt sich die Straße. Folgen Sie der linken Straße über die Brücke (Beschilderung Guddal). Nach weiteren 1 km erreichen Sie Guddalstunet. Fahren Sie hinauf und folgen Sie dem Privatschild „Guddalstunet".

Rom i Rambergstunet

Your host:
Signy Eikeland

Address:
Rambergstunet
N - 5244 Fana
Phone: 55 91 52 40
Fax: 55 91 71 32
Mobil: 93 03 87 78

Best time to call:
08.00 - 18.00

Twin room:	**450,-**	Tosengsrom:	**450,-**	Zweibettzimmer:	**450,-**
No. of rooms: 4		Antal rom: 4		Anzahl Zimmer: 4	
Full breakfast		Full frukost		Volles Frühstück	
Laid breakfast table		Dekka frukostbord		Serv.: Frühstückstisch	
Open year round		Ope heile året		Ganzjährig geöffnet	
No smoking inside		Inga røyking innomhus		Kein Rauchen im Haus	
Summer only:		Bare om sommaren:		Sommer:	
Familyroom in old log cabin house for 4-6 persons, self-catering possible.		Familierom finns i gamal tømmerstove for 4-6 pers. med høve til sjølvhushald.		Familienzimmer in altem Blockhaus für 4-6 Pers., Selbsthaushalt möglich.	
English spoken				Sprechen etwas Deutsch	

At Rambergstunet, the Eikelands have for 40 years arranged traditional wedding feasts for tourists which consist of Hardanger-fiddle music, folk dancing and such traditional food as bridal porridge, flatbread and dried meats. Now rooms are available to travellers. There are quaint log cabins, a loft and a large, newly built banquet hall. You'll find Rambergstunet 20 km south of the center of Bergen and well worth the visit.

På Rambergstunet har dei arrangert tradisjonsrike bryllaupsgjestebod for turistar og tilreisande i 40 år, med hardingfeletonar, folkedans, bruragraut, flatbrød og spekemat. No er også rom tilleige for vegfarande.
Tunet har gamle, lafta stover, bur og loft, og ei nyare storstove til større arrangement. Inne er det nok av gamle ting.
Tunet ligg 20 km sør for Bergen sentrum, og er sjåverdig i seg sjølv.

Auf dem Hof Ramberg veranstaltet man seit 40 Jahren für Gäste traditionelle Bräuche zu Hochzeiten mit Musik, Volkstanz u. traditioneller Kost. Nun vermietet man auch Unterkünfte. Der Hof hat gut erhaltene, alte Blockhäuser u. Speicher, die mit vielen alten Gegenständen eingerichtet sind.
Der Hof liegt 20 km südl. vom Zentrum Bergen und ist absolut sehenswert.

A rose only becomes beautiful and blesses others when it opens up and blooms. Its greatest tragedy is to stay in a tight-closed bud, never fulfilling its potential. -Author Unknown

Lerkebo

Your host:
Solveig & Jan-Georg Klausen

Address:
Sætervegen 40
N - 5236 Rådal
Phone: 55 13 38 50
Fax: 55 13 62 44 / 55 13 62 55
Mobil: 40 40 21 56 / 40 40 21 53
E-mail:
solveig.klausen@netcom.no
Web: www.lerkebo.no
Best time to call: 08.00 - 24.00

Double room:	**650,-**	Dobbeltrom:	**650,-**	Doppelzimmer:	**650,-**
Room for 2 pers.:	**700,-**	Rom for 3 pers.:	**700,-**	Zimmer für 2 Pers.:	**700,-**
Single room:	**350,-**	Enkeltrom:	**350,-**	Einzelzimmer:	**350,-**
Extra bed:	**175,-**	Ekstraseng:	**175,-**	Extrabett:	**175,-**

No. of rooms: 6	Antall rom: 6	Anzahl Zimmer: 6
Full breakfast	Full frokost	Volles Frühstück
Breakfast buffet	Servering: Frokostbuffét	Serv.: Frühstücksbüfett
Open year round	Åpent hele året	Ganzjährig geöffnet
TV available	TV tilgjengelig	Zugang zu TV
Yard/terrace/deck access	Hage/terrasse/uteplass	Garten/Terrasse/Aussenplatz
Bike for rent	Sykkelutleie	Fahrrad zu mieten
Trampoline and outdoor grill	Trampoline og utegrill	Trampolin und Außengrill
Internet accsess available	Tilgang til Internett	Internetzugang vorhanden
No smoking inside	Ingen røking innendørs	Kein Rauchen im Haus
English & French spoken		Sprechen Deutsch

Lerkebo - where chirping birds may be heard during light summer nights - is a modern and spacious detached home that is located in a quiet, suburban area on a private cul-de-sac 12 km from downtown Bergen. Your hosts love to meet people and take pride in making conditions optimal for their guests. Here you are welcome to just relax after a hectic day of running between Bergen's many attractions.

Lerkebo - kanskje med litt fugle-kvitter gjennom lyse sommernet-ter - er en moderne og romslig enebolig som ligger i et stille for-stadsområde i en privat blindvei 12 km fra Bergen sentrum. Vertskapet liker å møte menne-sker, og setter sin stolthet i å gjøre det best mulig for gjestene. Her er du velkommen til å slappe av etter en hektisk dag løpende mellom Bergens mange attraksjoner.

Lerkebo bietet neben Vogelge-zwitscher in hellen Sommer-nächten ein modernes und ge-räumiges Einfamilienhaus in einer privaten Sackgasse eines ruhigen Vororts. 12 km bis Bergen. Die Gastgeber sind sehr aufgeschlos-sen und tun alles zum Besten für die Gäste. Nach dem Besuch vieler Sehenswürdigkeiten in Bergen kann man sich hier bestens erholen.

Utsikten

Your host:
Vigdis & Arvid Bergesen

Address:
**Osvegen 121
N - 5227 Nesttun**
Phone: **55 91 29 92**
Fax: **55 10 55 50**
Mobil: **90 13 71 64**
E-mail: **berlex@online.no**

Best time to call:
08.00 - 23.00

Double room in rental apartment	Dobbeltrom i utleieleilighet	Doppelzimmer in Wohnung
Price per room: **270,-/300,-**	Pris pr. rom: **270,-/300,-**	Preis pro Zi.: **270,-/300,-**
Shared bath and kitchen	Delt bad og kjøkken	Gemeins. Bad u. Küche
Bed linen fee: **25,-**	Tillegg for sengetøy: **25,-**	Mieten von Bettwäsche: **25,-**
Open year round	Åpent hele året	Ganzjährig geöffnet
TV available	TV tilgjengelig	Zugang zu TV
Yard/terrace	Hage/terrasse/uteplass	Garten/Terrasse/Aussenplatz
Guests with pets are welcome	Kjæledyr tillatt	Haustiere erlaubt
No smoking inside	Ingen røking innendørs	Kein Rauchen im Haus
English and some French spoken		Sprechen etwas Deutsch

Situated in peaceful surroundings between Bergen and Os, just south of Nesttun along E-39, the Bergesen family welcomes guests. The detached house is surrounded by plenty of grounds and has a wonderful view.
The family has enjoyed receiving guests for over ten years.
Welcome!

I fredelige omgivelser midt mellom Bergen og Os, litt sør for Nesttun, langs E-39, tar familien Bergesen imot innlosjerende. Eneboligen ligger fritt og fint med en storslagen utsikt.
Familien har trivdes med å ta imot gjester i over ti år. Kona i huset er lærer, mannen er kjemi-ingeniør.
Velkommen!

In ruhiger Umgebung, mitten zwischen Bergen und Os, an der E-39 empfängt Familie Bergersen seit über 10 Jahren Übernachtungsgäste.
Das Haus hat eine schöne, freie Lage und herrliche Aussicht. Der Mann ist Chemie-Ingenieur und die Frau Lehrerin.
Willkommen!

Directions:
From Bergen: Take E-39 southward towards Stavanger/Hallhjem. Take a right after 12 km (2.5 km past Nesttun) at the sign marked "ROM" (about 30 m before coming to the cross-walk and bus shelter). Walk 150 m up the hill and you are there!

Veibeskrivelse:
Fra Bergen: Ta E-39 sørover mot Stavanger/Hallhjem. Etter 12 km (2,5 km forbi Nesttun) ta av til høyre ved Rom-skilt (ca. 30 m før fotgjengerovergang og busslomme). Etter 150 m oppover bakken er du framme.

Wegbeschreibung:
Von Bergen auf der E-39 südlich in Richtung Stavanger/Hallhjem. Nach 12 km (2,5 km hinter Nesttun) beim Schild "Rom" rechts ab (ca. 30 m vor dem Fußgängerüberweg und der Bushaltebucht). Dann noch 150 m bergan.

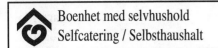
Astrid's økohage

Your host:
Astrid Strømme

Address:
Indre Sædal 16
N - 5098 Bergen
Phone: **55 28 52 69**

Best time to call:
08.00 - 11.00 / 18.00 - 23.00

Small apartment for 2-4 persons	Hybelleilighet for 2-4 personer	Kl. Wohnung für 2-4 Personen
Shared bath, kitchen, LR	Delt bad, kjøkken, stue	Gemeins. Bad, Küche, Stube
Price per pers.: **120,-**	Pris pr. pers.: **120,-**	Preis pro Pers.: **120,-**
Bed linen fee: **25,-**	Tillegg for sengetøy: **25,-**	Mieten von Bettwäsche: **25,-**
Breakfast service: **50,-**	Frokost kan serveres: **50,-**	Frühstück auf Bestellung: **50,-**
Open year-round	Åpent hele året	Ganzjährig geöffnet
Yard/deck access/terrace/garden	Terrasse/uteplass/hage	Garten/Aussenplatz
Pets welcome	Kjæledyr tillatt	Haustiere willkommen
No smoking inside	Ingen røyking innendørs	Kein Rauchen im Haus
Suitable for handicapped	Handikapvennlig	Behindertengerecht
English spoken		Sprechen etwas Deutsch

Astrid's Økohage (Organic Garden) is located 15 min. from downtown Bergen in partially rural surroundings and close to excellent terrain for mountain walks and hikes.
Your hostess is in the process of making her home and garden more ecological. She also hopes to soon be able to offer bicycle rentals. Ample parking.

Directions:
RV 585 to Birkelundstoppen. Turn off towards Sædalen. E-39: Exit towards Paradis. Drive towards Fantoft Stave Church, continue until Sædalen. Bus: Route 22 to the last bus stop.

Astrids Økohage finner du 15 min. fra Bergen sentrum, i delvis landlige omgivelser like ved flott fjellturterreng. Verten vil utvikle hus og hage i økologsk retning. Hun arbeider også for å få stand sykkelutleie. Gode parkeringsforhold.

Veibeskrivelse:
RV 585 til Birkelundstoppen. Ta av til Sædalen. E-39: Ta av til Paradis. Kjør retning Fantoft stavkirke, fortsett til Sædalen. Fra flyplassen: Følg skilting til Bergen, kjør som over nevnt etter å ha tatt til høyre etter Troldhaugtunnellen. Buss: Rute 22 til endeholdeplassen.

Astrids Økohage liegt ca. 15 Minuten von Bergen entfernt, in teilweise ländlicher Umgebung, unweit eines reizvollen Wandergebietes.
Die Gastgeberin versucht, Haus und Garten nach ökologischen Gesichtspunkten zu gestalten. Darüber hinaus ist sie bestrebt, eine Fahrradvermietung aufzubauen. Gute Parkmöglichkeiten.

Wegbeschreibung:
Fahren Sie die Str. 585 bis "Birkelundstoppen" und zweigen Sie dort in Richtung Sædalen ab. Bus: Linie 22 bis zur Endstation.

Skiven Gjestehus

Your host:
E. Kvale & Alf M. Heskja

Address:
Skivebakken 17
N - 5018 Bergen
Phone: 55 3130 30 Fax: 55 3130 90
Mobil: 90 05 30 30
E-mail: mail@skiven.no
Web: www.skiven.com

Best time to call:
08.00 - 23.00

Double room:	**350,-**	Dobbeltrom:	**350,-**	Doppelzimmer:	**350,-**
1 pers. in double room:	**250,-**	1 pers. i dobbeltrom:	**250,-**	1 Pers. im Doppelzi.:	**250,-**
Extra bed:	**100,-**	Ekstraseng:	**100,-**	Extrabett:	**100,-**
No. of rooms: 4		Antall rom: 4		Anzahl Zimmer: 4	
Shared bath, WC and kitchen		Delt bad, WC og kjøkken		Gemeins. Bad u. Küche	
Open year round		Åpent hele året		Ganzjährig geöffnet	
No smoking inside		Ingen røyking innendørs		Kein Rauchen im Haus	
VISA accepted		Vi tar VISA		Wir nehmen VISA	
English and some Italian spoken				Sprechen etwas Deutsch	

Skivebakken, where Skiven Gjestehus is located, is said to be one of the most painted streets in Bergen by artists who captured on canvas the charm of this lane and the view across its rooftops. Skivebakken is quiet, without through traffic.

The town center, market, quayside and railway station are all within 5-10 minute walk. The host family of 4 lives on the 1st floor and guest rooms on the ground floor. Built in 1896, the house has been restored to its original style.

Skivebakken, hvor Skiven Gjestehus ligger, sies å være Bergens mest malte gate. Her har kunstnere stått med sine staffelier og fanget bygatens idyll og den flotte utsikten over husrekkene. Skivebakken er en rolig gate uten gjennomgangstrafikk.

Bykjernen, torget, bryggen og jernbanestasjonen er innenfor 5-10 min. gange.

Utleierommene er i 1. etasje og vertskapet, en familie på fire, bor i 2. etasje. Huset ble bygd i 1896 og er nylig rehabilitert med respekt for det opprinnelige.

Skivebakken wird als bunteste Strasse von Bergen bezeichnet. Hier standen Maler, um die Idylle der Stadt und den herrlichen Blick über die Häuserreihen einzufangen. Skivebakken ist eine ruhige Strasse ohne Durchgangsverkehr. Der Stadtkern, der Markt, die Brücke und der Bahnhof sind zu Fuss innerhalb von 5-10 Min. zu erreichen. Die Mieträume befinden sich im Erdgeschoss, während die Gastgeber den 1. Stock bewohnen. Das Haus wurde 1896 erbaut und kürzlich pietätsvoll restauriert.

Sir, I look upon every day to be lost, in which I do not make a new acquaintance. –Samuel Johnson, in *'Life of Johnson'*

Kjellersmauet Gjestehus

Your host:
Sonja Krantz

Address:
Kjellersmauet 22
N - 5011 Bergen
Phone: 55 96 26 08
Mobil: 90 52 34 33
E-mail: kj-gj@online.no
Web: www.gjestehuset.com

Best time to call:
09.00 - 19.00

A: Apartment for 2 persons
Private bath, kitchenette
No. of apt.: 2
Price per unit: **600,-/700,-**

B: Apartment for 2-5 persons
Private bath, kitchen, LR
No. of apt.: 4
Price per unit: **700,-/1.100,-**

Bed linen included
Open all year
TV
No smoking indoors
VISA, MC accepted
Discount for children
Extra bed: **100,-**
English spoken

A: Leilighet for 2 personer
Eget bad, og minikjøkken
Antall leiligheter: 2
Pris pr. leilighet: **600,-/700,-**

B: Leilighet for 2-5 personer
Eget bad, kjøkken og stue
Antall leiligheter: 4
Pris pr. leilighet: **700,-/1.100,-**

Sengetøy er inkludert
Åpent hele året
TV
Ingen røking innendørs
Vi tar VISA, MC
Rabatt for barn
Ekstraseng: **100,-**

A: Wohnung für 2 Personen
Eig. Bad, Küchenecke
Anzahl Wohnungen: 2
Preis pro Einheit: **600,-/700,-**

B: Wohnung für 2-5 Personen
Eig. Bad, Küche, Stube
Anzahl Wohnungen: 4
Preis pro Einheit: **700,-/1.100,-**

Inkl. Bettwäsche
Ganzjährig geöffnet
TV
Kein Rauchen im Haus
Wir nehmen VISA, MC
Ermässigung für Kinder
Extrabett: **100,-**
Sprechen etwas Deutsch

Popular area in the midst of downtown Bergen with idyllic, narrow passages and the old, small wooden houses that are so characteristic of Bergen. Kjellersmauet Gjestehus is a newly renovated house with 6 separate rental apartments and its central location means only a two-minute walk to Den Nasjonale Scene: Bergen's theatre. Bryggen (the Wharf) and Akvariet (the Aquarium) are also within walking distance. Welcome to popular and charming apartments in the heart of the city!

Populært område midt i Bergen sentrum, med idylliske trange smau og gamle små trehus som er så typisk for Bergen. Kjellersmauet Gjestehus er et nyopppusset hus med 6 selvstendige utleieleiligheter, og ligger sentralt plassert med bare to minutter til Den Nasjonale Scene; teateret i Bergen. Bryggen og Akvariet er også innen gangavstand. Velkommen til populære og sjarmerende leiligheter i hjertet av byen!

Beliebte Gegend im Zentrum Bergens mit idyllischen engen Gassen und den für die Stadt so typischen kleinen Holzhäusern. Ein frisch renoviertes Haus, das 6 Ferienwohnungen bietet. Zentrale Lage, nur zwei Minuten bis zum bekannten Bergenser Theater "Den Nasjonale Scene". Hanseviertel "Bryggen" und Aquarium sind ebenfalls nicht weit entfernt. Willkommen in unseren schönen Ferienwohnungen im Herzen der Stadt!

Klosteret 5

Your host:
Elisabet Kaltenborn

Address:
Klosteret 5
N- 5005 Bergen
Phone: **55 31 55 50**
Mobil: **95 05 14 30**
E-mail: **ekaltenb@online.no**

Best time to call:
08.00 - 23.00

Apartment for 5 persons	Leilighet for 5 personer	Wohnung für 5 Personen
No. of bedrooms: 2	Soverom: 2	Anzahl Schlafräume: 2
Own bath and LR w/fireplace	Eget bad og peisestue	Eig. Bad und Stube mit Kamin
Price for whole unit: **800,-**	Pris for hele enheten: **800,-**	Ganze Einheit: **800,-**
Price per pers.: **300,-**	Pris pr. pers.: **300,-**	Preis pro Pers.: **300,-**
Bed linen included	Sengetøy inkl.	Inkl. Bettwäsche
Open 1 May - 30 Sep.	Åpent 1. mai - 30. sep.	Geöffnet 1. Mai - 30. Sep.
TV available	TV tilgjengelig	Zugang zu TV
No smoking inside	Ingen røking innendørs	Kein Rauchen im Haus
Pets welcome by agreement	Kjæledyr tillatt etter avtale	Haustiere nach Vereinbarung
Tea and coffe available	Te og kaffe tilgjengelig	Tee und Kaffee erhältlich
For breakfast: Neigborhood Café	For frokost: Caféen over gaten	Frühstück im gegen überl. Café
English spoken		Sprechen Englisch

Klosteret 5 is situated in a cozy, old alley among old wooden houses onNordnes, which is a peninsula that makes up a part of downtown Bergen. Walking distance to all facilities. Parks, aquarium and swimming pool are nearby. An affordable breakfast café is just across the street and a variety of eateries nearby.

Directions:
On routes into Bergen: Follow the signs towards "Akvariet", and continue back around towards downtown. Look for Klosteret 100 m past the avenue which has trees along each side.

Klosteret 5 ligger i et koselig "smau" i gammel bebyggelse på Nordnes, en halvøy som utgjør en del av Bergen sentrum. Gangavstand til alle fasiliteter. Park, akvarium og svømmebasseng like i nærheten. Rimelig frokostkafé over gaten, en rekke restauranter nær.

Veibeskrivelse:
Fra Puddefjordsbroen: Kjør mot sentrum, ta til høyre ved Teateret og til deretter til venstre. Se etter Klosteret 200 m etter Citypark P-hus. Alle andre innkjørsler til Bergen: følg skilt til Akvariet, fortsett tilbake mot sentrum, se etter Klosteret 100 m etter alléen.

Klosteret 5 liegt in Nordnes, inmitten enger, reizvoller Gassen in der Altstadt von Bergen. Nordnes ist eine Halbinsel, die einen Teil des Stadtzentrum ausmacht. Kurze Entfernung zu allen Angeboten wie: Stadtpark, Aquarium und Schwimmbad. Preiswertes Frühstückscafè gegenüber, mehrere Restaurants ganz in der Nähe.

Wegbeschreibung:
Folgen Sie der Beschilderung zum Aquarium, anschließend geht es zurück Richtung Zentrum. Achten Sie 100 m hinter der Allee auf Klosteret 5.

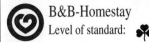
Boge
Bed & Breakfast

Your host:
Tove Margrete
& Per Nordmark

Address:
Boge
N - 5725 Vaksdal
Phone/Fax: 56 59 72 01
Mobil: 99 64 23 17
E-mail: tovemn@online.no

Best time to call:
08.00 - 22.00

Double room:	**400,-**	Dobbeltrom:	**400,-**	Doppelzimmer:	**400,-**
1 pers. in double room:	**250,-**	1 pers. i dobbeltrom:	**250,-**	1 Pers. im Doppelzi.:	**250,-**
No. of rooms: 3		Antall rom: 3		Anzahl Zimmer: 3	
Full breakfast		Full frokost		Volles Frühstück	
Laid breakfast table or -buffet		Dekket frokostbord eller -buffét		Serv.: Frühstückstisch oder -Büfett	
Open 10 June - 30 Aug.		Åpent 10. juni - 30. aug.		Geöffnet 10. Juni - 30. Aug.	

Guesthouse for 2-5 pers. (selfcat.)		Gjestehus for 2-5 pers. (selvhush.)		Gästehaus für 2-5 Pers. (Selbst.h.h)	
Own bath, kitchenette, LR		Eget bad tekjøkken, stue og hems		Eig. Bad, Küchenecke, Stube	
Price for whole unit:	**500,-**	Pris for hele enheten:	**500,-**	Ganze Einheit:	**500,-**
Bed linen fee:	**25,-**	Tillegg for sengetøy:	**25,-**	Mieten von Bettwäsche:	**25,-**

TV available	TV tilgjengelig	Zugang zu TV
Terrace/garden	Terrasse/uteplass/hage	Terrasse/Aussenplatz/Garten
Boat for rent	Båtutleie	Boot zu mieten
No smoking inside	Ingen røking innendørs	Kein Rauchen im Haus
VISA, MC accepted	Vi tar VISA, MC	Wir nehmen VISA, MC
English & French spoken		Sprechen Deutsch

In typically steep-sloped west coast Norway terrain, 40 minutes from Bergen and on E-16, Boge Bed & Breakfast presides over a majestic view of the fjord, 1.5 km from Vaksdal center with grocery, post, bank and gas station.
The guests have free access to the garden and the rowboat on the fjord. A good base for Bergen trips, and hikes in the wild west coast nature. The hosts are a family of five.

I et typisk vestlandsk bratthell, 40 min. fra Bergen, langs E-16, ligger Boge B&B, med flott utsikt over Veafjorden, 1,5 km fra Vaksdal sentrum med butikk, post, bank og bensinstasjon.
Gjestene disponerer uteplasser i hagen og robåt på fjorden.
Godt egnet som base for Bergensbesøk og for turer i vill og vakker vestlandsnatur. Vertskapet er en familie på fem.

40 Min. von Bergen, an der E-16, liegt Boge B&B am Steilhang mit prächtiger Aussicht über den Fjord; 1,5 km von Vaksdal Zentr. mit Geschäft, Post, Bank und Tankstelle.
Als Gast können Sie Garten und Ruderboot auf dem Fjord benutzen. Günstige Lage für Ausflüge nach Bergen und in die wilde, schøne Vestland-Natur. Die Gastgeber sind eine fünfköpfige Familie.

Aadland Gardsferie

Your host:
Solvor Aadland Olsnes

Address:
Samnanger
N - 5658 Årland
Phone: 56 58 78 14
Mobil: 93 42 43 61

E-mail:
solvadl@hotmail.com

Best time to call:
07.00 - 09.00 / 17.00 - 23.00

Twin room:	600,-	Tosengsrom:	600,-	Zweibettzimmer:	600,-
No. of rooms: 2		Antal rom: 2		Anzahl Zimmer: 2	
Full breakfast		Full frukost		Volles Frühstück	
Laid breakfast table		Dekka frukostbord		Serv.: Frühstückstisch	
Open 1 May - 15 Sept.		Ope 1. mai - 15. sept.		Geöffnet 1. Mai - 15. Sept.	
Terrace/dekk access		Terrasse/uteplass		Terrasse/Aussenplatz	
Yard/garden		Hage		Garten	
No smoking inside		Inga røyking innomhus		Kein Rauchen im Haus	
Selfcatering possible		Høve for sjølvhushald		Selbsthaushalt möglich	
English and some French spoken				Sprechen Deutsch	

Aadland Gardsferie is located in a nice rural district near the Samnanger Fjord, 42 km from downtown Bergen. The farm is run by seven family members, all of whom enjoy new people, cultures, languages and outdoor activities. A farm with older-style operations and cozy, old houses. Meals may be taken around the long table in the main kitchen. There are nice walking trails nearby, farm animals and rental boats for cruising the fjord. It is also possible to overnight at an old cotter's farm.

Aadland Gardsferie ligg i ei fin bygd ved Samnangerfjorden, 42 km frå Bergen sentrum. Garden er eit familiebruk med sju medlemmar, som alle er glade i mennesker, kultur, språk og friluftsliv.
Gard med litt gammaldags drift og gamle koselege hus. Eventuelle måltid blir inntatt rundt langbordet på kjøkenet.
Det er dyr på garden, fine turstiar i området og ein kan leiga båt og koma seg på fjorden.
Det er og høve til å overnatta på ein gamal husmannsplass.

Aadland Gardsferie liegt in einer kleinen Gemeinde am Samnangerfjord, 42 km von Bergen entfernt. Eine siebenköpfige Familie, die gern auf Menschen zugeht sowie an Kultur, Sprachen und Natur interessiert ist. Traditionell bewirtschafteter Bauernhof mit älteren gemütlichen Häusern. Eventuelle Mahlzeiten werden an einem großen Tisch in der Küche eingenommen. Außerdem: reizvolle Wanderwege, Tiere auf dem Hof, Bootsverleih.
Wer mag, kann in einer alten Kleinbauernkate übernachten.

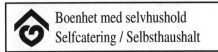
A: Apartment for 2-3 persons
No. of bedrooms: 1
Shared bath, own kitchenette
Price for whole unit: **350,-**

B: 'Store-house' for 3-4 persons
Sleeping acove
Shared bath, own kitchenette
and LR
Price for whole unit: **350,-**

Applies to all rental units:
Bed linen fee: **50,-**
Open May - Sept.
Yard/garden/terrace/deck access
No smoking inside
Breakfast service available: **50,-**
English and some French spoken

A: Husvære for 2-3 personar
Antal soverom: 1
Delt bad, eige tekjøken
Pris for heile eininga: **350,-**

B: Stabbur for 3-4 personar
Sovealkove
Delt bad, eige tekjøken
og stove
Pris for heile eininga: **350,-**

For alle einingar gjeld:
Tillegg for sengetyg: **50,-**
Ope mai - sept.
Hage/terrasse/uteplass
Inga røyking innomhus
Frukost kan serverast: **50,-**

A: Wohnung für 2-3 Personen
Anzahl Schlafräume: 1
Gemeins. Bad, Eig.Küchenecke
Ganze Einheit: **350,-**

B: 'Vorratshaus' für 3-4 Pers.
Schlafalkoven
Gemeins. Bad, Eig.Küchenecke
und Stube
Ganze Einheit: **350,-**

Für alle Einheiten gilt:
Mieten von Bettwäsche: **50,-**
Geöffnet Mai - Sept.
Garten/Terrasse/Aussenplatz
Kein Rauchen im Haus
Frühstück auf Bestellung: **50,-**
Sprechen Deutsch

Directions:
From Bergen: Follow E-16 towards Hardanger. 42 km from Bergen you arrive at Trengereid and exit to the right onto RV 7. After driving 9 km you come to the church in Samnanger. Aadland Gardsferie is located nearby. Look for the sign marked "Gardsferie".

Vegforklaring:
Frå Bergen følg E-16 mot Hardanger. 42 km frå Bergen kjem du til Trengereid, ta av til høgre og følg RV 7 vidare. Etter 9 km vil du kunne finne kyrkja i Samnanger. Aadland Gardsferie ligg like ved, sjå etter skilt med "Gardsferie".

Wegbeschreibung:
Von Bergen: E-16 Richtung Hardanger folgen. 42 km von Bergen erreicht man Trengereid, wo man rechts auf Strasse 7 abzweigt. Nach 9 km kommt man zur Kirche von Samnanger. Aadland Gardsferie liegt gleich nebenan. Siehe Schild "Gardsferie".

It is good to have an end to journey toward;
but it is the journey that matters, in the end.

-Ursula LeGuin

They can conquer who believe they can.
He has not learned the first lesson of life
who does not every day surmount a fear.

-Ralph Waldo Emerson

Have the courage to face a difficulty
lest it kick you harder than you bargain for.

-Leszczynski Stanislaus

Skjerping Gård

Your host:
Elinor Skjerping
& Jan Inge Wold

Address:
Skjerping
N - 5282 Lonevåg
Phone: 56 39 02 91
Fax: 56 39 25 67
Mobil: 91 34 99 25
E-mail: info@skjerping.net
Web: www.skjerping.net

Best time to call:
08.00 - 23.00

A: Guesthouse for 2-5 persons
No. of bedrooms: 2
Own bath, kitchen, LR
Price for whole unit: **600,-**

B: Apartment for 2-4 persons
No. of bedrooms: 2
Own kitchen and LR, shared bath
Price for whole unit: **500,-**

Bed linen included
Open year round
Terrace/deck access/yard
Bike for rent
No smoking inside
Breakfast service available
English spoken

A: Gjestehus for 2-5 personer
Antall soverom: 2
Eget bad, kjøkken, stue
Pris for hele enheten: **600,-**

B: Leilighet for 2-4 personer
Antall soverom: 2
Eget kjøkken og stue, delt bad
Pris for hele enheten: **500,-**

Sengetøy er inkludert
Åpent hele året
Terrasse/uteplass/hage
Sykkelutleie
Ingen røking innendørs
Frokost kan serveres

A: Gästehaus für 2-5 Personen
Anzahl Schlafräume: 2
Eig. Bad, Küche, Stube
Ganze Einheit: **600,-**

B: Wohnung für 2-4 Personen
Anzahl Schlafräume: 2
Eig. Küche u. Stube, gemeins. Bad
Ganze Einheit: **500,-**

Inkl. Bettwäsche
Ganzjährig geöffnet
Terrasse/Aussenplatz/Garten
Fahrrad zu mieten
Kein Rauchen im Haus
Frühstück auf Bestellung
Sprechen etwas Deutsch

The farm is located on Osterøya, Norways's largest landlocked island, which is often called "a miniature Norway". 35 min. drive from downtown Bergen. Three generations live on the farm. The Old Farmer cottage is rented to tourists, along with an apartment in the old main farmhouse. The farm hosts many animals also: oxen, horse, calves, goats, hens, ducks, rabbits, dogs and cats. Lovely hiking areas with freshwater fishing and a salmon river. Nice farm village museum and other cultural attractions.

Gården ligger på Osterøya, Norges største innlandsøy som blir kalt "et Norge i miniatyr", 35 min. kjøretur fra Bergen sentrum. Det bor tre generasjoner på gården. Kårhuset leies ut til turister, pluss en leilighet i det gamle hovedhuset. Det er også mange dyr på gården; okser, hest, kalver, geiter, høns, ender, kaniner, hund og katt. Stor trampoline i hagen. Nydelig turterreng med fiskemuligheter i fjellvann og lakseelv. Flott bygdemuseum og andre kulturtilbud.

Der Hof liegt auf Osterøya, der größten Halbinsel des Landes, oft auch "Norwegen en Miniature" genannt (35 Min. Autofahrt ab Bergen). Auf dem Hof leben 3 Generationen gemeinsam. Neben dem Altenteil-Haus wird eine Wohnung im Haupthaus vermietet. Ochsen, Pferde, Kälber, Ziegen, Hühner, Enten, Kaninchen, Hund und Katzen. Schönes Wandergebiet; Angeln in Bergseen und Lachsflüssen. Interessantes Freilichtmuseum sowie weitere kulturelle Angebote.

Vikinghuset

Your host:
Olaug Fagerbakke
& Helge Terje Fosse

Address:
Lid i Bergsdalen
N - 5722 Dalekvam
Phone: **56 59 89 34**
Mobil: **945 52 592**
E-mail: **helge.terje.fosse@c2i.net**

Best time to call:
08.00 - 22.00

Guesthouse for 2-9 persons	Gjestehus for 2-9 personer	Gästehaus für 2-9 Personen
No. of bedrooms: 3	Antal soverom: 3	Anzahl Schlafräume: 3
Own bath, kitchen, DR, LR	Eige bad, kjøken, spisestove, stove	Eig. Bad, Küche, Sp.Zi., Stube
Price for whole unit: **600,-**	Pris for heile eininga: **600,-**	Ganze Einheit: **600,-**
Bed linen fee: **50,-**	Tillegg for sengetyg: **50,-**	Mieten von Bettwäsche: **50,-**
Breakfast service available: **50,-**	Frukost kan serverast: **50,-**	Frühstück auf Bestellung: **50,-**
Open year round.	Ope heile året	Ganzjährig geöffnet
Yard/terrace/deck access	Terrasse/uteplass	Garten/Terr./Aussenplatz
Boat and bike for rent	Båt- og sykkelutleige	Boot u. Fahrrad zu mieten
No pets from other countries	Norske kjæledyr tillatt	Keine Haustiere aus dem Ausland
No smoking inside	Inga røyking innomhus	Kein Rauchen im Haus
Suitable for handicapped	Tilhøve for gjester med handikap	Behindertengerecht
Some English spoken		Sprechen etwas Deutsch

Lid in Bergsdalen valley is situated between Dale and Voss. The farm is about 450 meters above sea level. The house was renovated and expanded in 1998. High standard. A family of six lives on the farm and there are sheep and cows here, too. Child-friendly outdoor environment. Excellent terrain for mountain excursions by foot or bicycle. Fishing in rivers or lakes. Good skiing areas.

Lid i Bergsdalen ligg mellom Dale og Voss, og garden Lid ligg ca. 450 meter over havet. Huset er bygd ca. 1930, og vart restaurert og påbygd i 1998. Høg standard. På Lid bur det ein familie på seks, og det er sau og kyr på garden. Bornevennleg utemiljø. Gode høve til turar i fjellet, til fots eller på sykkel. Fiske i elvar og vatn. Godt skiterreng.

Das ca. 1930 erbaute Gehöft Lid liegt auf 450 m Höhe in Bergs-dalen zwischen Dale und Voss. 1998 wurde die Anlage renoviert, außerdem hat man angebaut. Hoher Standard. Lid beherbergt eine 6-köpfige Famile, darüber hinaus sind dort Schafe und Kühe anzutreffen. Kinderfreundliches Terrain. Gut Möglichkeiten zum Bergwandern und Radfahren. Angeln in Flüssen und Seen. Gutes Skigebiet.

Where there's a will there's a way. –Proverb

B&B-Homestay
Level of standard:

NBT-member
NBT-inspected

page **144**
Hordaland

Skjelde Gård

Your host:
Bitten Linde

Address:
Bulken
N - 5700 Voss
Phone: **56 51 42 90**
Mobil: **99 25 34 86**

Best time to call:
09.00 - 21.00

Double room:	**530,-/540,-**	Dobbeltrom:	**530,-/540,-**	Doppelzimmer:	**530,-/540,-**
Twin room:	**530,-/540,-**	Tosengsrom:	**530,-/540,-**	Zweibettzimmer:	**530,-/540,-**
Single room:	**360,-/370,-**	Enkeltrom:	**360,-/370,-**	Einzelzimmer:	**360,-/370,-**

No. of rooms: 7	Antall rom: 7	Anzahl Zimmer: 7
Full breakfast	Full frokost	Volles Frühstück
Breakfast buffet	Servering: Frokost buffét	Serv.: Frühstücksbüfett
Open 15 May - 10 Sept.	Åpent 15. mai - 10. sept	Geöffnet 15. Mai - 10. Sept.
TV available	TV tilgjengelig	Zugang zu TV
Terrace/garden	Terrasse/uteplass/hage	Terrasse/Aussenplatz/Garten
Boat for rent	Båtutleie	Boot zu mieten
Bike for rent in the area	Sykkelutleie i nærheten	Fahrradausleihe in der Nähe
No smoking inside	Ingen røking innendørs	Kein Rauchen im Haus
VISA, MC accepted	Vi tar VISA, MC	Wir nehmen VISA, MC
Discount for children	Rabatt for barn	Ermässigung für Kinder
Selfcatering possible	Selvhushold er mulig	Selbsthaushalt möglich
English spoken		Sprechen Deutsch

Skjelde gård is beautifully situated by the Vang lake in the pretty village of Voss. This old farm has been in the family for many generations. Finds from the Viking period show that people have been living here way back in history. The hostess has been receiving bed and breakfast guests since 1949. Wonderful hiking country, lots to see in the village.

Skjelde gård ligger vakkert til ved Vangsvatnet i den vakre Vossebygden. Det er en gammel slektsgård som har vært i familien i mange generasjoner. Funn fra vikingtiden viser at det har vært bosetning her langt tilbake i historien.
Vertskapet har drevet pensjonat på gården siden 1949.
Ypperlig turterreng, rikelig med severdigheter i bygden.

Skjelde gård liegt sehr reizvoll am See Vangsvatn in der schönen Gegend von Voss. Der alte Erbhof befindet sich seit vielen Generationen in dieser Familie. Funde aus der Wikingerzeit beweisen eine ganz frühe Besiedlung. Die Besitzer haben seit 1949 eine Pension auf dem Hof betrieben. Ausgezeichnetes Wandergelände und viele Sehenswürdigkeiten in der Gegend.

Sollia

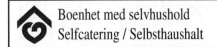

Your host:
Judith & Arnljot Møster

Address:
N - 5730 Ulvik
Phone: 56 52 63 87
Mobil: 90 95 65 57
E-mail: arnljot.moster@ulvik.org

Best time to call:
09.00 - 22.00

A: Apartment for 2-4 persons		**A:** Leilighet for 2-4 personer		**A:** Wohnung für 2-4 Personen	
LR w/convertable double bed sofa		Stue med dobbel sovesofa		Stube mit Doppelsofa	
Bunkbeds in kichen		Køysenger på kjøkkenet		Kojenbetten in der Küche	
Own bath		Eget bad		Eig. Bad	
Price for 2 pers.:	**500,-**	Pris for 2 pers.:	**500,-**	Preis für 2 Pers.:	**500,-**
3-4 pers.: price per pers.:	**200,-**	3-4 pers.: pris pr. pers.:	**200,-**	3-4 Pers.: Preis pro Pers.:	**200,-**
B: Room for 2 pers.:	**400,-**	**B:** Rom for 2 pers.:	**400,-**	**B:** Zimmer für 2 Pers.:	**400,-**
Room for 1 pers.:	**300,-**	Rom for 1 pers.:	**300,-**	Zimmer für 1 Pers.:	**300,-**
No. of rooms: 4		Antall rom: 4		Anzahl Zimmer: 4	

Bed linen included
Open 15 May - 15 Sep.
TV available
Yard/terrace/deck access
No smoking inside
English spoken

Sengetøy er inkludert
Åpent 15. mai - 15.sept.
TV tilgjengelig
Hage/terrasse/uteplass
Ingen røking innendørs

Inkl. Bettwäsche
Geöffnet 15. Mai - 15. Sept.
Zugang zu TV
Garten/Terrasse/Aussenplatz
Kein Rauchen im Haus
Sprechen etwas Deutsch

You will find Ulvik at the end of the Hardangerfjord, and 10 km from the ferry quay in "Bruravik." The main road runs through a tunnel from Bruravik and westward. Ulvik is therefore quietly situated between the mountains and the fjord. Marked hiking trails. Boat and bicycle rentals at local Tourist Office. Ulvik Church is worth a visit.
The Møster's have had summer guests in their home for over 25 years. In the winter they run a painting business.

Innerst i Hardangerfjorden ligger Ulvik, 10 km fra fergekaien i Bruravik. Hovedveien er lagt i tunnel vestover. Ulvik ligger derfor skjermet og fredelig til med fjell og fjord tett på.
Det er fint turterreng med skiltede turstier og muligheter for leie av sykler og båt ved det lokale turistkontoret. Ulvik kirke er verd et besøk.
Familien Møster har tatt imot gjester i sitt hjem i over 25 somre. Om vinteren driver de egen malervirksomhet.

Weit drinnen im Hardangerfjord liegt Ulvik, 10 km vom Fährkai Bruravik. Von hier aus verläuft die Hauptstr. nach Bergen im Tunnel. Ulvik liegt daher abgeschirmt und ruhig zwischen Berg und Fjord. Schönes Ausflugsgebiet mit markierten Pfaden Sie können Fahrräder und Boot im örtlichen Touristbüro mieten. Besuchen Sie die Kirche in Ulvik. Fam. Møster empfängt seit über 25 J. Sommergäste. Im Winter haben sie einen eigenen Malerbetrieb.

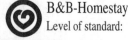
Brandseth Fjellstove

Your host:
Erling Brandseth

Address:
Haugsvik,
N - 5713 Vossestrand
Phone: 56 53 05 00
Fax: 56 53 05 01
Mobil: 93 20 67 51
E-mail: brandseth@c2i.net

Best time to call:
09.00 - 21.00

Twin room:	**590,-/650,-**	Tosengsrom:	**590,-/650,-**	Zweibettzimmer:	**590,-/650,-**
1 pers. in double room:	**395,-/450,-**	1 pers. i dobbeltrom:	**395,-/450,-**	1 Pers. in Doppelzi:	**395,-/450,-**

No. of rooms: 7	Antal rom: 7	Anzahl Zimmer: 7
Full breakfast	Full frukost	Volles Frühstück
Breakfast buffet	Servering: Frukostbuffét	Serv.: Frühstücksbüfett
Other meals served upon request	Andre måltid kan bestellast	Andere Mahlzeiten nach Vereinb.
Open 15 Feb. - 25 Apr.	Ope 15. feb. - 25. april	Geöffnet 15. Feb. - 25. April
and 1 June - 30 Aug.	og 1. juni - 30. aug.	und 1. Juni - 30. Aug.
TV available	TV tilgjengeleg	Zugang zu TV
Terrace/deck access	Terrasse/uteplass	Terrasse/Aussenplatz
Discount for children	Rabatt for born	Ermäßigung für Kinder
No smoking indoors	Inga røyking innomhus	Kein Rauchen im Haus
VISA accepted	Vi tek VISA	Wir nehmen VISA
Access to telephone/fax/Internet	Adgang til telefon/faks/Internett	Zugang Telefon/Fax/Internet
English spoken		Sprechen Deutsch

Charming mountain lodge half-way between Voss and Flåm, in the heart of fjord country, 2.5 km from E-16 and the "Norway in a Nutshell"-route. The Brandseth Fjellstove lodge is nicely situated with a view of the town and near good terrain for walks. An excellent starting point for fjord tours. The lodge kitchen is known for its tasty home-style cooking. All rooms include shower and WC.
Directions: From Voss: Look for the sign to Brandseth Fjellstove after you pass Haugsvik.

Triveleg fjellstove midt mellom Voss og Flåm, i hjartet av fjord-Norge, 2,5 km frå E-16 og "Norway in a Nutshell"-ruta. Fjellstova ligg fint til med utsyn over bygda og med flott tur-terreng. Godt utgangspunkt for turar til fjordane. Kjøkenet er kjend for god heimelaga mat. Alle rom har dusj og WC.
Vegforklaring: Frå Voss: Etter Haugsvik; sjå etter skilt til Brand-seth Fjellstove. Frå Flåm: Sjå etter skiltet etter tunnellane ved Stal-heim.

Gemütlicher Berggasthof im Herzen Fjordnorwegens, auf halbem Weg zwischen Voss und Flåm. Nur 2,5 km zur Hauptstraße E-16 und der bekannten Rundreise "Norway in a Nutshell". Der Berg-gasthof bietet eine sehr schöne Aussicht über die Siedlung und das reizvolle Wandergebiet. Guter Ausgangspunkt für Touren zu den Fjorden. Der Gasthof ist bekannt für seine gute Küche. Alle Zimmer mit Dusche und WC.
Wegbeschreibung: Ab Voss: Ach-ten Sie hinter Haugsvik auf die Be-schilderung "Brandseth Fjellstove".

Haugen Gard

Your host:
**Elisabeth Holth &
Kåre Magnar Trefall**

Address:
**Haugen, Eksingedalen
N - 5728 Eidslandet**
Phone: **56 59 58 33**
E-mail: **elisabeth.holth@c2i.net**

Best time to call:
18.00 - 23.00

A: Guesthouse for 2-9 persons	**A:** Gjestehus for 2-9 personar	**A:** Gästehaus für 2-9 Personen
No. of bedrooms: 3	Antal soverom: 3	Anzahl Schlafräume: 3
Own bath, kitchen, LR	Eige bad, kjøken, stove	Eig. Bad, Küche, Stube
Price for up to 6 persons: **600,-**	Pris for opp til 6 pers.: **600,-**	Preis bis 6 Pers: **600,-**
Price per pers. (over 6 pers.) **100,-**	Pris pr. pers. (over 6 pers.): **100,-**	Preis pro Pers. (über 6 Pers.) **100,-**
B: 'Stølshus' (cabin) for 2-6 pers.	**B:** Stølshus for 2-6 personar	**B:** Sennhütte für 2-6 Personen
1 bedroom and 1 loft-bedroom	1 soverom og 1 sovehems	1 Schlafraum und 1 Schlafboden
No running water, biological toilet	Ikkje innlagt vatn, biologisk toalett	Kein fl. Wasser, bio. Toilette
Washbasin in room, kitchenette	Vaskefat på romma, tekjøken	Waschschüssel im Zi., Kl. Küche
Price for whole unit: **600,-**	Pris for heile eininga: **600,-**	Ganze Einheit: **600,-**
Bed linen fee: **50,-**	Tillegg for sengetyg: **50,-**	Mieten von Bettwäsche: **50,-**
Open year round	Ope heile året	Ganzjährig geöffnet
Yard/terrace/deck access	Hage/terrasse/uteplass	Garten/Terrasse/Aussenplatz
No smoking inside	Inga røyking innomhus	Kein Rauchen im Haus
Breakfast service available: **50,-**	Frukost kan serverast: **50,-**	Frühstück auf Bestellung: **50,-**
Some English spoken		Sprechen etwas Englisch

The farm is located in the middle of Eksingedalen Valley. You will enjoy an excellent view of the valley and there are many nice options for mountain and fishing day-trips. The host family runs milk and meat production. Visit the cows, dogs and cats. Participate in an active farming environment! The cabin is situated 4 km from the farm with easy access by car. This newly renovated 'stølshus' (summer cabin) is surrounded by excellent walking/hiking trails.

Garden ligg midt i Eksingedalen, 2 km frå riksvegen. Det er fin utsikt utover dalen og det er gode høve til både fjell- og fisketurar. Vertskapet driv med mjølk- og kjøtproduksjon. Her kan du helse på kyr, hunder og katter. Du kan ta del i det aktive gardsmiljøet. Stølen ligg 4 km frå garden med god bilveg heilt fram. Det nyoppussa stølshuset ligg i eit fint turterreng.

Der Hof liegt in Eksingedalen, 2 km von der Hauptstraße entfernt. Schöne Aussicht; gute Möglichkeiten zu Fjell- und Angeltouren. Die Gastgeber betreiben Milch- und Fleischproduktion. Kühe, Hunde und Katzen auf dem Hof. Die Gäste können aktiv am Leben auf dem Bauernhof teilhaben. Die Alm liegt ca. 4 km vom Bauernhof entfernt (gute Straße bis zur Hütte). Die frisch renovierte Hütte befindet sich in einem reizvollen Wandergebiet.

Godmorstova

Your host:
Berit Vetlejord

Address:
Vetlejord, Eksingedalen
N - 5728 Eidslandet
Phone: 56 59 64 19
E-mail: vetlejord@c2i.net
Web: www.go.to/godmorstova

Best time to call:
08.00 - 23.00

Guesthouse for 2-6 persons	**A:** Gjestehus for 2-6 personer	**A:** Gästehaus für 2-6 Personen
No. of bedrooms: 1	Antall soverom: 1	Anzahl Schlafräume: 1
Own bath, kitchen and LR	Eget bad, kjøkken og stue	Eig. Bad, Küche und Stube
Price for whole unit: **430,-**	Pris for hele enheten: **430,-**	Ganze Einheit: **430,-**
B: Room for 2 pers., shared bath	**B:** Rom for 2 personer m/delt bad	**B:** Zimmer für 2 Pers., gem. Bad
No. of rooms: 2	Antall rom: 2	Anzahl Zimmer: 2
Price per pers.: **150,-**	Pris pr. pers.: **150,-**	Preis pro Pers.: **150,-**
Bed linen fee: **50,-**	Tillegg for sengetøy: **50,-**	Mieten von Bettwäsche: **50,-**
Open 1 March - 31 October	Åpent 1. mars - 31. oktober	Geöffnet 1. Marz - 31. Oktober
Yard/terrace/deck access	Hage/uteplass	Garten/Aussenplatz
Boat and bike for rent	Båt- og sykkelutleie	Boot und Fahrrad zu mieten
No smoking inside	Ingen røking innendørs	Kein Rauchen im Haus
Breakfast service available	Frokost kan serveres	Frühstück auf Bestellung
English and some French spoken		Sprechen etwas Deutsch

Godmorstova is the Old Farmer cottage on the Vetlejord farm. The house dates from 1871 and has housed 11 generations. Recently renovated in traditional style and is full of character and uniqueness with a rocking chair, spinning wheel and antique "Push Bed" from 1874. The modern additions are a new bathroom and heated floor in bathroom and kitchen. Two rooms are also rented out in the main farmhouse. Beautiful mountain areas surround the farm. Both river and lake fishing. Hiking trails and forest roads.

Godmorstova er kårhuset på gården Vetlejord. Huset er fra 1871 og har vært i familien i 11 generasjoner. Det er nylig oppusset og holdt i gammel stil, fullt av sjel og særpreg med gyngestol, rokk og gammel skuvseng fra 1874. Det moderne tilsnittet er et nytt bad og gulvvarme både på kjøkken og bad. To rom leies også ut i hovedhuset. Gården er omgitt av fine fjellområder. Fiske i elv og vann. Turstier og skogsveier.

Godmorstova ist ein Altenteil-Haus auf dem Hof Vetlejord aus dem Jahr 1871, seit 11 Generationen von der gleichen Familie bewirtschaftet. Das kürzlich renovierte Hau hat eine historische Atmosphäre mit Schaukelstuhl, Spinnrad und "Schiebebett" (breitenverstellbar) von 1874. Modernes Bad, Fußbodenheizung in Küche und Bad. Im Haupthaus zwei Zimmer zu vermieten. Reizvolle Gebirgsregion. Angeln in Flüssen und Seen. Wald- und Wanderwege.

Straume's Romutleige

Your host:
Aud Sørtun & Harald Nygard

Address:
**Straume
N - 5729 Modalen**
Phone: **56 59 98 37**

Best time to call:
20.00 - 23.00

Guesthouse for 2-8 persons	Gjestehus for 2-8 personar	Gästehaus für 2-8 Personen
No. of bedrooms: 2	Antal soverom: 2	Anzahl Schlafräume: 2
Bath, kitchen, LR	Eige bad, kjøken, stove	Bad, Küche, Stube
Price per pers.: **150,-**	Pris pr. pers.: **150,-**	Preis pro Pers.: **150,-**
Bed linen fee: **50,-**	Tillegg for sengetyg: **50,-**	Mieten von Bettwäsche: **50,-**
Open year round	Ope heile året	Ganzjährig geöffnet
TV available	TV tilgjengeleg	Zugang zu TV
Garden	Uteplass	Aussenplatz
No smoking inside	Inga røyking innomhus	Kein Rauchen im Haus
Discount for children	Rabatt for born	Ermässigung für Kinder
Some English spoken		Sprechen etwas Englisch

Straume's is located in Modalen which is one of the smallest localities in Norway with only 340 inhabitants, two general stores and a gas station. The hosts' son, John Sigurd, is a hiking enthusiast and, when coming home for summer vacations, offers guided tours of the area's mountains and wonderful west coast geography. Fishing, berry-picking, and skiing opportunities in their respective seasons. Check out the area's School Museum and old church. The hosts run a dairy farm, they also raise poultry and have cats.

Straumes romutleige ligg i Modalen kommune som er den nest minste kommunen i Noreg med 340 innbyggjarar. Det er to butikkar og sal av bensin.
Flott vestlandsnatur gir høve til fine turar. Sonen i huset, John Sigurd, er godt kjent i fjellet. Når han er heime i feriar kan han mot betaling ta med gjester på guida turar "med utsikt over halve Vestlandet".
Andre aktivitetar er fiske, bærplukking eller skitur, alt etter årstida. Det er skulemuseum og ei gammal kyrkje i bygda.
Det er kyr og kalvar på garden, pluss høner og kattar.

Straumes Zimmervermietung liegt in Modalen, Norwegens zweitkleinster Gemeinde mit 340 Einwohnern, 2 Geschäften und Tankstelle.
Machen Sie Ausflüge in die herrliche Landschaft von West-Norwegen. In seinen Ferien kann der Sohn der Fam. zu Aussichtspunkten in die Bergwelt führen.
Andere Aktivitäten: Angeln, Beerensammeln, Skilaufen, je nach Jahreszeit. Besuchen Sie das Schulmuseum und die alte Kirche. Milchkühe, Kälber, Hühner und Katzen auf dem Hof.

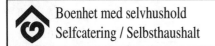
Hosteland feriehus

Your host:
Anne M. & Kaspar Wergeland

Address:
N - 5987 Hosteland
Phone: 56 36 73 79
Mobil: 97 65 90 54
E-mail: kasparw@c2i.net
Web:
http://www.scandion.no/hf.html

Best time to call:
16.00 - 23.00

Guesthouse for 2-9 persons	Gjestehus for 2-9 personer	Gästehaus für 2-9 Personen
No. of bedrooms: 4	Antall soverom: 4	Anzahl Schlafräume: 4
Own bath, kitchen, LR, DR	Eget bad, kjøkken, stue, spisestue	Eig. Bad, Küche, Stube, Sp.Zi.
Utility room and extra shower	Vaskerom og ekstra dusj	Waschraum u. Extradusche
Price per pers.: **150,-**	Pris pr. pers.: **150,-**	Preis pro Pers.: **150,-**
Bed linen fee: **50,-**	Tillegg for sengetøy: **50,-**	Mieten von Bettwäsche: **50,-**
Open year round	Åpent hele året	Ganzjährig geöffnet
TV available	TV tilgjengelig	Zugang zu TV
Yard/terrace/garden	Terrasse/uteplass/hage	Garten/Aussenplatz
Boat for rent	Båtutleie	Boot zu mieten
No smoking in rooms	Ingen røyking på rom	Kein Rauchen im Zimmer
English spoken		Sprechen Deutsch

The hosts at Hosteland Feriehus has been receiving guests since 1995. The rental house is situated in a farm complex near a road with minimal traffic. Beautiful nature area near both the sea, mountains and forest. Fishing, berry-picking and hikes. Excellent bicycling terrain. Good base for daytrips to Bergen and Sognefjorden.

Directions:
E-39 from Knarvik. After passing the Jernfjell Tunnel, exit towards Duesund. At the Mollandseid crossing, drive towards Rutledal and exit towards Brekke. First house on the left.

Vertskapet ved Hosteland Feriehus har tatt mot gjester siden 1995. Utleiehuset ligger i et gårdstun ved vei med liten trafikk. Naturskjønt område nær sjø, fjell og skog. Fiske, bærplukking og turer. Fine sykkelturmuligheter. God base for dagsturer til Bergen og Sognefjorden.

Veibeskrivelse:
E-39 fra Knarvik. Etter passering Jernfjelltunnelen, ta av mot Duesund. I kryss Mollandseid, kjør mot Rutledal, ta av mot Brekke. Første hus vs. Alternativt: Ta RV 57, ferge til Sløvåg, kjør mot Duesund. Første vei til venstre etter Hostelandtunellen.

Die Gastgeber von Hosteland Feriehus empfangen seit 1995 Übernachtungsgäste. Das Haus liegt auf einem Hof an einer Straße mit geringem Verkehr. Landschaftlich reizvolles Gebiet nah an Meer, Gebirge und Wald. Angeln, Beeren sammeln, Wander- touren. Gute Möglichkeiten zum Radfahren. Ideal für Autotouren nach Bergen und zum Sognefjord.

Wegbeschreibung:
E-39 ab Knarvik. Biegen Sie nach Jernfjelltunnel nach Duesund ab. An der Kreuzung Mollandseid Richtung Rutledal und nach Brekke abzweigen. Erstes Haus links.

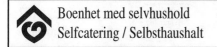

Flåm Camping & Vandrarheim

Your host:
Gjertrud & Erling Håland

Address:
Flåm, Postboks 8
N - 5743 Flåm
Phone: 57 63 21 21
Fax: 57 63 23 80
E-mail:
camping@flaam-camping.no

Best time to call:
08.00 - 20.00

A: Cabins for 4 persons (4x)	**A:** Hytte for 4 personer (4x)	**A:** Hütten für 4 Personen (4x)
No. of bedrooms: 2	Antall soverom: 2	Schlafräume: 2
Own bath, kitchen,	Eget bad, kjøkken	Eig. Bad, Küche
Price for whole unit: **650,-**	Pris for hele enheten: **650,-**	Ganze Einheit: **650,-**
B: Cabins for 4 persons (11x)	**B:** Hytter for 4 personer (11x)	**B:** Hütten für 3 Personen (11x)
Studio cabin	Ettromshytte	Zimmer: 1
Price for whole unit: **400,-/450,-**	Pris for hele enheten: **400,-/450,-**	Ganze Einheit: **400,-/450,-**
C: Rooms at the hostel	**C:** Rom i vandrehejemmet	**C:** Zimmer in der Jugendherberge
Double room: **350,-/450,-**	Dobbeltrom: **350,-/450,-**	Zweibettzimmer: **350,-/450,-**
Price per person	Pris pr. person	Preis pro Person
in four-bedded room **115,-/200,-**	i firesengsrom **115,-/200,-**	in Vierbettzimmer: **115,-/200,-**
Applies to all rental units:	For alle enhetene gjelder:	Für alle Einheiten gilt:
Bed linen fee: **50,-**	Tillegg for sengetøy: **50,-**	Mieten von Bettwäsche: **50,-**
Yard/terrace/deck access	Terrasse/uteplass/hage	Garten/Terrasse/Aussenplatz
Open 1 May - 1 Oct.	Åpent 1. mai - 1. okt.	Geöffnet 1. Mai - 1. Okt.
No smoking inside	Ingen røking innendørs	Kein Rauchen im Haus
English spoken		Sprechen Deutsch

Terminal station for the Flåm Railway. Fjordcruises to Gudvangen and Bergen. Excellent base for walking tours in the valleys of Flåm and Aurland, as well as daytrips by boat, bus and train. Bicycle tours on the Rallarvegen, etc. 300 m from the Flåm Railway Station.	Endestasjon for Flåmsbanen. Fjordcruise til Gudvangen og Bergen. Fint utgangspunkt for fotturer i Flåmsdalen og Aurlandsdalen, samt dagsturer med båt, buss og tog, sykkelturer på Rallarvegen m.m. 300 m frå Flåm stasjon.	Endstation der Flåmbahn. Fjordkreuzfahrt nach Gudvangen und Bergen. Guter Ausgangpunkt für Wanderungen in Flåmsdal und Aurlandsdal, sowie für Tagestouren mit Boot, Bus und Bahn. Fahrradtouren auf der Hardangervidda. Speisestätte in der Nähe. 300 m vom Bahnhof Flåm entfernt.

Eri Gardshus

Your host:
Anlaug Eri & Rolf Jakobsen

Address:
N - 6887 Lærdal
Phone: 57 66 65 14
Fax: 57 66 61 81
Mobil: 91 34 44 18
E-mail: rolfa@online.no
Web:
www.mamut.com/erigardshus

Best time to call:
08.00 - 21.00

A: 'Jesastova'
Guesthouse for 2-9 persons
No. of bedrooms: 3
Own bath, kitchen, LR
Price for whole unit: **600,-**
Price per pers.: **200,-**

B: 'Kvitastova'
Guesthouse for 2-13 persons
No. of bedrooms: 5
Own kitchen and two baths
Price for whole unit: **1.000,-**
Price per pers.: **200,-**

C: 'Store-house' for 2 persons
Shared bath and kitchen
Price for whole unit: **300,-**

Bed linen fee: **50,-**
Open year round
TV available
Yard/terrace/deck access
Boat for rent
No smoking in rooms
Discount for children
English spoken

The hosts of Eri Gardshus are involved in pork and milk production. The Eri farm is located 3.5 km from Lærdal city center. The rental cottage is situated 1 km from the main farm and has its own courtyard.

A: 'Jesastova'
Gjestehus for 2-9 personer
Antall soverom: 3
Eget bad, kjøkken, stue
Pris for hele enheten: **600,-**
Pris pr. pers.: **200,-**

B: 'Kvitastova'
Gjestehus for 2-13 personer
Antall soverom: 5
Eget kjøkken og to bad
Pris for hele enheten: **1.000,-**
Pris pr. pers.: **200,-**

C: Stabbur for 2 personer
Delt bad og kjøkken
Pris for hele enheten: **300,-**

Tillegg for sengetøy: **50,-**
Åpent hele året
TV tilgjengelig
Hage/terrasse/uteplass
Båtutleie
Ingen røking på rom
Rabatt for barn

Vertskapet på Eri Gardshus driv med svin- og mjølkeproduksjon. Garden Eri ligg 3,5 km frå Lærdal sentrum. Utleigehusa ligg i eit eige tun 1 km frå garden.

A: 'Jesastova'
Gästehaus für 2-9 Personen
Anzahl Schlafräume: 3
Eig. Bad, Küche, Stube
Ganze Einheit: **600,-**
Preis pro Pers.: **200,-**

B: 'Kvitastova'
Gästehaus für 2-13 Personen
Anzahl Schlafräume: 5
Eig. Küche und zwei Bäder
Ganze Einheit: **1.000,-**
Preis pro Pers.: **200,-**

C: 'Vorratshaus' für 2 Personen
Gemeins.. Bad und Küche
Ganze Einheit: **300,-**

Mieten von Bettwäsche: **50,-**
Ganzjährig geöffnet
Zugang zu TV
Garten/Terrasse/Aussenplatz
Boot zu mieten
Kein Rauchen im Zimmer
Ermässigung für Kinder
Sprechen etwas Deutsch

Die Gastgeber betreiben Schweine- und Milchproduktion. Der Hof liegt 3,5 km vom Ort Lærdal entfernt. Das Ferienhaus liegt ca. 1 km entfernt auf einem eigenen Hofgrundstück.

B&B-Homestay
Level of standard: ♣ ♣

NBT-member
NBT-inspected

page **153**
Sogn & Fjordane

Amla Nedre

Your host:
Eldbjørg & Hallvard
David Falck Husum

Address:
Amla Nedre
N - 6854 Kaupanger
Phone: 5767 8401 Fax: 5767 8659
Mobil: 90 65 24 64
E-mail: post@hallvard-david.no
Web: www.hallvard-david.no

Best time to call:
08.00 - 21.00

Double room:	550,-/650,-	Dobbeltrom:	550,-/650,-	Doppelzimmer:	550,-/650,-
Twin room:	475,-	Tosengsrom:	475,-	Zweibettzimmer:	475,-
Single room:	375,-	Enkeltrom:	375,-	Einzelzimmer:	375,-

No. of rooms: 4	Antal rom: 4	Anzahl Zimmer: 4
Full breakfast	Full frukost	Volles Frühstück
Breakfast buffet	Servering: Frukostbuffé	Serv.: Frühstücksbüfett
Open 1 June - 1 September	Ope 1. juni - 1. sept	Geöffnet 1. Juni - 1. Sept.
TV available	TV tilgjengeleg	Zugang zu TV
Terrace/deck access/yard	Terrasse/uteplass/hage	Terrasse/Aussenplatz/Garten
Boat for rent	Båtutleige	Boot zu mieten
No smoking in rooms	Inga røyking på romma	Kein Rauchen im Zimmer
Discount for children	Rabatt for born	Ermässigung für Kinder
English spoken		Sprechen etwas Deutsch

This is an old district officer's farm built in 1844 and restored in 1965. The main house is built in Biedermeier style and now historically recognized. Amla Nedre has been awarded "Olavsrosa" for its historic quality. At the farm they breed cattle. It is beautifully situated close to the Sognefjord with views extending to the community of Kaupanger. There is a private beach and a boat.

Ein gamal lensmannsgard, bygd i 1844 og restaurert i 1965. Hovedhuset er bygd i Biedermeierstil og er freda. Amla Nedre er tildelt Olavsrosa for sin historiske miljøkvalitet. Produksjonen på garden er kjøttproduksjon på ammeku. Garden ligg fint til tett ved Sognefjorden med utsikt over det vesle samfunnet Kaupanger. Eiga badestrand og båt.

Alter Gutshof aus 1844, 1965 restauriert. Das Haupthaus im Biedermeierstil steht unter Denkmalschutz. Der Hof wurde aufgrund seiner historischen Milieuqualität mit der Olavsrose ausgezeichnet. Viehzucht für Fleischproduktion auf dem Hof. Herrliche Lage und Aussicht direkt am Sognefjord mit eigenem Badestrand und Boot.

Travel broadens the mind. –Proverb

Urnes Gard

Your host:
Britt & Odd John Bugge

Address:
N - 6870 Ornes
Phone: 57 68 39 44
Fax: 57 68 37 19
Mobil: 94 50 80 88 / 93 42 63 99
E-mail: urnes-gard@urnes.no
Web: www.urnes.no

Best time to call:
08.00 - 22.00

Double room:	**490,-/590,-**	Dobbeltrom:	**490,-/590,-**	Doppelzimmer:	**490,-/590,-**
1 pers. in double room:	**245,-/295,-**	1 pers. i dobbeltrom:	**245,-/295,-**	1 Pers. im Doppelzi.:	**245,-/295,-**

Double room: **490,-/590,-**	Dobbeltrom: **490,-/590,-**	Doppelzimmer: **490,-/590,-**
1 pers. in double room: **245,-/295,-**	1 pers. i dobbeltrom: **245,-/295,-**	1 Pers. im Doppelzi.: **245,-/295,-**
No. of rooms: 4	Antal rom: 4	Anzahl Zimmer: 4
Full breakfast	Full frukost	Volles Frühstück
Breakfast buffet	Servering: Frukostbuffét	Serv.: Frühstücksbüfett
Open 1 June - 1 Sept.	Ope 1. juni - 1. sept.	Geöffnet 1. Juni - 1. Sept.
TV available	TV tilgjengeleg	Zugang zu TV
Terrace/deck access	Terrasse/uteplass	Terrasse/Aussenplatz
Boat for rent	Båtutleige	Boot zu mieten
No smoking inside	Inga røyking innomhus	Kein Rauchen im Haus
Discount for children under 10	Rabatt for born under 10 år	Ermässigung für Kinder unter 10
English spoken		Sprechen etwas Deutsch

Urnes Gard lies on the south side of Lusterfjorden and is adjacent to the Urnes Stave Church, which is Norway's oldest. Your hosts use the farm for berry production including rasberry, strawberry, cherry and blueberry, in addition to having sheep, two horses and three dogs. In short, there is a lot of activity! Britt and Odd John also run a farm cafe and a farm shop where they sell farm products and handicrafts.

Urnes Gard ligg på sørsida av Lusterfjorden, og er næraste nabo til Urnes stavkyrkje som er den eldste i Noreg.
På garden driv vertskapet bærproduksjon med bringebær, jordbær, moreller og blåbær, og i tillegg har dei sauer, to hestar og tre hundar. Så her kan det gå livleg for seg.
I tillegg driv Britt og Odd John ein gardskafé og ein gardsbutikk med utsal av gardsprodukt og husflid.

Der Hof liegt an der Südseite des Lusterfjords, als unmittelbarer Nachbar der Urnes Stabkirche, der ältesten Norwegens.
Die Gastgeber betreiben Beerenproduktion (Himbeeren, Erdbeeren, Kirschen und Blaubeeren), darüber hinaus kann man auf dem Hof Schafe, zwei Pferden und drei Hunden erleben. Es geht hier also durchaus lebhaft zu.
Darüber hinaus betreiben Britt und Odd John ein Bauernhofcafé sowie ein kleines Geschäft (Lebensmittel aus eigenem Anbau; Kunsthandwerk).

A: Apartment for 2-6 persons	**A:** Husvære for 2-6 personar	**A:** Wohnung für 2-6 Personen
No. of bedrooms: 2	Antal soverom: 2	Anzahl Schlafräume: 2
Own bath, kitchen, LR	Eiget bad, kjøken, stove	Eig. Bad, Küche, Stube
Price for whole unit: **600,-**	Pris for heile eininga: **600,-**	Ganze Einheit: **600,-**
B: 'Store-house' for 2-5 persons	**B:** Stabbur for 2-5 personar	**B:** 'Vorratshaus' für 2-5 Pers.
No. of bedrooms: 2	Antal soverom: 2	Anzahl Schlafräume: 2
Own kitchen and LR	Eige kjøken og stove	Eig. Küche u. Stube
Toilet and shower in annex	WC og dusj i anna bygning	Toilette u. Dusche im Annex
Price for whole unit: **450,-**	Pris for heile eininga: **450,-**	Ganze Einheit: **450,-**
C: 'Eldhus' for 2-5 persons	**C:** Eldhus for 2-5 personar	**C:** Beckhaus für 2-5 Pers.
1 room, hand basin w/H&C water	1 rom, vaskeservant m/V&K vatn	1 Zi. m/Handwaschbecken (W&K)
Kitchennook	Kjøkenkrok	Küchenecke
Toilet and shower in annex	WC og dusj i anna bygning	Toilette u. Dusche im Annex
Price for whole unit: **350,-**	Pris for heile eininga: **350,-**	Ganze Einheit: **350,-**
Applies to all rental units:	For alle einingar gjeld:	Für alle Einheiten gilt:
Bed linen fee: **45,-**	Tillegg for sengetyg: **45,-**	Mieten von Bettwäsche: **45,-**
Open 1 June - 1 Sept.	Ope 1. juni - 1. sept.	Geöffnet 1. Juni - 1. Sept.
TV	TV	TV
Terrace/deck access	Terrasse/uteplass	Terrasse/Aussenplatz
Boat for rent	Båtutleige	Boot zu mieten
No smoking inside	Inga røyking innomhus	Kein Rauchen im Haus
Breakfast service available	Frukost kan serverast	Frühstück auf Bestellung
English spoken		Sprechen etwas Deutsch

Directions:
From the village of Sogndal: take RV 55 towards Sognefjellet. Exit towards the ferry stop at Solvorn after 17 km, where you can take a ferry every hour during daytime. If you drive over Sognefjellet on RV 55: take a left in Skjolden and follow signs to Ornes, driving 30 km out along the fjord.

Vegforklaring:
Frå tettstaden Sogndal køyrer ein RV 55 mot Sognefjellet. Etter 17 km tek ein av til fergestaden Solvorn, der det går ferge kvar time på dagtid.
Hvis ein kjem over Sognefjellet, langs RV 55, tek ein til venstre i Skjolden, skilta til Ornes, og køyrer 30 km utover langs fjorden.

Wegbeschreibung:
Von der Ortschaft Sogndal auf der Straße 55 Richtung Sognefjell. Nach 17 km abbiegen zum Fähranleger Solvorn, von wo tagsüber stündlich eine Fähre verkehrt. Aus Richtung Sognefjell: Auf der Straße 55 bis Skjolden; dort links ab beim Schild "Ornes" und dann 30 km am Fjord entlang.

A person is happy so long as he chooses to be happy and nothing can stop him. –Alexander Solzhenitsyn

Happiness? That's nothing more than health and a poor memory.
–Albert Schweitzer (1875 – 1965)

Lunden Ferieleiligheter

Your host:
Bjørg & Jon Lidal

Address:
N - 6859 Slinde
Phone: 57 67 91 88
Mobil: 90 93 04 71
E-mail: post@lundenferie.no
Web: www.lundenferie.no

Best time to call:
16.00 - 23.00

Apartment for up to 4 pers.		Husvære for inntil 4 pers.		Wohnung für bis zu 4 Pers.	
No. of bedrooms: 2		Antal soverom: 2		Anzahl Schlafräume: 2	
Own bath, LR w/kitchen		Eige bad, stove m/kjøkenkrok		Eig. Bad, Stube mit Küche	
Price per Apt.:	**550,-**	Pris pr. leil.:	**550,-**	Preis pro Wohnung.:	**550,-**
No. of apartments: 4		Antal einingar: 4		Anzahl Wohnungen: 4	
Bed linen fee:	**50,-**	Tillegg for sengetyg:	**50,-**	Mieten von Bettwäsche:	**50,-**
Open year round		Ope heile året		Ganzjährig geöffnet	
TV in all apt.		TV i alle einingar		TV in allen Wohnungen	
Terrace/veranda		Terrasse/veranda		Terrasse/Veranda	
Yard with BBQ		Uteplass med grill		Aussenplatz mit Grill	
Boat available		Båt tilgjengeleg		Zugang zu Boot	
Discount off-season		Rabatt utanom sesong		Ermässigung Nebensaison	
English spoken				Sprechen etwas Deutsch	

Lunden Vacation Apartments is beautifully situated in the Slinde farming community on the north side of the Sognefjord. Here you will enjoy fruit orchards and a panoramic view of the fjord and lofty, perennially snow-capped mountain peaks.

The rental house includes 4 high standard apartments, and lies on Sognefjorden. There is a pier and two boats available.

Jon is a full-time fruit grower and Bjørg works part-time for the County government. They bid you welcome to a pleasant stay along the Sognefjord.

Lunden ferieleiligheter ligg vakkert til, i bygda Slinde, på nordsida av Sognefjorden. Her er fine frukthagar og panoramautsikt mot fjord og høge fjell med evig snø på toppane.

Utleigehuset inneheld 4 leiligheter av høg standard, og ligg like ved Sognefjorden. Det er eiga brygge med to båtar tilgjengeleg for gjester.

Jon er fruktdyrkar på heiltid, Bjørg jobbar deltid i Fylkeskommunen. Dei ønsker velkommen til eit hyggelig opphald ved Sognefjorden.

Reizvolle Lage in der Gemeinde Slinde, an der Nordseite des Sognefjords. Schöne Obstgärten in der Umgebung; Panoramaaussicht auf Fjord und hohe Gipfel, die mit ewigem Schnee bedeckt sind.

Das Haus enthält 4 Wohnungen von hohem Standard. Herrliche Lage am Sognefjord mit eigenem Bootsteg und zwei Booten.

Der Gastgeber Jon ist Obstbauer, Ehefrau Bjørg arbeitet in der Provinzverwaltung. Beide heißen ihre Gäste herzlich zu einem erholsamen Aufenthalt am Sognefjord willkommen.

B&B-Inn
Level of standard: ♣♣ & ♣♣♣

NBT-member
NBT-inspected

page **157**
Sogn & Fjordane

Sognefjord Gjestehus

Your host:
Kirsten & Odd E.Vangsnes

Address:
N - 6894 Vangsnes
Phone: **5769 6722** Fax: **5769 6275**
Mobil: **97 16 16 05**
E-mail: **vangpens@online.no**
Web:
www.sognefjord-gjestehus.com

Best time to call:
08.00 - 22.00

Double-/Twin room:	**570,-/670,-**	Dobbelt-/tosengsrom:	**570,-/670,-**	Doppel-/Zweib.zi.:	**570,-/670,-**
Single room:	**390,-**	Enkeltrom:	**390,-**	Einzelzimmer:	**390,-**
No. of rooms: 9		Antall rom: 9		Anzahl Zimmer: 9	
Family room, per pers.:	**250,-**	Familierom, pr. pers.:	**250,-**	Familienzi., pro Pers.:	**250,-**
Extra bed:	**140,-**	Ekstraseng:	**140,-**	Extra Bett:	**140,-**
Full breakfast		Full frokost		Volles Frühstück	
Breakfast buffet		Servering: Frokost buffét		Serv.: Frühstücksbüfett	
Open year round		Åpent hele året		Ganzjährig geöffnet	
TV		TV		TV	
Boat for rent		Båtutleie		Boot zu mieten	
No smoking in rooms		Ingen røking på rom		Kein Rauchen im Zimmer	
VISA, MC, AmEx accepted		Vi tar VISA, MC, AmEx		Wir nehmen VISA, MC, AmEx	
Discount for children		Rabatt for barn		Ermässigung für Kinder	
Some English spoken				Sprechen etwas Deutsch	

Sognefjord Guesthouse is situated near the ferry dock at Vangsnes with views out towards Sognefjord and Kvinnefossen waterfall on the opposite side. Sognefjord Guesthouse is a good base for visiting the many attractions along the Sognefjord. Among others, you can enjoy stave churches, glacier tours and day-trips by express boat to Flåm and Fjærland (the Jostedalsbreen glacier). The Guesthouse has a full liquor license.

Sognefjord gjestehus ligger ved Vangsnes fergekai med utsikt mot Sognefjorden og Kvinnefossen på andre siden av fjorden.
Sognefjord gjestehus er et godt utgangspunkt for å besøke de mange attraksjonene langs Sognefjorden. Her kan det nevnes blant annet stavkirker, brevandring og dagsturer med ekspressbåt til Flåm og Fjærland (Jostedalsbreen).
Gjestehuset har alle serveringsrettigheter.

Sognefjord Gjestehus liegt am Kai in Vangsnes und bietet eine schöne Aussicht auf den Sognefjord und den Wasserfall Kvinnefossen am anderen Fjordufer. Das Gästehaus ist ein guter Ausgangspunkt, um die vielen Sehenswürdigkeiten am Sognefjord mitzuerleben. Man kann z.B. Stabkirchen besichtigen, Gletscherwanderungen unternehmen oder eine Tagestour mit dem Schnellboot nach Flåm oder Fjærland buchen (Abstecher zum Gletscher Jostedalsbreen).
Das Gästehaus verfügt über alle Schankrechte.

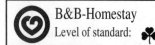
Flesje Gard

Your host:
Torunn Grut & Rune Andersen

Address:
N - 6899 Balestrand
Phone: 57 69 14 28
Fax: 57 69 16 82
E-mail: flesje.gard@balestrand.
online.no

Best time to call:
08.00 - 10.00 / 16.00 - 22.00

Double room: **600,-/700,-**	Dobbeltrom: **600,-/700,-**	Doppelzimmer: **600,-/700,-**
No. of rooms: 1	Antal rom: 1	Anzahl Zimmer: 1
Full breakfast	Full frukost	Volles Frühstück
Laid breakfast table	Dekka frukostbord	Serv.: Frühstückstisch
Open 1 May - 31 Sept.	Ope 1. mai - 31. sept.	Geöffnet 1. Mai - 31. Sept.
Yard/garden	Hage	Garten
No smoking inside	Inga røyking innomhus	Kein Rauchen im Haus
English spoken		Sprechen etwas Deutsch

Balestrand has been popular with tourists and artists for over 100 years; choose an active or relaxing visit.
Flesje is located 4 km from Balestrand city center. The farm dates from the 1700s and is idyllically and peacefully situated on the banks of the Sognefjord. Flesje has been the residence of both the county bailiff and various military men. There are 12 old structures on the farm property including a restored millhouse. There is only limited farming today: mostly vegetables and berries for personal consumption. Your room is on the second floor of the main farmhouse and is newly renovated with a beautiful view of the fjord. A family of five welcomes you: two adults, three children and a friendly Golden Retriever.

Balestrand har vore besøkt av turistar og kunstnerar i over 100 år, og her kan du ha både eit aktivt og eit roleg opphald.
Flesje ligg 4 km frå Balestrand sentrum. Garden er frå 1700-talet og ligg idyllisk og fredeleg til, heilt nede ved Sognefjorden.
Flesje har vore bustad for både futar og militærfolk.
Det er 12 gamle hus på garden, blant dei eit restaurert kvernhus. No er det lite gardsdrift att; berre grønsaker og bær til eige bruk. Utleierommet ligg i 2. høgda på hovudhuset, er nyopppussa og har ein flott utsikt mot fjorden.
Familien på fem ynskjer dykk velkommen; to vaksne, tre born og ein snill Golden retriver.

Balestrand wird seit über 100 Jahren von Touristen und Künstlern besucht. Besucher können selbst bestimmen, ob sie einen Aktiv- oder Erholungsurlaub verleben möchten. Flesje liegt 4 km von Balestrand Zentrum entfernt. Der Hof stammt aus dem 18. Jahrhundert und liegt idyllisch und friedlich direkt am Sognefjord. Unter den 12 Gebäuden befindet sich auch ein restauriertes Mühlenhaus. Heute wird kaum mehr Landwirtschaft betrieben (nur Gemüse und Beeren für den Eigenbedarf). Das zu vermietende Zimmer befindet sich im 1. Stock des Haupthauses, ist frisch renoviert und bietet eine schöne Aussicht auf den Fjord. Die fünfköpfige Familie (2 Erw., 3 Kinder und 1 freundlicher Golden Retriever) heißt sie herzlich willkommen!

Thue romutleige

Your host:
Britt Thue & Jan Henry Olsen

Address:
N - 6899 Balestrand
Phone: **57 69 15 95**
Fax: **57 69 15 33**
Mobil: **91 34 09 17**

Best time to call:
17.00 - 23.00

Room for 2 pers.:	**350,-**

No. of rooms: 5
Shared; one bath, two toilets,
kitchen and LR with TV

Bed linen fee:	**25,-**

Open 20 June - 20 Aug.
Three rooms have a balcony each
No smoking in LR
English spoken

Rom for 2 pers.:	**350,-**

Antal rom: 5
Deles: eit bad, to toalett, kjøken
og TV-stove

Tillegg for sengetyg:	**25,-**

Ope 20. juni - 20. aug.
Tre rom har balkong
Inga røying på stova

Zimmer für 2 Pers.:	**350,-**

Anzahl Zimmer: 5
Gemeins. Bad, zwei WCs, Küche
und Stube mit TV

Mieten von Bettwäsche:	**25,-**

Geöffnet 20. Juni - 20. Aug.
Drei Räume mit Balkon
Kein Rauchen in der Stube
Sprechen etwas Deutsch

Thue Room Rentals is situated along the fjord in the middle of Balestrand town center. The house consists of two levels in which your hostess operates a hair salon on the ground floor and the rental rooms are on the second floor. The Tourist Office is only two houses away.

Balestrand is known for the elegant, old Kvikne Hotel. There are many classic, old wooden buildings in the Kaiser Wilhelm style, built early in the 1900's, and which feature lovely gardens. The Aquarium is also worth a visit. You can rent a boat and take a ride on the fjord. The local hills have trails that are well suited for a leisurely hike.

Thue romutleige ligg ved fjorden, midt i sentrum av Balestrand. Huset er i 2 etasjar kor vertinna har frisørsalong i 1. etasje, utleigeromma er i 2. etasje. To hus nedanfor ligg turistkontoret. Balestrand er kjend for det gamle og staselege Kvikne hotell. Her er mange fine gamle trehus i Keiser Wilhilm-stil, bygd tidleg på 1900-talet, og med fine hagar. Her er også eit interessant akvarium. Det er mogeleg å leiga båt for ein tur på fjorden. I heiene omkring er det stiar og fine høve til fotturar.

Das Haus liegt in Fjordnähe, mitten im Zentrum von Balestrand. In dem zweigeschossigen Haus betreibt die Gastgeberin im Erdgeschoss einen Frisiersalon, im 1. Stock wird vermietet. Die örtliche Touristeninformation befindet sich zwei Häuser weiter. Balestrand ist bekannt für das historische und stattliche Kvikne Hotel. Darüber hinaus findet man in Balestrand viele reizvolle Holzhäuser mit schönen Gärten, die Anfang des 20. Jahrhunderts im Kaiser-Wilhelm-Stil erbaut wurden. Der Ort bietet auch ein interessantes Aquarium. Wer eine Tour auf dem Fjord unternehmen möchte, kann ein Boot mieten. In den Bergen ringsum finden Wanderfreunde gute Wanderwege.

B&B-Inn
Level of standard: ♣ ♣

NBT-member
NBT-inspected

page **160**
Sogn & Fjordane

Skilbrei Ungdomsenter

Your host:
Alfhild Bringeland

Address:
N - 6975 Skilbrei
Phone: 57 71 87 62
Fax: 57 71 87 15
Mobil: 41 50 79 33

Best time to call:
09.00 - 15.00

Double-/Twin room: **620,-**	Dobbelt-/tosengsrom: **620,-**	Doppel-/Zweibettzi.: **620,-**
Single room: **410,-**	Enkeltrom: **410,-**	Einzelzimmer: **410,-**
Family rooms: **830,-/980,-/1.190,-**	Familierom: **830,-/980,-/1.190,-**	Familienzi.: **830,-/980,-/1.190,-**
No. of rooms: 15	Antall rom: 15	Anzahl Zimmer: 15
Full breakfast	Full frokost	Volles Frühstück
Breakfast buffet	Servering: Frokostbufffét	Serv.: Frühstücksbüfett
Open 1 May - 31 Aug.	Åpent 1. mai - 31. aug.	Geöffnet 1. Mai - 31. Aug.
Terrace/deck access/yard	Terasse/uteplass/hage	Terrasse/Aussenplatz/Garten
No smoking inside	Ingen røking innendørs	Kein Rauchen im Haus
VISA, MC accepted	Vi tar VISA, MC	Wir nehmen VISA, MC
English spoken		Sprechen etwas Deutsch

Skilbrei Pensjonat offers reasonable accommodations for tourists. The hosts maintain a comfortable and domestic atmosphere.
The pension is located in an area of great natural beauty where it is possible to fish, swim and go hiking summer and winter. Here are many lovely summer pastures which are 1 - 3 hours away by foot.
An old post road runs close by.
NOTE: The inn is sometimes closed a few hours around midday.

Skilbrei Pensjonat tilbyr rimelig og enkel overnatting for turister. Vertskapet sørger for en personlig og hjemmekoselig atmosfære.
Pensjonatet ligger i et naturskjønt område med muligheter for fiske, bading og fjellturer sommer og vinter. Her er mange koselige støler innenfor 1-3 timers fottur. En gammel postvei ligger like ved.
Merk: pensjonatet kan av og til være stengt noen timer midt på dag.

Skilbrei Pensjonat bietet Touristen einfache, preiswerte Übernachtung. Die Gastgeber sorgen für eine persönliche und gemütliche Atmosphäre. Die Pension liegt landschaftlich sehr schön mit Möglichkeiten für Angeln und Baden, sowie für Bergtouren Sommer und Winter. Viele malerische Almen in 1-3 Stunden Wanderung zu erreichen.
Alter Postpfad in der Nähe.
Bitte beachten: Die Pension kann an manchen Tagen tagsüber einige Stunden geschlossen sein.

Practice what you preach. –Proverb

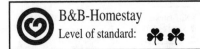
Rom i Jølster

Your host:
Halrid Sætveit

Address:
Storetrævegen 50
N - 6847 Vassenden
Phone: 57 72 74 70

Best time to call:
08.00 - 10.00 / 20.00 - 23.00

Twin room:	**500,-**	Tosengsrom:	**500,-**	Zweibettzimmer.:	**500,-**
Single room:	**250,-**	Enkeltrom:	**250,-**	Einzelzimmer:	**250,-**
No. of rooms: 2		Antall rom: 2		Anzahl Zimmer: 2	
Full breakfast		Full frokost		Volles Frühstück	
Laid breakfast table		Dekket frokostbord		Serv.: Frühstückstisch	
Open year round		Åpent hele året		Ganzjährig geöffnet	
Terrace/deck access/yard		Terrasse/uteplass/hage		Terrasse/Aussenplatz/Garten	
Bike for rent		Sykkelutleie		Fahrrad zu mieten	
Discount for children		Rabatt for barn		Ermässigung für Kinder	
Selfcatering possible		Selvhushold er mulig		Selbsthaushalt möglich	
English spoken				Sprechen Englisch	

Vassenden is located at the far end of Jølstra Lake, about 20 km east of the village Førde, along State Highway 1. Halrid's "Rom i Jølster" is situated in the upper part of a recent dwelling area, with the forest next door.

In winter, a lit trail for crosscountry skiers is just behind the house. Bjørklia Alpine Ski Center is on the opposite side of the valley. Fishing, swimming and boat rental available.

Vassenden finner du i enden av Jølstravatnet, langs riksvei 1, ca. 20 km øst for Førde. Halrids hus ligger øverst i et moderne byggefelt, med skog og friluft som nærmeste nabo.

Vinterstid er det lysløype bak huset og videre innover. Bjørklia skisenter ligger rett over dalen og har stor alpinbakke.

Fiske i elven Jølstra og bading i Jølstravatnet. Båtutleie flere steder.

Der Ort Vassenden liegt am Ende des Sees Jølstravatn an der Strasse 1, ca 20 km vor Førde. "Rom in Jølster" liegt am oberen Rand eines modernen Wohnviertels, umgeben von Wald und frischer Luft. Im Winter beginnt eine beleuchtete Skiloipe direkt hinter dem Haus. Unweit zu Bjørklia Skisenter mit grosser Alpinanlage. Angeln im Fluss und Baden im See. Bootsverleih an mehreren Stellen.

Success is having a flair for the thing that you are doing;
knowing that is not enough, you have got to have hard work
and a sense of purpose. -Margaret Thatcher

B&B-Homestay
Level of standard: ♣ ♣

NBT-member
Inspected by NBT

page **162**
Sogn & Fjordane

Årseth Hytter

Your host:
Kjellrun Årseth

Address:
N - 6847 Vassenden
Phone: 57 72 72 46
kjaarse@frisurf.no

Best time to call:
09.00 - 10.00 / 12.00 - 13.00
16.00 - 17.00 / 20.00 - 22.00

Double-/Twin room: **500,-**	Dobbelt-/tosengsrom: **500,-**	Doppel-/Zweibettzi.: **500,-**
No. of rooms: 4	Antal rom: 4	Anzahl Zimmer: 4
Full breakfast	Full frukost	Volles Frühstück
Laid breakfast table	Dekka frukostbord	Serv.: Frühstückstisch
Open year round	Ope heile året	Ganzjährig geöffnet
TV available	TV tilgjengeleg	Zugang zu TV
Terrace/deck access	Terrasse/uteplass	Terrasse/Aussenplatz
No smoking in rooms	Inga røyking på romma	Kein Rauchen im Zimmer
Some English spoken		Sprechen etwas Englisch

This farm is nestled high in a crook of the mountainside surrounding Vassenden, with an excellent view of the valley and Jølstra Lake. Try river or lake trout fishing, or go to Stardalen Valley for rafting or glacier hikes. Fields and forests entice hikers in all directions.
In Fjærland, you'll find a glacier museum, a gallery and a historical museum.
You can also enjoy driving on day trips to the quaint villages of Sogndal, Selje, Stryn, Florø or Førde.

Garden ligg høgt oppe i lia over Vassenden med flott utsikt over dalen og Jølstravatnet.
Det er mogleg å fiska aure både i elv og vatn, eller ein kan dra til Stardalen for rafting eller breturar. Skog og mark inviterer til turar på alle kanter.
I Fjærland er det isbremuseum, galleri og historisk museum. Her kan ein også reise på dagsturar med bil til Sogndal, Selje, Stryn, Florø eller Førde.

Der Hof liegt hoch oben am Hang über Vassenden mit schöner Aussicht über das Tal und den See Jølstervatn. Möglichkeit zum Forellenangeln in See und Fluss. Man kann auch nach Skardalen zum Raften oder Gletscherwandern fahren. Wald und Wiesen laden zum Wandern ein. In Fjærland gibt es ein Gletschermuseum, ein historisches Museum und man kann eine Galerie besuchen. Auch Autoausflüge nach Sogndal, Selje, Stryn, Florø oder Førde sind möglich.

Travel, in the younger sort, is a part of education; in the elder,
a part of experience. –Francis Bacon (1561 – 1626)

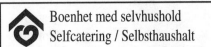
A: Guesthouse for 2-8 persons
No. of bedrooms: 3
Own bath, kitchen, LR
Price for whole unit: **500,-**

B: Cabin for 2 persons
Kitchenette
Bath in another building
Own dekk
Price for whole unit: **200,-**

Applies to all rental units:
Bed linen fee: **50,-**
Open year round
TV available
Terrace/deck access
No smoking in rooms
Some English spoken

A: Gjestehus for 2-8 personar
Antal soverom: 3
Eige bad, kjøken, stove
Pris for heile eininga: **500,-**

B: Hytte for 2 personar
Tekjøken
Bad i anna bygning
Eigen uteplass
Pris for heile eininga: **200,-**

Gjeld alle einingar:
Tillegg for sengetyg: **50,-**
Ope heile året
TV tilgjengeleg
Terrasse/uteplass
Inga røyking på romma

A: Gästehaus für 2-8 Personen
Anzahl Schlafräume: 3
Eig. Bad, Küche, Stube
Ganze Einheit: **500,-**

B: Hütte für 2 Personen
Kleine Küche
Bad in anderen Gebäude
Eig. Aussenplatz
Ganze Einheit: **200,-**

Gilt für alle Einheiten:
Mieten von Bettwäsche: **50,-**
Ganzjährig geöffnet
Zugang zu TV
Terrasse/Aussenplatz
Kein Rauchen im Zimmer
Sprechen etwas Englisch

Directions:
Centrally located between Bergen and Ålesund about 4 hours drive from either city. 20 km from both Førde and Skei in Jølster. Alongside E-39 in the direction of Førde, about 500 m from the end of Jølstravatnet Lake and Jølster Hotel, look for the sign for "Årseth Hytter". Continue about 1 km up the curvy road.

Vegforklaring:
Lægje midt mellom Bergen og Ålesund, - ca. 4 timar med bil til kvar by. 20 km frå Førde og 20 km til Skei i Jølster. Langs E-39 i retning Førde, ca. 500 meter frå enden av Jølstravantet og Jølster Hotell, finn du skiltet "Årseth Hytter". Du følgjer dette 1 km opp på svingete veg.

Wegbeschreibung:
Årseth liegt auf halbem Wege zwischen Bergen und Ålesund, von beiden ca. 4 Autostunden entfernt. Der Ort ist ca. 20 km von Førde und 20 km von Skei i Jølster entfernt. Anreise entlang der E-39 in Richtung Førde. Ca. 500 vom Ende des Sees Jølstravatnet und vom Jølster Hotel entfernt der Beschilderung "Årseth Hytter" folgen. Der Weg führt ca. 1 km eine kurvige Straße hinauf.

Von
Rom & Frokost

Your host:
Anny Eikås Strømmen

Address:
Michael Sarsgate 23
N - 6900 Florø
Phone: 57 74 14 46

Best time to call:
15.00 - 22.00

Twin room:	**550,-**	Tosengsrom:	**550,-**	Zweibettzimmer:	**550,-**
1 pers. in twin room:	**350,-**	1 pers. i tosengsrom:	**350,-**	1 Pers. im Zweibettzi.:	**350,-**
No. of rooms: 3		Antal rom: 3		Anzahl Zimmer: 3	
Full breakfast		Full frukost		Volles Frühstück	
Laid breakfast table		Dekka frukostbord		Serv.: Frühstückstisch	
Open 1 June - 31 Aug.		Ope 1. juni - 31. aug.		Geöffnet 1. Juni - 31. Aug.	
TV available		TV tilgjengeleg		Zugang zu TV	
Terrace/deck access		Terrasse/uteplass		Terrasse/Aussenplatz	
No smoking inside		Inga røyking innomhus		Kein Rauchen im Haus	
Discount for children		Rabatt for born		Ermässigung für Kinder	
English spoken				Sprechen etwas Deutsch	

Florø, a city community where visitors can enjoy the smell of salt water and coastal Norway. Here you are close to the majestic ocean, inviting you from just beyond the small islands and skerries. Anny welcomes guests to her row house built in 1994. The house is easily found 10 min. walk from the bus station and 2 min. from city center. A beautiful setting and an old neighborhood give the area its special character. We recommend visitors to Florø to take a day-trip by boat to the island Kinn west of Florø. Here you can see Kinnakyrkja, a Romanesque stone church from the middle ages and connected to the legend of St. Sunniva and the Selje men.

Florø, bysamfunnet som får besøkande til å kjenne lukta av saltvatn og norsk hav. Her ligg sjølvaste "storhavet" rett utanfor holmane og skjæra og lurer. Anny tek imot gjester i sitt rekkjehus bygd i 1994. Huset finn du i 10 minutters gange frå bussstasjonen, og 2 min. frå sentrum. Vakre omgjevnader og eit gammalt villastrøk pregar området rundt. Er du i Florø, kan vi anbefale ein dagstur med båt til øya Kinn vest for Florø. Her finn du Kinnakyrkja, ei romansk steinkyrkje frå middelalderen knytta til legenden om St. Sunniva og Seljumennene.

Florø ist genau der richtige Ort für alle Urlauber, die Meeresluft und die norwegische Küste mögen. Genau hier, jenseits der Schären und kleinen Inseln, beginnt der Nordatlantik. Die Gastgeberin Anny empfängt ihre Gäste in einem Reihenhaus von 1994. Das Haus liegt nur 10 Minuten Fußweg von der Bushaltestelle entfernt (2 Min. z. Zentrum). Die Umgebung ist von reizvollen alten Villen geprägt. Wer Florø besucht, sollte eine Tagestour mit dem Boot zur Insel Kinn westlich der Stadt nicht versäumen. Hier steht die "Kinnakyrkja", eine romantische Steinkirche aus dem Mittelalter, an der die Legende von der Heiligen Sunniva und den Seljemännern anknüpft.

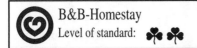
Stranda
Rom & Frukost

Your host:
Liv & Reidunn Byrkjeland

Address:
Strandavegen
N - 6900 Florø
Phone: **57 74 06 23 / 57 74 25 65**
Fax: **57 74 06 61**
Mobil: **99 22 96 29 / 48 13 11 88**
E-mail: **stranda@adel.no**
Web: **http://adel.no/stranda**

Best time to call:
08.00 - 11.00 / 18.00 - 22.00

Double room:	**550,-**	Dobbeltrom:	**550,-**	Doppelzimmer:	**550,-**
Single room:	**350,-**	Enkeltrom:	**350,-**	Einzelzimmer:	**350,-**
No. of rooms: 4		Antal rom: 4		Anzahl Zimmer: 4	
Full breakfast		Full frukost		Volles Frühstück	
Laid breakfast table		Dekka frukostbord		Serv.: Frühstückstisch	
Open 15 June - 15 Aug.		Ope 15. juni - 15. aug.		Geöffnet 15. Juni - 15. Aug.	
Open weekends 15 Aug. - 1 Oct.		Ope helgar 15. aug - 1. okt		Wochenenden 15. Aug. - 1. Okt.	
TV available		TV tilgjengeleg		Zugang zu TV	
Terrace/yard		Terrasse/uteplass		Terrasse/Aussenplatz	
No smoking inside		Inga røyking innomhus		Kein Rauchen im Haus	
Discount for children, min. 2 nights		Rabatt for born (min. 2 netter)		Ermässigung für Kinder	
Clothes-washing service		Klesvask kan ordnast		Wäschewaschservice	
English and some French				Sprechen etwas Deutsch	

Florø is the town in Norway which lies on an island furthest to the west, at the end of Route 5. The area has 11,300 inhabitants.

The sisters Liv and Reidunn share a semi-detached house, located only 500 m from the boat terminal and the town center, and 300 m from the busstation.

Here you can fish, go on a lighthouse safari or boat-trip to the islands. Kinnakyrkja (church) and the Coastal Museum are also well worth a visit. You will also enjoy excellent walks near downtown and your hostess Liv will happily take her guests on a walking tour of the area.

Florø er den vestlegaste byen i Noreg og ligg på ei øy ved enden av riksveg 5. Bykommunen har 11.300 innbyggjarar.

Systrene Liv og Reidunn Byrkjeland deler ein tomannsbustad, bygd i 1994. Den ligg berre 500 m frå båtterminalen og sentrum, og 300 m frå busstasjonen.

Her er tilbod om fiske, fyrsafari og båtturar til øyane. Kinnakyrkja og kystmuseet er og vel verd eit besøk.

Her er fint turterreng nær sentrum, og Liv tek gjerne med gjester på fotturar.

Florø ist die westlichste Stadt Norwegens, auf einer Insel, am Ende der Strasse 5. Die Stadt hat 11.300 Einwohner.

Die Schwestern Liv und Reidunn Byrkjeland teilen ein Zweifamilienhaus, gebaut 1994, 500 m vom Zentrum, nahe Schiffsterminal und Busstation.

Angebote: Angeln, Leuchtturmsafari, Bootstouren zu den Inseln. Einen Besuch wert sind auch Küstenmuseum und Kirche Kinnakyrkja. Schönes Wandergebiet in Ortsnähe. Die Gastgeberin Liv nimmt Gäste mit zum Wandern.

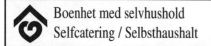
Friheten

Your host:
Dagfinn Giil

Address:
Strandavegen
N - 6900 Florø
Mobil: **90 82 25 77**

Best time to call:
08.00 - 11.00 / 18.00 - 22.00

Room for 2 pers.:	**450,-**	Rom for 2 pers.:	**450,-**	Zimmer für 2 Pers.:	**450,-**
Extra mattress:	**125,-**	Ekstra madrass:	**125,-**	Extramatratzen:	**125,-**
No. of bedrooms: 2		Antal rom: 2		Anzahl Zimmer: 2	
Shared bath, kitchen, LR		Delt bad, kjøken, stove		Gemeins. Bad, Küche, Stube	
Bed linen included		Sengetyg er inkludert		Inkl. Bettwäsche	
Open year round		Ope heile året		Ganzjährig geöffnet	
TV available		TV tilgjengeleg		Zugang zu TV	
Yard/terrace/deck access		Hage/terrasse/uteplass		Garten/Terrasse/Aussenplatz	
No smoking inside		Inga røyking innomhus		Kein Rauchen im Haus	
English spoken				Sprechen Englisch	

You will find "Friheten" (Freedom) on a quiet street with minimal traffic, only 40 m from the sea with a view of the harbor. Guests enjoy access to the entire house, which can accommodate groups up to 6 persons or each room may be rented out separately where guests share the common room.

I ei stille gate utan nevneverdig trafikk, berre 40 m frå sjøen og med utsikt over hamna finn du "Friheten". Gjestene får nytta heile boligen, den kan husa ei gruppe på opptil 6 personer, eller kvart rom leiges ut for seg og fellesromma deles.

In einer ruhigen Straße ohne besonderen Verkehr, nur 40 m vom Meer entfernt und mit Aussicht auf den Hafen, liegt "Friheten" (Freiheit). Die Gäste können die gesamte Wohnung nutzen, die bis zu 6 Personen faßt. Alternativ kann auch jedes Zimmer für sich vermietet werden. Der Gemeinschaftsraum steht dann allen zur Verfügung.

> The people who try to do something and fail are infinitely better than those who try to do nothing and succeed.
> -Lloyd James

Eltvik Havstover

Your host:
Aslaug Mikkelsen

Address:
Eltvik
N - 6750 Stadtlandet
Phone: **57 85 98 89**
Fax: **57 85 98 89**
Mobil: **91 69 44 43**

Best time to call:
09.00 - 23.00

Double-/Twin room:	**600,-**	Dobbelt-/tosengsrom:	**600,-**	Doppel-/Zweibettzi.:	**600,-**
Single room:	**300,-**	Enkeltrom:	**300,-**	Einzelzimmer:	**300,-**
No. of rooms: 2		Antall rom: 2		Anzahl Zimmer: 2	
Full breakfast		Full frokost		Volles Frühstück	
Laid breakfast table		Dekket frokostbord		Serv.: Frühstückstisch	
Open year round		Åpent hele året		Ganzjährig geöffnet	
TV available		TV tilgjengelig		Zugang zu TV	
Terrace/yard		Terrasse/hage		Terrasse/Garten	
Boat for rent		Båtutleie		Boot zu mieten	
No smoking inside		Ingen røking innendørs		Kein Rauchen im Haus	
Discount off season		Rabatt utenom sesong		Rabatt Nebensaison	
Selfcatering possible		Selvhushold er mulig		Selbsthaushalt möglich	
Some English spoken				Sprechen etwas Englisch	

Aslaug and her family extend hearty welcomes to people visiting this holiday paradise located between mountains and the ocean. The fishing possibilities are many; both from the shore and by boat. For anyone preferring both feet on dry land, hiking in the beautiful mountain areas is a better choice. Eltvikbakken has been in Aslaug's family for six generations. It is located to the north of Stadtlandet and overlooking the ocean.

Aslaug og familie ønsker gjester hjertelig velkommen til dette ferieparadiset mellom fjell og hav. Fiskemulighetene er mange både fra strandkanten og fra båt. For landkrabber kan fjellturer være mer fristende i flott natur og frisk og ren havluft.
Eltvikbakken har vært i Aslaugs familie i seks generasjoner. Den ligger helt nord på Stadtlandet og vender ut mot Storhavet.

Familie Mikkelsen heisst Gäste zu diesem Urlaubsparadies zwischen Gebirge und Meer herzlich willkommen. Ausgezeichnete Angelmöglichkeiten von Strand und Boot. Die herrliche Umgebung lädt zu Bergwanderungen in frischer, reiner Meeresluft ein. Eltvikbakken liegt nördlich von Stadtlandet, gegen das Meer gewendet. Aslaug und Familie sind die 6. Generation auf dem Hof.

Haste is only good for catching flies. –Origin unknown

B&B-Inn
Level of standard: ♣ ♣ ♣

NBT-member
NBT-inspected

page **168**
Sogn & Fjordane

Hammersvik Gjestehus

Your host:
Doris & Jan Hammersvik

Address:
N - 6740 Selje
Phone: **57 85 62 63**
Fax: **57 85 67 60**

Best time to call:
08.00 - 21.00

Double room:	**600,-**	Dobbeltrom:	**600,-**	Doppelzimmer:	**600,-**
1 pers. in dbl. room:	**500,-**	1 pers. i dobbeltrom:	**500,-**	1 Pers. im Doppelzi.:	**500,-**
No. of rooms: 3		Antal rom: 3		Anzahl Zimmer: 3	
Full breakfast		Full frukost		Volles Frühstück	
Breakfast buffet		Servering: Frukostbufét		Serv.: Frühstücksbüfett	
Open 1 May - 30 Sept.		Ope 1. mai - 30. sept.		Geöffnet 1. Mai - 30. Sept.	
TV available		TV tilgjengeleg		Zugang zu TV	
Yard/garden		Hage		Garten	
Boat for rent		Båtutleige		Boot zu mieten	
No smoking in rooms		Inga røyking på romma		Kein Rauchen im Zimmer	
Some English spoken				Sprechen Deutsch	

Hammersvik Gjestehus is located in Selje, in Nordfjord, in far western Norway and toward the open sea. Here you'll see the changing patterns of nature alongside some of the country's oldest historic monuments, including the ruins of Benedictine's Convent from 1103. Near Vestkapp, white beaches are found amidst green inlets.
The rooms are in a recently renovated house. The hosts run a farm and guest house side by side. Jan runs a boat route to Selje cloister.

Hammersvik Gjestehus ligg i Selje, i Nordfjord, heilt ute mot ope hav, lengst vest i Noreg. Her er ein særprega, skiftande natur og nokre av dei eldste kulturhistoriske minna i landet. Selje var eit av dei tre første bispeseta i landet, her er ruinane etter Benedictiner Kloster frå år 1103.
I områda rundt Vestkapp finn ein kritkvite strender langs grøne viker.
Romma er i det nyrestaurerte kårhuset på garden. Vertskapet driv gard og gjestehus ilag. Jan driv båtturar til Selje Kloster.

Hammersvik Gästehaus liegt in Selje, Nordfjord, an Norwegens äusserster Westküste. Sie finden eine gewaltige und abwechslungsreiche Natur, weisse Sandstrände an grünen Buchten, alte kulturhistorische Stätten.
Besuchen Sie in Selje, einem der 3 frühesten Bischofssitze im Lande, die Ruinen eines Benediktinerklosters von 1103.
Sie wohnen im restaurierten Haus auf dem Hof von Doris (aus Deutschl.) und Jan. Jan veranstaltet Boottouren zum Selje Kloster.

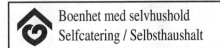
Huset Vårt overnatting

Your host:
Kjellaug Haugen
& Aashild Sætren

Address:
N - 6761 Hornindal
Phone: 57 87 94 82
Fax: 57 87 94 56
Mobil: 90 67 68 45
E-mail: husetvaart@c2i.net

Best time to call:
10.00 - 14.00

Room for 2 pers.:	**320,-**	Rom for 2 pers.:	**320,-**	Zimmer für 2 Pers.:	**320,-**
Room for 1 pers.:	**160,-**	Rom for 1 pers.:	**160,-**	Zimmer für 1 Pers.:	**160,-**
Shared bath, kitchen, LR		Delt bad, kjøken, stove		Gemeinsch. Bad, Küche, Stube	
Bed linen fee:	**50,-**	Tillegg for sengetyg:	**50,-**	Mieten von Bettwäsche:	**50,-**
No. of rooms: 4		Antal rom: 4		Anzahl Zimmer: 4	
Open year round		Ope heile året		Ganzjährig geöffnet	
TV available		TV tilgjengeleg		Zugang zu TV	
Terrace/dekk access		Terrasse/uteplass		Terrasse/Aussenplatz	
No smoking inside		Inga røyking innomhus		Kein Rauchen im Haus	
Breakfast service available:	**60,-**	Frukost kan serverast:	**60,-**	Frühstück auf Bestellung:	**60,-**
Other meals available		Andre måltider kan bestellast		Andere Mahlzeiten auf Anfrage	
Some English spoken				Sprechen etwas Englisch	

Huset Vårt is a multi-activity house. The structure consists of an old log house in neo-classic style with pleasant atmosphere, which has been renovated during recent years. Our House is operated by a property management group that bids guests welcome all year round. Central location faciliates day-trips to Geiranger, Briksdalsbreen, Vestkapp and Ålesund. Hornindalen is rich in folk music, woodcarving and traditional crafts with museums and galleries. Svor Museum is next door. Hornindalsvatnet is Europe's deepest lake. Fine hiking trails and dairies in the mountains.

Huset Vårt er eit allaktivitetshus. Bygningen er eit gamalt tømmerhus i nyklassisistisk stil med triveleg atmosfære og som i seinere år er pussa opp. Huset blir drive av ei driftsgruppe som tar imot gjester heile året.
Ein sentral overnattingsstad for dagsturar til Geiranger, Briksdalsbreen, Vestkapp og Ålesund. Hornindalen er rik på folkemusikktradisjonar, treskjering og kunsthandverk. Her er museum og galleri. Svormuseet ligg like ved. Hornindalsvatnet er den djupaste innsjøen i Europa. Turbåtar om sommeren. Fint turterreng og fine gamle setrer inne på fjellet.

Huset Vårt ist ein Betrieb mit zahlreichen Aktivitätsmöglichkeiten. Es handelt sich um ein renoviertes, altes Blockhaus im neuklassizistischen Stil. Einladende Atmosphäre, das ganze Jahr über für Gäste geöffnet.
Zentrale Lage für Tagestouren nach Geiranger, Briksdalsbreen, Vestkap und Ålesund. Hornindal bietet Kunsthandwerk, Volksmusiktradition, Holzschnitzerei, Galerie und Museum (in der Nähe Svor-Museum). Hornindalsvatnet ist Europas tiefster Binnensee. Schiffsverkehr im Sommer. Herrliche Wandergegend mit schönen, alten Almen.

B&B-Inn
Level of standard: ♣ ♣

NBT-member
NBT-inspected

page **170**
Sogn & Fjordane

Skipenes Gard

Your host:
Sigdis Skipenes
& Arild Andersen

Address:
N - 6770 Nordfjordeid
Phone: **57 86 08 24**
Fax: **57 86 00 89**
Mobil: **40 20 09 26**
E-mail: **aria@online.no**

Best time to call:
10.00 - 18.00 / 20.00 - 22.00

Double-/Twin room:	**600,-**	Dobbelt-/tosengsrom:	**600,-**	Doppel-/Zweibettzi.:	**600,-**
1 pers. in double room:	**500,-**	1 pers. i dobbeltrom:	**500,-**	1 Pers. im Doppelzi.:	**500,-**
Single room:	**400,-**	Enkeltrom:	**400,-**	Einzelzimmer:	**400,-**
No. of rooms: 5		Antal rom: 5		Anzahl Zimmer: 5	
Full breakfast		Full frukost		Volles Frühstück	
Laid breakfast table		Dekka frukostbord		Serv.: Frühstückstisch	
Open year round		Ope heile året		Ganzjährig geöffnet	
TV available		TV tilgjengeleg		Zugang zu TV	
Terrace/deck access/yard		Terrasse/uteplass/hage		Terrasse/Aussenplatz/Garten	
Boat for rent		Båtutleige		Boot zu mieten	
No smoking inside		Inga røyking innomhus		Kein Rauchen im Haus	
VISA accepted		Vi tek VISA		Wir nehmen VISA	
Discount for children		Rabatt for born		Ermässigung für Kinder	
English spoken				Sprechen Deutsch	

An old farm typical of the West Coast of Norway, with the dwelling house dating back to the 18th and 19th centuries. Breakfast is served in the formal dining room which has been restored to the old style.

This farm features milk production and you can even get to participate and get to know the animals. Horseback riding can also be arranged. Skipenes Gard lies 800 m from Nordfjordeid city center, close to a salmon river called Eidselva.

Ein gamal vestlandsgard med hus frå 1700- og 1800-talet. Frukost serverast i bestestova som er restaurert i gamal stil.

Dei driv mjølkeproduksjon på garden, og du kan få vere med og helse på dyra. Tur med hest kan også formidlast.

Skipenes Gard ligg 800 meter frå Nordfjordeid sentrum, like ved den laseførande Eidselva.

Ein alter Vestlands-Hof mit Gebäuden aus dem 18. und 19. Jh. Frühstück wird in der "guten Stube" serviert, die in altem Stil restauriert ist.

Auf dem Hof wird Milchproduktion betrieben. Wer mag, kann mithelfen und die Tiere kennenlernen. Darüber hinaus können Reittouren organisiert werden. Skipenes Gard liegt 800 m von Nordfjordeid Zentrum entfernt, direkt am Lachsfluß Eidselva.

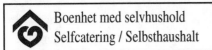
A: Apartment for 2-4 persons
No. of bedrooms: 2
Own bath, kitchen, LR
Price for whole unit: **800,-**

B: 2 Cabins for 2-5 persons
No. of bedrooms: 2
Own bath, kitchen, LR
Price for whole unit: **1.000,-**

Discount for unused bed: **-50,-**
Bed linen included
Open year round
TV available
Terrace/deck access/yard/garden
Boat and bike for rent
No smoking inside
VISA accepted
Discount for children
Breakfast service available: **60,-**
English spoken

A: Husvære for 2-4 personar
Antal soverom: 2
Eige bad, kjøken, stove
Pris for heile eininga: **800,-**

B: 2 Hytter for 2-5 personar
Antal soverom: 2
Eige bad, kjøken, stove
Pris for heile eininga: **1.000,-**

Avslag pr. seng ikkje i bruk: **-50,-**
Sengetøy er inkludert
Ope heile året
TV tilgjengeleg
Terrasse/uteplass/hage
Båt- og sykkelutleige
Inga røyking innomhus
Vi tek VISA
Rabatt for born
Frukost kan serverast: **60,-**

A: Wohnung für 2-4 Pers.
Anzahl Schlafräume: 2
Eig. Bad, Küche, Stube
Ganze Einheit: **800,-**

B: 2 Hütten für 2-5 Personen
Anzahl Schlafräume: 2
Eig. Bad, Küche, Stube
Ganze Einheit: **1.000,-**

Ermäss.f. nicht gebrauch. Bett **-50,-**
Inkl. Bettwäsche
Ganzjährig geöffnet
Zugang zu TV
Terrasse/Aussenplatz/Garten
Boot und Fahrrad zu mieten
Kein Rauchen im Haus
Wir nehmen VISA
Ermässigung für Kinder
Frühstück auf Bestellung: **60,-**
Sprechen Deutsch

Directions:
From Førde: The distance to Nordfjordeid is 108 km. Take E-39 northward to the ferry dock for Anda - Lote. Continue from Lote and drive through a tunnel. After the downgrade following the tunnel, make a right turn before coming to the bridge. Skipenes Gard is 100 m from the bridge on the left side.

Vegforklaring:
Frå Førde: Kjøyr E-39 nordover. Avstand til Nordfjordeid er 108 km. Turen inkluderer fergestrekninga Anda - Lote. Etter Lote kjøyrer du gjennom ein tunell, så kjem ei nerstigning etter tunellen. Etter bakkane ser du ei bru, sving til høgre før brua. Skipenes Gard ligg 100 m frå brua, på venstre side av vegen.

Wegbeschreibung:
Von Førde aus sind es 108 km bis Nordfjordeid. Fahren Sie auf der E 39 in Richtung Norden. Von Anda nach Lote verkehrt eine Fähre. Von Lote aus führt die Strecke durch einen Tunnel. Nach dem Gefälle hinter dem Tunnel biegen Sie vor der Brücke rechts ab. Ca. 100 m weiter liegt auf der linken Seite Skipenes Gard.

One hour's sleep before midnight, is worth two after.
–Proverb

Laugh and the world laughs with you; snore and you sleep alone.
–Anthony Burgess

After all, tomorrow is another day.
–Margaret Mitchell

Loen pensjonat

Your host:
Erik & Åsta Bødal

Address:
N - 6789 Loen
Phone: 57 87 76 24
Fax: 57 87 76 78
Mobil: 94 55 29 92
E-mail: post@loen-pensjonat.com
Web: http://loen-pensjonat.com

Best time to call:
08.00 - 12.00 / 17.00 - 23.00

Double-/Twin room:	**450,-**	Dobbelt-/tosengsrom:	**450,-**	Doppel-/Zweibettzi.:	**450,-**
Single room:	**250,-/300,-**	Enkeltrom:	**250,-/300,-**	Einzelzimmer:	**250,-/300,-**
No. of rooms: 10		Antall rom: 10		Anzahl Zimmer: 10	
Full breakfast		Full frukost		Volles Frühstück	
Breakfast buffet		Servering: Frukostbufét		Serv.: Frühstücksbüfett	
Open 20 May - 10 Sept.		Ope 20. mai - 10. sept.		Geöffnet 20. Mai - 10. Sept.	
TV available		TV tilgjengeleg		Zugang zu TV	
Terrace/garden		Terrasse/uteplass/hage		Terrasse/Aussenplatz/Garten	
Boat for rent		Båtutleige		Boot zu mieten	
Bike for rent		Sykkelutleige		Fahrrad zu mieten	
No smoking inside		Inga røyking innomhus		Kein Rauchen im Haus	
Discount for children		Rabatt for born		Ermässigung für Kinder	
English spoken				Sprechen Deutsch	

Loen Pensjonat is 400 m from the centre of Loen, with a wonderful view of the fjord. The main building dates back to 1910 with several modern additions. There was an inn here from 1910-1940, and from 1956 until the present. A large garden surrounds the house. Beautiful hiking country and good fishing. There are sheep on the farm. Possibilities for glacier trekking.
Directions:
Loen is located 10 km from Stryn - towards Førde. Exit towards Lodalen in Loen and drive about 500 m. The guest house is situated just near the church in Loen.

Loen Pensjonat ligg 400 m frå sentrum, med fin utsikt over fjorden. Hovudbygninga er frå 1910 med fleire nyare tilbygg. Her har det vore dreve pensjonat i åra 1910-1940 og frå 1956 og fram til i dag. Ein stor hage ligg ikring huset.
På garden driv dei sauehald. Flott turterreng og gode høve for fiske. Muligheter for brevandring.

Vegforklaring:
Loen ligg 10 km frå Stryn i retning Førde. Ta av mot Lodalen i Loen og kjør ca. 500 m mot Lodalen. Pensjonatet ligg like ved kyrkja i Loen.

Loen Pensjonat liegt 400 m vom Zentrum Loen. Schöne Aussicht auf den Fjord. Die Pension ist von einem großen Garten umgeben. Das Hauptgebäude stammt von 1910. Schafzucht auf dem Hof. Herrliches Wandergelände. In der Nähe gute Möglichkeiten zum Angeln und zu Gletscherwanderungen.
Wegbeschreibung:
Loen liegt 10 km von Stryn entfernt in Richtung Førde. Biegen Sie dort in Richtung "Lodalen" ab und folgen Sie der Straße ca. 500 m geradeaus. Die Pension liegt in unmittelbarer Nähe der Kirche von Loen.

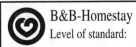
Olden romutleie

Your host:
Solbjørg Sætren

Address:
Olden
N - 6870 Olden
Phone: 57 87 31 93 / 57 87 25 02
Fax: 57 87 34 10 / 57 87 25 04

Best time to call:
08.00 - 23.00

Double room:	**390,-**	Dobbeltrom:	**390,-**	Doppelzimmer:	**390,-**
Single room:	**250,-**	Enkeltrom:	**250,-**	Einzelzimmer:	**250,-**

No. of rooms: 4	Antall rom: 4	Anzahl Zimmer: 4
Full breakfast	Full frokost	Volles Frühstück
Breakfast tray or buffet	Serv.: Frokostbrett eller -buffét	Serv.: Frühstückstablett o. -büfett
Open 1 May - 1 October	Åpent 1. mai - 1. okt.	Geöffnet 1. Mai - 1. Okt.
TV available	TV tilgjengelig	Zugang zu TV
Terrace/garden	Terrasse/uteplass/hage	Terrasse/Aussenplatz/Garten
Boat and bikes for rent	Båt- og sykkelutleie	Boot und Fahrrad zu mieten
Discount for children	Rabatt for barn	Ermässigung für Kinder
Selfcatering possible	Selvhushold er mulig	Selbsthaushalt möglich
Laundry facilities	Mulighet for klesvask	Zugang zu Waschmaschine
Some English spoken		Sprechen etwas Deutsch

Olden is located in the depths of Nordfjord. Daily tours to Olden's Historic Church and the gallery of a local painter.
"Isabella" is a boat taking tourists fishing several times a day. You can also take a bus 20 km to the Briksdalbreen Glacier where you'll find a restaurant, riding and a souvenir shop. Throughout the Olden area there are marked hiking trails.
Olden Room Rentals is centrally located in relation to the main highway, dock, bus stop, gas station and restaurant.

Olden ligger lengst inne i Nordfjord. Det er daglige omvisninger i Olden Gamle kirke og i heimen til en kunstmaler, hvor det også er utstilling.
Båten "Isabella" går flere ganger om dagen og tar turister med på fjordfiske. Det går også buss til Briksdalsbreen hvor det, foruten isbreen, er serveringssted, hesteskyss og suvenirforretning. Det er ellers oppmerkede stier for fotturister over hele Olden.
Olden romutleie ligger sentralt i forhold til hovedvei, kai, bussholdeplass, bensinstasjon og restaurant.

Der Ort Olden liegt am Ende des Nordfjords. Tägliche Führungen in der alten Kirche in Olden und in der Ausstellung eines lokalen Malers.
Auf dem Nordfjord nimmt das Schiff "Isabella" mehrmals täglich Touristen zum Fischfang mit. 20 Min. Busfahrt zum Briksdalsgletscher mit Pferdekutschen, Imbisslokal und Andenkenladen. Gut markierte Wanderpfade.
Olden Romutleie bietet eine zentrale Lage in der Nähe von Hauptstraße, Anlegestelle, Bushaltestelle,Tankstelle und Restaurant.

B&B-Inn
Level of standard: ♣ ♣

NBT-member
NBT-inspected

page **174**
Sogn & Fjordane

Trollbu

Your host:
Signe Aabrekk

Address:
N - 6791 Oldedalen
Phone: 57 87 38 38
Fax: 57 87 34 96
Mobil: 91 38 25 69
E-mail: sign-aab@online.no

Best time to call:
09.00 - 23.00

Twin room:	**500,-**	Tosengsrom:	**500,-**	Zweibettzimmer:	**500,-**
1 pers. in double room:	**400,-**	1 pers. i dobbeltrom:	**400,-**	1 Pers. im Doppelzi.:	**400,-**
No. of rooms: 2		Antal rom: 2		Anzahl Zimmer: 2	
Full breakfast		Full frukost		Volles Frühstück	
Laid breakfast table		Dekka frukostbord		Serv.: Frühstückstisch	
Open year round		Ope heile året		Ganzjährig geöffnet	
Terrace/deck access/yard		Terrasse/uteplass/hage		Terrasse/Aussenplatz/Garten	
Boat for rent		Båtutleige		Boot zu mieten	
No smoking in rooms		Inga røyking på romma		Kein Rauchen im Zimmer	
Member of Norsk Gardsmat		Medlem av Norsk Gardsmat		Mitglied v. Norsk Gardsmat	
Some English spoken				Sprechen etwas Deutsch	

Trollbu is on the Aabrekk farm in Oldedalen, Stryn. Three generations live on the dairy and meat farm, Signe and Rune, five children and grandparents.
The courtyard has 3 houses, one from 1992 and 2 newly restored houses from the 1700's and 1800's. The farm cafe sells coffee, traditional food and local handicrafts.
Guests are welcome to visit the farm and ride ponies. Take horse and cart rides to Briksdal glacier, hikes on Jostedal glacier, or go fishing or mountain hiking.

Trollbutunet ligg på garden Aabrekk i Oldedalen, Stryn. På garden bur tre generasjonar, Signe og Rune, fem born og besteforeldre.
Garden er i full drift med mjølke- og kjøtproduksjon. Trollbutunet består av tre hus, eitt frå 1992 og to eldre hus frå 1700- og 1800-talet som er nyrestaurerte.
Gardskafé med sal av tradisjonsrik mat, kaffi og husflid produsert i dalen.
Familien Aabrekk tek imot gjester på gardsbesøk; vitjing i fjøset og høve til å ri på fjordhest. Tur med hest og kjerre til Briksdalsbreen, bretur på Jostedalsbreen, fiske i vatn og merka turstier i fjellheimen.

Trollbutunet besteht aus zwei völlig restaurierten Häusern aus dem 18. Und 19. Jh., sowie einem Haus aus 1992. Die Häuser liegen auf dem Hof Aabrekk in Oldedalen, bei Stryn. Milch- und Viehwirtschaft. Auf dem Hof leben drei Generationen. Kaffee und Traditionskost, sowie Heimkunst werden im Cafe auf dem Hof angeboten. Die Familie bietet Hofbesichtigung, Reiten auf Fjordpferd, Ausflüge mit Pferd und Wagen zum Briksdals-Gletscher, sowie Touren auf dem Jostedalsgletscher an. Angeln in Bergseen und markierte Wanderstrecken in den Bergen.

Kneiken
Romutleie

Your host:
Ingebjørg Slyngstadli

Address:
Kneiken 2
N - 6007 Ålesund
Phone: 70 12 82 68
Mobil: 92 60 22 90

Best time to call:
09.00 - 23.00

Room for 2 pers.:	**400,-**	Rom for 2 pers.:	**400,-**	Zimmer für 2 Pers.:	**400,-**
Room for 1 pers.:	**300,-**	Rom for 1 pers.:	**300,-**	Zimmer für 1 Pers.:	**300,-**
One night stay only; add:	**50,-**	Ettdøgnstillegg:	**50,-**	Zuschlag f. 1 Tag:	**50,-**
No. of rooms: 2		Antall rom: 2		Anzahl Zimmer: 2	
Bed linen included		Sengetøy er inkludert		Inkl. Bettwäsche	
Shared bath and kitchen		Delt bad og kjøkken		Gemeins. Bad u. Küche	
Open year round		Åpent hele året		Ganzjährig geöffnet	
TV in rooms		TV på rom		TV im Zimmer	
Some English spoken				Sprechen etwas Englisch	

Kneiken lies on the hillside of the mountain that towers over Ålesund. A 10 min. walk brings you to Fjellstua where a unique panorama is revealed.
The place is a good base for day trips. The town center is only 20 min. walk away.
Ålesund lies on three islands, with a canal straight through the center. The town is best known for its architecture, in Jugend style.
Ålesund was reconstructed by the German emperor Wilhelm after being destroyed by the great fire in 1904.

Kneiken ligger i ås-siden av by-fjellet som kneiser over Ålesund. Det er 10 min. gange til Fjellstua hvor det åpenbarer seg en panoramautsikt av de sjeldne.
Stedet egner seg godt som utgangspunkt for dagsturer. Det er 20 min. gangavstand til sentrum.
Ålesund ligger på tre øyer med en kanal tvers gjennom sentrum. Byen er mest kjent for sin arkitektur, gjennomført i jugend-stil. Byen ble gjenreist av den tyske keiser Wilhelm etter den store by-brannen i 1904.

Kneiken liegt am Hang des Stadtbergs, der sich über Ålesund erhebt. 10 Min. Wanderung zum Restaurant Fjellstua mit einzigartiger Panoramaaussicht.
Günstige Lage für Tagesausflüge. 20 Min. zum Zentrum.
Ålesund liegt verteilt auf drei Inseln, wobei ein Kanal direkt durch das Zentrum verläuft. Die Stadt ist aufgrund ihrer einheitlichen Jugendstilbauten bekannt, die der deutsche Kaiser Wilhelm II nach dem grossen Stadtbrand 1904 errichten liess.

Early to bed and early to rise,
makes a man healthy, wealthy and wise.
–Proverb

Rønneberg Gard

Your host:
Astrid Ytreeide

Address:
Rønneberg
N - 6215 Eidsdal
Phone/Fax: 70 25 90 18
Mobil: 90 67 20 89

Best time to call:
07.00 - 12.00 / 20.00 - 23.00

Double room:	**500,-**	Dobbeltrom:	**500,-**	Doppelzimmer:	**500,-**
Twin room:	**450,-**	Tosengsrom:	**450,-**	Zweibettzimmer:	**450,-**
Single room:	**300,-**	Enkeltrom:	**300,-**	Einzelzimmer:	**300,-**
No. of rooms: 4		Antall rom: 4		Anzahl Zimmer: 4	
Full breakfast		Full frokost		Volles Frühstück	
Laid breakfast table		Dekket frokostbord		Serv.: Frühstückstisch	
Open 1 May - 10 August		Åpent 1. mai - 10. aug.		Geöffnet 1. Mai - 10. Aug.	
TV available		TV tilgjengelig		Zugang zu TV	
Terrace/yard		Terrasse/uteplass/hage		Terrasse/Aussenplatz/Garten	
No smoking inside		Ingen røking innendørs		Kein Rauchen im Haus	
English spoken				Sprechen etwas Deutsch	

Rønneberg Farm is located 7 km from Eidsdal city center along the highway to Geiranger. This mountain farm lies 420 meters above sea level and enjoys plenty of sunlight. The farm is situated on a side-trail 3 km from the spectacular "Golden Route" between Åndalsnes and Geiranger. Excellent hiking on un-crowded trails. Nearby lakes for fishing and small game hunting. Fishing license sold on the farm.
Large hydro electric station in Tafjord close by, with a museum and an outdoor swimming pool. Welcome to the Rønneberg's red house.

Rønneberg gard ligger 7 km fra Eidsdal sentrum på veien mot Geiranger. Fjellgården ligger 420 m.o.h. og det er ingen fjell som stenger for sola. Gården ligger på en 3 km avstikker fra den spektakulære turistruten "The Golden Route" mellom Åndalsnes og Geiranger .
Det er fine turmuligheter i et terreng lite brukt av turister. Gode fiskevann og småviltjakt. Fiskekort selges på garden.
I Tafjord finner du ellers en kraftstasjon med museum og utendørs svømmebaseng.
Velkommen til det røde huset på Rønneberg.

Der Hof befindet sich 7 km von Eidsdal Zentrum entfernt in Richtung Geiranger. Der Gebirgshof liegt auf 420 m Meereshöhe; kein Bergrücken versperrt den Blick auf die Sommersonne. Rønneberg liegt 3 km abseits der Touristenstraße "The Golden Route" zwischen Åndalsnes und Geiranger.
Schöne Wandermöglichkeiten in einem wenig touristischen Gebiet. Reizvolle Angelseen; Niederwildjagd. Angelschein auf dem Hof erhältlich.
E-Werk mit Museum und Schwimmbad (28 Grad) in Tafjord. Willkommen zum roten Haus von Rønneberg.

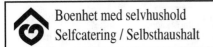
Cabins for 2-5 persons	Hytter for 2-5 personer	Hütten für 2-5 Personen
No. of bedrooms: 2-3	Antall soverom: 2-3	Anzahl Schlafräume: 2-3
Own bath, kitchen, LR	Eget bad, kjøkken, stue	Eig. Bad, Küche, Stube
Price for whole unit: **480,-**	Pris for hele enheten: **480,-**	Ganze Einheit: **480,-**
No. of cabins: 2	Antall hytter: 2	Anzahl Hütten: 2
Bed linen included	Sengetøy er inkludert	Inkl. Bettwäsche
Open 1 May - 30 Aug.	Åpent 1. mai - 30. aug.	Geöffnet 1. Mai - 30. Aug.
TV available	TV tilgjengelig	Zugang zu TV
Yard/terrace/deck access	Hage/terrasse/uteplass	Garten/Terrasse/Aussenplatz
Boat for rent	Båtutleie	Boot zu mieten
No smoking inside	Ingen røking innendørs	Kein Rauchen im Haus
Breakfast service available: **60,-**	Frokost kan serveres: **60,-**	Frühstück auf Bestellung: **60,-**
English spoken		Sprechen etwas Deutsch

Directions:	Veibeskrivelse:	Wegbeschreibung:
Drive 25 km from Geiranger towards Eidsdal on Ørneveien. Look for a sign marked "Rønneberg/Kilsti". Take the steep road 3 km up from main highway to get to farm. Look for the red house. From Eidsdal: about 7 km to the exit point "Rønneberg/Kilsti".	Kjør 25 km fra Geiranger mot Eidsdal over Ørneveien. Se etter skiltet "Rønneberg/Kilsti". Det er 3 km bratt vei fra riksvegen opp til gården. Se etter det røde huset. Fra Eidsdal er det ca. 7 km til avkjøring "Rønneberg/Kilsti".	Fahren Sie von Geiranger aus auf dem Ørneveien 25 km in Richtung Eidsdal. Achten Sie auf das Schild "Rønneberg/Kilsti". Von der Hauptstraße aus geht es 3 km steil bergan bis zum Hof. Halten Sie Ausschau nach einem roten Haus. Von Eidsdal aus sind es ca. 7 km bis zur Abzweigung "Rønneberg/Kilsti".

Mølsæter

Your host:
Oddrun Mølsæter

Address:
Mølsæter
N - 6216 Geiranger
Phone: 70 26 30 64

Best time to call:
17.00 - 22.00

Apartment for 2-4 persons	Husvære for 2-4 personar	Wohnung für 2-4 Personen
No. of bedrooms: 2	Antal soverom: 2	Anzahl Schlafräume: 2
Shared bath, kitchenette, LR	Delt bad, tekjøken, stove	Gemeins. Bad, Teeküche, Stube
Price per pers.: **200,-**	Pris pr. pers.: **200,-**	Preis pro Pers.: **200,-**
Bed linen fee: **20,-**	Tillegg for sengetyg: **20,-**	Mieten von Bettwäsche: **20,-**
Open 1 May - 31 Aug.	Ope 1. mai - 15. aug.	Geöffnet 1. Juni - 31. Aug.
Yard/terrace/deck access/garden	Terrasse/uteplass/hage	Garten/Terrasse/Aussenplatz
Pets welcome	Kjæledyr tillatt	Haustiere willkommen
No smoking inside	Inga røyking innomhus	Kein Rauchen im Haus
Some English spoken		Sprechen etwas Englisch

Mountain farm situated 400 meters above sea level with breathtaking view of nearby town, fjord and mountains. Non-operational farm with very quiet and peaceful surroundings. Close to hiking trails.

Directions:
6 km from Geiranger. Take RV 63 (Ørnevegen) towards Eidsdal. Look for the sign to Mølsæter. Red house with brown and white trim.

Fjellgard 400 meter over havet med flott utsikt over bygda, fjorden og fjella. Garden er ikkje i drift og her er svært stilt og roleg. Turstier i området.

Vegforklaring:
Frå Geiranger kjøyr Ørnevegen (RV 63) mot Eidsdal, 6 km. Sjå etter skilt til Mølsæter. Huset er raudt med brune og kvite lister.

Bergbauernhof, auf 400 m Meereshöhe gelegen. Reizvolle Aussicht über Siedlung, Fjord und Berge. Der Hof ist nicht mehr bewirtschaftet, daher sehr ruhige Atmosphäre. Wanderwege vorhanden.

Wegbeschreibung:
6 km von Geiranger entfernt. Folgen Sie der Passstraße "Ørnevegen" (Str. 63) in Richtung Eidsdal. Auf Schild nach Mølsæter achten. Das Haus ist rot gestrichen (braune und weiße Holzleisten!).

What was once thought can never be unthought.
–Friedrich Dürrenmatt (1921 – 1990)

Petrine's Gjestgiveri

Your host:
Kirsti Indreeide Dale

Address:
N - 6214 Norddal
Phone: **70 25 92 85**
Fax: **70 25 92 88**
E-mail: **petrines@petrines.com**
Web: **www.petrines.com**

Best time to call:
09.00 - 23.00

Double room: **600,-/800,-/900,-**	Dobbeltrom: **600,-/800,-/900,-**	Doppelzimmer: **600,-/800,-/900,-**
Single room: **450,-/550,-**	Enkeltrom: **450,-/550,-**	Einzelzimmer: **450,-/550,-**
No. of rooms: 12	Antal rom: 12	Anzahl Zimmer: 12
Full breakfast	Full frukost	Volles Frühstück
Breakfast buffet	Servering: Frukostbufffét	Serv.: Frühstücksbüfett
Open year round	Ope heile året	Ganzjährig geöffnet
Winter; reservations required	Vinter: kun best. på førehand	Winter: Vorbestellung nötig
TV available	TV tilgjengeleg	Zugang zu TV
Terrace/deck access/yard	Terrasse/uteplass/hage	Terrasse/Aussenplatz/Garten
VISA, MC accepted	Vi tek VISA, MC	Wir nehmen VISA, MC
Discount for children	Rabatt for born	Ermässigung für Kinder
English & some French spoken		Sprechen Deutsch

Petrine's Inn is by the fjord at Norddal, in the middle of "The Golden Route", 4 km from the Eidsdal ferry quay, along the road leading up to the beautiful Herdal mountain pastures.

The house was built in 1916 as a nursing home, and was converted to an inn in 1992 and renovated in "Carl-Larsson" style in 1999.

Your hostess' specialty is traditional, homemade Norwegian food including such dishes as kid (goat) meat, venison, carmel pudding and apple cake.

There is also a farm here with goats and horses.

Petrines Gjestgiveri ligg ved fjorden i Norddal, midt i "The Golden Route", 4 km frå ferjekaia i Eidsdal, ved vegen som fører opp til den vakre Herdalsetra. Huset vart bygd som aldersheim i 1916 og vart bygd om til gjestgiveri i 1992, og pussa opp i Carl-Larsson-stil i 1999.

Vertskapet sin spesialitet er tradisjonell heimelaga norsk mat, blandt anna kjekjøt, viltrettar, karamellpudding og eplekake. Dei har gard med geiter og hestar.

Petrines Gjestgiveri liegt am Fjord in Norddal, mitten in The Golden Route, 4 km vom Fährkai in Eidsdal, an der Strasse hinauf zur schönen Alm Herdalsetra. Das im Jahr 1916 als Altenheim erbaute Gebäude wurde 1992 zu einem Übernachtungsbetrieb umgebaut und 1999 im Stil des schwedischen Malers Carl Larsson renoviert. Die Gastgeber bieten traditionelle norwegische Kost an, z.B. Ziegenfleisch, Wildgerichte, Karamellpudding und Apfelkuchen.

Sie betreiben den Hof mit Ziegen und Pferden.

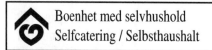
Strandhuset
Måndalen

Your host:
Elsa & John Vold

Address:
N - 6386 Måndalen
Phone: 71 22 33 25
Mobil: 90 87 59 72

Best time to call:
10.00 - 18.00

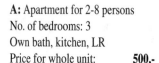

A: Apartment for 2-8 persons
No. of bedrooms: 3
Own bath, kitchen, LR
Price for whole unit: **500,-**

B: Apartment for 2-6 persons
No. of bedrooms: 2
Own bath, kitchen, LR
Price for whole unit: **400,-**

No. of apt.: 3
Bed linen fee: **50,-**
Open year round
TV available
Yard/terrace/deck access
Boat for rent
Some English spoken

A: Leilighet for 2-8 personer
Antall soverom: 3
Eget bad, kjøkken, stue
Pris for hele enheten: **500,-**

B: Leilighet for 2-6 personer
Antall soverom: 2
Eget bad, kjøkken, stue
Pris for hele enheten: **400,-**

Antall leiligheter: 3
Tillegg for sengetøy: **50,-**
Åpent hele året
TV tilgjengelig
Hage/terrasse/uteplass
Båtutleie

A: Wohnung für 2-8 Personen
Anzahl Schlafräume: 3
Eig. Bad, Küche, Stube
Ganze Einheit: **500,-**

B: Wohnung für 2-6 Personen
Anzahl Schlafräume: 2
Eig. Bad, Küche, Stube
Ganze Einheit: **400,-**

Anzahl Wohnungen: 3
Mieten von Bettwäsche: **50,-**
Ganzjährig geöffnet
Zugang zu TV
Garten/Terrasse/Aussenplatz
Boot zu mieten
Sprechen etwas Deutsch

Måndalen lies by Romsdals Fjord, a side valley flanked by high mountains. The river Måna, which carries salmon and trout, has its mouth here. Further up the valley are good fishing lakes and logging roads.
The hosts run a farm. The house for rent lies by a dock on the sea with a boathouse and boats that can be used for fishing.
Short distance to post office, bank, cafeteria and several stores.

Ved Romsdalsfjorden ligger Måndalen, en sidedal som er omgitt av høye fjell. Fiskeelven Måna med laks og ørret renner ut i havet her. Lenger oppe i dalen er det fine fiskevann og skogsbilveier.
Vertskapet driver gårdsbruk. Utleiehuset ligger ved en brygge nede ved sjøen med naust og båter som kan benyttes til fjordfiske.
Kort vei til post, bank, kafeteria og flere butikker.

Am Romsdalsfjord liegt Måndalen, ein von hohen Bergen umgebenes Seitental. Hier mündet der Angelfluss Måna mit Lachs und Seeforelle in den Fjord. Weiter talaufwärts gibt es Forststrassen und gute Fischwasser. Die Gastgeber bewirtschaften einen Bauernhof. Das Miethaus liegt an der Bootbrücke am Fjord, wo Boote zum Angeln benützt werden können. Unweit zu Postamt, Bank und Geschäften.

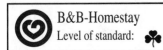
Romsdal Skysstation

Address:
Jernbanegata 3
N - 6800 Åndalsnes
Phone: 71 22 21 00
Fax: 71 22 21 01
Mobil: 99 74 17 44
E-mail:
alpehotel@sensewave.com
Web: www.alpehotel.no
Best time to call:
10.00 - 15.00 / 21.00-23.00

Double-/Twin room:	**450,-**	Dobbelt-/tosengsrom:	**450,-**	Doppel-/Zweibettzimmer:	**450,-**
1 pers. in double room:	**375,-**	1 pers. i dobbeltrom:	**375,-**	1 Pers. in Doppelzimmer:	**375,-**
Single room:	**300,-**	Enkeltrom:	**300,-**	Einzelzimmer:	**300,-**
No. of rooms: 17		Antall rom: 17		Anzahl Zimmer: 17	
Continental breakfast		Kontinental frokost		Kontinentales Frühstück	
Breakfast tray		Servering: Frokostbrett		Serv.: Frühstückstablett	
Other meals served upon request		Andre måltider ved bestilling		Andere Mahlzeiten nach Vereinb.	
Open year round		Åpent hele året		Ganzjährig geöffnet	
TV available		TV tilgjengelig		Zugang zu TV	
Garden		Hage		Garten	
Bike for rent		Sykkelutleie		Fahrrad zu mieten	
Discount for children		Rabatt for barn		Ermäßigung für Kinder	
No smoking inside		Ingen røking innendørs		Kein Rauchen im Haus	
VISA, MC, AmEx, DC accepted		Vi tar VISA, MC, AmEx, DC		Wir nehmen VISA, MC, AmEx, DC	
Access to telephone/fax/internet		Tilgang på telefon/faks/Internett		Zugang Telefon/Fax/Internet	
Pets welcome		Kjæledyr tillatt		Haustiere willkommen	
English spoken				Sprechen Deutsch	

Near Trollstigen, Trollveggen and the museum train. Fishing boat trips. Optional sightseeing tours by hotel car in Romsdalen at reasonable prices.

Directions:
In Åndalsnes town center, 20 meters from the railway and bus stations. Visitors traveling by car should follow posted signs to Åndalsnes town center.

Nær Trollstigen, Trollveggen og museumstog. Fiskebåtturer. Tilbud om sightseeing i Romsdalen med hotellets bil til fornuftige priser.

Veibeskrivelse:
I Åndalsnes sentrum, 20 meter fra jernbanestasjonen og bussstasjonen. Reisende med bil følger skilting til Åndalsnes sentrum.

Sehenswürdigkeiten in der Nähe: Passstraße Trollstigen, Felswand Trollveggen, Museumseisenbahn. Touren mit Fischerboot, Preiswerte Sightseeingtouren mit dem hoteleigenen Fahrzeug durch das Romsdal.

Wegbeschreibung:
Im Zentrum von Åndalsnes gelegen, nur 20 m von Bahnhof und Bushaltestelle entfernt. Anreise mit dem Auto: Schild nach Åndalsnes Zentrum folgen.

Trollstigen
Camping & Gjestegård

Your host:
Milouda & Edmund Meyer

Address:
N - 6300 Åndalsnes
Phone: 71 22 11 12
Fax: 71 22 22 48
Mobil: 92 49 84 62
E-mail: ed-mey@online.no
Web: www.trollcamp.no

Best time to call:
08.00 - 22.00

Double room:	**510,-**	Dobbeltrom:	**510,-**	Doppelzimmer:	**510,-**
Single room:	**330,-**	Enkeltrom:	**330,-**	Einzelzimmer:	**330,-**
3 bedded room:	**660,-**	Tresengsrom:	**660,-**	Dreibettzimmer:	**660,-**
4 bedded room:	**880,-**	Firesengsrom:	**880,-**	Vierbettzimmer:	**880,-**

No. of rooms: 15	Antall rom: 15	Anzahl Zimmer: 15
Full breakfast	Full frokost	Volles Frühstück
Breakfast buffet	Servering: Frokostbuffé	Serv.: Frühstücksbüfett
Restaurant, fully-licensed	Restaurant, alle rettigheter	Restaurant, alle Schankrechte
Open year round	Åpent hele året	Ganzjährig geöffnet
TV available	TV tilgjengelig	Zugang zu TV
Terrace/garden	Terrasse/uteplass/hage	Terrasse/Aussenplatz/Garten
Boat for rent	Båtutleie	Boot zu mieten
VISA, MC accepted	Vi tar VISA, MC	Wir nehmen VISA, MC
Discount for children	Rabatt for barn	Ermässigung für Kinder
Member of Norsk Gardsmat	Medlem av Norsk Gardsmat	Mitglied v. Norsk Gardsmat
English, Arabic and some French spoken		Sprechen etwas Deutsch

Trollstigen Camping & Gjestegård is at Istedalen, along Route 63 in the direction of Trollstigen. The farm has a dairy and cattle herds along with potatoe and Christmas tree production. River fishing: Your hosts have their own salmon/trout river including an outdoor shelter and boat. Canoe rental, fjord fishing by boat and rent of hunting rights.

Trollstigen Camping & Gjestegård ligger i Istedalen, 10 km fra Åndalsnes langs RV 63 mot Trollstigen.
På gården er det produksjon av kjøtt, melk, poteter og juletrær. Elvefiske, utleier har egen laks- og ørretelv med gapahuk og båt. Utleie av jaktrettigheter, og kanoutleie. Fjordfiske fra båt er også mulig.

Trollstigen Camping & Gjestegård liegt in Istedalen, an der Strasse 63 gegen Trollstigen. Auf dem Hof gibt es Milchwirtschaft, Viehzucht, Kartoffeln und Christbaumpflanzungen. Flussangeln möglich. Der Gastgeber ist Besitzer eines eigenen Lachs- und Forellenflusses mit Schutzhütte und Boot. Jagdrechte, Kanuvermietung. Ebenfalls möglich: Fjordangeln vom Boot aus.

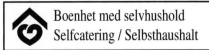
A: Cabins for 2-5 persons
Trollstigen Camping & Gjestegård
No. of cabins: 8
Own bath, kitchen, LR, bedroom
Price for whole unit: **550,-**
Bed linen fee: **55,-**
Open year round
TV available
Yard/terrace/deck access
Free sauna
Boat for rent
VISA, MC accepted
Discount for children
Restaurant

B: Apartment for 2-4 persons
Trollstigen Gjestegård - Meyer
No. of bedrooms: 2
Own bath, kitchen, LR
Price for whole unit: **500,-**
Bed linen fee: **55,-**
English, French and Arabic spoken

A: Hytter for 2-5 personer
Trollstigen Camping & Gjestegård
Antall hytter: 8
Eget bad, kjøkken, stue, soverom
Pris for hele enheten: **550,-**
Tillegg for sengetøy: **55,-**
Åpent hele året
TV tilgjengelig
Hage/terrasse/uteplass
Gratis badstu
Båtutleie
Vi tar VISA, MC
Rabatt for barn
Restaurant

B: Leilighet for 2-4 personer
Trollstigen Gjestegård - Meyer
Antall soverom: 2
Eget bad, kjøkken, stue
Pris for hele enheten: **500,-**
Tillegg for sengetøy: **55,-**

A: Hütte für 2-5 Personen
Trollstigen Camping & Gjestegård
Anzahl Hütten: 8
Eig. Bad, Küche, Stube, Schlafzi.
Ganze Einheit: **550,-**
Mieten von Bettwäsche: **55,-**
Ganzjährig geöffnet
Zugang zu TV
Garten/Terrasse/Aussenplatz
Gratis Sauna
Boot zu mieten
Wir nehmen VISA, MC
Ermässigung für Kinder
Restaurant

B: Wohnung für 2-4 Personen
Trollstigen Gjestegård - Meyer
Anzahl Schlafräume: 2
Eig. Bad, Küche, Stube
Ganze Einheit: **500,-**
Mieten von Bettwäsche: **55,-**
Sprechen etwas Deutsch

Unit A is located in Istedalen, 10 km from Åndalsnes, direction Trollstigen. The name here is "Trollstigen Camping og Gjestegård". There is also a restaurant that serves both breakfast and dinner, plus a sauna and canoe rental.
Unit B, Trollstigen Gjestegård, is where your hosts live and is located at Sogge, 6 km from Åndalsnes towards Trollstigen.

Directions:
The facility is located 10 km from Åndalsnes along highway E-136. Take RV 63 towards Trollstigen and drive 5 km. Look for an exit sign marked "Trollstigen Gjestegård".
From Geiranger: Look for the first tourist facility after descending from Trollstigen.

Enhet A ligger i Istedalen, 10 km fra Åndalsnes, retning Trollstigen. Navnet her er Trollstigen Camping og Gjestegård. Her er det også restaurant med frokost og middagservering, badstu og kanoutleie.
Enhet B, Trollstigen Gjestegård hvor vertskapet selv bor, ligger på Sogge, 6 km fra Åndalsnes mot Trollstigen.

Veibeskrivelse:
Anlegget ligger 10 km fra Åndalsnes langs E-136. Ta RV 63 mot Trollstigen og kjør 5 km. Se etter avkjørselsskiltet som er merket med "Trollstigen Gjestegård". Fra Geiranger er det det første turistanlegget etter at du kommer ned fra Trollstigen.

Wohneinheit A befindet sich im Istedalen, 10 km von Åndalsnes entfernt in Richtung Paßstraße "Trollstigen". Gasthof mit Campingplatz. Frühstück und Abendessen werden angeboten, außerdem Sauna und Kanuvermietung.
Wohneinheit B - hier wohnen die Gastgeber selbst - liegt in Sogge, 6 km von Åndalsnes entfernt in Richtung Paßstraße Trollstigen.

Wegbeschreibung:
Der Gasthof befindet sich 10 km von Åndalsnes entfernt an der E-136. Folgen Sie der Straße 63 Richtung Trollstigen 5 km weit. Achten Sie auf das Schild mit der Aufschrift "Trollstigen Gjestegård".
Aus Richtung Geiranger ist es die erste Ferienanlage nach der Abfahrt von Trollstigen.

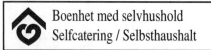

Gråhaugen Fjellstue

Your host:
Anne & Jon Erik Moen

Address:
Folldalen
N - 6653 Øvre Surnadal
Phone: 71 66 25 00
Fax: 71 66 10 27
E-mail: jerimoen@online.no

Best time to call:
08.00 - 23.00

A: Cabins for 2-4 persons	**A:** Hytter for 2-4 personer	**A:** Hütten für 2-4 Personen
No. of bedrooms: 1	Antall soverom: 1	Anzahl Schlafräume: 1
Living room and kitchenette	Stue og tekjøkken	Stube und Teeküche
No running water in cabin	Ikke innlagt vann i hytten	Kein fliess. Wasser
Sanitary facilities in unit B	Sanitæranlegg i enhet B	Sanitäranlage in Einheit B
Price for whole unit: **400,-**	Pris for hele enheten: **400,-**	Ganze Einheit: **400,-**
B: Cabin for 26 persons	**B:** Fjellstue for 26 personer	**B:** Hütte für 26 Personen
Please contact your host for prices and other information.	Ta kontakt med vertskap for pris og mer informasjon	Preise und Auskünfte erhalten Sie von den Vermietern.
Open March - October	Åpent mars - oktober	Geöffnet März - Oktober
Bed linen fee: **40,-**	Tillegg for sengetøy: **40,-**	Mieten von Bettwäsche: **40,-**
Terrace/deck access	Terrasse/uteplass	Terrasse/Aussenplatz
Boat for rent	Båtutleie	Boot zu mieten
Reservations required	Forhåndsbestilling nødvendig	Vorbestellung nötig
English spoken		Sprechen Deutsch

Three small cabins and one large are located 16 km from RV 65, at Gråsjø lake, inside Trollheimen which is a Nature Reserve. Here you find yourself in the middle of the mountain wilds and will enjoy ideal conditions for all sorts of outdoor activities.

Tre små hytter og en stor ligger 16 km fra RV 65, ved Gråsjø, inne i Trollheimen som er et naturreservat. Her er du midt inne i fjellheimen og finner ideelle forhold for alle typer friluftsaktiviteter.

3 kleine Hütten und 1 grosse Hütte liegen ca. 16 km von der Strasse RV65 entfernt. Reizvolle Lage inmitten des Trollheimen-Gebirges (Naturpark) mit idealen Bedingungen für alle Aktivitäten an der frischen Luft.

Friendship is unnecessary, like philosophy, like art…
It has no survival value; rather it is one of those things that give value to survival.

–C. S. Lewis (1898 – 1963)

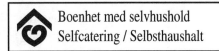
Øien Gård

Your host:
Anna & Arne Myren

Address:
N - 6570 Smøla
Phone: **71 54 03 13**
Fax: **71 54 02 58**

Best time to call:
09.00 - 22.00

A: Guesthouse for 2-4 persons No. of bedrooms: 2 Own bath, kitchen, LR Price for whole unit: **700,-**	**A:** Gjestehus for 2-4 personer Antall soverom: 2 Eget bad, kjøkken, stue Pris for hele enheten: **700,-**	**A:** Gästehaus für 2-4 Personen Anzahl Schlafräume: 2 Eig. Bad, Küche, Stube Ganze Einheit: **700,-**
B: Guesthouse for 2-8 persons No. of bedrooms: 4 Own bath, kitchen, LR Price for whole unit: **800,-**	**B:** Gjestehus for 2-8 personer Antall soverom: 4 Eget bad, kjøkken, stue Pris for hele enheten: **800,-**	**B:** Gästehaus für 2-8 Personen Anzahl Schlafräume: 4 Eig. Bad, Küche, Stube Ganze Einheit: **800,-**
Applies to all rental units: Bed linen fee: **50,-** Open year round TV available Yard/terrace/deck access Boat for rent English spoken	For alle enhetene gjelder: Tillegg for sengetøy: **50,-** Åpent hele året TV tilgjengelig Terrasse/uteplass Båtutleie	Für alle Einheiten gilt: Mieten von Bettwäsche: **50,-** Ganzjährig geöffnet Zugang zu TV Terrasse/Aussenplatz Boot zu mieten Sprechen etwas Deutsch

The accommodations are situated along the shoreline with excellent fishing and outdoor walks in Smøla's unique nature. Museums located nearby. The farm has sheep that graze near the farm year round. The rental units are fully furnished.

Directions:
Ferry Seivika-Tustna and ferry Tustna-Edøy. From Edøy: Follow RV 669 to Hopen/Veidholmen. Take marked exit to Øien Gard. Distance: Edøy 30 km.

Anlegget ligger like ved havet, med gode muligheter for fiske og turer i Smølas særegne natur. Museer i området. Gården har sauer som går nær gården hele året. Boenhetene er fullt utstyrte.

Veibeskrivelse:
Ferge Seivika-Tustna og ferge Tustna-Edøy. Fra Edøy, følg RV 669 til Hopen/Veidholmen, Skiltet avkjøring til Øien Gard. Avstand: Edøy 30 km.

Der Hof befindet sich direkt am Meer. Smøla bietet sehr gute Möglichkeiten für Angeln und Wandern in der reizvollen Natur der Insel. Mehrere Museen in der Umgebung. Die Ferienwohnungen sind komplett ausgestattet.

Wegbeschreibung:
Fähre Seivika – Tustna/Tustna – Edøy. Folgen Sie ab Edøy der Straße 669 nach Hopen/Veidholmen, dort ist der Weg zum Hof Øien Gård ausgeschildert. 30 km von Edøy.

Inger Stock
Bed & Breakfast

Your host:
Inger Stock Yesükan

Address:
Porsmyra 18
N - 7091 Tiller, Trondheim
Phone/Fax: 72 88 83 19
Mobil: 91 51 37 23

Best time to call:
08.00 - 22.00

Double-/Twin room:	**400,-**	Dobbelt-/tosengsrom:	**400,-**	Doppel-/Zweibettzi.:	**400,-**
Single room:	**320,-**	Enkeltrom:	**320,-**	Einzelzimmer:	**320,-**
No. of rooms: 5		Antall rom: 5		Anzahl Zimmer: 5	
Full breakfast		Full frokost		Volles Frühstück	
Laid breakfast table		Dekket frokostbord		Serv.: Frühstückstisch	
Open 1 May - 15 October		Åpent 1. mai - 15. oktober		Geöffnet 1. Mai - 15. Okt.	
TVavailable		TV tilgjengelig		Zugang zu TV	
No smoking inside		Ingen røking innendørs		Kein Rauchen im Haus	
Discount for children		Rabatt for barn		Ermässigung für Kinder	
Selfcatering possible		Selvhushold er mulig		Selbsthaushalt möglich	
Evening meal available:	**45,-**	Kveldsmat kan bestilles:	**45,-**	Abendbrot auf Bestellung:	**45,-**
English & some Italian and Turkish spoken				Sprechen Deutsch	

Inger Stock's Bed & Breakfast is in Tiller, 12 minutes drive south on E-6 from Trondheim's city center. Historically, Trondheim is an important city. Nidaros Cathedral is one of Scandinavia's largest buildings from the Middle Ages. Invaluable art and history collections in the city's museums. At the end of July, there is an annual celebration with concerts and exhibitions. Trondheim also offers many other attractions and good restaurants.

Inger Stocks Bed & Breakfast ligger på Tiller, 12 min. kjøring i sørlig retning på E-6 fra Trondheim sentrum.
Trondheim er en historisk viktig by. Den har mye å tilby av severdigheter, museer, kunst, konserter, og her er en rekke restauranter. Nidarosdomen er et av Nordens største middelalderbygg, Olavsdagene er et årlig arrangement i slutten av juli med konserter og utstillinger. Flere muséer har betydelige kunst- og historiske samlinger.

Inger Stocks Bed & Breakfast liegt in Tiller, 12 Min. südwärts auf der E-6 von Trondheim. Trondheim ist historisch bedeutsam und hat viele Sehenswürdigkeiten, Museen, Konzerte, Restaurants. Der Nidarosdom ist eines der grössten Mittelalterbauwerke in Skandinavien. Ende Juli finden jedes Jahr die Olavstage mit Konzerten und Ausstellungen statt. Mehrere Museen haben bedeutende Sammlungen aus Kunst und Geschichte.

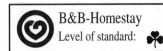
Sommerbo

Your host:
Liv Aldstedt

Address:
Enromveien 160
N - 7026 Trondheim
Phone/Fax: 72 56 02 65
Mobil: 99 55 33 40 / 93 20 82 25
E-mail: aldstedt@stud.ntnu.no

Best time to call:
08.00 - 23.00

A: Dobbeltrom: 400,-	**A:** Double room: 400,-	**A:** Doppelzimmer: 400,-
Mulighet for ekstraseng	Extra bed available	Extrabett möglich
Antall rom: 2	No. of rooms: 2	Anzahl Zimmer: 2
Full frokost	Full breakfast	Volles Frühstück
Servering: Frokostbord	Laid breakfast table	Serv.: Frühstückstisch
Åpent 1. juni - 31. aug.	Open 1 June - 31 Aug.	Geöffnet 1. Juni - 31. Aug.
TV tilgjengelig	TV available	Zugang zu TV
Terrasse/uteplass	Terrace/deck access	Terrasse/Aussenplatz
Ingen røking innendørs	No smoking inside	Kein Rauchen im Haus
B: Leilighet for 2-3 personer	**B:** Apartment for 2-3 persons	**B:** Wohnung für 2-3 Personen
Antall soverom: 1	No. of bedrooms: 1	Anzahl Schlafräume: 1
Eget bad, kjøkken, stue	Own bath, kitchen, LR	Eig. Bad, Küche, Stube
Pris for hele enheten: 550,-	Price for whole unit: 550,-	Ganze Einheit: 550,-
Mulighet for ekstraseng	Extra bed available	Extrabett möglich
Sengetøy er inkludert	Bed linen included	Inkl. Bettwäsche
Åpent 1. juli - 31. juli	Open 1 July - 31 July	Geöffnet 1. Juli - 31. Juli
TV	English spoken	Sprechen Englisch

Sommerbo ligger på Stavset, på Byåsen, 20 min. sør for Trondheim sentrum. Vertinnen er hageentusiast, dyrevenn, har reist mye og liker å lage mat. Hjemlig atmosfære i stille strøk.
Veibeskrivelse:
Ta av fra E-6 mot "Byåsen", etter ca. 3 km kommer du til en rundkjøring, du ser Rema Stormarked rett fram. Her tar du til høyre og dette er Enromveien. Du finner en snuplass for buss og Sommerbo er 2dre hus på venstre side.

Sommerbo is located at Stavset, near Byåsen, 20 min. south of downtown Trondheim. Your hostess is a gardening enthusiast, animal lover, has traveled extensively and enjoys preparing food. A homelike atmosphere in quiet surroundings. Directions: Exit from E-6 towards "Byåsen" and drive ca. 3 km till a roundabout, you will see a Rema supermarket straight ahead. Turn right onto Enromveien. Find a turn for buses, then it is the 2nd house on the left.

Sommerbo liegt in Stavset, Byåsen, 20 Min. südlich vom Stadtzentrum Trondheims. Die Gastgeberin ist garten- und tierbegeistert, weitgereist und liebt es zu kochen. Gemütliche Atmosphäre in ruhiger Wohngegend.
Wegbeschreibung: Biegen Sie bei Byåsen von der E-6 ab. Nach ca. 3 km gelangen Sie zu einem Kreisverkehr (am Supermarkt „Rema"). Dort biegen Sie rechts ab auf die Straße „Enromveien". Nach dem Buswendeplatz 2. Haus, links.

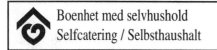
Åse's Romutleie

Your host:
Åse L. Andersen

Address:
Nedre Møllenberggt. 27
N - 7014 Trondheim
Phone: 73 51 15 40
Mobil: 41 20 86 50

Best time to call:
08.00 - 22.30

A: Apartment for up to 8 pers.: No. of rooms: 4. Shared: 2 baths, kitchen, DR, LR Room for 2 pers.: **340,- to 380,-** Room for 1 pers.: **230,-**	**A:** Leilighet for opp til 8 pers.: Antall rom: 4 Deles: 2 bad, spisestue, stue, kjk. Rom for 2 pers.: **340,- til 380,-** Rom for 1 pers.: **230,-**	**A:** Wohnung bis zu 8 Pers.: Anzahl Zimmer: 4 Gemeins.: 2 Bad, Küche, Stube Zi. für 2 Pers.: **340,- bis zu 380,-** Zi. für 1 Pers.: **230,-**
B: Apartment for 2-4 persons Bath, kitchen, LR, sleeping alcove Price per pers.: **200.-**	**B:** Leilighet for 2-4 personer Bad, kjøkken, stue, sovealkove Pris pr. person **200,-**	**B:** Wohnung für 2-4 Personen Bad, Küche, Stube, Alkoven Preis pro Pers.: **200,-**
Applies to all rental units: Bed linen fee: **30,-** Open 10 June - 20 Aug. TV available Yard/terrace Garden Pets welcome Family discount Baby free No smoking inside Parking in yard English spoken	For alle enhetene gjelder: Tillegg for sengetøy: **30,-** Åpent 10. juni - 20. aug. TV tilgjengelig Terrasse/uteplass Hage Kjæledyr tillatt Familierabatt Baby gratis Ingen røking innendørs. P-plasser på gårdsplass	Für alle Einheiten gilt: Mieten von Bettwäsche: **30,-** Geöffnet 10. Juni - 20. Aug. Zugang zu TV Terrasse/Aussenplatz Garten Haustiere willkommen Ermäßigung für Familien Baby kostenlos Kein Rauchen im Haus Parkraum im Hof Sprechen etwas Deutsch

In old town area and featuring renovated or newly built houses in the "Møllenberg" style. Many cozy cafés and restaurants nearby. Most of Trondheim's attractions are within walking distance.

I gammel bydel med rehabiliterte eller nybygde hus i møllenberg-stil. Mange hyggelige kafeer og restauranter i bydelen. De fleste av Trondheims severdigheter ligger i gangavstand.

Reizvolle Lage in der Altstadt mit sanierten Gebäuden im Møllen-berg-Stil. In der Nähe viele gemüt-liche Cafès und Restaurants. Die meisten Sehenswürdigkeiten Trondheims sind zu Fuß zu erreichen.

Trøabakken

Your host:
Sigrun & Per Storholmen

Address:
Leksdal
N - 7650 Verdal
Phone: 74 04 24 69
Mobil: 95 05 88 02
E-mail: per.storholmen@c2i.net

Best time to call:
07.00 - 09.00 / 16.00 - 23.00

A: Room for 1 pers.: **100,-**	**A:** Rom for 1 pers.: **100,-**	**A:** Zimmer für 1 Pers.: **100,-**
B: Apartment for 2-6 persons	**B:** Leilighet for 2-6 personer	**B:** Wohnung für 2-6 Personen
No. of bedrooms: 1	Antall soverom: 1	Anzahl Schlafräume: 1
Own bath, kitchenette, LR	Eget bad, tekjøkken, stue	Eig. Bad, kleine Küche, Stube
Price for whole unit: **400,-**	Pris for hele enheten: **400,-**	Ganze Einheit: **400,-**
Bed linen included	Sengetøy er inkludert	Inkl. Bettwäsche
Open year round	Åpent hele året	Ganzjährig geöffnet
TV available	TV tilgjengelig	Zugang zu TV
Yard/garden	Hage	Garten
Boat for rent	Båtutleie	Boot zu mieten
No smoking inside	Ingen røking innendørs	Kein Rauchen im Haus
Breakfast service available: **30,-**	Frokost kan serveres: **30,-**	Frühstück auf Bestellung: **30,-**
Some English spoken		Sprechen etwas Deutsch

Trøabakken is in Leksdal, in the northeastern part of Verdal, about 8 km from Stiklestad which is known for its history of kings. Summer tourist activities in Stiklestad are visits to the church, museum, cultural center, the Olsok play, historical tours, and concerts. There is commercial salmon fishing in the Verdal River, with a salmon ladder and a salmon studio. The Leksdal Lake provides good fishing both summer and winter, and a boat can be provided.

Leksdal, hvor man finner Trøabakken, ligger i nord-østre del av Verdal, ca. 8 km fra Stiklestad som er kjent for sin kongehistorie. Aktuelle turistaktiviteter på Stiklestad sommerstid er; besøk ved kirken, museet, kulturhuset, Olsokspelet, historiske turer, konserter. I Verdalselva drives det laksefiske, der er laksetrapp med laksestudio. På Leksdalsvatnet kan man fiske både sommer og vinter, båt kan skaffes til veie.

Trøabakken liegt in Leksdal, im nordöstlichen Teil von Verdal, etwa 8 km vom historischen Ort Stiklestad entfernt. Stiklestad bietet im Sommer: Besuch der alten Kirche, des Museums und Kulturhauses, das Spiel vom Hl. Olav, historische Wanderungen und Konzerte.
Verdalselva heisst der bekannte Lachsfluss mit Lachstreppe und Lachsstudio. Der See Leksdalsvatnet bietet Angelmöglichkeiten. Boot kann beschafft werden.

B&B-Homestay
Level of standard: ♣ ♣ & ♣ ♣ ♣

NBT-member
NBT-inspected

page **190**
Nord-Trøndelag

Skartnes Gård & Familieferie

Your host:
Aud & Per Sandnes

Address:
Skartnes, N - 7760 Snåsa
Phone: 7415 2526 Fax: 7415 2546
Mobil: 90 63 98 90
E-mail: sandnes@skartnes.no
Web: www.skartnes.no

Best time to call:
19.00 - 22.00

Double room/Apt.:	**550,-/600,-**	Dobbeltrom/leilighet:	**550,-/600,-**	Doppelzi./Wohnung:	**550,-/600,-**
Twin room:	**450,-**	Tosengsrom/hems:	**450,-**	Zweibettzi./Schlafboden:	**450,-**
1 pers. in double room:	**350,-**	En pers. i dobbeltrom:	**350,-**	1 Pers. im Doppelzi.:	**350,-**
No. of rooms: 5		Antall rom: 5		Anzahl Zimmer: 5	
Full breakfast		Full frokost		Volles Frühstück	
Laid breakfast table		Dekket frokostbord		Serv.: Frühstückstisch	
Open year round		Åpent hele året		Ganzjährig geöffnet	
TV available		TV tilgjengelig		Zugang zu TV	
Boat for rent		Båtutleie		Boot zu mieten	
No smoking inside		Ingen røking innendørs		Kein Rauchen im Haus	
Discount for children		Rabatt for barn		Ermässigung für Kinder	
English spoken				Sprechen etwas Deutsch	

Skartnes Farm and Family Vacation Center is a cow-farm in the southern Lapland area along the highway to Gressåsmoen National Park in Snåsa. Your hosts bid you welcome to a comfortable apartment with all-natural wood interior and a fireplace in the lower level of the main dwelling, or to cozy rooms that share a common 50's-style living room in the rental house. Also possibilities to rent a loft room in the main dwelling. The farm is situated in peaceful surroundings with no through traffic and a hilly wilderness area nearby. The hosts serve a breakfast based on Norwegian and Lapland food traditions.

Skartnes Gård og Familieferie er en gård med kyr i et sør-samisk område på veien til Gressåsmoen nasjonalpark i Snåsa.
Vertene ønsker dere velkommen i en trivelig trehvit leilighet med peisestue i sokkelen på hovedhuset eller i trivelige rom m/fellesstue i 50-talls stil i utleiehuset. I tillegg er det også mulighet for innlosjering på et hemsrom i hovedhuset.
Gården ligger i rolige omgivelser uten gjennomgangstrafikk og med villmarksheia like ved.
Vertskapet byr på særegen frokost bygd på norske- og samiske mattradisjoner.

Der Hof betreibt Viehwirtschaft und liegt in südsamischer Landschaft in Snåsa, auf dem Weg zum Nationalpark Gressåmoen. Die Gastgeber erwarten ihre Gäste in einer einladenden Wohnung mit Kaminstube im Untergeschoss des Hauphauses sowie in gemütlichen Zimmern im Stil der 50er Jahre mit Gemeinschaftsraumim Miethaus. Ausserdem gibt es eine Übernachtungsmöglichkeit auf einem Schlafboden im Hauphaus. Skartnes Gård liegt in ruhiger Umgebung ohne Durchgangsverkehr umgeben von unberührter Natur. Die Gastgeber bieten ein Frühstück, geprägt von norweg. und samischer Tradition.

Guesthouse for up to 14 persons	Gjestehus for opptil 14 pers.	Gästehaus für bis zu 14 Pers.
No. of bedrooms: 5	Antall soverom: 5	Anzahl Schlafräume: 5
Own bath, kitchen, LR	Eget bad, kjøkken, stue	Eig. Bad, Küche, Stube
Price per pers.: **175,-/200,-**	Pris pr. pers.: **175,-/200,-**	Preis pro Pers.: **175,-/200,-**
Bed linen included	Sengetøy er inkludert	Inkl. Bettwäsche
Open year round	Åpent hele året	Ganzjährig geöffnet
TV available	TV tilgjengelig	Zugang zu TV
Yard/terrace/deck access	Hage/terrasse/uteplass	Garten/Terrasse/Aussenplatz
Boat for rent	Båtutleie	Boot zu mieten
No smoking in rooms	Ingen røking på rom	Kein Rauchen im Zimmer
Discount for children		Ermässigung für Kinder
English spoken		Sprechen etwas Deutsch

Directions:
From Steinkjær: Take RV 763 and follow the signs to Snåsa. Once in Snåsa city center, look for the sign to Skartnes. Continue on RV 763 for 8 km until you reach Øverbygda town center and see its school and store. Take a left here towards Gressåsmoen, and drive 2 km until you see a sign marked Skartnes gård (farm). Look for modern, red farmhouse.

Veibeskrivelse:
Fra Steinkjær ta RV 763 og følg skilt til Snåsa. I Snåsa sentrum ser du skilt til Skartnes. Etter 8 km på RV 763 er du i Øverbygda grendesentrum med skole og butikk. Her tar du av til venstre mot Gressåsmoen og kjører 2 km til du møter skilt til Skartnes gård. Rødt moderne gårdshus.

Wegbeschreibung:
Von Steinkjær fahren Sie auf der Straße 763 und folgen der Abzweigung nach Snåsa. In der Ortsmitte von Snåsa zweigen Sie nach Skartnes ab. Nach etwa 8 km auf der Straße 763 erreichen Sie Øverbygda mit Schule und Geschäft. Hier biegen Sie ab in Richtung Gressåsmoen, bis Sie nach 2 km Skartnes Gård erreichen, ein modernes, rotes Bauernhaus.

Gjestehuset Nora
Kvinneuniversitetet Nord

Your host:
Berit Woie Berg

Address:
N - 8286 Nordfold
Phone: 75 77 90 50
Fax: 75 77 90 70
E-mail: KUN.Nord@kun.nl.no
Web: www.kun.nl.no

Best time to call:
08.00 - 16.00

Double room:	660,-	Dobbeltrom:	660,-	Doppelzimmer:	660,-
Twin room:	495,-/605,-	Tosengsrom:	495,-/605,-	Zweibettzimmer:	495,-/605,-
Single room:	385,-/495,-	Enkeltrom:	385,-/495,-	Einzelzimmer:	385,-/495,-

No. of rooms: 10 / Antall rom: 10 / Anzahl Zimmer: 10

Full breakfast	Full frokost	Volles Frühstück
Laid breakfast table	Dekket frokostbord	Serv.: Frühstückstisch
Open year round	Åpent hele året	Ganzjährig geöffnet
TV available	TV tilgjengelig	Zugang zu TV
Terrace/deck access	Terrasse/uteplass	Terrasse/Aussenplatz
Selfcatering possible	Selvhushold er mulig	Selbsthaushalt möglich
English spoken		Sprechen etwas Deutsch

A naturally beautiful setting with mountains and fjords as your neighbors is where you will find a cozy and pleasant Nora Guesthouse. From here you can look out over the Foldafjord and see Hellalsisen: Steigen's highest mountain. The guesthouse serves as an excellent base for assorted mountain trips and your hosts gladly assist with the planning of each visitor's outing.

I naturskjønne omgivelser, med fjell og fjord som nabo, finner du det hjemlige og trivelige Gjestehuset Nora. Herifra kan man se ut på Foldafjorden og bort på Hellalsisen; Steigens høyeste fjell. Gjestehuset er et godt utgangspunkt for varierte turer i fjellet, og vertskapet kan være behjelpelig med å finne ruter som passer den enkelte.

In landschaftlich reizvoller Umgebung, mit Fjord und Gebirge als nächsten Nachbarn, liegt das gemütliche Gästehaus Nora. Schöne Aussicht auf den Foldafjord, sowie zum Hellalsisen, dem höchsten Berg in Steigen.
Das Gästehaus ist ein sehr guter Ausgangspunkt für Bergwanderungen. Die Gastgeber sind den Gästen gern dabei behilflich, eine geeignete Wanderroute festzulegen.

The best things come in small parcels. –Proverb

He who hesitates is lost. –Proverb

Nordbua

Your host:
Unni & Jan E. Horn

Address:
Rishaugveien 3
N - 8340 Stamsund
Phone: **76 08 91 85**
Mobil: **95 72 95 88**
E-mail: **unnihorn@frisurf.no**

Best time to call:
18.00 - 23.00

Guesthouse for 2-8 pers.		Gjestehus for 2-8 pers.		Gästehaus für 2-8 Pers.
No. of bedrooms: 4		Antall soverom: 4		Anzahl Schlafräume: 4
Own bath, LR w/kitchen		Eget bad, stue m/kjk.krok		Eig. Bad, Stube m/Küche.
Price for whole unit:	**600,-**	Pris for hele enheten:	**600,-**	Ganze Einheit: **600,-**
Bed linen fee:	**50,-**	Tillegg for sengetøy:	**50,-**	Mieten von Bettw.: **50,-**
Open year round		Åpent hele året		Ganzjährig geöffnet
TV available		TV tilgjengelig		Zugang zu TV
Small boat available		Liten båt tilgjengelig		Kleines Boot zu leihen
Discount off-season		Rabatt utenom sesong		Ermässigung Nebensaison
Some English spoken				Sprechen etwas Deutsch

Stamsund has grand scenery, towering mountains, rich birdlife and good fishing. Midnight sun and dark days, too, depending on the time of year. Nordbua is centrally located in Stamsund. It has its own jetty and guests can use the boats between 15 May and 30 September. Freezer space and fish-cleaning facilities are available as well, making this a good holiday for fishing enthusiasts. The best times of year are May - September, and during the traditional Lofoten fishing season from 15 February until 15 April.

I Stamsund er det flott natur, høye, bratte fjell, fugleliv og fiske. Det er midnattsol og mørketid, alt etter årstiden.
Nordbua ligger sentralt i Stamsund. Den har egen kai og båt som kan disponeres av gjester i perioden 15. mai til 30. september. Gjester har også tilgang til fryseboks og rom for sløying av fisk. Her ligger alt til rette for den ivrigste feriefiskeren.
Den beste sesongen er mai - september, samt fra 15. februar til 15. april under Lofotfisket, da er her mindre turister enn i sommermånedene.

Stamsund ist ein Ort mit prachtvoller Landschaft, hohen, steilen Bergen, mannigfaltigen Vogelarten, Mitternachtssonne, aber auch Dunkelheit, je nach Jahreszeit. Nordbua liegt im Zentrum von Stamsund, hat eigenen Kai und vom 15. Mai bis 30. September Boot für Gäste zur Verfügung. Eigener Raum für Fischausnehmen, sowie Zugang zu Tiefkühler. Die beste Saison ist Mai - September, sowie von 15. Februar bis 15. April, wo die bekannte Lofotfischerei stattfindet.

Norumgården
Bed & Breakfast

Your host:
Marit & Tor Mikalsen

Address:
Framnesveien 127
N - 8516 Narvik
Phone/Fax: 76 94 48 57
Mobil: 97 50 59 70
Web:
http://norumgaarden.narviknett.no

Best time to call:
08.00 - 15.00 / 18.00 - 22.00

Double room:	**500,-/600,-**	Dobbeltrom:	**500,-/600,-**	Doppelzimmer:	**500,-/600,-**
Single room:	**350,-**	Enkeltrom:	**350,-**	Einzelzimmer:	**350,-**
1 pers. in dbl. room:	**400,-**	1 pers. i dobbeltrom:	**400,-**	1 Pers. im Doppelzi.:	**400,-**
No. of rooms: 4		Antall rom: 4		Anzahl Zimmer: 4	
Full breakfast		Full frokost		Volles Frühstück	
Laid breakfast table		Dekket frokostbord		Serv.: Frühstückstisch	
Open year round		Åpent hele året		Ganzjährig geöffnet	
TV/radio in all rooms		TV/radio på alle rom		TV/Radio in allen Räumen	
Terrace/dekk access/yard		Terasse/uteplass/hage		Terrasse/Aussenplatz/Garten	
No smoking inside		Ingen røking innendørs		Kein Rauchen im Haus	
VISA accepted		Vi tar VISA		Wir nehmen VISA, MC, DC	
Discount for children		Rabatt for barn		Ermässigung für Kinder	
Selfcatering possible		Selvhushold mulig		Selbsthaushalt möglich	
White bathrobes in rooms		Hvite morgenkåper på alle rom		Bademäntel in allen Räumen	
English spoken				Sprechen etwas Deutsch	

Norumgården was named after the master builder who erected it in 1925. 15 years of restoration have brought the building back to its original splendour. The restoration work has brought the owners several prizes. The house also has period furniture. Antique shop on premises.
The Norumgården is a 15 minutes walk from the town centre.
Narvik is best known for its war history, but can also offer skiing, sea fishing and hiking in the summer.

Norumgården har sitt navn etter byggmesteren som bygget huset i 1925. De siste 15 års restaurering har brakt det tilbake til sin fordums prakt. Restaureringsarbeidet har medført at eierne er tildelt flere priser. Huset er innredet med tidsriktige møbler. Egen antikvitetsbutikk.
Norumgården ligger 15 min. gange fra Narvik sentrum. Narvik, mest kjent for sin krigshistorie, tilbyr også skisport, fjordfiske og turmuligheter.

Das Haus aus 1925 ist nach dem Baumeister benannt. Nach 15 Jahren Restaurierung ersteht es nun mit zeitgerechtem Interieur in seinem ehemaligen Glanz, was den Besitzern mehrere Preise eingetragen hat. Eigener Antiquitätenladen.
15 Min. zu Fuss zum Zentrum Narvik, bekannt für seine Kriegsgeschichte. Reiche Möglichkeiten für Angeln und Wandern im Sommer, sowie für Skisport im Winter.

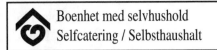
Sjøgata Gjestehus

Your host:
Tove & Arne Hjalmar Hansen

Address:
Sjøgata 4
N - 8480 Andenes
Phone: 76 14 16 37
Fax: 76 14 14 53
Mobil: 90 61 72 64
E-mail: tovekhan@online.no
Web:
http://welcome.to/gjestehuset
Best time to call:
08.00 - 23.00

Room for 1-4 persons	Rom for 1-4 personer	Zimmer für 1-4 Personen
No. of rooms: 4	Antall rom: 4	Anzahl Zimmer: 4
Shared bath, kitchen and LR	Delt bad, kjøkken og stue	Gemeins. Bad, Küche und Stube
Price per room: **300,- to 450,-**	Pris pr. rom: **300,- til 450,-**	Preis pro Zi.: **300,- zu 450,-**
Bed linen fee: **50,-**	Tillegg for sengetøy: **50,-**	Mieten von Bettwäsche: **50,-**
Open 20 May - 15 Sept.	Åpent 20. mai - 15. sept.	Geöffnet 20. Mai - 15. Sept.
TV available	TV tilgjengelig	Zugang zu TV
Terrace/deck access	Terrasse/uteplass	Terrasse/Aussenplatz
No smoking inside	Ingen røking innendørs	Kein Rauchen im Haus
English spoken		Sprechen etwas Deutsch

Sjøgata Guest House is a wooden house over a hundred years old, renovated in 1991. It is centrally located in Andenes, just 200 m from the tourist office and Whaling Center.

Besides the whaling exhibits and whale safaris, there is the midnight sun, much natural beauty, long beaches and saltwater fishing. International saltwater fishing festival in the beginning of July. Daily boat tours around Bleiksøya Island, where 80,000-90,000 pairs of birds are nesting.

Sjøgata Gjestehus er et over hundre år gammelt trehus som ble renovert i 1991. Huset ligger sentralt i Andenes, bare 200 m fra turistkontoret/Hvalsenteret. Foruten hvalutstilling og hvalsafari er her også midnattssol, sjø, lange sandstrender og havfiske. I begynnelsen av juli hvert år arrangeres internasjonal havfiskefestival.
På fuglefjellet Bleiksøya hekker 80-90.000 fuglepar. Det går daglige båtturer rundt øya.

Das Holzhaus ist über 100 Jahre alt und wurde 1991 renoviert. Es liegt zentral in Andenes, nur 200 m vom Touristbüro/Hvalsenter mit einer Walausstellung, entfernt. Hier kann Walsafari gebucht werden. Mitternachtssonne, lange Sandstrände und reiche Angelmöglichkeiten. Anfang Juli: internationaler Angelwettbewerb. Auf der Vogelinsel "Bleikøya" hecken jedes Jahr 80-90.000 Vogelpaare. Tägliche Schiffsrundfahrten.

The only way to be sure of catching a train
is to miss the one before it.
–G. K. Chesterton

Bakkemo Gård

Your host:
Jorunn Hanssen

Address:
Selnes
N - 9470 Gratangen
Phone: **77 02 11 20**
Fax: **76 95 28 60**
Mobil: **48 06 51 96 / 91 69 50 97**

Best time to call:
08.00 - 23.00

Double room:	**450,-**	Dobbeltrom:	**450,-**	Doppelzimmer:	**450,-**
Single room:	**320,-**	Enkeltrom:	**320,-**	Einzelzimmer:	**320,-**
No. of rooms: 4		Antall rom: 4		Anzahl Zimmer: 4	
Guest's common living room		Gjestestue		Aufenthaltsraum	
Full breakfast		Full frokost		Volles Frühstück	
Laid breakfast table		Dekket frokostbord		Serv.: Frühstückstisch	
Open year round		Åpent hele året		Ganzjährig geöffnet	
Garden		Hage		Garten	
Boat for rent		Båtutleie		Boot zu mieten	
Bike for rent		Sykkelutleie		Fahrrad zu mieten	
Selfcatering possible		Selvhushold er mulig		Selbsthaushalt möglich	
Some English spoken				Sprechen Deutsch	

Bakkemo Farm, built in 1870 and fully restored in 1994, is in Gratangen municipality, a 30 km trip from E-6 and 90 km from Evenes Airport. Gratangen is known for its coastal culture, mountain hikes, fjord fishing, lakes, rivers and hunting. Historic sailing tours can be arranged on a "Fembøring" from 1846.

Also available; two solar heated cabins with 3/6 beds and outhouse, and the restored "Stone Cottage" from 1942 for two people which is located an hour's walk from the main road.

Bakkemo Gård ligger i Gratangen kommune, en avstikker på ca. 30 km fra E-6 og 90 km fra Evenes flyplass.
Bakkemo ble bygd i 1870 og restaurert i gammel stil i 1994. Gratangen er kjent for sin kystkultur. Rike muligheter til jakt og friluftsliv, fjellturer, fiske i fjorden, innsjøer og elver.
Seilturer med fembøring fra 1846 kan arrangeres.
Vertskapet leier også ut til solenergioppvarmede hytter med 3/6 soveplasser og uthus, pluss den restaurerte "Steinhytta" som ligger en drøy times krevende gangtur fra veien.

Bakkemo Gård liegt in der Gemeinde Gratangen, 30 km von der E-6 und 90 km vom Flugplatz Evenes.
Gratangens herrliche Natur mit Küste und Bergen bietet Wanderungen, Salz- und Süsswasserangeln, sowie Jagd.
Segeltouren mit altem Schiff (1846) werden veranstaltet. Das Haus aus 1870 wurde im alten Stil renoviert. Der Besitzer hat 2 Hütten mit 3 bzw. 6 Schlafplätzen, Solar-Strom u. Aussentoilette zu vermieten. 1 St. anspruchsvolle Wanderung zu restaurierter Steinhütte mit 2 Schlafstellen.

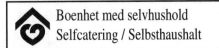

Gunn's Turistutleie

Your host:
Gunn Jensen

Address:
Nordjordveien 37
N - 9110 Sommarøy
Phone: 77 64 02 26
Mobil: 99 70 13 60

Best time to call:
08.00 - 23.00

Apartment for 2-7 persons	Leilighet for 2-7 personer	Wohnung für 2-7 Personen
No. of bedrooms: 2	Antall soverom: 2	Anzahl Schlafräume: 2
Own bath, kitchen, LR	Eget bad, kjøkken, stue	Eig. Bad, Küche, Stube
Price for whole unit: **500,-**	Pris for hele enheten: **500,-**	Ganze Einheit: **500,-**
Bed linen fee: **25,-**	Tillegg for sengetøy: **25,-**	Mieten von Bettwäsche: **25,-**
Open year round	Åpent hele året	Ganzjährig geöffnet
TV available	TV tilgjengelig	Zugang zu TV
Yard/terrace/deck access	Hage/terrasse/uteplass	Garten/Terrasse/Aussenplatz
No smoking inside	Ingen røking innendørs	Kein Rauchen im Haus
English spoken		Sprechen Englisch

Sommarøy (Summer Island) is a tiny sea village 60 km from Tromsø of about 600 residents, most of whom work in the fishing industry on land or at sea. The village has a bank, store, post office, pub and bakery. There is a village museum, handicrafts store and an animal and bird park. Excellent fishing both from the shore and by boat, and the whole of Sommarøy is ringed with white, sandy beaches. On Kvaløya, only 5 km away, you find hiking trails of all varieties. Gunn rents out a cozy cellar 50 m² apartment.

Sommarøy er et lite tettsted, 60 km fra Tromsø, med ca. 600 innbyggere. De fleste arbeider i fiskeindustrien på land eller ute på havet. På stedet finnes det bank, butikk, postkontor, kro og bakeri. Det finnes et bygdemuseum, husflidshus og en smådyrs- og fuglepark.
Det er gode fiskemuligheter både fra land og til havs, flotte kalksandstrender omringer hele Sommarøy. På Kvaløya, bare 5 km unna, er det turterreng for enhver smak.
Gunn leier ut en koselig kjellerleilighet på ca. 50 m² i sin enebolig.

Sommarøy ist eine kleine Insel mit ca. 600 Einwohnern, ca. 60 km von Tromsø entfernt. Die meisten Bewohner sind in der Fischindustrie beschäftigt, entweder an Land oder als Fischer auf dem Meer. Sommarøy bietet Bank, Geschäft, Post, Gasthof und Bäckerei, außerdem Heimatmuseum, Kunstgewerbeladen sowie einen Kleintier- und Vogelpark. Gute Angelmöglichkeiten von Land oder vom Meer aus. Sommarøy ist von reizvollen Kalksandstränden umgeben. Auf Kvaløya, nur 5 km entfernt, gibt es Wandermöglichkeiten für jeden Geschmack. Die Gastgeberin Gunn vermietet eine gemütliche Wohnung (ca. 50 m²) im Untergeschoß ihres Einfamilienhauses.

Forsøket

Your host:
Raymond Abrahamsen

Address:
Borgermester Eidemsgate 1
N - 9009 Tromsø
Phone: **77 69 90 20**
Fax: **77 69 54 83**
Mobil: **90 85 32 86**
E-mail: **r.abraham@c2i.net**

Best time to call:
09.00 - 19.00

Double room: **400,-/450,-**	Dobbeltrom: **400,-/ 450,-**	Doppelzimmer: **400,-/450,-**
1 pers. in double room: **300,-/ 350,-**	En pers. i dobbeltrom: **300,-/ 350,-**	1 Pers. im Doppelzi.: **300,-/ 350,-**
No. of rooms: 2	Antall rom: 2	Anzahl Zimmer: 2
Full breakfast	Full frokost	Volles Frühstück
Breakfast tray	Servering: Frokostbrett/kurv	Serv.: Frühstückstablett
Open year round	Åpent hele året	Ganzjährig geöffnet
No smoking inside	Ingen røking innendørs	Kein Rauchen im Haus
Selfcatering possible	Selvhushold er mulig	Selbsthaushalt möglich
English spoken		Sprechen Englisch

On Tromsø island's eastside, near downtown is where you find a reasonable lodging alternative hosted by Raymond. 10-min. walk to the heart of town. Tromsø, also called the Nordic Paris, offers sightseeing, shopping and restaurants and cafés to active visitors. This part of Tromsø was previously inhabited mostly by fishermen and other sea-hunters, but is now marked by a generational transition. The guest home is a townhouse from 1960 and is located in an area where some traffic noise can be heard from the rooms.

På Tromsøyas østside, ved sentrum, finner du et rimelig alternativ hos Raymond. Det er 10 minutter gange til hjertet av sentrum. Tromsø, også kalt Nordens Paris, har både severdigheter, shopping og resturanter og kaféer å tilby den nysjerrige reisende.
Denne delen av Tromsø hadde tidligere en høy andel av fiskere og fangstfolk, mens den i dag er preget av et generasjonsskifte. Huset er en tomannsbolig fra 1960, og ligger i et område med noe trafikkstøy som vil kunne merkes fra rommene.

Auf der Ostseite der Insel Tromsøya bietet das Haus eine preiswerte Übernachtungsmöglichkeit. Nur 10 Minuten Fußweg bis zum Stadtzentrum. Tromsø, auch "Paris des Nordens" genannt, bietet den interessierten Gästen Sehenswürdigkeiten, Shopping, Restaurants und Cafès.
Dieser Teil Tromsøs verzeichnete früher einen hohen Anteil von Fischern, heute scheint ein Generationenwechsel stattzufinden. Das Zweifamilienhaus von 1960 liegt in einem Gebiet, durch das ein wenig Verkehr fließt, den man auch auf den Zimmern hören kann.

Travel is glamorous only in retrospect. –Paul Theroux

Det røde huset

Your host:
Sollaug Bessesen

Address:
Vågnes
N - 9022 Krokelvdalen
Phone: 77 69 00 88
Mobil: 97 13 55 88
Fax: 77 64 53 90
E-mail: detrodehuset@mail.no
Web:
www.destinasjontromso.no/drh

Best time to call:
07.00 - 22.00

A: Apartment for 2 persons
Own LR, sleeping alcove
Shared bath and kitchen
B: Apartment for 3 persons
No. of bedrooms: 1
Own LR, shared bath and kitchen
A og B: Price per pers.:   **250,-**

C: Guesthouse for 5 persons
Price for whole unit: **1.000,-**

Bed linen included
Open 1 June - 31 Aug.
Terrace/deck access
Boat and bike for rent
No smoking inside
Breakfast service available: **60,-**
English spoken

A: Leilighet for 2 personer
Egen stue, sovealkove
Delt bad og kjøkken
B: Leilighet for 3 personer
Antall soverom: 1
Egen stue, delt bad og kjøkken
A og B: Pris pr. pers.:   **250,-**

C: Gjestehus for 5 personer
Pris for hele enheten: **1.000,-**

Sengetøy er inkludert
Åpent 1. juni - 31. aug.
Terrasse/uteplass
Båt- og sykkelutleie
Ingen røking innendørs
Frokost kan serveres: **60,-**

A: Wohnung für 2 Personen
Eig. Stube, Schlafalkoven
Gemeins. Bad und Küche
B: Wohnung für 3 Personen
Anzahl Schlafräume: 1
Eig. Stube, gem. Bad u. Küche
A og B: Preis pro Pers.:   **250,-**

C: Gästehaus für 5 Personen
Ganze Einheit: **1.000,-**

Inkl. Bettwäsche
Geöffnet 1. Juni - 31. Aug.
Terrasse/Aussenplatz
Boot und Fahrrad zu mieten
Kein Rauchen im Haus
Frühstück auf Bestellung: **60,-**
Sprechen etwas Deutsch

The Bessesen Family welcomes visitors in the summertime to their beautifully furnished 100-year old timber home with character. Situated by the fjord, there is a magnificent sea view from the 1st floor. Rowboat for rent. You may go fishing in either of two rivers a few kilometers away. Breathtaking nature. Vågnes is located on the mainland, 23 km northeast of Tromsø. Sollaug, your hostess, has her own furniture restoration workshop and Atle works at the university.

I et nydelig innredet 100 år gammelt tømmerhus med sjel tar familien Bessesen vel imot gjester på sommerstid. Huset ligger like ved fjorden. Fra utkikksrommet i 2. etasje er det fin utsikt utover sjøen.
En robåt er til leie. Noen kilometer unna gir to elver muligheter for fiskefangst. Naturen er storslagen i distriktet. Vågnes ligger på fastlandet 23 km nord-øst for Tromsø. Vertinnen Sollaug har møbelrestaurerings verksted og Atle er universitetsansatt.

In einem wunderschön eingerichtetem, 100 Jahre altem Blockhaus mit Seele empfängt die Familie Bessesen im Sommer gerne Gäste. Das Haus liegt direkt am Fjord. Vom 1. Stock hat man gute Aussicht aufs Meer. Ruderboot zu vermieten. Einige Kilometer entfernt laden zwei Flüsse zum Angeln ein. Großartige Landschaft ringsum. Vågnes liegt 23 km nordöstlich von Tromsø auf dem Festland. Die Gastgeberin Sollaug restauriert Möbel, Atle ist Universitätsangestellter.

Laksefiskerens krypinn

Your host:
Harald-Erik & Ragnhild Rognmo

Address:
Rognmo
N - 9151 Storslett
Phone/Fax: 77 76 54 55
Mobil: 94 81 83 91
E-mail: haralro@online.no

Best time to call:
08.00 - 23.00

Cabin for 2-6 persons	Hytte for 2-6 personer	Hütte für 2-6 Personen
No. of bedrooms: 3	Antall soverom: 3	Anzahl Schlafräume: 3
Bath, kitchen	Bad, kjøkken	Bad, Küche
Price per pers.: **200,-**	Pris pr. pers.: **200,-**	Preis pro Pers.: **200,-**
Price for hole unit.: **1.200,-**	Pris for hele enheten: **1.200,-**	Ganze Einheit: **1.200,-**
Bed linen included	Sengetøy er inkludert	Inkl. Bettwäsche
Open 1 June - 30 Sept.	Åpent 1. juni - 30. sept.	Geöffnet 1. Juni - 30. Sept.
TV available	TV tilgjengelig	Zugang zu TV
Deck access	Uteplass	Aussenplatz
Sauna	Badstu	Sauna
Boat for rent	Båtutleie	Boot zu mieten
No smoking inside	Ingen røking innendørs	Kein Rauchen im Haus
Breakfast service available	Frokost kan serveres	Frühstück auf Bestellung
Finish and some English spoken		Sprechen etwas Englisch

Mountains rise up to 4000 feet on both sides of Storslett. The valley is exceptionally lush even though so far north. You can find Norway's third highest waterfall at 840 feet in Reisa National Park. "The Salmon Fisher's Hut" lies on Reisa River, with good fishing for salmon, char and trout. Fishing licenses can be purchased during the summer. The Rognmos have a small farm with 2.3 km of shoreline, well-suited for boat and hiking trips.

Storslett er sentrum i Nordreisa kommune. Reisadalen har fjell opp til 1300 m.o.h. på begge sider. Til å ligge så langt nord, er dalen særdeles frodig. Norges tredje-høyeste foss på 260 m finner du i Reisa nasjonalpark. "Laksefiskerens krypinn" ligger ved Reisaelva, en god fiske-elv med laks, røye og ørret. Fiskekort kan kjøpes i sommersesongen. Fam. Rognmo har et småbruk med 2,3 km strandlinje. Området egner seg til båtturer og fotturer.

Storslett ist Zentrum der Gemeinde Nordreisa. Berge bis zu 1300 m ü.d.M. In dem für seine nördliche Lage fruchtbaren Tal liegt Reisa Nationalpark mit Norwegens dritthöchstem Wasserfall (260 m). Die "Lachsfischer-Hütte" liegt am Fluss Reisaelva. Gute Fangmöglichkeiten für Lachs, Saibling und Seeforelle. Angelkarten. Fam. Rognmo sind Kleinbauern und verfügen über 2,3 km Strandlinie. Boottouren u. Wanderungen.

Simonsen Gårdsferie

Your host:
Nelly & Willy Simonsen

Address:
Storeng, N - 9161 Burfjord
Phone: 77 76 93 86
Fax: 77 76 93 65
Mobil: 91 16 83 20
E-mail: simonsen@simongard.no
Web: www.simongard.no

Best time to call:
09.00 - 22.00

A: "Naustet"
Guesthouse for 2-5 persons
No. of bedrooms: 2
Own bath, kitchen, LR
Price for whole unit: **870,-**

B: "Bestefarshuset"
Guesthouse for 2-11 persons
No. of bedrooms: 4
Own bath, kitchen, LR
Price for whole unit: **995,-**
Price per room.:   **340,-**
Bed linen fee: **50,-**

C: "Nyheim"
Guesthouse for 2 persons
No. of bedrooms: 1
Own bath, kitchen, LR
Price for whole unit: **600,-**

D: "Røysa"
Guesthouse for 2-6 persons
No. of bedrooms: 2
Own bath, kitchen, LR
Price for whole unit: **715,-**

Applies to all rental units:
Bed linen incl., but not for unit B
Breakfast service avaiable: **50,-**
Other meals served
Open year round
Yard/garden
Boat for rent, freezer available
Discount after 3 days
English spoken

A: "Naustet"
Gjestehus for 2-5 personer
Antall soverom: 2.
Eget bad, kjøkken, stue
Pris for hele enheten: **870,-**

B: "Bestefarshuset"
Gjestehus for 2-11 personer
Antall soverom: 4
Eget bad, kjøkken, stue
Pris for hele enheten: **995,-**
Pris pr. rom: **340,-**
Tillegg for sengetøy: **50,-**

C: "Nyheim"
Gjestehus for 2 personer
Antall soverom: 1
Eget bad, kjøkken, stue
Pris for hele enheten: **600,-**

D: "Røysa"
Gjestehus for 2-6 personer
Antall soverom: 2
Eget bad, kjøkken, stue
Pris for hele enheten: **715,-**

For alle enhetene gjelder:
Sengetøy inkl, unntatt for enhet B
Frokost kan serveres: **50,-**
Andre måltider kan bestilles
Åpent hele året
Uteplass/hage
Båtutleie, fryseboks tilgjengelig
Rabatt ved leie over 3 dager

A: "Naustet"
Gästehaus für 2-5 Personen
Anzahl Schlafräume: 2
Eig. Bad, Küche, Stube
Ganze Einheit: **870,-**

B: "Bestefarshuset"
Gästehaus für 2-11 Personen
Anzahl Schlafräume: 4
Eig. Bad, Küche, Stube
Ganze Einheit: **995,-**
Preis pro Zimmer: **340,-**
Mieten von Bettwäsche: **50,-**

C: "Nyheim"
Gästehaus für 2 Personen
Anzahl Schlafräume: 1
Eig. Bad, Küche, Stube
Ganze Einheit: **600,-**

D: "Røys"
Gästehaus für 2-6 Personen
Anzahl Schlafräume: 2
Eig. Bad, Küche, Stube
Ganze Einheit: **715,-**

Für alle Einheiten gilt:
Inkl. Bettw., ausser für Einheit B
Frühstück auf Bestellung: **50,-**
Serv.: Andere Mahlzeiten
Ganzjährig geöffnet
Aussenplatze
Boot zu mieten, Tiefkühler
Ermäßigung: ab 3 Übernachtungen
Sprechen Deutsch

Karen's Rorbuer

Your host:
Svein & Karen-Anna Christoffersen

Address:
Komagfjord
N - 9536 Korsfjorden
Phone: 78 43 92 81
Fax: 78 44 51 66
E-mail: firma@rorbuer.com
Web: www.rorbuer.com

Best time to call:
16.00 - 22.00

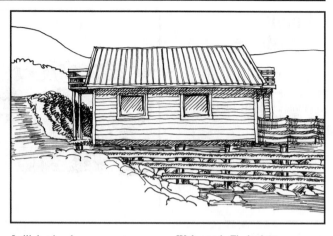

Apartment in Fisherman's cabin for 2-4 (family: 6) persons	Leilighet i rorbu for 2-4 (familie 6) personer	Wohnung in Fischerhütte für 2-4 (Familie: 6) Personen
No. of bedrooms: 1	Antall soverom: 1	Anzahl Schlafräume: 1
Own bath, sleeping alcove, LR with kitchenette/kitchen nook	Bad, sovealkove, oppholdsrom med tekjøkken/kjøkkenkrok	Eig. Bad, Schlafalkoven, Stube mit Teeküche/Küchenecke
Price for whole unit: **750,-**	Pris for hele enheten: **750,-**	Ganze Einheit: **750,-**
Bed linen fee: **50,-**	Tillegg for sengetøy: **50,-**	Mieten von Bettwäsche: **50,-**
Breakfast service available: **70,-**	Frokost kan serveres: **70,-**	Frühstück auf Bestellung: **70,-**
Other meals on request	Andre måltider kan bestilles	Andere Mahlzeiten nach Vereinb.
Open year round	Åpent hele året	Ganzjährig geöffnet
TV available	TV tilgjengelig	Zugang zu TV
Yard/terrace/garden	Terrasse/uteplass/hage	Garten/Terrasse/Aussenplatz
Boat for rent	Båtutleie	Boot zu mieten
Pets welcome	Kjæledyr tillatt	Haustiere willkommen
No smoking inside	Ingen røking innendørs	Kein Rauchen im Haus
Some English spoken		Sprechen etwas Deutsch

Fisherman's cabins by the sea in Komagfjord are near excellent fishing areas. Boat rental, independent activities. Store and gas stations. Activities include: ice-fishing, ski trips, grouse hunting, freshwater fishing, diving and berry and mushroom picking, among others.

Directions:
Exit E-6 at Leirbotvann towards Nyvoll via RV 883. Ferry from Nyvoll to Korsfjord. Then drive 4 km to Komagfjord.

Rorbuer ved sjøen i Komagfjord, nær gode fiskeplasser. Båtutleie, selvaktivisering.
Butikk og bensinstasjoner. Muligheter for isfiske, skiturer, rypejakt, ferskvannsfiske, dykking, sopp- og bærsanking m.m.

Veibeskrivelse:
Ta av fra E-6 ved Leirbotvann mot Nyvoll RV 883. Ferge fra Nyvoll, 10 min til Korsfjord. Deretter 4 km til Komagfjord.

Fischerhütten direkt am Meer, in der Nähe einiger guter Angel-plätze. Bootsverleih (teilweise Selbstinitiative). Geschäft, Tank-stellen. Möglichkeiten zum Eis-angeln und Skiwandern. Außerdem: Schneehuhnjagd, Binnenangeln, Tauchen, Beeren- und Pilze sammeln.

Wegbeschreibung:
Biegen Sie bei Leirbotvann von der E-6 auf die Straße 883 nach Nyvoll ab. Ab Nyvoll verkehrt eine Fähre nach Korsfjord. Anschließend 4 km bis Komagfjord.

Havstua

Your host:
Ester S. N. Hansen

Address:
**Kamøyvær
N - 9750 Honningsvåg**
Phone: 78 47 51 50
Fax: 78 47 51 91
Mobil: 90 97 69 21
E-mail: havstua@havstua.no
Web: www.havstua.no

Best time to call:
09.00 - 22.00

Double room:	**760,-**	Dobbeltrom:	**760,-**	Doppelzimmer:	**760,-**
1 pers. in double room:	**570,-**	1 pers. i dobbeltrom:	**570,-**	1 Pers. in Doppelzimmer:	**570,-**
Full breakfast		Full frokost		Volles Frühstück	
Laid breakfast table		Servering: Frokostbord		Serv.: Frühstückstisch	
Summer: À la carte dinner menu		Sommer: á la carte middagsmeny		Sommer: à la carte-Speisekarte	
B&B Open 1 May - 31 Aug.		B&B åpent 1. mai - 31. aug.		B&B: Geöffnet 1. Mai - 31. Aug.	
Self-catering open all year		Selvhushold åpent hele året		Selbsthaushalt: Ganzjährig geöffn.	
Yard		Uteplass		Aussenplatz	
Private dock		Egen kai		Eigene Anlegestelle	
Boat for rent		Båtutleie		Boot zu mieten	
Self-catering possible		Selvhushold er mulig		Selbsthaushalt möglich	
No smoking indoors		Ingen røking innendørs		Kein Rauchen im Haus	
VISA, MC accepted		Vi tar VISA, MC		Wir nehmen VISA, MC	
Access to telephone/fax/internet		Tilgang på telefon/faks/Internett		Zugang Telefon/Fax/Internet	
Suitable for handicapped		Handikapvennlig		Behindertengerecht	
English and some French spoken				Sprechen Deutsch	

Overnight accommodations in a small yet active and vibrant fishing village with 120 local inhabitants. The Havstua is built upon a pier directly above the sea and is idyllicly situated with waves washing in below your feet and the shrill of seagulls on the rooftop...

Directions:
About 24 km from the actual North Cape plateau. Kamøyvær is situated along the main route to the North Cape, 2 km from E-69, 10 km from Honningsvåg.

Overnatting i et lite, men aktivt og levende fiskevær med 120 innbyggere. Anlegget står på påler ute i sjøen, og ligger nydelig til med bølgesvulp under føttene og måkeskrik på taket ...

Veibeskrivelse:
Ca 24 km fra selveste Nordkappplatået. Kamøyvær er på veien til Nordkapp, 2 km fra E-69, 10 km fra Honningsvåg.

Übernachtungsmöglichkeiten in einem kleinen, aber durchaus lebhaften Fischerdorf mit 120 Einwohnern. Die Anlage wurde als Pfahlbau direkt am Wasser erbaut. Genießen Sie das leichte Plätschern der Wellen unter den Füßen, eingerahmt vom charakteristischen Schreien der Möwen auf dem Dach!

Wegbeschreibung:
Ca. 24 km bis zum Nordkapfelsen. Kamøyvær liegt auf dem Weg dorthin, ca. 2 km von der E-69 und 10 km von Honningsvåg entfernt.

Barbara's Bed & Breakfast

Your host:
Barbara Lund

Address:
Henrik Lunds gate 13
N - 9900 Kirkenes
Phone: 78 99 32 07
Mobil: 41 46 11 30
E-mail: barbara@trollnet.no
Web:
http://home.trollnet.no/barbara

Best time to call:
16.00 - 23.00

Double-/Twin room: **450,-/500,-**	Dobbelt-/tosengsrom: **450,-/500,-**	Doppel-/Zweibettzi.: **450,-/500,-**
1 pers. in double room: **275,-/300,-**	En pers. i dobbeltrom: **275,-/300,-**	1 Pers. im Doppelzi.: **275,-/300,-**
No. of rooms: 2	Antall rom: 2	Anzahl Zimmer: 2
Full breakfast	Full frokost	Volles Frühstück
Laid breakfast table	Dekket frokostbord	Serv.: Frühstückstisch
Open year round	Åpent hele året	Ganzjährig geöffnet
TV in rooms	TV på rommene	TV im Zimmer
Terrace/deck access/yard/garden	Terrasse/uteplass/hage	Terrasse/Aussenplatz/Garten
Discount for children	Rabatt for barn	Ermässigung für Kinder
Selfcatering possible	Selvhushold er mulig	Selbsthaushalt möglich
English & French spoken		Sprechen Deutsch

Within walking distance from Kirkenes city center and the Coastal Express quay, you will find shelter at Barbara's Bed & Breakfast. The rooms are situated in the loft level of a 50 year-old house and are in excellent condition. The two rooms share one bathroom. Barbara gladly welcomes motorcycle-tourists and people who didn't have the heart to leave their dog at home. Your hostess has her own dog. Kirkenes is the final stop for the Coastal Express on its long northern journey along the Norwegian coastline. The city is also a border town unlike any other in Norway, and it is also possible to travel over to both Finland and Murmansk in Russia.

I gangavstand til Kirkenes sentrum og hurtigrutekaia, kan du søke ly hos Barbaras Bed & Breakfast. Rommene ligger i loftetasjen i et 50 år gammelt hus og er fullt oppusset. Badet deles mellom de to utleierommene. Barbara tar gjerne imot MC-turister og folk som ikke hadde hjerte til å la hunden være igjen hjemme. Vertinnen har hund selv. Kirkenes er siste stoppested for hurtigruten på sin lange ferd langs norskekysten. Byen er også grensebyen fremfor noen i Norge, og det kan være muligheter for å dra videre både til Finnland og til Murmansk i Russland.

Unweit von Kirkenes Zentrum und der Anlegestelle der Hurtigruten-Schiffe bietet Barbara ihren Gästen Unterkunft. Die Zimmer befinden sich im Dachgeschoß eines 50 Jahre alten Hauses und sind vollständig renoviert. Das Bad wird von beiden Mietern gemeinsam genutzt. Barbara empfängt gerne MC-Touristen und alle, die es nicht übers Herz bringen, ihren Hund zu Hause zu lassen. Sie hat selbst einen Hund. Kirkenes ist der letzte Hafen der Postschiffe auf ihrem langen Weg die norwegische Küste hinauf., und ausserdem bekannte Grenzstadt im hohen Norden. Ausflüge nach Finnland sowie nach Murmansk in Rußland.

Page 41 Villa Antique

The house is located 1 km from the Norway/Sweden border near the Svinesund Bridge, and is easily visible from E-6. Close to the Shell Gas Station.

Huset ligger 1 km inn i Norge fra Svinesundbroen. Huset er lett synlig fra E-6, ved Shell bensinstasjon.

Page 42 Pia's Gjestehus

Exit onto RV 21 from E-6 towards Halden to the roundabout before the bridge in the town. Exit the roundabout to the left and drive about 600 m to the complex marked "Norske Skog". Brattveien starts just across from the main entrance to Norske Skog.

Kjør RV-21 fra E-6 mot Halden til rundkjøring før broen inne i byen. Ta til venstre ut av rundkjøringen og kjør ca. 600 m til anlegg med skilt Norske Skog. Brattveien begyner vis a vis hovedporten.

Page 43 Bed & Breakfast in Moss

From Moss city center: Follow the signs to Jeløy. After crossing the canal, take your first right at the intersection. Follow the signs up Rambergveien to Jeløy Chapel ("kapell"). Then take your first left after the chapel. Stjerneveien 10 is the next to last house on the left-hand side.

Fra Moss sentrum følg skilt til Jeløy. Etter at du har krysset kanalen, ta første vei til høyre i lyskrysset. Følg skilt til Jeløy kapell opp Rambergveien. Ta så første til venstre etter kapellet. Stjerneveien 10 ligger som nest siste hus på venstre hånd.

Page 44 Østre Tveter Gård

From Moss: Follow RV 120 towards Våler. Get on RV 115 at the Rødsund Bru and continue straight ahead, while RV 120 veers in another direction. Keep driving until you see a sign for Våler kirke, and turn left towards the church. Note: Just before the church, turn right towards Mørk and drive 6.5 km until you see a sign for Østre Tveter Gård.

Fra Moss ta RV 120 mot Våler. Ved Rødsund Bru, hvor RV 120 svinger av, skal du fortsette rett fram på RV 115. Kjør til du ser skilt med Våler kirke, ta til venstre mot kirken, men like før kirken tar du til høyre, mot Mørk, og kjører 6,5 km til du ser skilt til Østre Tveter Gård.

Page 47 Solveig's Bed & Breakfast

Just north of Ring 3 in northeast central Oslo. About 5 km north of Central Station. Public transportation: Take Metro Line number 5 towards Sognsvann to Tåsen Station. Walk uphill on Tåsenveien about one block. Turn left into Tåsen Terrasse. Approx. 5 min. walk.

Just north of Ring 3 in north-east central Oslo. Ca 5 km north of Central Station. Public transportation: Take Metro Line number 5 towards Sognsvann to Tåsen Station. Walk Tåsenveien (uphill), about one block. Turn left into Tåsen Terrasse. Appr. 5 min. walk.

Page 48 Evjen Bed & Breakfast

From Ring 3: Take the exit for Holmenkollen/Vindern. From Majorstua: Take Slemdalsveien to Holmenveien. At Vindern trolley station, cross the train tracks and drive straight ahead through the next intersection. Number 16 B is a single-level, white house on the left side.

Fra Ring 3: Ta av ved avkjørsel til Holmenkollen/ Vinderen. Fra Majorstua: Kjør Slemdalsveien til Holmenveien. Ved Vindern stasjon, kryss T-banesporet og kjør rett frem gjennom neste kryss, Nr. 16B er en hvit énetasjes villa på venstre side.

Vom Ring 3: Abfahrt Holmenkollen/Vinderen. An der Bahnstation "Vindern stasjon" die U-Bahn überqueren und anschließend geradeaus über die nächste Kreuzung fahren. Nr. 16 b ist eine eingeschossige, weiße Villa und liegt auf der linken Seite.

Page 49 Mary's Bed & Breakfast

By car: Drive towards Frognerseteren/Holmenkollen. About 9 km from downtown: turn left at the sign marked "Trollvasshytta", the road is called Sætravei, which is just before the overpass at Besserud. After another 2 km, you come to the next overpass at Voksenlia trolley station. Turn left before the underpass onto Jerpefaret. Follow the sign marked "Jerpefaret 11-17" to the right and drive across the stream and then look for the second house on the right (long stairway up to the house).

Med bil: Kjør mot Frognerseteren/Holmenkollen. Ca. 9 km fra sentrum, ta av til venstre hvor skilt viser "Trollvasshytta", veien heter Sætravei, dette er like

før undergang ved Besserud. Etter ca 2 km kommer du til neste undergang, ved Voksenlia stasjon. Ta da til venstre før undergangen og du er i Jerpefaret. Følg skiltet med Jerpefaret 11-17 til høyre, og kjør så over bekken og deretter finn andre huset på høyre (lang trapp opp til huset).

Page 51 Anna's Place

Follow E-18 to Lysaker. Exit towards Jar. Drive 3 km and turn right at the end of the road (Vollsveien). Then take your first left onto Ringstabekkveien and turn left after the 5th speed bump onto Myrveien. Anna's Place is the 2nd house. Walking time to trolley and Metro: 7 min.

Følg E-18 til Lysaker. Ta av mot Jar. Kjør 3 km og i enden av veien ta til høyre (Vollsveien). Så tar du første vei til venstre som er Ringstabekkveien, og etter 5. fartsdump tar du til venstre til Myrveien. Anna's Place er 2. hus. 7 min. å gå fra hus til trikk og T-bane.

Page 53 The Blue Room

From Oslo: E-18 southward towards Drammen. Exit towards Billingstad and Nesøya. Turn left at the first roundabout and drive straight through the second roundabout. Drive about 1 km on a road called Billingstadsletta until you get to Nesbru. Drive under the main highway and you will see the Viking Towing Yard on the right-hand side. Opposite the Viking station (on your left as you drive in this direction), there is a small bridge that takes you to Nesåsen. Look for number 11 C, a brown house.

Fra Oslo: E-18 sørover mot Drammen, ta av mot Billingstad og Nesøya. Ved første rundkjøring, ta til venstre, og i andre rundkjøring kjør rett fram. Kjør ca 1 km på veien kalt Billingstadsletta til du kommer til Nesbru. Kjør under hovedveien, og på høyre side er det en Viking bilborttauingsstasjon. På motsatt side av Viking stasjonen (til venstre når du kommer kjør ende) er det en smal bru som vil føre deg til Nesåsen. Finn nummer 11 C, et brunt hus.

Page 58 Trugstadloftet

From Oslo: Follow E-6 northward to Skedsmokorset where you will exit onto RV 120 towards Nannestad. Drive though Gjerdrum to the roundabout near the Rimi grocery store and gas station. Drive straight ahead for about 2 km towards Nannestad. Then turn left at the sign marked "Trugstad gård". Drive 800 m and you are here!

Fra Oslo: Følg E-6 nordover til Skedsmokorset hvor du tar RV 120 mot Nannestad. Kjør kjennom Gjerdrum til rundkjøring ved Rimi-butikk og bensinstasjon. Fortsett rett fram mot Nannestad ca. 2 km. Ta så av til venstre hvor skilt sier Trugstad gård. Kjør 800 m og du er framme.

Page 59 Aarholt-tunet

From E-18 at Tønsberg: Exit towards Andebu, drive 3.5 km and then exit towards Vennerød and drive 2.7 km. From Vennerød skole (school), drive 1.7 km towards Gjein. Turn right at Holt towards Aarholt. Drive 1 km on the gravel road.

Fra E-18 ved Tønsberg; ta av mot Andebu, kjør 3,5 km og ta av mot Vennerød, kjør så 2,7 km. Ved Vennerød skole skal du kjøre videre mot Gjein, 1,7 km. Ved Holt ta til Høyre mot Aarholt. Kjør 1 km på grusvei.

Page 62 Heggelund's rom og frokost

Location: 45 km from Elverum and 60 km from Kongsvinger. From Flisa town center: Drive towards Elverum from the roundabout, then take your first road and your first right again. Here you will find Heggelund's Bed & Breakfast, an ochre yellow house.

Beliggenhet: 45 km fra Elverum og 60 km fra Kongsvinger. Fra Flisa sentrum: Fra rundkjøringen ta mot Elverum, så første vei til høyre og første til høyre igjen. Der finner du Heggelund's rom og frokost, et okergult hus.

Page 64 Spitalengen

From E-6: Follow E-6 to a point about 6 km south of Espa. Exit towards Trautskogen and drive about 5.5 km. Look for the sign marked "Spitalen Nord", then drive to the left and follow the road uphill about 550 m (keep to your left in the intersection). Come to the farm situated down on the right-hand side. From RV 24: Drive to Bruvold in Nord Odalen, and look for the sign marked for "Løkker" on RV 24, then drive 1 km, and follow the sign to "Trøftskogen".

Drive about 15 km. Drive uphill to the right at the sign on the left-hand side marked "Spitalen Nord", and follow the road about 550 m. Follow the above directions the rest of the way.

Fra E-6: kjør E-6 til ca 6 km sør for Espa. Ta av i retning Trautskogen og følg denne veien ca 5.5 km. Skilt på høyre side "Spitalen Nord". Ta til venstre og følg veien oppover ca 550 m (hold til venstre i krysset). Henvend dere til gården som ligger ned til høyre. Fra RV 24: Kjør til Bruvold i Nord Odalen, skilt "Løkker" på RV 24, kjør 1 km, følg skilt til "Trøftskogen". Følg veien ca 15 km. Skilt på venstre side "Spitalen Nord", ta opp til høyre og følg veien oppover ca. 550 m, og resten som ovenfor.

Page 65 Skogholtet utleie

From the Norsk skogbruksmuseum (Forestry Museum): Turn left onto RV-20, then make two right turns. Follow Grindalsbakken 1 km past the block apartments on the left-hand side. Take your first right onto Dagfinn Grønnosets vei. Then turn left immediately and look for a brown-stained duplex as the road curves.

Fra Norsk skogbruksmuseum; ta til venstre ut på RV-20, så til høyre to ganger. Følg Grindalsbakken 1 km forbi boligblokker på venstre side. Ta første til høyre som er Dagfinn Grønnosets vei. Ta så straks til venstre og finn en brunbeiset tomannsbolig i svingen.

Page 69 Overskotts B&B

Exit E-6 just south of Hamar. Follow the sign towards Ottestad 500 meters westward to RV 222, then turn right and drive 100 m towards the Shell gas station. Follow the signs towards Sandvika/HIAS. Drive past Ideal-Wasa and make your first left turn onto Rundvegen. Drive 100 m then turn right onto Parallellvegen and drive until you meet Buevegen. From Hamar city center: Follow RV 222 over the Stangebrua bridge to the Shell station.

Ta av fra E-6 like sør for Hamar. Følg skilt Ottestad 500 meter vestover til RV 222, ta til høyre 100 m ned til Shell stasjonen. Følg skilt Sandvika/HIAS. Kjør forbi Ideal-Wasa og ta

første vei til venstre; Rundvegen. Kjør 100 m, ta så til høyre inn Parallellvegen og kjør til du finner Buevegen. Fra Hamar sentrum tar du RV 222 over Stangebrua til Shell-stasjonen.

Page 71 Strandhagen

From E-6 / Brumunddal N: Exit towards Nes. Follow RV 212 to Stavsjø. Turn left onto RV 213 and drive to Tignes. From Tignes take the bridge over to Helgøya, then make your first right onto Skavangvegen. Drive past a large red farm building and up to your left. Here the road curves to the right into a woodsy area, but you should keep to your left and drive down to the farm with mostly red houses and one brown wooden house.

Fra E-6 / Brumunddal N. ta av til Nes. Kjør RV 212 til Stavsjø. Ta til venstre, RV 213, til Tignes. Ved Tignes tar du brua over til Helgøya, ta så til høyre med en gang og kjør Skavangvegen. Du kjører forbi et stort rødt uthus og opp til venstre. Veien svinger så til høyre, inn i et skogholt, men her tar du til venstre og kjører ned til gården med røde og ett brunt tømmerhus.

Page 72 Solbakken gjestegård

From Oslo: Follow E-6 towards Lillehammer. Drive past the exit for Brummunddal and turn right at the sign marked "Brumunddal N./Nes 212". After 300 m, turn right at the sign marked "Brumunddal 212". After another 300 m, turn left at the sign marked "Økelsrud". After 2 km, turn right at the sign marked "Veldre". After 800 m, turn right at the sign marked "Hageberg". Drive 200 m and you are here!

Fra Oslo, følg E-6 i retning Lillehammer. Passér avkjøring til Brumunddal og ta til høyre ved skilt til "Brumunddal N./Nes 212". Etter 300 m: ta til høyre ved skilt "Brumunddal 212". Etter 300 m: ta til venstre ved skilt "Økelsrud". Etter 2 km: ta til høyre ved skilt "Veldre". Etter 800 m: ta til høyre ved skilt "Hageberg". Etter 200 m er du framme.

Page 76 Høvren Gård

Exit E-6 towards Øyer Nord about 20 km north of Lillehammer. Drive onto old highway E-6 near the Statoil gas station. Turn left at this intersection and drive about 50 meters. Look for the sign marked "Høvren 3.5 km". Follow the signs uphill through the town.

Ca. 20 km nord for Lillehammer; ta av fra E-6 mot Øyer

Nord. Kjør inn på gammle E-6 ved Statoil. Ta til venstre i dette krysset og kjør ca. 50 meter. Se skilt merket Høvren 3,5 km. Følg skiltene oppover bygda.

Page 77 Skåden Gard

Exit E-6 towards Øyer Nord. Look for the sign marked Skåden Gard just a few yards before you come to the Statoil gas station, then drive 4 km up into the hills.

Ta av E-6 ved skilt mot Øyer N. Noen meter nord for Statoil bensinstasjon er det skiltet videre til Skåden Gard, 4 km oppover i lia.

Page 80 Glomstad Gård

Glomstad is located at Tretten, 5 km from town center on the east side of the river, 30 km north of Lillehammer. Drive through the town center and exit the main road towards Glomstad just after passing the Kiwi grocery store on the right-hand side. Remaining distance: 5 km.

Glomstad ligger på Tretten, 5 km fra sentrum på østsiden av elven, 30 km nord for Lillehammer. Kjør gjennom sentrum, og like etter at du passerer en Kiwi-butikk på høyrehånd, tar du av til Glomstad, 5 km.

Page 81 Valberg Fjellgard

Follow E-6 from Lillehammer for about 60 km to Sør-Fron in Gudbrandsdalen. About 5 km north of Sør-Fron town center and about 7 km from Vinstra, you exit at the sign marked "Kvarvet". From E-6 there is a 12 km stretch of good roads up to Valberg Fjellgard. There is a sign marking the location of the farm.

Følg E-6 fra Lillehammer til Sør-Fron i Gudbrandsdalen, ca. 60 km. Ca. 5 km nord for Sør-Fron sentrum og ca. 7 km fra Vinstra, tar du av hvor skilt viser "Kvarvet". Fra E-6 er det 12 km god vei opp til Valberg Fjellgard. Det er skilt ved gården.

Page 82 Skåbu Hytter og Camping

From Vinstra and E-6: Take RV 255 towards Skåbu and drive 25 km. The farm is 4 km from the center of Skåbu.

Fra Vinstra og E-6; ta RV 255 mot Skåbu og kjør 25 km. Plassen ligger 4 km før Skåbu sentrum.

Aus Richtung Vinstra (E 6): Fahren Sie auf der Straße 255 nach Skåbu (ca. 25 km). Der Campingplatz liegt etwa 4 km vom Zentrum entfernt.

Page 83 Storrusten Gjestehus

Situated along E-6, about 7 km south of Otta and 3 km north of Sjoa.

Langs E-6 ca 7 km sør for Otta, 3 km nord for Sjoa.

Page 87 Sørre Hemsing

From Fagernes: Take E-16 towards Lærdal and take a right turn over Hemsing bridge at Vang in Valdres. Drive approx. 1 km climbing towards Heensåsen church. (Do not exit before having driven along Vangsmjøsa lake, about 2 km).

Fra Fagernes: E-16 mot Lærdal, i Vang i Valdres ta til høyre over Hemsing bru og kjør ca. 1 km oppover mot Heensåsen kirke. (En skal ikke ta av før en har kjørt langs Vangsmjøsa, ca 2 km).

Von Fagernes: Auf der E 16 Richtung Lærdal, in Vang i Valdres rechts ab, über die Brücke Hemsing bru und dann ca. 1 km bergan zur Heensåsen-Kirche (biegen Sie erst ab, nachdem Sie 2 km am See Vangsmjøsa entlanggefahren sind).

Page 89 Fagernes B&B

Fagernes Bed & Breakfast is located in Fagernes town center. From E-16: Drive 20 km along RV 51 towards Beitostølen, then turn left and drive up Gamlevegen. Drive about 100 meters to Gamlevegen 4.

Fagernes Bed & Breakfast ligger i Fagernes sentrum. Fra E-16, kjør 20 m langs RV 51 retning Beitostølen, ta deretter av til venstre opp Gamlevegen. Kjør ca. 100 meter til Gamlevegen 4.

Fagernes Bed & Breakfast liegt im Zentrum von Fagernes. Zweigen Sie von der E-16 ab und fahren Sie 20 m auf der Str. 51 in Richtung Beitostølen. Anschließend biegen Sie nach links ab ("Gamlevegen"). Nach ca. 100 m sind Sie vor Ort ("Gamlevegen 4").

Page 90 Holthe Gård

From Gjøvik: Drive towards Minnesund (Lena) and after 15 km you will exit at the roundabout onto RV 246 towards Lena and drive about 1 km. Follow RV 244 into Lena town center and stay on RV 244 for

about 12-13 km. At the S-markedet grocery store, there is a sign for Holthe Gård. From Oslo: RV-4 towards Gjøvik, exit after 90 km towards Lena.

Fra Gjøvik; Kjør mot Minnesund (Lena), etter 15 km, i en rundkjøring; ta av mot Lena RV 246 og kjør ca 1 km. Ta RV 244 inn til Lena sentrum og gjennom videre RV 244 ca 12-13 km. Ved S-markedet står skilt til Holthe Gård. Fra Oslo: RV-4 mot Gjøvik, etter 90 km ta av mot Lena.

Page 92 Kronviksætra

From Gjøvik: Follow RV-33 14 km towards Fagernes /Dokka. Exit towards Kronviksætra /Landåsbygda onto Fylkesvei-132, and drive 6 km. Follow the signs the rest of the way.

Fra Gjøvik; følg RV-33 mot Fagernes /Dokka 14 km. Ta av mot Kronviksætra /Landåsbygda på Fylkesvei-132, følg denne 6 km. Det er skiltet helt frem.

Page 99 Fjellheim Bed & Breakfast

From Larvik: Drive northeastward on E-18 and exit onto RV 30 about 12 km from Larvik and proceed towards Langangen. After 1.5 km you will see a sign marked B&B. From Porsgrunn: Drive southwestward from Porsgrunn city center on RV 30 about 12 km and exit to Langangen near the Telemarksporten. If you are driving on E-18 towards Oslo from Kristiansand, exit about 8 km past the Telemarksporten towards Langangen after bridges and follow RV 30 (about 1.5 km, look for the B&B sign).

Fra Larvik: Ca 12 km fra Larvik nord/øst på E18, ta av til Langangen og følg deretter RV 30 ca 1,5 km der du finner skilt til B&B. Fra Porsgrunn: Ca 12 km fra Porsgrunn sentrum på RV 30. Ta av til Langangen ved Telemarksporten. Kjører du E-18 fra Kristiansand mot Oslo er det ca 8 km fra Telemarksporten. Ta av til Langangen etter broene og følg RV 30 (ca 1,5 km, så finner du skilt B&B).

Page 100 Åkerveien Bed & Breakfast

Åkerveien is located about 3 km south of Porsgrunn city center. From the city center: take Deichmannsgate to Flåtten and then get on Stridsklev ring. Turn right at Bryhns gartneri (nursery). Take your first left and then your first right and Åkerveien 11 is the house on the corner. From E-18: Exit at Skjelsvik.

Drive towards Håvet Strids-Klev. Take Stridsklev ring to Bryhns Gartneri (nursery) and then follow the above directions.

Åkerveien ligger ca. 3 km fra Porsgrunn sentrum mot syd. Fra sentrum, ta Deichmannsgate til Flåtten og derifra Stridsklev ring. Sving til høyre ved Bryhns gartneri. Ta deretter første vei til venstre og så første vei til høyre, der ligger Åkerveien 11 på hjørnet. Fra E-18, ta av ved Skjelsvik. Kjør mot Håvet Strids-Klev. Kjør Stridsklev ring til du kommer til Bryhns Gartneri og så videre etter beskrivelsen over.

Page 104 Huldrehaug

From Notodden, take RV-134 to Flatdal. Look for Nutheim Gjestgiveri (Guesthouse) among the hills down close to Flatdal. Huldrehaug is located up on the right, 250 m further down. Look for sign: "Seng og frokost" (i.e. bed and breakfast).

Fra Notodden følges RV-134 til Flatdal. I bakkene ned mot Flatdal skal du se etter Nutheim Gjestgiveri. Huldrehaug ligger opp til venstre, 250 m lenger nede. Skilt med "Seng og frokost".

Von Notodden fahren Sie auf der Straße 134 bis Flatdal. Bei der Abfahrt hinunter in Richtung Flatdal achten Sie auf den Gasthof "Nutheim Gjestgiveri". Huldrehaug liegt 250 m weiter talwärts auf der linken Seite. Dort steht ein Schild mit der Aufschrift "Seng og frokost" (Übernachtung m. Frühstück).

Page 108 Templen B&B

Exit from E-18 at the Bjorbekk/ Hisøy sign, west of Arendal. Turn left in the Bjorbekkrysset (crossing) towards Hisøy. Drive about 1-2 km on road 407 to a plumbing service on the right roadside (Egil Bringsverd). Turn right onto the side-road called Gamle Bievei. The road splits into two: you take Vestre Bievei to the left and continue on a gravel road and up a small hill. The house will be visible straight ahead.

Ta av fra E-18 ved Bjorbekk/Hisøy-skiltet vest for Arendal. I Bjorbekkrysset sving til venstre mot Hisøy. Kjør ca 1-2 km på RV 407 til en rørleggerforretning (Egil Bringsverd) på høyre side. Her svinger du inn på en sidevei til venstre som heter Gamle Bievei. Denne deler seg i to; og du følger så Vestre Bievei. Kjør Vestre Bievei til venstre, så inn på en grusvei,

opp en liten bakke, og da ser dere huset rett fremfor dere.

Biegen Sie westlich von Arendal von der E-18 ab in Richtung Bjorbekk/Hisøy. An der Kreuzung Bjorbekkrysset links ab nach Hisøy. Nach 1-2 km (Str. 407) liegt auf der rechten Seite ein Installateurbetrieb (Rørlegger Egil Bringsverd). Dort nach links auf eine kleine Straße einbiegen (Gamle Bievei). An der Gabelung dem Vestre Bievei nach links folgen, dann in einen Kiesweg einbiegen und einen kleinen Hang hinauf bis zum Haus.

Page 112 Vatne Gård

From E-39 at Lyngdal: Exit E-39 onto RV 43 towards Farsund and proceed to Vanse town center. Turn left towards Lunde at the Kiwi grocery store and drive 900 m. Turn left about 70 m past Hydro Texaco. Look for the sign marked Vatne Gård.

Fra E-39 ved Lyngdal: Sving av E-39 mot Farsund på RV 43, og fortsett til Vanse sentrum. Sving til venstre mot Lunde ved Kiwi-butikken, og kjør 900 m. Sving til venstre ca 70 m etter Hydro Texaco. Se etter skilt med Vatne Gård.

Page 113 Skipperhuset seng & mat

From Egersund: Follow RV 44 towards Flekkefjord and exit onto RV 469 towards Hidra. Ferry over to Rasvåg and Skipperhuset is easy to find. From Flekkefjord: Take RV 44 towards Egersund and exit onto RV 469 towards Hidra. Otherwise same directions as above.

Fra Egersund: Følg RV 44 mot Flekkefjord, ta av til RV 469 til Hidra. Ferge over til Hidra. Kjør til Rasvåg, og du finner enkelt Skipperhuset. Fra Flekkefjord: Kjør RV 44 mot Egersund, ta av til RV 469 til Hidra. Resten som over.

Von Egersund: Auf der Straße 44 Richtung Flekkefjord, dann abbiegen nach Hidra auf die Straße 469. Mit der Fähre nach Hidra übersetzen. Richtung Rasvåg fahren, das Skipperhuset ist dann leicht zu finden. Von Flekkefjord: Auf der Straße 44 Richtung Egersund, abbiegen auf die Straße 469 nach Hidra. Weiter wie oben.

Page 116 Magne Handeland

Exit E-39 3 km north of Moi to the right towards

Hovsherad. Drive 5 km and look for Bjørnestad. It is the third house on the right-hand side.

Langs E-39, 3 km nord for Moi tar du til høyre mot Hovsherad. Kjør 5 km og se etter Bjørnestad. Det er det 3dje hus på høyre hånd.

Page 120 Den Gamle Stallen

Look for the house marked Villa Blidensol. We are located in the north end of Gamle (Old) Stavanger, just near the concert house (konserthuset) in Bjergsted with its adjoining park.

Huset er skiltet med Villa Blidensol. Det ligger i nordre ende av Gamle Stavanger, like ved konserthuset i Bjergsted og tilhørende park.

Page 122 Kleivå Gardscamping

From Haugesund: take E-134 to Aksdal, then take E-39 towards Arsvågen. After passing Bokna-sundsbru (bridge), go right at first crossing. Follow signs to Kleivå Camping about 3 1/2 km from E-39.

Fra Haugesund; kjør E-134 til Aksdal, ta E-39 mot Arsvågen, og etter å ha passert Bokna-sundsbru, ta til høyre i første kryss. Følg skilting til Kleivå Camping ca 3.5 km fra E-39.

Von Haugesund: Auf der E-134 nach Aksdal, dann auf der E-39 Richtung Arsvågen. Wenn Sie die Brücke Broknasundbru passiert haben, biegen Sie an der ersten Kreuzung rechts ab. Folgen Sie der Beschilderung "Kleivå Camping". Von der E-39 aus sind es etwa 3,5 km.

Page 123 Anne Grete's husrom

From Haugesund: take RV-47 southward until the roundabout where you continue on E-134. From there, take a right in the next roundabout onto highway 831 and drive 9.2 km to Røyksund. After a blue sign "Røyksund", take the first left and then another left after the bus-stop onto Soldalveien. Take the first right after the post boxes. House number 3.

Fra Haugesund; kjør sørover langs RV-47 til en rundkjøring hvor du videre tar E-134. Deretter tar du til høyre i første rundkjøring, vei nr. 831, og kjører 9,2 km til Røyksund. Etter blått skilt "Røyksund", ta første vei til venstre, deretter til venstre etter et busskur og inn Soldalveien. Etter postkassene ta første vei til høyre. Huset har nr. 3.

Von Haugesund: Auf der Straße 47 in Richtung Süden bis zum Kreisverkehr. Dort auf die E-134. Am ersten Kreisverkehr nach rechts auf die Straße 831 nach Røyksund (9,2 km) abbiegen. Hinter dem blauen Schild "Røyksund" die erste Straße links, dann hinter dem Bushäuschen links in den Soldalsveien. Nach den Briefkästen in die erste Straße rechts bis zum Haus Nr. 3.

Page 127 Øysteinbu

From Stavanger: the easiest way to Sauda is via Rennfast. This includes two undersea tunnels and one ferry. The road over Rødalsfjellet is closed winters. New: RV520 from Sauda going northwards. You arrive in Øysteinbu after 16 km.

Fra Stavanger kommer en seg lettest til Sauda via Rennfast. Dette innebærer to undersjøiske tuneller, samt ei ferje. Veien over Rødalsfjellet er vinterstengt. Ny: RV 520 fra Sauda i nordgående retning. Du er fremme ved Øysteinbu etter 16 km.

Von Stavanger aus gelangt man am leichtesten über Rennfast nach Sauda. Auf dieser Strecke durchquert man zwei Fjordtunnels und setzt einmal mit der Fähre über. Die Strecke über das Rødalsfjell ist im Winter gesperrt. Neu ist die Straße von Sauda Richtung Norden (Str. 520). Nach 16 km erreichen Sie Øysteinbu.

Page 129 Koløens Bondegårdsferie

From RV 545: follow the signs towards Koløyholmen from the crossing at Rydland for 1 3/4 km. Then take a right towards Fitjar, again 1 3/4 km. Take another right and drive about 300 m to the top of the hill. You will then arrive at a large farm courtyard with a new, red service building and an older, white farmhouse.

Fra RV 545, i krysset på Rydland; følg skilt mot Koløyholmen, 1,7 km. Der tar du til høyre mot Fitjar, 1,7 km. Ta til høyre igjen og kjør ca. 300 m til toppen av bakken. Der vil du komme til et romslig tun med en ny, rød driftsbygning og et eldre, hvitt våningshus.

Von der Straße 545 folgen Sie an der Kreuzung bei Rydland dem Schild Richtung Koløyholmen (1,7 km). Dort rechts ab nach Fitjar (1,7 km). Dort wieder rechts und ca. 300 m eine Anhöhe hinauf. Koløen's ist ein großer Hof mit einem neuen roten Wirtschaftsgebäude und einem älteren weißen Wohnhaus.

Page 133 Lerkebo

From Bergen: take RV 553 towards Flesland airport. Take RV580, Fanavegen, towards Nesttun from the roundabout nearest Lagunen shopping centre and then make a right in the first lighted intersection onto Sætervegen. Look for a sign with "40-64 Sætervegen" and turn left here. Enter the driveway just past the post boxes.

Fra Bergen: ta RV 553 mot Flesland flyplass. I rundkjøringen ved Lagunen senter ta RV 580, Fanavegen, mot Nesttun og ta så til høyre i første lyskryss, dette er Sætervegen. Se så etter skilt med "40-64 Sætervegen" og ta til venstre her. Kjør inn oppkjørselen rett etter poststativet.

Von Bergen: Auf der Straße 553 Richtung Flughafen Flesland. Am Kreisverkehr beim Lagunen-Center auf die Straße 580 (Fanavegen) Richtung Nesttun, und dann an der ersten Ampelkreuzung nach rechts in die Straße "Sætervegen". Am Schild "Sætervegen 40-64" links ab. Nehmen Sie die Einfahrt gleich hinter dem Briefkastengestell.

Page 136 Skiven Gjestehus

By foot from the railway station: a short city block north of the station, take Kong Oscarsgate to the left towards downtown and then turn right on the second street Dankert Krohnsgate. This road ends after about 150 m and from here the steps lead up to Skivebakken. You will find number 17 is the first house to the left of the steps. It is also possible to get here by car: Take Kong Oscarsgate towards downtown and turn right four city blocks past the railway station onto Heggebakken. Skivebakken is 100 m down the road on your right-hand side.

Til fots fra jernbanestasjonen; ett lite kvartal nord for stasjonen: ta Kong Oscarsgate til venstre mot sentrum, deretter andre gate, Dankert Krohnsgate, til høyre. Ved enden av denne, etter ca. 150 m, leder en trapp opp til Skivebakken. Du finner nr. 17 som det første huset til venstre for trappen. Det er også mulig å kjøre bil helt fram; kjør Kong Oscarsgate mot sentrum, fire kvartaler etter jernbanestasjone; sving til høyre, inn Heggebakken, etter 100 m finner du Skivebakken til høyre.

Page 142 Skjerping Gård

Exit E-16 onto RV 566 at the sign marked "Osterøybrua". From Bergen: You will find the turn-off past the Arnanipa Tunnel. From Voss: The turn-off is past the small towns of Dale, Vaksdal and Trengereid. Drive over the bridge and follow the signs towards Lonevåg. After the tunnel, you will drive about 4-5 km and look for a private road to the right with a sign marked "Skjerping", which is situated alongside a group of mailboxes with a grass-covered roof.

Når du kjører E-16 skal du ta av ved skilt som sier "Osterøybrua" RV 566. Fra Bergen finner du avkjørselen etter Arnanipatunnellen. Fra Voss er det etter tettstedene Dale - Vaksdal - Trengereid. Kjør så over brua og følg skilt i retning Lonevåg. Etter en tunnell kjører du ca. 4-5 km og se etter en privat vei til høyre med skiltet "Skjerping" plassert sammen med et postkassestativ med gress på taket.

Page 144 Skjelde Gård

From Bergen: Follow E-16 towards Voss and exit towards Bulken 10 km before Voss. From Voss: Follow E-16 westward to the end of Vangsvatnet (lake) and exit towards Bulken. Drive across the bridge, turn left and look for the sign to Skjelde Gård, which is the first farm on the left-hand side. Distances to Bulken: From Bergen, 90 km; From Voss, 100 km.

Fra Bergen; kjør E-16 mot Voss og ta av til Bulken 10 km før Voss.

Fra Voss; kjør E-16 vestover til enden av Vangsvatnet og ta av til Bulken. Kjør over broen, kjør til venstre og se etter skilt med Skjelde Gård, som er første gården på venstre side. Fra Bergen er det 90 km til Bulken, 100 km til Voss.

Page 145 Sollia

Drive into Ulvik town center. Take the road towards Granvin and drive about ca. 200 m. The house is situated just near a large, red meeting hall. There is a sign marked "Rom" near the road and on the house itself.

Kjør inn til Ulvik sentrum. Ta veien mot Granvin og kjør ca. 200 m på denne. Huset ligger like ved et stort rødt forsamlingshus. Der er "Rom"-skilt ved veien og på huset.

Page 147 Haugen Gard

From Dale: take RV 569 to Romarheim/Mo. Continue past Stamnes and then left in the crossing towards Gullbrå. Drive to and past Eidslandet, Høvik, Flatekval and Lavik. Take a left, 1 km past Lavik to Fjellanger. Look for a sign marked "Rom". Keep left at the first crossing. Drive 1.8 km and turn right when you come upon an open area with houses and a barn.

Fra Dale; ta RV 569 mot Romarheim/Mo. Kjør forbi Stamnes, i krysset ta til venstre mot Gullbrå. Kjør mot og forbi Eidslandet, Høvik, Flatekval og Lavik. Ca. 1 km etter Lavik ta til venstre mot Fjellanger. Her står også skiltet "Rom". Hold til venstre i første veikryss. Kjør 1,8 km. Du kommer opp på en flate. Ta til høyre hvor du ser noen hus og et fjøs.

Von Dale auf Str. 569 Richtung Romarheim/Mo. An Stamnes vorbei, an der Kreuzung links Richtung Gullbrå. Weiter nach Eidslandet, Høvik, Flatekval und Lavik. Ca. 1 km nach Lavik links nach Fjellanger (Schild"Rom"). An der ersten Kreuzung links 1,8 km auf eine Ebene hinauf. Bei einigen Häusern u. einem Stall nach rechts.

Page 148 Godmorstova

From Bergen (Option 1): Follow E-39 towards Romarheim, then continue on RV 569 to Modalen, through the tunnel to Eksingedalen, then turn left onto FV 344, and look for the sign marked Vetlejord after 3 km. From Bergen (Option 2): Follow E-16 to Dale, proceed towards Dalseid, but exit left onto RV 569 just before Dalseid, at the sign marked Romarheim-Mo. Turn left towards Gullbrå (Eksingedalen) once past Stamnes. From Voss: Follow E-16 westward, exit towards Evanger. Exit to your right onto FV 313 in Evanger and follow the signs towards Eksingedalen. Turn left onto FV 344 at the intersection in Nesheim and drive downhill into the valley until you reach the sign marked Vetlejord.

Fra Bergen kan du ta E-39 til Romarheim, fortsett på RV 569 til Modalen, gjennom tunnellen til Eksingedalen, ta så til venstre, FV 344, og finn skilt til Vetlejord etter 3 km. Eller du kan fra Bergen ta E-16 til Dale, videre mot Dalseid, men like før Dalseid ta RV 569, avkjøring til venstre, med skilt mot Romarheim-Mo. Etter Stamnes, ta til venstre ved skilt

mot Gullbrå (Eksingedalen). Fra Voss følger du E-16 vestover, ta av mot Evanger, i Evanger tar du av til høyre, FV 313, og følger skilt til Eksingedalen. I krysset ved Nesheim tar du til venstre, inn FV 344 og nedover dalen til du ser skilt med Vetlejord.

Page 149 Straume's Romutleige
From Bergen: Drive across the Nordhordlandsbrua (bridge), and follow E-39 towards Romarheim, where you will exit to your right onto RV 569 towards Modalen. Drive through Modalen, then uphill to Straume where you will find Straumes Romutleie, about 15 km from Mo.

Fra Bergen kan du kjøre over Nordhordlandsbrua, følg E-39 til Romarheim, der du tar av til høyre på RV 569 til Modalen. Du kjører gjennom Modalen, opp til Straume, der finner du Straumes Romutleie, ca. 15 km frå Mo.

Page 152 Eri Gardshus
The Eri Gardshus is located 4 km from Lærdal town center, towards Fagernes. The house is clearly visible from the highway. The illustration in the guide is of the old farmyard, which is situated a bit farther up in the valley.

Eri Gardshus ligger 4 km fra Lærdal sentrum i retning Fagernes. Huset er lett synlig fra veien. Tegningen i boken er gamle-tunet som ligger litt lenger opp i dalen.

Page 153 Amla Nedre
Exit the main highway 10 km east of Sogndal town center and drive towards Kaupanger. From the Kaupanger ferry quay: Drive 1 km along the fjord and you will see the house in front of you.

10 km øst for Sogndal sentrum tar du av fra riksveien og kjører mot Kaupanger. Fra Kaupanger fergekai kjører du 1 km langs fjorden, så vil du se huset fremfor deg.

Page 156 Lunden ferieleiligheter
Slinde is located along RV 55 between Sogndal and Hermansverk/Hella. Distances to Slinde: 15 km from Sogndal; 6 km from Hermansverk; 22 km from Hella. Look for the red house near the shoreline. It is easy to see from the road.

Slinde ligger langs RV 55 mellom Sogndal og Hermansverk/Hella. 15 km fra Sogndal, 6 km fra Hermansverk og 22 km fra Hella. Det rødmalte huset ligger like i strandkanten og er lett synlig fra veien.

Page 157 Sognefjord Gjestehus
From Bergen: Drive past Voss, Vinje and over Vikafjellet to Vik, then proceed to Vangsnes. From Oslo: Drive via Gol, Hol, Aurland, Vinje and proceed to Vangsnes. Express Boat from Bergen to Vangsnes (Vik): Approx. 4 hours.

Fra Bergen: kjør til Voss, Vinje og over Vikafjellet til Vik og videre ut til Vangsnes. Fra Oslo: kjør via Gol, Hol, Aurland, Vinje og videre til Vangsnes. Ekspressbåt fra Bergen til Vangsnes (Vik) Ca. 4 timer.

Page 158 Flesje Gard
4.5 km from Balestrand town center. Follow RV 55 towards Høyanger.

4,5 km frå Balestrand sentrum, følg RV 55 i retning Høyanger.

Page 160 Skilbrei Pensjonat
The Skilbrei Pensjonat is located along E-39 between Ålesund and Bergen, 13 km south of Førde. There is a sign marked Skilbrei and "overnatting" 400 m ahead of the turn-off.

Skilbrei Pensjonat ligger langs E-39, på veien mellom Ålesund og Bergen, 13 km sør for byen Førde. Det er merket med skilt for overnatting 400 m før avkjørsel. Det er også merket med skilt: Skilbrei ved avkjørsel.

Page 161 Rom i Jølster
From Førde: Follow RV-39 for 20 km until you reach a Statoil gas station and a "Spar" grocery store. Turn left and drive about 500 m then turn right onto Storetrærvegen. Our house is at the end of the road.

Fra Førde: 20 km langs RV-39 til du kommer til en Statoil-stasjon og en "Spar"-butikk. Ta til venstre, kjør ca. 500 m og ta til høyre - inn på Storetrærvegen. Huset ligger i enden av veien.

Page 164 Von Rom & Frokost
Follow RV 5 towards downtown. Exit left towards

the airport (flyplass). Take your second right and then turn right at the first turn-off into the parking area. Michael Sarsgate 23 is the green house with yellow trim.

Følg RV 5 til sentrum. Ta til venstre ved skilting til flyplass. Ta andre veg til høgre og første avkjørsel til høgre inn på parkeringsplass. Michael Sarsgate 23 er grønnmalt med gule lister.

Page 165 / 166 Stranda Rom & Frukost / Friheten

Follow RV (Riksveg) 5 to Florø. Drive straight through the town center and turn left just past the bus station at the sign marked "Vestlandshus". Drive 300 m on Strandavegen. About 50 m past the 'Vestlandshus', you will see two double-family homes on a small hilltop on the left-hand side. Our sign is mounted on the wall of the house on the left.

Følg Riksveg 5 til Florø. Køyr tvers gjennom sentrum, ta til venstre rett etter bussstasjonen ved skilt som viser til "Vestlandshus". Køyr 300 m langs Strandavegen. Ca 50 m etter 'Vestlandshus', på ein liten bakketopp, ligg to tomannsbustader på venstre side. Då ser du skiltet vårt på husveggen på huset til venstre.

Page 168 Hammersvik Gjestehus

From Otta: Follow Stamvei 15 past Stryn and Nordfjordeid to Maurstad. Follow R-61 from Maurstad to Åheim, then proceed on RV-619 to Kjøde and then RV-618 to Selje. Hammersvik Gjestehus is about 1 km before Selje town center.

Fra Otta; kjør Stamvei 15 over Stryn og Nordfjordeid til Maurstad. Fra Maurstad på R-61 til Åheim, videre på RV-619 til Kjøde og på RV-618 til Selje. Hammersvik Gjestehus er ca. 1 km før Selje sentrum.

Page 169 Huset Vårt overnatting

From Oslo: Follow E-6 to Otta, then RV 15 to Kjøsbru, then RV 60 from Kjøsbru to Grodås town center where you will find Huset Vårt overnatting.

Fra Oslo: Følg E-6 til Otta, deretter RV 15 til Kjøsbru, så RV 60 fra Kjøsbru til Grodås sentrum hvor Huset Vårt overnatting ligger like i nærheten.

Page 173 Olden romuteleie

Located just near the grocery store and Statoil gas station in the center of Olden. Ask at the Statoil station about how to contact the B&B hostess.

Like ved en butikk og en bensinstasjon (Statoil), like ved sentrum av Olden. Spør etter B&B-vertinnen på Statoil-stasjonen.

Page 174 Trollbu

From Olden: Drive about 20 km towards Oldedalen/Briksdal. Look for the sign alongside the road marked "Trollbu".

Fra Olden skal du kjøre mot Oldedalen/Briksdal, ca. 20 km. Det er skilt ved veien som sier "Trollbu".

Page 175 Kneiken Romutleie

Look for the sign marked "Fjellstua" before entering Ålesund city center. Follow the signs uphill along the mountainside until you reach a 4-way crossing with a Spar grocery store on the left-hand side. Turn left and drive downhill about 50 meters, then take your first right and drive uphill about 50 meters. Kneiken 2 is on the right-hand side of the road.

Før du kommer inn til sentrum av Ålesund vil du se skilt med "Fjellstua". Følg disse skitlene et stykke oppover fjellsiden til du kommer til et kryss med 4 veier og med Spar marked til venstre i krysset. Ta til venstre nedover ca. 50 meter, deretter første vei opp til høyre ca. 50 meter, og du har Kneiken 2 på høyre side av veien.

Page 179 Petrines Gjestgiveri

Situated along the fjord in Norddal. Located 30 km fra Geiranger along "The Golden Route".

Ligger ved fjorden i Norddal, 30 km fra Geiranger langs "The Golden Route".

Page 180 Strandhuset Måndalen

The house is located in Måndalen town center, down near the water. Easy to find and clearly visible from E-136. Look for the sign marked "Rom/overnatting".

Huset ligger i sentrum av Måndalen, nede ved sjøen. Lett å finne og godt synlig fra E-136. Se etter skilt med "Rom/overnatting".

Page 184 Gråhaugen Fjellstue

Exit RV 65 towards "Trollheimshytta" as indicated by the sign at the border between Rindal and Surnadal, near Kvammen in Øvre Surnadal. This is a toll road (kr. 50). Follow this road about 16 km into Folldalen. First drive along Follsjøen (lake) and the cabins are located at the second lake, Gråsjøen.

På RV 65 ved grensen mellom Rindal og Surnadal, ved Kvammen i Øvre Surnadal, skal du ta av i retning skilt som viser "Trollheimshytta". Dette er bomvei (kr. 50,-). Du følger denne ca. 16 km innover Folldalen. Du kjører først langs Follsjøen, og ved den andre sjøen, Gråsjøen, ligger hyttene.

Page 186 Inger Stock B&B

From the south: Exit E-6 towards Tillerbyen. Turn left at the lighted intersection near the Rema-1000 grocery store and then turn right at the next stoplight towards Tiller kirke (church). Take John Aaes vei, then take your third right onto Porsmyra. From the north: Follow E-6 towards Oslo and exit towards Tillerbyen. Stay in the middle lane at the first lighted intersection, then drive straight ahead and Porsmyra will be your third right.

Fra sør: ta av ved skilt på E-6 mot Tillerbyen. Ved lyskryss ved Rema-1000 ta til venstre, neste lyskryss ta til høyre i retning Tiller kirke. Følg John Aaes vei, tredje gate til høyre er Porsmyra. Fra nord: E-6 retning Oslo, ta av til Tillerbyen, hold i midtre fil ved første lyskryss, så rett frem og Porsmyra er tredje gate til høyre.

Page 189 Trøabakken

From Stiklestad kirke: Follow RV 759 about 8 km to Leksdal near the Leksdalsvatnet lake. Turn right at "Lund". Trøabakken is situated 600 m from Lund and RV 759.

Fra Stiklestad kirke følg veg nr. 759 ca. 8 km til Leksdal ved Leksdalsvatnet. Ta veg til høyre ved "Lund". Trøabakken ligger 600 m fra Lund og riksveg 759.

Page 192 Gjestehuset Nora

The nearest town is Fauske. From Fauske: Follow E-6 northward to Tømmernes (107 km), and exit onto RV 835 towards Nordfold. From Tømmerhus to Nordfold is 65 km. Gjestehuset Nora has a sign marked "Kvinneuniversitetet Nord". There is also Express Boat service to Lofoten and Bodø via Steigen.

Nærmeste tettsted/by er Fauske, og fra Fauske følg E-6 nordover til Tømmernes (107 km), der du tar av på RV 835 mot Nordfold. Fra Tømmerhus til Nordfold er det 65 km. Gjestehuset er merket med Kvinneuniversitetet Nord. Det går også hurtigbåt til Lofoten og Bodø via Steigen.

Page 193 Nordbua

When approaching Stamsund by car: Drive past the church on the left-hand side and then pass by Svarholt skole (school). Turn right onto Skolegata (towards the mountains) and then take your first left onto Rishaugveien. We live in number 3. We will then escort you to Nordbua. (Please call in advance so we can meet you at Nordbua or otherwise arrange a meeting place).

Når du kommer inn mot Stamsund med bil; passér kirken på venstre side, passér Svarholt skole, ta til høyre inn Skolegata (i retning fjellene) og ta deretter første vei til venstre Rishaugveien. Vi bor i nr. 3. Så tar vi deg med til Nordbua. (Ring gjerne, så møtes vi ved bua eller avtaler et møtested).

Page 194 Norumgården B&B

Drive over the bridge from the main square in Narvik. Follow the signs towards the airport. Once you have passed Narvik kirke (church), you will drive straight ahead for about 200 m. The house is on the right-hand side and has a large white fence. Our nearest neighbor is the nursery school.

Fra torget i Narvik; kjører over broen. Følg skilt i retning flyplassen. Når du har passert Narvik kirke, kjør ca. 200 m rett frem. Huset ligger på høyre side, med et stort hvitt gjerde rundt. Nærmeste nabo er en barnehage.

Page 195 Sjøgata Gjestehus

Andenes Harbor, situated about 200 meters from the Hvalsenteret (Whaling Center).

Andenes havn, ca. 200 meter fra Hvalsenteret.

Page 197 Gunn's Turistutleie

The first landmark you can see from the bridge over to Sommarøy is a nursery school painted like a caterpillar. Follow the sign marked Unn-Tones Kro at the intersection and the first house (yellow) on the right-hand side is Nordjordveien 37.

Fra brua over til Sommarøy er det første du ser en barnehage malt som tusenbein. Ved krysset følg skiltet Unn-Tones Kro og det første huset på høyre hånd er Nordjordveien 37, en gulmalt enebolig.

Page 198 Forsøket

Follow Skippergata northward over the Tromsøbrua (bridge) to Stakkevollveien on which you continue north and then turn left at the first lighted intersection onto Søren Zakariassens gate. This road curves uphill at the top and becomes Borgermester Eidems gate. Reddish brown house with green window trimming.

Fra Tromsøbrua følges Skippergata nordover til Stakkevollveien. Denne følges videre nord til første lyskryss, og det tas til venstre opp Søren Zakariassens gate. Den dreier til venstre på toppen, og man er inne i Borgermester Eidems gate. Rødbrunt hus med grønn vindusbelistning.

Page 199 Det røde huset

Take your second right in the roundabout situated 6-700 m before the Tromsøbrua (bridge) and drive past the Shell gas station, proceed under the bridge and then 23 km further to the north. Look for the sign marked Vågnes after passing Movik and Tønsvik. Drive on for precisely 3.5 km. Look for a light-color-

ed yellow-brown house with red window trimming and two small red houses on the same property. Drive up alongside the triple garage.

I en rundkjøring 6-700 m før Tromsøbrua skal du ta andre vei til høyre, forbi Shellstasjon, under brua og 23 km videre nordover. Etter å ha passert Movik, Tønsvik, kommer skiltet Vågnes. Kjør videre ganske nøyaktig 3,5 km. Se etter et lyst gul-brunt hus med røde karmer og to små, røde hus på samme tomten. Kjør opp ved trippel-garasjen.

Page 200 Laksefiskerens krypinn

From Storslett: Exit E-6 onto RV-865 and drive towards Bilto, Reisa Nasjonalpark. Rognmo is located about 23 km from Storslett.

Ved Storslett; ta av fra E-6 og inn på RV-865 følg denne mot Bilto, Reisa Nasjonalpark. Rognmo ligger ca. 23 km fra Storslett.

Page 204 Barbara's B&B

Once you get to Kirkenes, you should follow E-6 through town until you reach the Volkswagen dealership on the right-hand side. Turn in to the right and then turn left onto Henrik Lunds gate. The first house on the left-hand side is Barbara's and the house is yellow with red trim.

Når du kommer til Kirkenes skal du følge E-6 gjennom byen til du kommer til Volkswagen på høyre side av veien. Der svinger du inn til høyre, tar så andre veien til venstre (Henrik Lunds gate). Det første huset på venstre side er Barbara's og huset er gult med røde lister.

Øien Gård, Smøla, Møre & Romsdal, page 185

Evaluation / Evaluering / Beurteilung

To present even better updates of this B&B book we are interested in hearing from you. Please share of your experiences and opinions after you have been our guest.

For å kunne presentere et enda bedre B&B-tilbud i neste utgave av denne boken tar vi gjerne imot dine synspunkter og erfaringer etter at du har vært vår gjest.

Damit die nächste Ausgabe des B&B-Buches noch besser werden kann, möchten wir gerne Ihre Ansichten und Erfahrungen nach Ihrem Aufenthalt wissen und bitten Sie, diesen Fragebogen an obige Adresse zu senden.

Jeg var gjest hos: / I was a guest at: / Ich war als Gast bei:

....

1. Living standard and cleanliness / Bostandard og renhet / Wohnstandard und Sauberkeit
2. Breakfast and food / Frokost og servering / Frühstück und Servierung
3. Hospitality and service / Gjestfrihet og service / Gastlichkeit und Service
4. Price and value / Pris i forhold til standard / Preis im Verhältnis zum Standard
5. B&B book's information / B&B bokens informasjon / Information im B&B-Buch

Commentary / Kommentarer / Kommentare:

....
....
....
....
....
....
....
....
....
....
....
....
....
....
....
....

Your name: ....

Address: ....

(we appreciate anonymous letters too) ....

Norsk Bygdeturisme (NBT) ble stiftet i februar 1997 og er en bransjeorganisasjon for småskala- og temabaserte reiselivsbedrifter. Målsettingen er å ivareta bedriftenes interesser på følgende måter:

* Være et talerør for medlemsbedriftene i forhold til myndighetene og andre som setter næringens rammevilkår.
* Legge til rette for faglig samarbeid både nasjonalt, i landsdeler og i regioner.
* Fremme kollegialt samhold og samarbeid innenfor næringen og virke for at bedriftene skal ha best mulig sosiale, markedsmessige og økonomiske rammebetingelser.

NBT er i ferd med å bygge opp et landsdekkende nettverk av regionale- og fylkesvise NBT-avdelinger. Følgende NBT-regioner er på plass eller under etablering høsten 2001: Sørlandet (Aust- og Vest-Agder), Telemark, Buskerud, Hedmark/Oppland, Vestlandet (Rogaland, Hordaland og Sogn og Fjordane), Møre og Romsdal, Trøndelag (Sør- og Nord-Trøndelag), Finnmark.

Medlemmene har tilhørighet til ulike tema- og produktgrupper som bed & breakfast, hest i turisme, hytteutleie, besøksgårder og fiskeferie.

NBT arbeider med bransjespørsmål (rammebetingelser m.v.) samt med kompetanseheving og kvalitetssikring. Dessuten er det samarbeid med bookingselskaper, Norges Turistråd (gjennom markedsføringssamarbeidet landbruket / Norges Turistråd) og andre om markedsføring og salg av bygdeturismeproduktene. Det arbeides kontinuerlig med å få mange og gode medlemsfordeler for de bedriftene som er medlemmer av NBT.

NBT har en samarbeidsavtale med Norges Bondelag og leier også lokaler i Landbrukets Hus i Oslo. Daglig leder i NBT er Ole Jonny Trangsrud. Nærmere informasjon om bransjeorganisasjonen:

Norsk Bygdeturisme
Postboks 9354 Grønland
0135 OSLO
Telefon: 22 05 46 40   Telefaks: 22 17 17 87
E-post: norsk.bygdeturisme@bondelaget.no
Internett: www.norsk-bygdeturisme.no

Start din egen attåtnæring: privat rom-utleie for turister.

Du leier kanskje ut rom allerede, eller ønsker å starte med det. Har du et ledig soverom, eller kanskje flere? Liker du mennesker og kan tenke deg å ta imot reisende i ditt hjem? Det er ikke mer som skal til. Da kan du starte din egen romutleie-binæring. Som deltaker i The Norway Bed & Breakfast Book og eventuelt som medlem i NBT-produktgruppe for B&B, får du markedsført dine rom og mulighet til å møte mennesker fra fjerne himmelstrøk. For mer informasjon om å delta i denne boken; send noen ord til: **B&B Norway AS, Østerdalsgaten 1J, 0658 Oslo, Tlf.: 22 67 30 80, Fax: 22 19 83 17, E-post: bbnorway@online.no**

Navn: ....

Adresse: ....

Postnr./-sted: ....

Telefon:.. **E-post:** ....

This edition of The Norway Bed & Breakfast Book has been put together by a devoted group of professionals. Thanks to:

Co-editor Jan Hanchen Michelsen, Bergen, Norway

Jeff McLean, Bolga, Norway - for English translation

Andreas Schmitt, Lemgo, Germany - for German translation

Bodil Sandøy, Oslo, Norway - for illustrations on page 47, 48, 56, 86, 88, 89, 106, 128, 133, 143, 185, 197, 198 and 204.

Gertraud Lynau, Oslo, Norway - for proof-reading of German text

Roy Evarson, Oslo, Norway - for proof-reading of English text